T0181601

Statistical Mechanics of Learning

Statistical Mechanics of Learning

A. Engel

Otto von Guericke University, Magdeburg, Germany

C. Van den Broeck

Limburgs Universitair Centrum, Diepenbeek, Belgium

CAMBRIDGE
UNIVERSITY PRESS

CAMBRIDGE UNIVERSITY PRESS
Cambridge, New York, Melbourne, Madrid, Cape Town, Singapore,
São Paulo, Delhi, Dubai, Tokyo

Cambridge University Press
The Edinburgh Building, Cambridge CB2 8RU, UK

Published in the United States of America by Cambridge University Press, New York

www.cambridge.org
Information on this title: www.cambridge.org/9780521774796

© Cambridge University Press 2001

First published 2001

A catalogue record for this publication is available from the British Library

ISBN 978-0-521-77307-2 Hardback
ISBN 978-0-521-77479-6 Paperback

Transferred to digital printing 2010

Contents

Preface

Understanding intelligent behaviour has always been fascinating to both laymen and scientists. The question has become very topical through the concurrence of a number of different issues. First, there is a growing awareness of the computational limits of serial computers, while parallel computation is gaining ground, both technically and conceptually. Second, several new non-invasive scanning techniques allow the human brain to be studied from its collective behaviour down to the activity of single neurons. Third, the increased automatization of our society leads to an increased need for algorithms that control complex machines performing complex tasks. Finally, conceptual advances in physics, such as scaling, fractals, bifurcation theory and chaos, have widened its horizon and stimulate the modelling and study of complex non-linear systems. At the crossroads of these developments, *artificial neural networks* have something to offer to each of them.

The observation that these networks can learn from examples and are able to discern an underlying rule has spurred a decade of intense theoretical activity in the statistical mechanics community on the subject. Indeed, the ability to infer a rule from a set of examples is widely regarded as a sign of intelligence. Without embarking on a thorny discussion about the nature or definition of intelligence, we just note that quite a few of the problems posed in standard IQ tests are exactly of this nature: given a sequence of objects (letters, pictures, ...) one is asked to continue the sequence "meaningfully", which requires one to decipher the underlying rule. We can thus hope that a theoretical study of learning from examples in simple, well understood scenarios will shed some light on how intelligent behaviour emerges or operates.

Artificial systems which can learn from examples also offer a very appealing alternative to rule and program-driven systems in cases where explicit algorithms are difficult to find. After all, most of the things we do have been learned from experience and are hard to formulate in terms of rules. A simple example is the sorting of passport photographs according to whether the person shown is male or female. Every human more than five years old performs extraordinarily well on this task, with respect to both error rate and speed. Yet no present-day computer can handle this problem. This is *not* because of its limited speed or power, but due to the inability of the programmer to convey to the machine what to do. It is an extremely attractive idea in problems as complex as the above pattern recognition task to instruct the computer by means of a learning session using examples.

Furthermore, machines which learn from examples typically operate in a parallel and distributed fashion, and therefore share several fundamental characteristics with the human brain, such as fault tolerance, flexibility, and high computational power. With the promise of parallel computers tackling the hardest computational problems, one may hope to bridge the increasing gap between hardware and software by studying how to construct and train machines which learn from examples. At the same time, detailed neural networks have been constructed that mimic quite well the functioning of their biological counterparts. These biologically inspired networks together with their fully artificial counterparts are increasingly being used in a variety of practical applications, from robotics through speech and image processing to control and decision making.

The topic under consideration is in fact old and carries a distinct interdisciplinary flavour. The theory of learning is a classic subject in psychology, philosophy, and pedagogy. But it is also being addressed in other scientific disciplines. Computational learning theory explores the theoretical boundaries of how well simple devices like the Turing machine or more abstract constructions, such as classifier systems, can learn. Mathematical statistics and information theory tell us how much we can infer from observed data. Even though neural networks have become an active subfield of research in statistical mechanics, extending well beyond the incipient connection between associative memories and spin glasses, it is a newcomer in the field compared to the classical disciplines involved. Correspondingly it is only able to deal with rather simple learning scenarios so far. Nevertheless, starting from the new central dogma that information processing in artificial neural networks is a *collective* property well beyond the ability of the individual constituents, and borrowing from an impressive arsenal of both conceptual and technical tools developed over the last hundred years, it is beginning to contribute stimulating new results from a fresh point of view.

The present book is about the statistical mechanics of learning, providing an introduction both to the basic notions and to the relevant techniques used to obtain quantitative results. Care has been taken to make most of the concepts accessible without following all calculations in detail. On the other hand, being a part of theoretical physics, the field relies on mathematical modelling and thorough understanding will be impossible without having control of the relevant techniques.

A major part of the book deals with the perceptron, which is the basic building block for neural networks. While the computational capabilities of the perceptron are very limited, all its properties can be discussed in full analytic detail. After elucidating various aspects of perceptron learning, including a detailed description of the basic setup, a review of the most pertinent learning rules, the storage problem, and discontinuous, unsupervised, and on-line learning in chapters 1–11, we discuss multilayer networks in chapters 12 and 13. These chapters are supplemented by problems forming an integral part of the material. In the discussion section at the end of every chapter, we include a brief review of the literature. These references are cited for guidance and reflect our own interest and background. We apologize to authors whose work is not cited adequately. In the final chapter we glance at some related problems from the statistical mechanics of complex systems such as support vector machines, computationally hard problems, error-correcting codes, and game theory. Most of the more technical aspects have been collected in the appendices, where the basic computational techniques are presented in great detail.

We would like to take the opportunity to express our gratitude to the many friends and colleagues together with whom our understanding of the field has been shaped, notably to Michael Biehl, Marc Bouten, Nestor Caticha, Mirta Gordon, Geza Györgyi, John Hertz, Ido Kanter, Wolfgang Kinzel, Reimar Kühn, Rémi Monasson, Manfred Opper, Juan Manuel Parrondo, Peter Reimann, Lüder Reimers, Pál Rujan, David Saad, Holm Schwarze, Sara Solla, Timothy Watkin, Michael Wong, Richardo Zecchina, Annette Zippelius as well as to our students Ioana Bena, Johannes Berg, Geert Jan Bex, Mauro Copelli, Wolfgang Fink, Eddy Lootens, Peter Majer, Doerthe Malzahn, Jan Schietse and Martin Weigt. We regret not having had the privilege of meeting Elizabeth Gardner, whose groundbreaking contributions will continue to inspire the whole field of neural networks.

We are indebted to Alexander Schinner for helpful assistance in all kinds of computer problems. We would also like to thank Michael Biehl, Mauro Copelli, Stephan Mertens, and Richard Metzler for reading preliminary versions of parts of this book and making useful comments. Special thanks are due to Johannes Berg, who literally read every line of the manuscript (except for these), pointed out mistakes, tracked down inconsistencies, removed colons, improved arguments, corrected misspellings, and suggested references.

Part of the work related to this book was performed during a stay in 1999 at the Max-Planck-Institut für komplexe Systeme in Dresden, whom we would like to thank for hospitality and excellent working conditions.

1

Getting Started

In the present chapter we introduce the basic notions necessary to study learning problems within the framework of statistical mechanics. We also demonstrate the efficiency of learning from examples by the numerical analysis of a very simple situation. Generalizing from this example we will formulate the basic setup of a learning problem in statistical mechanics to be discussed in numerous modifications in later chapters.

1.1 Artificial neural networks

The statistical mechanics of learning has been developed primarily for networks of so-called *formal neurons*. The aim of these networks is to model some of the essential information processing abilities of biological neural networks on the basis of artificial systems with a similar architecture. Formal neurons, the microscopic building blocks of these artificial neural networks, were introduced more than 50 years ago by McCulloch and Pitts as extremely simplified models of the biological neuron [1]. They are bistable linear threshold elements which are either *active* or *passive*, to be denoted in the following by a binary variable $S = \pm 1$. The state S_i of a given neuron i changes with time because of the signals it receives through its *synaptic couplings* J_{ij} from either the "outside world" or other neurons j.

More precisely, neuron i sums up the incoming activity of all the other neurons weighted by the corresponding synaptic coupling strengths to yield the *post-synaptic potential* $\sum_j J_{ij} S_j$ and compares the result with a threshold θ_i specific to neuron i. If the post-synaptic potential exceeds the threshold, the neuron will be active in the next time step, otherwise it will be passive

$$S_i(t+1) = \text{sgn}\left(\sum_j J_{ij} S_j(t) - \theta_i\right), \tag{1.1}$$

where the sign function is defined by $\text{sgn}(x) = 1$ if $x > 0$ and $\text{sgn}(x) = -1$ otherwise.

The McCulloch–Pitts neuron is clearly an extreme oversimplification of its biological prototype. In fact, for every objection raised against it, it is easy to find an additional one. However, the emphasis in statistical mechanics of neural networks is on issues that are complementary to those of neurophysiology. Instead of focusing on the single neuron, the main objectives are the *collective* properties that emerge in *large* assemblies of neurons. Previous experience with complex *physical* systems such as magnets, liquid crystals and superfluids has shown that often these collective properties are surprisingly insensitive to many of the microscopic details and thus the use of extremely simplified models for the constituents is often appropriate to describe the macroscopic properties of the system. A central hypothesis in the statistical mechanics of learning is hence that learning from examples *is* such a collective emerging property and that it can be studied in large networks of McCulloch–Pitts neurons.

There are several ways of connecting formal neurons to create a network, characterized by the connectivity graph of the synaptic matrix J_{ij}. Figure 1.1 shows some simple possibilities for small systems.

A mathematical analysis is, however, possible for some extreme architectures only. Two types of connectivities will be of special interest. In the first one every neuron is connected with every other neuron, see fig. 1.1b. The dynamics (1.1) is then highly recurrent and will in general result in a chaotic sequence of different activity patterns of the neurons. For a suitably chosen set of couplings J_{ij}, however, the situation can be much simpler. Consider, e.g., the case of symmetric couplings $J_{ij} = J_{ji}$. It is then easy to show that the function

$$H(\mathbf{S}) = -\sum_{i,j} J_{ij} S_i S_j \tag{1.2}$$

with $\mathbf{S} = \{S_i\}$ denoting the complete vector of neuron activities, can never *increase* under the dynamics (1.1). Since $H(\mathbf{S})$ cannot become arbitrarily small, the system will eventually approach configurations which minimize H and then remain in these *attractor states*. In fact, by suitably choosing the couplings J_{ij} these attractors can be *prescribed* to be certain desired neuron configurations $\boldsymbol{\xi}^\mu = \{\xi_1^\mu, \ldots, \xi_N^\mu\}$, $\xi_i^\mu = \pm 1$. The index μ labels the different coexisting attractor states and runs from 1 to p. If the network is now initialized in some configuration $\mathbf{S}$ which is similar to one of these embedded patterns, $\boldsymbol{\xi}^1$ say, the dynamics will in most cases tend to this attractor and thereby *restore* the complete pattern $\boldsymbol{\xi}^1$. In this sense, attractor neural networks may function as *associative memories* which are able to retrieve a stored pattern $\boldsymbol{\xi}^1$ if initially stimulated by a noisy or incomplete variant $\mathbf{S}$ of this pattern. The parallel and distributed character

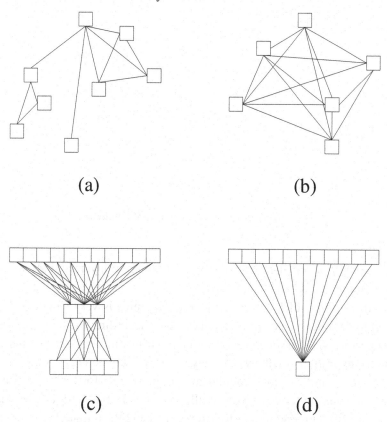

Fig. 1.1. Different types of networks of formal neurons. (a) general architecture, (b) fully connected attractor neural network, (c) feed-forward network with one hidden layer, (d) single layer perceptron.

of such a memory is rather reminiscent of the human brain and very different from present-day electronic memory devices. Central questions in the statistical mechanics of attractor neural networks concern the maximal possible number p_c of patterns ξ^μ that can be stored, the properties of different learning rules fixing the values of the synaptic couplings as functions of the stored patterns, the typical basins of attraction quantifying the maximally admissible difference of the stimulus from the desired pattern, and the interference of different patterns in the retrieval process. There are several textbooks dealing with the statistical mechanics analysis of these systems [2, 3, 4, 5].

The other extreme type of architecture, called *feed-forward neural network*, is shown in fig. 1.1c. In such a network, the neurons can be arranged in layers $l = 1, \ldots, L$ such that every neuron in layer l only receives inputs from neurons of layer $(l-1)$ and in turn only feeds neurons in layer $(l+1)$. The first layer, $l = 1$,

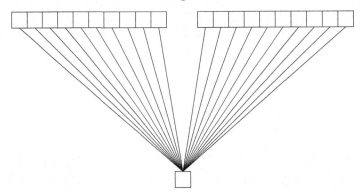

Fig. 1.2. Simple perceptron used to rank dual numbers.

is called the *input* layer; the last one, $l = L$; the *output* layer; and all layers with $1 < l < L$ are referred to as *hidden* layers.

Due to the absence of feedback loops the dynamics is very simple. The input is mapped to the output via successive time steps according to (1.1). The network therefore performs a *classification* of the input strings into classes labelled by the different configurations of the output layer. This architecture is well suited for learning from examples. In particular the simplest feed-forward neural net, the perceptron, having no hidden layers at all, as shown in fig. 1.1d, can be analysed in great detail. Its introduction by Rosenblatt in 1962 [6] initiated a first period of euphoria about artificial neural networks. The attractive features of the perceptron as a simple model for some basic cognitive abilities of the human brain also stimulated some speculations widely overestimating its relevance. So this period ended surprisingly abruptly in 1969 when some rather obvious limitations of the perceptron were clearly stated [7].

Nevertheless the perceptron is a very interesting and valuable model system. In the statistical mechanics of learning it has become a kind of "hydrogen atom" of the field and hence it will often be the focus of attention in this book. In later chapters we will discuss the application of the techniques developed for the perceptron to the more powerful *multilayer networks* having one or more hidden layers.

1.2 A simple example

It is certainly appropriate to introduce learning from examples by discussing a simple example. Consider the perceptron shown in fig. 1.2. It has $N = 20$ input units S_i each connected directly to the single output σ by real valued couplings J_i.

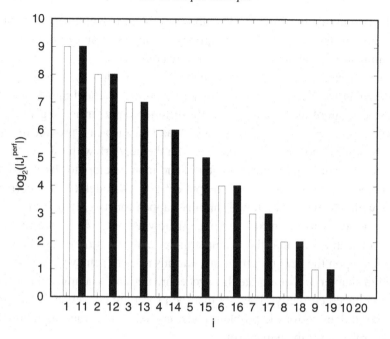

Fig. 1.3. Graphical representation of the perfect couplings for a perceptron to rank dual numbers as given by (1.4). $J_1, \ldots, J_{10}$ (white) are positive, $J_{11}, \ldots, J_{20}$ (black) are negative, cf. (1.4).

For any input vector **S** the output is determined by the rule

$$\sigma = \mathrm{sgn}\left(\sum_i J_i S_i\right), \tag{1.3}$$

which is a special case of (1.1).

We would like to use the network to rank 10-digit dual numbers.[1] To this end we require the output to be $+1 \, (-1)$ if the dual number represented by the left ten input bits is larger (smaller) than the one given by the right ten inputs. For simplicity we ignore for the moment the possibility of the two numbers being equal.

It is easy to construct a set of couplings that does the job perfectly. Consider the coupling values

$$J_i^{\mathrm{perf}} = 2^{10-i} \qquad \text{if} \qquad i = 1, \ldots, 10$$
$$J_i^{\mathrm{perf}} = -J_{i-10}^{\mathrm{perf}} \qquad \text{if} \qquad i = 11, \ldots, 20, \tag{1.4}$$

displayed also in fig. 1.3. This choice gives, as it should, a larger weight in the superposition (1.3) to the leftmost bits in the two subfields of the input. On the other hand it ensures that less significant bits are able to tip the balance if the first

---

[1] A 3-digit dual number with dual code $(-1, 1, -1)$ is equal to $0 \cdot 2^2 + 1 \cdot 2^1 + 0 \cdot 2^0$.

bits of the two numbers coincide. The above problem is simple enough for us to guess the appropriate values of the couplings. Doing so is an example of explicit programming as used in almost all present-day computers.

However, we can apply another, more interesting procedure to solve the problem, namely learning from examples. Let us first initialize the couplings J_i at random. We then select, out of the total of $2^{20} \simeq 10^6$ different input strings, a given number p of input vectors $\boldsymbol{\xi}^\mu, \mu = 1, \ldots, p$ at random and for each case provide the *correct output*, which we denote by σ_T^μ. Next, we *train* the network with this set $\{\boldsymbol{\xi}^\mu, \sigma_T^\mu\}$. To this end we sequentially present each of the input vectors to the network and verify whether the resulting network output σ^μ given through (1.3) is correct, i.e. coincides with σ_T^μ. If so, which will initially happen for roughly half of the cases, we simply proceed to the next example. If however $\sigma^\mu \neq \sigma_T^\mu$ we modify the couplings in such a way that the example under consideration is less likely to be misclassified upon the next presentation. Various rules to achieve this goal will be presented in chapter 3.[2] We iterate this procedure until all examples of the training set are reproduced correctly. The fact that the procedure converges is *a priori* not obvious, but it does so for the problem under consideration: ranking numbers is a *learnable* problem for the perceptron.

The success on the training set, however, does not tell us whether the network has really learned the *rule* behind the examples. To answer this question the performance on *so far unseen* inputs has to be investigated.[3] A quantitative measure of the degree of generalization from the examples to the rule can be obtained by determining the fraction of wrong outputs when running through the *complete* set of 2^{20} different inputs. This fraction is called the generalization error ε and is one of the central quantities in the analysis of learning problems.

Figure 1.4 shows ε as a function of the size p of the training set as resulting from simulations as described above. Note that ε is a random variable which depends on the particular choice of the training set. In fig. 1.4, we have reproduced the average over 1000 random realizations of the training set.

The general behaviour is as expected. For $p = 0$ the network has no information at all about the target rule. By chance half of the examples are classified correctly, $\varepsilon = 0.5$, which is the known success rate for pure guessing. With increasing p the generalization error decreases monotonically and for $p \to \infty$ it must, of course, vanish. However, the surprising fact is that the generalization error already becomes rather small for p of the order of a few hundred, which is *much less* than the total number of different input vectors! In other words, the network is able to generalize rather well in the sense that it can approximate the desired rule on the basis of a very limited set of examples.

---

[2] In the simulations shown below we used the randomized perceptron learning rule discussed in section 3.2.

[3] This is also the reason why exercises are to be found at the end of most chapters of this book.

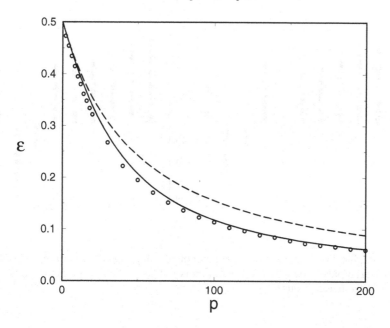

Fig. 1.4. Simulation results (circles) for the generalization error of a perceptron learning from examples to rank dual numbers. The results are averaged over 1000 realizations of the training set, and the statistical error is smaller than the symbol size. The full line gives the analytic result of the quenched calculation, the dashed line that of the annealed approximation. Both are discussed in detail in chapter 2.

In a similar way, one can show that a somewhat more complicated network made of Boolean gates is able to learn the addition of numbers from examples [8]. Another striking demonstration of learning from examples in artificial neural networks is the ability of a multilayer neural net to read English text aloud [9], and many more examples have been documented [10].

At first sight it may seem somewhat enigmatic that a system as simple as the perceptron should be "intelligent enough" to decipher a rule behind examples. Nevertheless the explanation is rather simple: the perceptron can only implement a very limited set of mappings between input and output, and the ranking of numbers happens to be one of them. Given this limitation it is therefore comparatively easy to select the proper mapping on the basis of examples. These rather vague statements will be made more precise in the following chapters.

To get a more concrete idea of how the perceptron proceeds in the above problem, it is instructive to look at the evolution of the couplings J_i as a function of the size p of the training set. In fig. 1.5 the couplings are shown for $p = 50$ and $p = 200$. In both cases we have normalized them such that $J_1 = 2^9$ in order to facilitate comparison with the target values given in (1.4) and fig. 1.3. As one easily

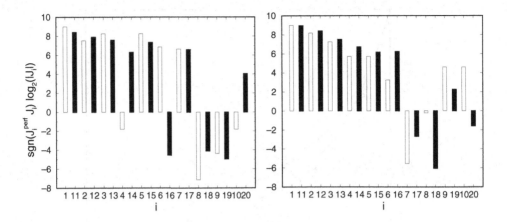

Fig. 1.5. Graphical representation of the perceptron couplings after learning 50 (left) and 200 (right) examples. The signs of the columns indicate whether the couplings have the same sign as the perfect couplings of fig. 1.3 or not.

realizes, the relation between the most important couplings J_1, J_2, J_3, J_{11}, J_{12}, J_{13} is fixed first. This is because they decide the output for the large majority of input patterns, both in the training and in the complete set. Considering that correct values for J_1, J_2, J_3, J_{11}, J_{12} and J_{13} yield a correct output for 15/16 of all patterns already, one understands how the initial efficiency of the learning process is achieved. By the same token, one expects that inputs which give information about the couplings J_9, J_{10}, J_{19} and J_{20} are rare, with a rather slow asymptotic decay of the generalization error to zero as a result.

We have included in fig. 1.4 the generalization error as obtained from two analytic treatments of the learning problem within the framework of statistical mechanics (an approximate one called "annealed" and the exact one referred to as "quenched"). The concepts and techniques necessary to produce curves such as these are the main subject of this book.

1.3 General setup

We are now ready to formulate the basic scenario for learning problems in the statistical mechanics of artificial neural networks. To this end we consider a feed-forward network of formal neurons with N input units denoted by S_i, $i = 1, \ldots, N$ and one output σ. We restrict ourselves to networks with a single output unit merely for simplicity. Since there are no couplings between neurons in the same layer, networks with several outputs are not significantly more complex than those with a single one.

The input–output mapping performed by the network is specified by a vector $\mathbf{J} = \{J_1, \ldots, J_N\}$ of synaptic couplings. The network is required to *adapt* these couplings in order to perform a certain target mapping which will be generally referred to as the *rule*. It is often convenient to think of the target mapping as being represented by another feed-forward neural net characterized by a synaptic vector $\mathbf{T} = \{T_1, \ldots, T_N\}$. Although the *teacher* network $\mathbf{T}$ and the *student* network $\mathbf{J}$ must, of course, have the same number N of inputs and a single output they may, in general, differ in their architecture.

In his task to approximate the teacher neither the detailed architecture nor the components of the teacher vector $\mathbf{T}$ are known to the student. The only accessible information about the target rule is contained in the *training set* composed of p inputs $\boldsymbol{\xi}^\mu$, $\mu = 1, \ldots, p$ with $\boldsymbol{\xi}^\mu = \{\xi_i^\mu = \pm 1, i = 1, \ldots, N\}$ and their corresponding outputs $\sigma_T^\mu = \pm 1$, $\mu = 1, \ldots, p$ provided by the teacher. The prescription $\{\boldsymbol{\xi}^\mu, \sigma_T^\mu\} \mapsto \mathbf{J}$ which specifies a suitable student coupling vector $\mathbf{J}$ on the basis of the training set is called a *learning rule*. The most obvious requirement for a learning rule is to generate a student vector which approximates the teacher as well as possible. But there are also other important features such as the time needed for the determination of $\mathbf{J}$ and the flexibility with respect to the incorporation of new inputs added to the training set.

A crucial question is how the examples of the training set are selected. This is quite important since different training sets of the same size may well convey a different amount of information about the target rule. In many practical situations one cannot design the training set at will since its elements are determined by some experimental procedure. In order to model these situations one therefore assumes that the examples of the training set are selected *independently at random* according to some probability distribution $P_S(\mathbf{S})$ defined on the input space. Throughout this book we will use simple distributions such as

$$P_S(\mathbf{S}) = \prod_i \left[\frac{1}{2}\delta(S_i + 1) + \frac{1}{2}\delta(S_i - 1) \right], \tag{1.5}$$

which implies that the individual components S_i of the inputs are ± 1 with equal probability and independently of each other. Some properties of the δ-function $\delta(x)$ are summarized in appendix 1.

Analogously to considering a training set compiled at random it is often sensible not to concentrate on *one specific* target rule $\mathbf{T}$ but to assume that also the target is chosen at random from a *rule space* according to some probability distribution $P_T(\mathbf{T})$. The results of the analysis will then characterize a whole class of learning problems rather than singling out the performance on one particular task.

Finally, many learning rules involve random elements in order to facilitate convergence. As a result, the training set leads not to a unique $\mathbf{J}$-vector but to a whole distribution $P_{\mathbf{J}}(\mathbf{J})$. The learning process is then conveniently described as a reshaping of this probability distribution on the basis of the information gained from the examples [11, 12].

In conclusion there are several sources of randomness in a generic learning problem and the different ways of dealing with this probabilistic nature result in different approaches to a mathematical analysis of learning.

In order to quantify the success of the student in approximating the teacher we first need a measure of similarity or dissimilarity between two networks. Let us present the same input vector $\mathbf{S}$ to both networks and denote by σ_T and σ the corresponding output of the teacher and the student respectively. For binary outputs the quantity

$$d(\mathbf{J}; \mathbf{S}, \mathbf{T}) = \theta(-\sigma_T \sigma) \tag{1.6}$$

is an appropriate distance measure since with the θ-function defined by $\theta(x) = 1$ if $x > 0$ and $\theta(x) = 0$ otherwise (cf. (A1.17)) it is 1 in case of an error (output different from target output) and 0 otherwise.[4] We may then quantify the performance of the student on the training set by calculating the so-called *training error*

$$\varepsilon_t(\mathbf{J}; \{\boldsymbol{\xi}^\mu\}, \mathbf{T}) = \frac{1}{p} \sum_{\mu=1}^{p} d(\mathbf{J}; \boldsymbol{\xi}^\mu, \mathbf{T}) \tag{1.7}$$

which just gives the fraction of misclassified patterns of the training set. The training error is an important ingredient of most learning rules and we will see in later chapters that it is often (but not always) a good idea to choose a student vector with small training error.

On the other hand the training error is clearly not suitable for determining how well the student really approximates the target rule. This is measured by the *generalization error* $\varepsilon(\mathbf{J}; \mathbf{T})$, which is defined as the *average* of d over the *whole set* of possible inputs $\mathbf{S}$

$$\varepsilon(\mathbf{J}; \mathbf{T}) = \sum_{\{\mathbf{S}\}} P_{\mathbf{S}}(\mathbf{S}) \, d(\mathbf{J}; \mathbf{S}, \mathbf{T}). \tag{1.8}$$

Equivalently we may interpret ε as the probability that the student classifies a *randomly drawn* input differently from the teacher. It is sometimes also referred to as "probability of mistake" or "expected 0–1 loss". Note that it is natural to sample the test input from the *same* probability distribution $P_{\mathbf{S}}$ as the training examples.

From the definition of ε_t and ε it is clear that the problem of learning from examples shares some features with a standard problem in mathematical statistics,

---

[4] For continuous outputs $d(\mathbf{J}; \mathbf{S}, \mathbf{T}) = (\sigma_T - \sigma)^2/4$ is a suitable generalization.

namely the convergence of frequencies to probabilities. In fact the training error ε_t can be interpreted as an estimate for the generalization error ε on a *test set* of examples ξ^μ. As such it has to converge to the generalization error with growing size p of this set. Since we have control over the training error by choosing $\mathbf{J}$ appropriately (in learnable situations we may ensure $\varepsilon_t = 0$) the details of this convergence will yield information on the asymptotic behaviour of the generalization error for large training set size p.

Specifically, the decrease of the probability

$$\mathcal{P} = \text{Prob}(|\varepsilon_t - \varepsilon| > \delta) \tag{1.9}$$

that the difference between training and generalization error exceeds a given threshold δ can be used to characterize the ability of the system under consideration to learn from examples. Note that two parameters are necessary to describe this ability, a tolerance δ, since usually only an approximation to the target rule can be realized for finite p, and a confidence $\mathcal{P}$ guarding against unfortunate realizations of the training set. This is the concept of *probably almost correct* or *PAC* learning [13], which is central to many investigations of learning problems in mathematical statistics and computer science. A subtle point of this approach is the proper treatment of the correlations between the inputs ξ^μ and the student couplings $\mathbf{J}$ introduced by the learning rule. Due to these correlations the training set is not just a simple independent test set and somewhat more advanced techniques of mathematical statistics are needed to determine the behaviour of $\mathcal{P}$ as a function of p.

We will elucidate some aspects of the *PAC* approach in chapter 10. Here we just note that it allows one to derive very general *bounds* for the performance of learning scenarios by studying *worst case* situations. These worst cases generally include the worst possible choice of the student vector for a given value of the training error, the worst choice of the target rule and the worst realization of the training set. It is hence quite possible that the results obtained are over-pessimistic and may not characterize the average or most probable behaviour.

The theoretical description of learning from examples outlined in the present book is based on concepts different from PAC learning. Contrary to mathematical statistics, statistical mechanics tries to describe the *typical* behaviour *exactly* rather than to *bound* the worst case. In statistical mechanics *typical* means not just *most probable* but in addition it is required that the probability for situations different from the typical one can be made arbitrarily small. This remarkable property is achieved by what is called the *thermodynamic limit*. In this limit the number N of degrees of freedom tends to infinity, and the success of statistical mechanics rests on the fact that the probability distributions of the relevant quantities become sharply peaked around their maximal values in this limit.

In the statistical mechanics of learning the degrees of freedom are the couplings J_i of the student network. In most situations studied in this book their number is identical with the dimension N of the input space. In biological as well as in many technical realizations of neural networks this number is indeed large and we may expect to describe relevant situations by considering the limit $N \to \infty$. We will see later that in fact even the behaviour for moderate values of N is often already near to the asymptotic result (cf. fig. 1.4).

Since in the thermodynamic limit the number of adjustable parameters grows large, one expects that learning from examples will remain possible only if the number p of training examples also grows. In fact it turns out that the appropriate scaling of the training set size is given by

$$p = \alpha N, \tag{1.10}$$

such that in the thermodynamic limit both N and p diverge with their ratio α remaining of order 1.

In order to implement the machinery of statistical mechanics for the analysis of learning problems one hence has to determine typical values of interesting quantities such as the generalization error. It is, however, in general rather difficult to calculate the most probable values since this requires one more or less to calculate the complete probability distribution. Fortunately, for some quantities the most probable value coincides with the *average* value, which is much more easily accessible analytically. If additionally the variance of the probability distribution tends to zero in the thermodynamic limit such a quantity is called *self-averaging* since the probability for a value different from its average tends to zero in the thermodynamic limit. It is very important to always remember, however, that *not all* interesting quantities are automatically self-averaging.[5] We will therefore find that the *identification* of the self-averaging quantities is the first and rather crucial step in the statistical mechanics analysis of a learning problem.

To summarize, the mathematical analysis of learning from examples requires a proper treatment of the various probabilistic elements essential for such a problem. Statistical mechanics mainly considers the special scenario of a teacher and student neural network and aims at producing *exact* results for the *typical* learning behaviour. This becomes possible by considering the thermodynamic limit, in which both the number of adjustable couplings of the student network and the number of examples in the training set diverge. After identifying the self-averaging quantities of the problem the typical performance is characterized by calculating their averages over the relevant probability distributions.

---

[5] A popular counterexample is the income distribution. The typical income is well below the average one. See [14] for a nice discussion.

1.4 Problems

1.1 Show that for symmetric couplings $J_{ij} = J_{ji}$ the function $H(\mathbf{S})$ defined in (1.2) can only decrease or at most stay constant under the dynamics (1.1). Why is the restriction to symmetric couplings important? Try to construct an asymmetric coupling matrix J_{ij} that gives rise to cycles for the dynamics of the network.

1.2 Verify that if J_1, J_2, J_3, J_{11}, J_{12} and J_{13} of the ranking machine discussed in section 1.2 have taken on their perfect values given in (1.4) and all the others are still random 15/16 of all inputs are already classified correctly as stated in the main text. What is the probability for an input that conveys information on the values of J_{10} and J_{20}?

1.3 In addition to the probability distribution $P_{\mathbf{S}}(\mathbf{S})$ over the input space defined in (1.5) consider the distribution in which the components of $\mathbf{S}$ are Gaussian random variables with zero mean and unit variance and the distribution in which the endpoints of the N-dimensional vectors $\mathbf{S}$ are distributed with constant density on the N-dimensional sphere with radius $\sqrt{N}$. Show that all these three distributions have the same first and second moments $\langle\!\langle \mathbf{S} \rangle\!\rangle = 0$ and $\langle\!\langle \mathbf{S}^2 \rangle\!\rangle = N$ respectively.

1.4 Consider a system with a single parameter θ_T which classifies real numbers $S \in (0, 1)$ as $+1$ if $S > \theta_T$ and -1 otherwise. This so-called *high–low game* can be considered as an extremely simplified perceptron ($N = 1$) with dynamics (1.1). A student characterized by θ_J is supposed to guess the teacher threshold θ_T from the classification provided by the latter on a set of random examples ξ^μ. Assume that the threshold θ_T is drawn at random with constant density from the interval $(0, 1)$. Show that for a student chosen at random with equal probability from the set of numbers θ_J with zero training error, the generalization error is given by $\varepsilon = (\xi_{max} - \xi_{min})/3$ where ξ_{max} (ξ_{min}) is the smallest (largest) element of the training set that was classified $+1$ (-1) by the teacher.

2

Perceptron Learning – Basics

In this chapter we analyse step by step our paradigm of learning from examples, namely the case of a student perceptron learning a set of p training examples provided by a teacher perceptron. Gibbs learning is used as a simple scenario well suited for an introductory discussion. We start by giving an intuitive albeit approximate description of the learning process and then, as we go on, refine it by introducing the appropriate concepts and techniques from statistical mechanics.

2.1 Gibbs learning

To begin with let us introduce a simple geometric interpretation of the classification sgn($\mathbf{JS}$) of an input $\mathbf{S}$ by a perceptron $\mathbf{J}$. It is $+1$ or -1 depending on whether the angle between $\mathbf{S}$ and $\mathbf{J}$ is smaller or larger than $\pi/2$. Hence, the collection of points at which the classification switches from $+1$ to -1, also referred to as the *decision boundary*, is just the hyperplane orthogonal to $\mathbf{J}$ through the origin. For this reason, the classifications implementable by a perceptron are called *linearly separable*.

It is clear that the *lengths* of $\mathbf{J}$ and $\mathbf{S}$ have no effect on the classification. It has therefore become customary to normalize both couplings and inputs according to

$$\mathbf{J}^2 = \sum_{i=1}^{N} J_i^2 = N \qquad \text{and} \qquad \mathbf{S}^2 = \sum_{i=1}^{N} S_i^2 = N \tag{2.1}$$

respectively. Hence both types of vectors lie on the surface of an N-dimensional sphere with radius $\sqrt{N}$, which in the following we will call the N-sphere. The choice of this radius is consistent with the case of inputs having binary components $+1$ or -1 (cf. (1.5)) while the fact that the surface of such a sphere is exponential in N (cf. problem 2.1) gives a convenient scaling of the quantities to be introduced below.

In order to compare the classifications performed by a teacher perceptron $\mathbf{T}$ and a student perceptron $\mathbf{J}$, we project the input examples onto the plane spanned by

14

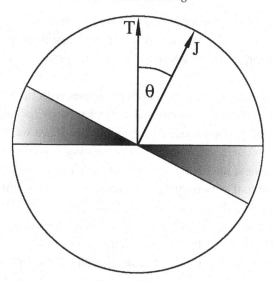

Fig. 2.1. Projection of the input space onto the plane spanned by the coupling vectors of teacher and student. Inputs with projection in the shaded region are classified wrongly by the student.

the coupling vectors of teacher and student (see fig. 2.1). One easily realizes that the projections lying in the shaded region originate from inputs which are classified differently by teacher and student. If the inputs are chosen at random, the probability of disagreement, which is precisely the generalization error ε, is just the probability that a projection falls into this region. Since the decision lines are orthogonal to the vectors $\mathbf{T}$ and $\mathbf{J}$, we conclude that $\varepsilon = \theta/\pi$, where θ is the angle between $\mathbf{T}$ and $\mathbf{J}$. The generalization error is therefore proportional to the geodesic distance between the two points on the N-sphere which correspond to the teacher and the student perceptron. It is convenient to introduce the so-called *teacher–student overlap*:

$$R = \frac{\mathbf{JT}}{N} = \frac{1}{N}\sum_i T_i J_i. \tag{2.2}$$

Since we fixed the lengths of the vectors equal to $\sqrt{N}$, R is nothing but the cosine of the angle θ between $\mathbf{J}$ and $\mathbf{T}$, and the generalization error can be written as

$$\varepsilon = \frac{1}{\pi}\arccos R. \tag{2.3}$$

We now turn to a simple strategy for fixing the student couplings during learning. Consider all the coupling vectors $\mathbf{J}$ which score on the examples exactly like the teacher. The set of these *compatible* students is called the *version space*. We ask for the generalization error of a vector **J** drawn *at random* from this version space. This simple prescription is called Gibbs learning.[1] It is interesting since the results to be found for this learning rule characterize the *typical performance of a compatible student*.

In Gibbs learning the generalization error decreases with increasing training set size because more and more couplings **J** are rejected as incompatible with the examples, causing the version space to shrink in size. If we were able to quantify the "survival chance" of a coupling when presenting a new example, we could infer the average behaviour of the generalization error as the training proceeds. This is indeed possible if we group the couplings into classes with respect to their overlap with the teacher. For all couplings **J** with overlap R defined in (2.2), the chance of producing the same output on a randomly chosen input as the teacher is $1 - (\arccos R)/\pi = 1 - \varepsilon$ by the very definition of the generalization error ε. Let $\Omega_0(\varepsilon)$ be the volume of coupling vectors **J** with overlap $R = \cos(\pi\varepsilon)$ before training has taken place. Since the examples are assumed to be independent, and each example will reduce this number on average by a factor $1 - \varepsilon$, we conclude that the *average* volume $\Omega_p(\varepsilon)$ of compatible students with generalization error ε after presentation of p training examples is given by

$$\Omega_p(\varepsilon) = \Omega_0(\varepsilon)(1 - \varepsilon)^p. \tag{2.4}$$

As discussed in the previous chapter we are interested in large networks describable by the thermodynamic limit $N \to \infty$. In this limit a simple calculation (cf. problem 2.2) gives to leading order in N

$$\Omega_0(\varepsilon) = \int d\mathbf{J}\, \delta(\mathbf{J}^2 - N)\delta\left(\frac{\mathbf{JT}}{N} - \cos(\pi\varepsilon)\right) \sim \exp\left(\frac{N}{2}[1 + \ln 2\pi + \ln \sin^2(\pi\varepsilon)]\right) \tag{2.5}$$

and from (2.4) and (2.5) we find, using the scaling $p = \alpha N$ of the training set size postulated in (1.10),

$$\Omega_p(\varepsilon) \sim \exp\left(N\left[\frac{1}{2}(1 + \ln 2\pi) + \frac{1}{2}\ln \sin^2(\pi\varepsilon) + \alpha \ln(1 - \varepsilon)\right]\right). \tag{2.6}$$

The expression in the square brackets is plotted in fig. 2.2 as a function of ε for several values of α. Note that although it is a smooth function of ε, the corresponding differences in values of $\Omega_p(\varepsilon)$ are exponentially amplified by the large prefactor N in (2.6). We therefore conclude that by choosing a student vector *at random* from the version space we will, for large N, with overwhelming probability pick one with the value of ε which *maximizes* the function shown in fig. 2.2. All other values of ε are realized by coupling vectors which are

---

[1] More precisely it is referred to as zero-temperature Gibbs learning, see section 4.2.

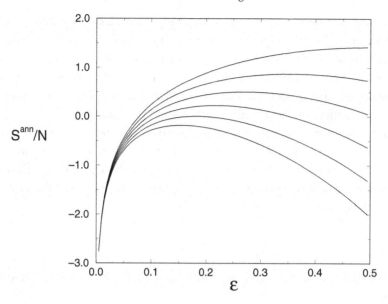

S^{ann}/N

Fig. 2.2. Expression in the square brackets of (2.6) as a function of ε for $\alpha = 0, 1, 2, 3, 4$ and 5 (from top to bottom)

exponentially rare. We therefore expect that the generalization error is, in the large N limit, given by

$$\varepsilon(\alpha) = \text{argmax}\left[\frac{1}{2}\ln\sin^2(\pi\varepsilon) + \alpha\ln(1-\varepsilon)\right]. \tag{2.7}$$

For $\alpha = 0$ the maximum of Ω_p occurs at $\varepsilon = 0.5$, corresponding to students "orthogonal" to the teacher. Clearly, without any further information, all the choices of $\mathbf{J}$ are equally probable, and those students who perform random guessing dominate exponentially in number over all the others. During the learning process, this effect is counterbalanced by a contribution incorporating information coming from the training set. In the present case of Gibbs learning this is the term $\alpha\ln(1-\varepsilon)$ in (2.6), which is of the required order if $\alpha = O(1)$, verifying our scaling assumption (1.10). For large training sets the generalization error becomes small and, as expected, we find $\varepsilon \to 0$ for $\alpha \to \infty$.

The above result also provides some qualitative insight about how artificial neural networks can learn from examples. Firstly, the specific architecture of the network implies a kind of *a priori* hierarchy of implementable mappings. "Easy" input–output relations are realized by many different coupling vectors, "difficult" ones require rather detailed microscopic configurations. One could call this hierarchy the prejudices of the system. Secondly, classifications which are incompatible with the training set are eliminated. This type of learning hence implies a trade-off between speed and flexibility. A system with equal ability for the implementation of all mappings can in principle learn any problem, but its generalization characteristics will be equally poor for all of them. A very specialized system on the other hand is able to learn a very restricted class of problems only, but it will do so rather quickly. In fact spectacular "Eureka"-like sudden transitions to perfect generalization can occur in such systems (cf. chapter 7).

In order to see how accurate our simple analysis of Gibbs learning is, we have included the result (2.7) as the dashed line in fig. 1.4. From the comparison with the simulation results we clearly see that although the qualitative behaviour is described correctly there are significant deviations. In particular for large α we find from (2.7)

$$\varepsilon \sim \frac{1}{\alpha}, \tag{2.8}$$

which although giving the correct scaling is quantitatively poor due to the wrong prefactor.

So what went wrong with our analysis? The main flaw is that we did not treat the randomness in the learning examples ξ^μ and the teacher couplings $\mathbf{T}$ correctly. Let us denote by $\Omega(\varepsilon; \xi^\mu, \mathbf{T})$ the volume of student coupling vectors making an angle $\pi\varepsilon$ with the teacher vector $\mathbf{T}$ which remain in the version space after learning the p examples ξ^μ. Due to the random choice of both $\mathbf{T}$ and the ξ^μ, $\Omega(\varepsilon; \xi^\mu, \mathbf{T})$ is also a random quantity. However, Ω_p as defined in (2.4) just describes its *average*. As discussed in section 1.3, in many situations dealing with random systems the average also gives a reasonable estimate for the *typical*, i.e. most probable, value of a random quantity. This is, however, not always the case and it is in particular *not true* for $\Omega(\varepsilon; \xi^\mu, \mathbf{T})$. As a result one finds for large N with overwhelming probability a value of $\Omega(\varepsilon; \xi^\mu, \mathbf{T})$ which is different from the average described by (2.6).

In order to demonstrate that the distribution of $\Omega(\varepsilon; \xi^\mu, \mathbf{T})$ is indeed badly characterized by its average for large N and, more importantly, to find a correct way to describe the *typical* behaviour of $\varepsilon(\alpha)$, it is useful to first reconsider the above approach within the framework of statistical mechanics. Building on this formulation we will then develop the central statistical mechanics techniques for the quantitative analysis of learning problems.

2.2 The annealed approximation

Let us rephrase the above learning scenario from the point of view of statistical mechanics. The microscopic variables are the components J_i of the student vector. They span the so called *phase space*. The generalization error ε is the relevant macro-variable. A given value of ε can be achieved by many different choices of the micro-variables **J**. The important quantity $\Omega(\varepsilon; \boldsymbol{\xi}^\mu, \mathbf{T})$ denotes the volume in phase space occupied by all the microscopic states which for given $\boldsymbol{\xi}^\mu$ and $\mathbf{T}$ realize the macroscopic state specified by ε. In statistical mechanics it is quantified by the *entropy S* which is nothing but the logarithm of this volume:

$$S(\varepsilon; \boldsymbol{\xi}^\mu, \mathbf{T}) = \ln \Omega(\varepsilon; \boldsymbol{\xi}^\mu, \mathbf{T}). \tag{2.9}$$

From (2.5) we hence find for the entropy before learning for large N

$$S_0(\varepsilon) \sim \frac{N}{2}[1 + \ln 2\pi + \ln \sin^2(\pi \varepsilon)]. \tag{2.10}$$

The entropy has the appealing property of being *extensive*,[2] i.e. it is proportional to the number of degrees of freedom N.

The first two terms in (2.10) are independent of ε and just correspond to the surface of the N-sphere (cf. problem 2.1). It is convenient to normalize $\Omega(\varepsilon; \boldsymbol{\xi}^\mu, \mathbf{T})$ with respect to this value. To this end we will use from now on the integration measure

$$d\mu(\mathbf{J}) := \frac{d\mathbf{J}\, \delta(\mathbf{J}^2 - N)}{\int d\mathbf{J}\, \delta(\mathbf{J}^2 - N)} \tag{2.11}$$

ensuring $\int d\mu(\mathbf{J}) = 1$. The renormalized entropy is then simply given by

$$S_0(\varepsilon) \sim \frac{N}{2}[\ln \sin^2(\pi \varepsilon)]. \tag{2.12}$$

As learning proceeds, more and more couplings **J** are rejected because they are incompatible with the training examples $\boldsymbol{\xi}^\mu$. The function

$$\chi(\mathbf{J}) = \prod_{\mu=1}^{p} \theta\left(\left(\frac{1}{\sqrt{N}}\mathbf{T}\boldsymbol{\xi}^\mu\right)\left(\frac{1}{\sqrt{N}}\mathbf{J}\boldsymbol{\xi}^\mu\right)\right) \tag{2.13}$$

is 1 if **J** classifies *all* examples exactly like the teacher and 0 otherwise. It may hence serve as an *indicator function* of the remaining couplings forming the version space.

The arguments of the θ-function have been normalized such that they remain $O(1)$ for $N \to \infty$. Although this is not absolutely necessary since the Heaviside function $\theta(x)$ depends only on whether its argument is bigger or smaller than zero it is quite helpful for keeping track of the order of different terms in the thermodynamic limit. It also facilitates the comparison with expressions for smooth, i.e. gradual, neuron characteristics in which the scaling of the argument

---

[2] The preservation of this property of the entropy was the reason for the special choice of the **J**-normalization (2.1).

is really important. Prefactors such as $1/\sqrt{N}$ will show up on various occasions in this book and as a rule they will not be indispensable but quite helpful.

Using the indicator function $\chi(\mathbf{J})$ the normalized volume of the whole version space after learning p examples may be written as

$$\Omega(\boldsymbol{\xi}^\mu, \mathbf{T}) = \int d\mu(\mathbf{J}) \prod_{\mu=1}^{p} \theta\left(\left(\frac{1}{\sqrt{N}}\mathbf{T}\boldsymbol{\xi}^\mu\right)\left(\frac{1}{\sqrt{N}}\mathbf{J}\boldsymbol{\xi}^\mu\right)\right). \tag{2.14}$$

It depends on the teacher vector $\mathbf{T}$ and the particular examples $\boldsymbol{\xi}^\mu$ forming the training set all being random variables. Let us calculate the *average* $\Omega_p = \langle\!\langle\Omega(\boldsymbol{\xi}^\mu, \mathbf{T})\rangle\!\rangle$ of the version space volume. Here and in the following the double angle $\langle\!\langle\cdots\rangle\!\rangle$ denotes the average over the training examples and the teacher couplings. The logarithm of Ω_p is called the *annealed* entropy

$$S_p^{\text{ann}} = \ln\langle\!\langle\Omega(\boldsymbol{\xi}^\mu, \mathbf{T})\rangle\!\rangle. \tag{2.15}$$

To calculate the average explicitly we will use the distribution (1.5) for the inputs. For the teacher we assume that her coupling vector $\mathbf{T}$ is chosen with constant probability from the N-sphere, i.e.

$$P_{\mathbf{T}}(\mathbf{T}) = (2\pi e)^{-N/2}\delta(\mathbf{T}^2 - N). \tag{2.16}$$

As we will see shortly, however, the average over the teacher is trivial since, after the $\boldsymbol{\xi}^\mu$-average has been found, almost all choices of $\mathbf{T}$ give the same result for the generalization error.

The random variables appear in (2.14) in a multiplicative manner and inside a function. Introducing the auxiliary variables

$$\lambda_\mu = \frac{1}{\sqrt{N}}\mathbf{J}\boldsymbol{\xi}^\mu \qquad \text{and} \qquad u_\mu = \frac{1}{\sqrt{N}}\mathbf{T}\boldsymbol{\xi}^\mu, \tag{2.17}$$

one can rewrite (2.14) as (cf. (A1.11))

$$\Omega_p = \int d\mu(\mathbf{J}) \int \prod_\mu d\lambda_\mu \, du_\mu \prod_\mu \theta(\lambda_\mu u_\mu)$$

$$\times \prod_\mu \left\langle\!\!\left\langle \delta\left(\lambda_\mu - \frac{1}{\sqrt{N}}\mathbf{J}\boldsymbol{\xi}^\mu\right)\delta\left(u_\mu - \frac{1}{\sqrt{N}}\mathbf{T}\boldsymbol{\xi}^\mu\right)\right\rangle\!\!\right\rangle. \tag{2.18}$$

At this point, one could formally proceed to represent the delta functions by their Fourier representation, to achieve a factorization over the components of the examples $\boldsymbol{\xi}^\mu$ (see appendix 1). We will however use a short cut. For fixed values of $\mathbf{J}$ and $\mathbf{T}$, both λ_μ and u_μ are sums of N independent terms and by the central limit theorem they obey a Gaussian distribution. With the help of (2.1), (2.2) and

(1.5) one easily finds (cf. problem 2.3)

$$\langle\!\langle \lambda_\mu \rangle\!\rangle = \langle\!\langle u_\mu \rangle\!\rangle = 0,$$
$$\langle\!\langle \lambda_\mu^2 \rangle\!\rangle = \langle\!\langle u_\mu^2 \rangle\!\rangle = 1, \qquad (2.19)$$
$$\langle\!\langle \lambda_\mu u_\mu \rangle\!\rangle = \frac{\mathbf{JT}}{N} = R.$$

To evaluate (2.18) we use the bi-Gaussian probability distribution determined by the moments (2.19) and find

$$\Omega_p = \int d\mu(\mathbf{J}) \int \prod_\mu \frac{d\lambda_\mu \, du_\mu}{2\pi\sqrt{1-R^2}}$$
$$\times \prod_\mu \theta(\lambda_\mu u_\mu) \exp\left(-\frac{1}{2(1-R^2)}\sum_\mu (\lambda_\mu^2 + u_\mu^2 - 2R\lambda_\mu u_\mu)\right), \quad (2.20)$$

where R is just a shorthand notation for $\mathbf{JT}/N$. To proceed, one notes that the $\mathbf{J}$- and λ_μ-u_μ-integrals are entangled through the combination $R\lambda_\mu u_\mu$. They can be decoupled by introducing an additional delta function $\delta(\mathbf{JT}/N - R)$ which effectively amounts to performing the $\mathbf{J}$-integration in slices of constant R, just as we did in the previous section.

In this way we get

$$\Omega_p = \int_{-1}^{1} dR \int d\mu(\mathbf{J}) \, \delta\left(\frac{\mathbf{JT}}{N} - R\right) \int \prod_\mu \frac{d\lambda_\mu \, du_\mu}{2\pi\sqrt{1-R^2}}$$
$$\times \prod_\mu \theta(\lambda_\mu u_\mu) \exp\left(-\frac{1}{2(1-R^2)}\sum_\mu (\lambda_\mu^2 + u_\mu^2 - 2R\lambda_\mu u_\mu)\right). \quad (2.21)$$

Now the λ_μ-u_μ-integrals factorize in μ and using

$$\frac{2}{\sqrt{1-R^2}}\int_0^\infty \frac{d\lambda}{\sqrt{2\pi}}\int_0^\infty \frac{du}{\sqrt{2\pi}}\exp\left(-\frac{(\lambda^2 + u^2 - 2R\lambda u)}{2(1-R^2)}\right) = 1 - \frac{1}{\pi}\arccos R$$
$$(2.22)$$

we find with (2.3) and (2.5)

$$\Omega_p = \int_{-1}^{1} dR \exp\left(N\left[\frac{1}{2}\ln(1-R^2) + \alpha \ln\left(1 - \frac{1}{\pi}\arccos R\right)\right]\right). \quad (2.23)$$

Similarly to (2.6) this expression shows that the restriction of the coupling vector to the version space introduces an extra term counterbalancing the purely entropic part (2.12). Due to our scaling $p = \alpha N$ of the training set size this new contribution is extensive, too. It is called the *energetic* part for reasons which will be elaborated on in chapter 4.

The asymptotic behaviour of the remaining R-integral in (2.23) in the thermodynamic limit $N \to \infty$ can now be determined by the saddle point method explained in appendix 1. This yields finally

$$S_p^{\text{ann}} = N \max_R \left[\frac{1}{2} \ln(1 - R^2) + \alpha \ln\left(1 - \frac{1}{\pi} \arccos R \right) \right]. \qquad (2.24)$$

This result implies in particular that the average phase space volume Ω_p is dominated by couplings with overlap

$$R = \text{argmax} \left[\frac{1}{2} \ln(1 - R^2) + \alpha \ln\left(1 - \frac{1}{\pi} \arccos R \right) \right]. \qquad (2.25)$$

Equations (2.23) and (2.25) reproduce (2.6) and (2.7) respectively. This is reasonable since we have in both cases analysed the *average* of the phase volume $\Omega(\xi^\mu, \mathbf{T})$. From (2.14), however, we infer that $\Omega(\xi^\mu, \mathbf{T})$ involves a *product* of many random contributions. Products of independent random numbers are known to possess distributions with long tails for which the average and the most probable value are markedly different (see problem 2.5). On the other hand, the logarithm of such a quantity is a large *sum* of independent terms and hence becomes Gaussian distributed so that its average and most probable value asymptotically coincide. Similarly, the *typical* value of $\Omega(\xi^\mu, \mathbf{T})$ is for large N given by[3]

$$\Omega^{\text{typ}}(\xi^\mu, \mathbf{T}) \sim \exp(\langle\!\langle \ln \Omega(\xi^\mu, \mathbf{T}) \rangle\!\rangle). \qquad (2.26)$$

This is in accordance with the general dogma of the statistical mechanics of disordered systems that *extensive* quantities such as entropy and energy are *self-averaging*, see [16, 17]. A reliable analysis of the typical generalization behaviour therefore requires the calculation of $\langle\!\langle \ln \Omega(\xi^\mu, \mathbf{T}) \rangle\!\rangle$ rather than $\langle\!\langle \Omega(\xi^\mu, \mathbf{T}) \rangle\!\rangle$. As we will see in the next section this indeed yields the correct result.

2.3 The Gardner analysis

As became clear at the end of the last section the annealed entropy $S^{\text{ann}} = \ln\langle\!\langle \Omega(\xi^\mu, \mathbf{T}) \rangle\!\rangle$ cannot be used to describe the *typical* generalization behaviour. A correct theory must instead be built on the so-called *quenched* entropy defined by

$$S = \langle\!\langle \ln \Omega(\xi^\mu, \mathbf{T}) \rangle\!\rangle. \qquad (2.27)$$

This involves the calculation of the average

$$\langle\!\langle \ln \Omega(\xi^\mu, \mathbf{T}) \rangle\!\rangle = \left\langle\!\!\!\left\langle \ln \int d\mu(\mathbf{J}) \prod_{\mu=1}^p \theta\left(\left(\frac{1}{\sqrt{N}} \mathbf{T}\xi^\mu \right) \left(\frac{1}{\sqrt{N}} \mathbf{J}\xi^\mu \right) \right) \right\rangle\!\!\!\right\rangle \qquad (2.28)$$

---

[3] This holds true although the different terms in $\Omega(\xi^\mu, \mathbf{T})$ are weakly correlated. See [15] for a rigorous proof.

over the random examples of the training set and over the random teacher vector. This quenched average is technically much less straightforward than the annealed one (2.18). The main problem is that the integration over $\mathbf{J}$ cannot be performed analytically for every individual realization of the examples. Only *after* averaging over the examples is the system "translationally invariant" in the sense that all neurons i are equivalent to each other so that the integral over $\mathbf{J}$ can be reduced to an integral over a single component J of $\mathbf{J}$. We hence have to interchange the average and the logarithm in (2.28) in some way. It is far from obvious how to accomplish this in a controlled fashion. Fortunately, quenched averages have been a central problem in the theory of disordered solids since the early 1970s and we can build on the techniques developed in this field. A way which – although by no means mathematically rigorous – has turned out to be successful in many situations is the so-called *replica trick* [18, 19, 20], relying on the simple identity

$$\ln x = \lim_{n \to 0} \frac{d}{dn} x^n = \lim_{n \to 0} \frac{x^n - 1}{n}. \tag{2.29}$$

Used for our problem it yields

$$\langle\!\langle \ln \Omega(\boldsymbol{\xi}^\mu, \mathbf{T}) \rangle\!\rangle = \lim_{n \to 0} \frac{\langle\!\langle \Omega(\boldsymbol{\xi}^\mu, \mathbf{T})^n \rangle\!\rangle - 1}{n} \tag{2.30}$$

and the calculation of $\langle\!\langle \ln \Omega(\boldsymbol{\xi}^\mu, \mathbf{T}) \rangle\!\rangle$ is transformed to that of $\langle\!\langle \Omega^n(\boldsymbol{\xi}^\mu, \mathbf{T}) \rangle\!\rangle$. For general real n this is, of course, as complicated as the original average. However, for *natural* numbers $n = 1, 2, 3, \ldots$ the average can be rewritten as

$$\langle\!\langle \Omega^n(\boldsymbol{\xi}^\mu, \mathbf{T}) \rangle\!\rangle = \left\langle\!\!\!\left\langle \left[\int d\mu(\mathbf{J}) \prod_{\mu=1}^{p} \theta\left(\left(\frac{1}{\sqrt{N}} \mathbf{T} \boldsymbol{\xi}^\mu\right) \left(\frac{1}{\sqrt{N}} \mathbf{J} \boldsymbol{\xi}^\mu\right) \right) \right]^n \right\rangle\!\!\!\right\rangle$$

$$= \left\langle\!\!\!\left\langle \int \prod_{a=1}^{n} d\mu(\mathbf{J}^a) \prod_{\mu=1}^{p} \prod_{a=1}^{n} \theta\left(\left(\frac{1}{\sqrt{N}} \mathbf{T} \boldsymbol{\xi}^\mu\right) \left(\frac{1}{\sqrt{N}} \mathbf{J}^a \boldsymbol{\xi}^\mu\right) \right) \right\rangle\!\!\!\right\rangle \tag{2.31}$$

which looks like the combined average of n different copies (*replicas*) of the original system with the *same* realization of the random examples. As we will see shortly, this average is only slightly more complicated than the annealed one calculated in the last section. The main question which remains is how to find the proper analytic continuation which allows one to determine the limit $n \to 0$ from the result for natural n. This can be a very hard problem.[4] For most of the systems considered in this book, fortunately a comparatively straightforward procedure is successful.

In the rest of this chapter we will discuss the application of the replica trick to our learning problem. We will mainly expound the basic lines of reasoning, with the corresponding calculations given in detail in appendix 2.

---

[4] An authoritative guide through the highways and byways of the replica method is [17].

To find the average of $\Omega^n(\xi^\mu, \mathbf{T})$ over the examples and the teacher we introduce auxiliary variables similarly to (2.17):

$$\lambda_\mu^a = \frac{1}{\sqrt{N}}\mathbf{J}^a\xi^\mu \qquad \text{and} \qquad u_\mu = \frac{1}{\sqrt{N}}\mathbf{T}\xi^\mu. \qquad (2.32)$$

For given $\mathbf{J}^a$ and $\mathbf{T}$ these are for large N again normally distributed random variables with moments

$$\langle\!\langle \lambda_\mu^a \rangle\!\rangle = \langle\!\langle u_\mu \rangle\!\rangle = 0,$$
$$\langle\!\langle (\lambda_\mu^a)^2 \rangle\!\rangle = \langle\!\langle (u_\mu)^2 \rangle\!\rangle = 1,$$
$$\langle\!\langle \lambda_\mu^a \lambda_\mu^b \rangle\!\rangle = q^{ab},$$
$$\langle\!\langle \lambda_\mu^a u_\mu \rangle\!\rangle = R^a, \qquad (2.33)$$

where

$$R^a = \frac{\mathbf{J}^a\mathbf{T}}{N} \qquad \text{and} \qquad q^{ab} = \frac{\mathbf{J}^a\mathbf{J}^b}{N}. \qquad (2.34)$$

Here the R^a denote the overlaps between the different students and the teacher. As before this parameter is directly related to the generalization error. The new parameters q^{ab} specify the mutual overlaps between two different student vectors and therefore characterize the *variability* which remains possible within version space.

As shown in detail in appendix 2 it turns out that similarly to the annealed calculation $\langle\!\langle \ln\Omega(\xi^\mu, \mathbf{T}) \rangle\!\rangle$ is dominated by $\mathbf{J}^a$-configurations with specific values of R^a and q^{ab}. Since all the replica variables play a completely symmetric role, it is natural to assume that these *typical* values will not depend on the replica indices, i.e. $R^a = R$ and $q^{ab} = q$. This is the crucial assumption of *replica symmetry* (cf. (A2.28)), which will simplify the following analysis considerably. It means that the overlap between a member $\mathbf{J}^a$, chosen at random in the version space, and the teacher always takes on the same value R with probability 1, while the typical mutual overlap between any pair of vectors $\mathbf{J}^a$ and $\mathbf{J}^b$ chosen at random in the version space has almost always the value q. We will discuss in chapter 6 how one can check whether the replica symmetric assumption is indeed valid. Here we just state that it is justified for the present learning problem.

In fact our special learning situation is characterized by an additional symmetry. The teacher $\mathbf{T}$ is chosen at random from a uniform distribution on the whole sphere (cf. (2.16)) and of course, by definition, lies within the version space. On the other hand our learning scenario consists of sampling student vectors at random with equal probability from the version space. Therefore the typical teacher–student overlap R should coincide with the typical student–student overlap q. This assumption is verified by the detailed calculation (see (A2.36)).

Using the Gaussian probability distribution corresponding to the moments (2.33) and exploiting $q^{ab} = R^a = R$ we find from (2.31) by similar manipulations as in the previous section

$$\langle\!\langle \Omega^n(\xi^\mu, \mathbf{T}) \rangle\!\rangle = \int_{-1}^1 dR \int \prod_a d\mu(\mathbf{J}^a) \left\langle\!\left\langle \prod_a \delta\left(\frac{\mathbf{J}^a \mathbf{T}}{N} - R\right) \right\rangle\!\right\rangle \prod_{(a,b)} \delta\left(\frac{\mathbf{J}^a \mathbf{J}^b}{N} - R\right)$$

$$\times \int \prod_{\mu,a} \frac{d\lambda_\mu^a}{\sqrt{2\pi(1-R)}} \int \prod_\mu \frac{du_\mu}{\sqrt{2\pi(1+nR)}} \prod_{\mu,a} \theta(\lambda_\mu^a u_\mu)$$

$$\times \exp\left(-\frac{1}{2(1-R)(1+nR)} \sum_\mu \left[(1 + (n-1)R)(u_\mu)^2\right.\right.$$

$$\left.\left. + (1 + (n-1)R)\sum_a (\lambda_\mu^a)^2 - 2Ru_\mu \sum_a \lambda_\mu^a - R\sum_{(a,b)} \lambda_\mu^a \lambda_\mu^b \right]\right). \quad (2.35)$$

The remaining average is over the teacher only and (a, b) denotes all pairs with $a \neq b$. For $n = 1$ one of course recovers (2.20).

This result can be further streamlined by exploiting again the symmetry between teacher and students. The average over the teacher couplings $\mathbf{T}$ gives rise to an additional integral $\int d\mu(\mathbf{T})$ which is of the same type as the $\mathbf{J}$-integrals. Analogously the u_μ-integrals are similar to the λ_μ^a-integrals. Moreover they factorize in μ. By calling $\mathbf{T} = \mathbf{J}^{n+1}$ and $u_\mu = \lambda_\mu^{n+1}$ one can thus rewrite (2.35) as

$$\langle\!\langle \Omega^n(\xi^\mu, \mathbf{T}) \rangle\!\rangle = \int_{-1}^1 dR \int \prod_a d\mu(\mathbf{J}^a) \prod_{(a,b)} \delta\left(\frac{\mathbf{J}^a \mathbf{J}^b}{N} - R\right)$$

$$\times \left[2\sqrt{\frac{1-R}{1+nR}} \int_0^\infty \prod_a \frac{d\lambda^a}{\sqrt{2\pi(1-R)}}\right.$$

$$\left. \times \exp\left(-\frac{1}{2(1-R)(1+nR)}\left((1 + (n-1)R)\sum_a(\lambda^a)^2 - R\sum_{(a,b)}\lambda^a\lambda^b\right)\right)\right]^{\alpha N}$$

$$(2.36)$$

with the significant difference that now a runs from 1 to $(n + 1)$ instead of only to n. The remaining $\mathbf{J}$-integral is Gaussian and can be calculated with the help of the methods of appendix 1 to give

$$\exp\left(N\left[\frac{n}{2}\ln(1-R) + \frac{1}{2}\ln(1+nR)\right]\right) \quad (2.37)$$

generalizing (2.5). The λ^a-integrals are also Gaussian. Taking into account the restricted interval of integration $0 \leq \lambda^a < \infty$ one finds that they are equal to

$$2 \int Dt \, H^{n+1}\left(-\sqrt{\frac{R}{1-R}} t\right), \tag{2.38}$$

where we have used the shorthand notations

$$Dt = \frac{dt}{\sqrt{2\pi}} \exp\left(-t^2/2\right) \quad \text{and} \quad H(x) = \int_x^\infty Dt \tag{2.39}$$

also introduced in section A1.1. Again (2.38) coincides for $n = 1$ with (2.22) as it should.

We are hence left with

$$\langle\!\langle \Omega^n(\boldsymbol{\xi}^\mu, \mathbf{T}) \rangle\!\rangle = \int_{-1}^1 dR \exp\left(N\left[\frac{n}{2}\ln(1-R) + \frac{1}{2}\ln(1+nR)\right.\right.$$
$$\left.\left. + \alpha \ln 2 \int Dt \, H^{n+1}\left(-\sqrt{\frac{R}{1-R}} t\right)\right]\right). \tag{2.40}$$

The limit $n \to 0$ is now easily found. Using (2.30) and noting that for $N \to \infty$ the remaining R-integral can be done by the saddle point method as explained in appendix A1.4 we finally obtain

$$S(\alpha) \sim N \max_R \left[\frac{1}{2}\ln(1-R) + \frac{R}{2}\right.$$
$$\left. + 2\alpha \int Dt \, H\left(-\sqrt{\frac{R}{1-R}} t\right) \ln H\left(-\sqrt{\frac{R}{1-R}} t\right)\right]. \tag{2.41}$$

Differentiating with respect to R we get as the condition for the maximum

$$\frac{R}{\sqrt{1-R}} = \frac{\alpha}{\pi} \int Dt \, \frac{\exp(-Rt^2/2)}{H(-\sqrt{R}t)}. \tag{2.42}$$

Equations (2.41) and (2.42) are equivalent to the results (A2.37) and (A2.36) respectively of the more detailed derivation performed in appendix 2.

Figure 2.3 shows the behaviour of the relevant quantities as they result from the numerical solution of (2.42) and subsequent use in (2.41) and (2.3). The qualitative behaviour is as in the annealed calculation. The teacher–student overlap R starts at $R = 0$ for $\alpha = 0$ and monotonically increases with α, tending asymptotically to $R = 1$ for $\alpha \to \infty$. Correspondingly the generalization error ε monotonically decreases from its "pure guessing" value $\varepsilon = 0.5$ to zero for $\alpha \to \infty$. The shrinkage of the version space with increasing number of training examples is quantified by the decrease of the quenched entropy with increasing α.

To test the quantitative accuracy of the Gardner approach we have included the result for $\varepsilon(\alpha)$ as the full line in fig. 1.4. As can be seen, the agreement with the

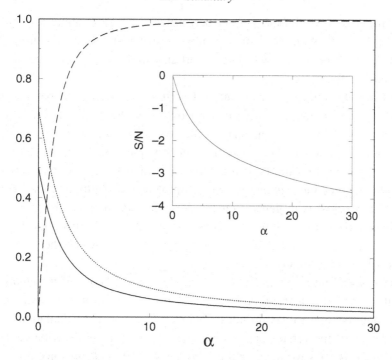

Fig. 2.3. Results for the teacher–student overlap R (dashed) and the generalization error ε (full) as functions of the training set size α. The inset shows the decrease of the quenched entropy per coupling with increasing α. The dotted line gives the behaviour of the information gain ΔI to be determined in problem 2.9.

simulation results is very good. The remaining differences for intermediate values of α are due to the fact that the simulations were done for $N = 20$ whereas the analytical calculations are strictly valid for $N \to \infty$ only. From the nevertheless good agreement between theory and simulation we may hope that the statistical mechanics analysis, which relies on the thermodynamic limit $N \to \infty$, often yields results that also describe finite systems quite accurately.

2.4 Summary

Let us briefly summarize the main points of this chapter. We introduced Gibbs learning as a natural and effective algorithm for a perceptron to learn from examples a target mapping specified by a teacher network. Starting from an *a priori* distribution of implementable classifications, which is mainly determined by the network architecture, learning is realized by simply rejecting all hypotheses which are at variance with at least one of the teacher classifications in the training set. For a large input dimension N the version space is then found to be dominated by coupling vectors with both perfect performance on the training set and large *a priori* probability. With increasing training set size α this balance is shifted more and more towards couplings with large overlap with the target coupling, resulting in a decreasing generalization error.

The basic problem of a quantitative description turns out to be the correct treatment of the randomness contained in the examples of the training set and the target mapping. Complementary to the worst case analysis central to many investigations in mathematical statistics and computer science, emphasis is in statistical mechanics on the typical behaviour, which for $N \rightarrow \infty$ occurs with probability 1. Since the calculation of the complete probability distribution of the quantities of interest is in general far too complicated, the typical behaviour has to be characterized by analytically accessible averages. To this end one has to identify quantities which are self-averaging, i.e. those for which the average and most probable value coincide.

We have seen that the volume of the version space is *not* self-averaging. Although its probability distribution becomes sharply peaked for $N \rightarrow \infty$, the most probable and average values do not coincide! The annealed calculation, resting on the average of the version space volume, therefore fails to describe the typical behaviour. Being easy to calculate it is nevertheless often useful since it may give insight into the qualitative behaviour of the system and can also yield fairly good quantitative approximations. In statistical mechanics, annealed averages describe systems in which *all* degrees of freedom show a stochastic dynamics which aims at minimizing the relevant thermodynamic potentials. For the learning problem this means that the annealed estimate corresponds to a learning scenario in which both the student couplings **J** *and the examples* ξ^μ of the training set are adapted to minimize the training error. In fact one can show [21] that within the annealed approximation, the distribution of the examples *after* learning is different from the distribution *before* learning. The degree of this modification determines the quantitative accuracy of the annealed approximation. In simple setups like the one analysed in the present chapter it may be rather good. However, as we will see in later chapters, it may also fail miserably.

The correct self-averaging quantity in the generalization problem turns out to be the *entropy* in phase space, i.e. the *logarithm* of the version space volume. Its analytical determination is possible for $N \rightarrow \infty$ using the replica trick borrowed from the statistical mechanics of disordered systems. The calculation is fairly straightforward within the replica symmetric ansatz, which we will always use in the first place for the investigation of a learning problem. One has to keep in mind, however, that a consistent treatment always requires checking the reliability of this ansatz. This question will be discussed in more detail in chapter 6. For the simple learning scenario discussed above the replica symmetric assumption yields correct results. This is related to the fact that the version space is connected,[5] meaning that for any two elements there is always a line connecting them that lies entirely inside the version space. Roughly speaking a connected version space is the equivalent to an ergodic dynamics, which in the theory of disordered systems is known to be correctly described by replica symmetry.

Let us finally quote the key references relevant to the present chapter. The annealed estimate of the generalization error as presented in the first section was proposed in [22] and [23]. The application of the replica method to networks of formal neurons was pioneered by Elizabeth Gardner in a series of seminal papers [24, 25, 26, 27]. The possibility of applying these techniques to rule inference problems was suggested in [28, 29, 27]. The special case of Gibbs learning in the teacher–student scenario was first studied in [30]. A detailed analysis of related situations is given in [21].

2.5 Problems

2.1 Show that the surface Ω_0 of an N-sphere is for large N to leading order given by

$$\Omega_0 = \exp\left(\frac{N}{2}[1 + \ln 2\pi]\right). \tag{2.43}$$

What is the exact result?

2.2 Evaluate the surface of a cap on the N-sphere defined by all vectors that make an angle smaller or equal to θ with a given direction. Show that this surface is dominated by the rim of the cap and verify in this way (2.5).

2.3 Show that the joint probability density $P(\lambda, u)$ for the variables defined in (2.17) is indeed Gaussian with moments given by (2.19). Start from

$$P(\lambda, u) = \left\langle\!\!\left\langle \delta\left(\lambda - \frac{1}{\sqrt{N}}\mathbf{J}\boldsymbol{\xi}\right)\delta\left(u - \frac{1}{\sqrt{N}}\mathbf{T}\boldsymbol{\xi}\right)\right\rangle\!\!\right\rangle \tag{2.44}$$

where the average is with respect to a randomly chosen example $\boldsymbol{\xi}$ on the N-sphere, and use the techniques introduced in appendix 1.

2.4 Show that the annealed entropy S^{ann} is never smaller than the quenched entropy S. When does equality hold?

2.5 Generate numerically M random numbers x each being the product of N independent random numbers equally distributed between 1 and 2 with M between 10^3 and 10^6 and N between 5 and 50. Approximate the distribution

---

[5] It is even convex, see problem 2.8.

of x by a histogram and compare the evolution with N of the most probable value x_{mp} of x with its average $\langle\langle x \rangle\rangle$ and the quantity $x_{typ} := \exp(\langle\langle \ln x \rangle\rangle)$. Could you give an argument why asymptotically (for $N \to \infty$) the most probable value and x_{typ} should coincide? Why is the most probable value always smaller than x_{typ} in the simulations?

(Hint: Compare the equations determining the most probable value of x and of $\ln x$.)

2.6 The number W of possible configurations of a system of p particles that can occupy N sites, with mutual exclusion and $p \leq N$, is given by the combinations of N elements in groups of p, $W = C_p^N = \binom{N}{p}$.

(a) Calculate the asymptotic behaviour of this quantity for $N \to \infty$ and $p \to \infty$ with fixed ratio $\alpha = p/N$ from the identity

$$W = \sum_{\{S_i\}} \delta\left(\sum_{i=0}^{N} S_i, p\right), \tag{2.45}$$

where $S_i = 0, 1$ with $S_i = 1$ corresponding to site i being occupied and $\sum_{\{S_i\}}$ denoting the sum over all the 2^N possible configurations of the S_i. Check the result with Stirling's formula.

(Hint: Use the exponential representation of the Kronecker-δ given by (A1.15).)

(b) Consider the same problem with sites blocked at random with probability ρ. If we introduce the random variables x_i, $i = 1, \ldots, N$, taking the value 0 for a blocked site, and 1 for an accessible site, the number of configurations is given by $W = \sum_{\{S_i\}} \delta(\sum_{i=0}^{N} S_i x_i, p)$. Evaluate the entropy $S = \ln W$ using both annealed and quenched averages. Check that only the quenched average is in agreement with the fact that the number of accessible sites is equal to $(1 - \rho)N$ with fluctuations of order $\sqrt{N}$.

2.7 The overlap R between teacher and student is, in contrast to the volume of the version space, a self-averaging quantity. It would thus seem at first that one can avoid the complicated replica calculation by directly evaluating the average overlap. The problem with this argument is that the version space volume appears now as a normalization factor

$$R = \left\langle\!\!\left\langle \frac{\mathbf{J}\mathbf{T}}{N} \right\rangle\!\!\right\rangle = \left\langle\!\!\left\langle \frac{\int d\mu(\mathbf{J}) \prod_\mu \theta\left((\frac{1}{\sqrt{N}}\mathbf{T}\boldsymbol{\xi}^\mu)(\frac{1}{\sqrt{N}}\mathbf{J}\boldsymbol{\xi}^\mu)\right)\mathbf{J}\mathbf{T}/N}{\int d\mu(\mathbf{J}) \prod_\mu \theta\left((\frac{1}{\sqrt{N}}\mathbf{T}\boldsymbol{\xi}^\mu)(\frac{1}{\sqrt{N}}\mathbf{J}\boldsymbol{\xi}^\mu)\right)} \right\rangle\!\!\right\rangle. \tag{2.46}$$

Show that by using $a^{-1} = \lim_{n\to 0} a^{n-1}$, the calculation is essentially reduced to the standard Gardner calculation in which the order parameter $R = \mathbf{J}\mathbf{T}/N$ is determined by the saddle point equation (2.42).

2.8 Show that the version space of the perceptron with real valued couplings obeying the spherical constraint (2.1) is convex. To this end show that for any two vectors $\mathbf{J}^{(1)}$ and $\mathbf{J}^{(2)}$ of the version space $\mathbf{J}(\gamma) = \gamma \mathbf{J}^{(1)} + (1 - \gamma)\mathbf{J}^{(2)}$ also corresponds to a vector of the version space for all $\gamma \in (0, 1)$. Take care with the normalization of $\mathbf{J}(\gamma)$.

2.9 Consider the expression

$$\Delta I = \left\langle\!\!\left\langle \ln \frac{\Omega(\boldsymbol{\xi}^1, \ldots, \boldsymbol{\xi}^{p-1}; \mathbf{T})}{\Omega(\boldsymbol{\xi}^1, \ldots, \boldsymbol{\xi}^p; \mathbf{T})} \right\rangle\!\!\right\rangle. \tag{2.47}$$

It describes the decrease of the version space volume induced by the p-th example in the training set. Since the logarithm of the relative reduction of the version space volume is nothing but the *additional information* about the teacher coupling gained from this example, ΔI is called the average *information gain*. From a comparison with (2.27) and (2.41) show that

$$\Delta I = S_{p-1} - S_p = -\frac{1}{N}\frac{dS(\alpha)}{d\alpha}$$

$$= -2 \int Dt\, H\!\left(-\sqrt{\frac{R}{1-R}}t\right) \ln H\!\left(-\sqrt{\frac{R}{1-R}}t\right), \tag{2.48}$$

and verify the behaviour of ΔI as a function of α as shown in fig. 2.3. Why does ΔI decrease with increasing α? Could you think of a learning scenario that ensures *constant* information gain for all examples? What kind of scaling of ε with α would you expect for such a case?

2.10 Determine the asymptotic behaviour of the quantities describing Gibbs learning for large training set size α. To this end show starting from (2.42) that

$$1 - R \sim \left[\frac{\alpha}{\pi}\int Dt\, \frac{e^{-t^2/2}}{H(-t)}\right]^{-2} \sim \frac{1.926}{\alpha^2} \tag{2.49}$$

and consequently

$$\varepsilon \sim \frac{\sqrt{2}}{\int Dt\,[\exp(-t^2/2)]/H(t)}\frac{1}{\alpha} \sim \frac{0.625}{\alpha}, \tag{2.50}$$

$$S \sim \frac{1}{2}\ln(1-R) \sim -\ln\alpha, \tag{2.51}$$

$$\Delta I \sim -\sqrt{\frac{2(1-R)}{\pi}}\int dt\, H(t)\ln H(t) \sim \frac{2.60}{\alpha}. \tag{2.52}$$

as follows from (2.3), (2.41) and (2.48).

2.11 Consider the so-called *nearest neighbour classifier*. It returns as the classification of a new input pattern $\mathbf{S}$ the teacher classification for that pattern $\boldsymbol{\xi}$ of the training set with the smallest angle with $\mathbf{S}$ (the nearest neighbour). Introducing the probabilities

$$P(a, b) = \left\langle\!\!\left\langle \delta\left(\frac{\boldsymbol{\xi}\mathbf{S}}{\sqrt{N}} - a\right)\delta\left(\frac{\boldsymbol{\xi}\mathbf{T}}{\sqrt{N}} - b\right)\right\rangle\!\!\right\rangle_{\!\xi\mu}, \tag{2.53}$$

$$P(a) = \left\langle\!\!\left\langle \delta\left(\frac{\boldsymbol{\xi}\mathbf{S}}{\sqrt{N}} - a\right)\right\rangle\!\!\right\rangle_{\!\xi\mu}, \tag{2.54}$$

show that the generalization error is given by

$$\varepsilon(p) = p\left\langle\!\!\left\langle \int_{-\infty}^{0} db \int da\, P(a, b)\left[\int_{-\infty}^{a} da'\, P(a')\right]^{p-1}\right\rangle\!\!\right\rangle_{\!\mathbf{S}}. \tag{2.55}$$

Calculate the limit of $\varepsilon(p)$ for $p = \alpha N \to \infty$. What can be inferred from the result about the performance of this learning algorithm in high-dimensional problems?

(Hint: Consult [31] in case of difficulty.)

3

A Choice of Learning Rules

The Gibbs rule discussed in the previous chapter characterizes the typical general-ization behaviour of the students forming the version space. It is hence well suited for a general theoretical analysis. For a concrete practical problem it is, however, hardly the best choice and there is a variety of other learning rules which are often more direct and may also show a better performance. The purpose of this chapter is to introduce a representative selection of these learning rules, to discuss some of their features, and to compare their properties with those of the Gibbs rule.

3.1 The Hebb rule

The oldest and maybe most important learning rule was introduced by D. Hebb in the late 1940s. It is, in fact, an application at the level of single neurons of the idea of Pavlov coincidence training. In his famous experiment, Pavlov showed how a dog, which was trained to receive its food when, at the same time, a light was being turned on, would also start to salivate when the light alone was lit. In some way, the coincidence of the two events, food and light, had established a connection in the brain of the dog such that, even when only one of the events occurred, the memory of the other would be stimulated. The basic idea behind the Hebb rule [32] is quite similar: strengthen the connection of neurons that fire together. As a result, the firing of a single one of them will stimulate the other neuron to fire as well.

The Hebb rule applied to the simple perceptron architecture takes on the following form. Let ξ_i^μ be the input of example $\boldsymbol{\xi}^\mu$ at the input channel J_i of the neuron. If the required output $\sigma_T^\mu = \mathrm{sgn}(\mathbf{T}\boldsymbol{\xi}^\mu)$ has the same sign as ξ_i^μ, we have coincidence and the connection has to be strengthened: $J_i^{(\mathrm{new})} = J_i^{(\mathrm{old})} + 1$. If they have different signs, the original Hebb rule prescribes no change. However, for symmetry reasons, we will decrease the connection strength: $J_i^{(\mathrm{new})} = J_i^{(\mathrm{old})} - 1$. With this convention the Hebb rule may be written in vector notation as $\mathbf{J}^{(\mathrm{new})} = \mathbf{J}^{(\mathrm{old})} + \boldsymbol{\xi}^\mu \sigma_T^\mu$. For a set of p training examples, each being presented once to the

33

network, one hence finds the coupling strength

$$\mathbf{J}^H = \frac{1}{\sqrt{N}} \sum_{\mu} \boldsymbol{\xi}^{\mu} \sigma_T^{\mu}, \tag{3.1}$$

where we have included a normalization factor that guarantees $\mathbf{J}^2 \sim N$ for large N.

The particularly simple structure of the Hebb rule allows us to find its training and generalization error rather easily. We start by defining the *stability* or *aligning field* Δ^{ν} of an input $\boldsymbol{\xi}^{\nu}$ by

$$\Delta^{\nu} = \frac{1}{\sqrt{N}} \mathbf{J} \boldsymbol{\xi}^{\nu} \sigma_T^{\nu}. \tag{3.2}$$

A correct classification of $\boldsymbol{\xi}^{\nu}$ is equivalent to the condition that the quantity Δ^{ν} be positive. To evaluate the probability for this to be the case, we use the explicit expression of the Hebb vector (3.1) to rewrite Δ^{ν} as

$$\Delta^{\nu} = 1 + \frac{1}{N} \sum_{\mu \neq \nu} \boldsymbol{\xi}^{\mu} \boldsymbol{\xi}^{\nu} \sigma_T^{\mu} \sigma_T^{\nu}. \tag{3.3}$$

The interpretation of this formula is clear. The first term in the r.h.s. is the so-called *signal* term, and derives from the contribution of example $\boldsymbol{\xi}^{\nu}$ to $\mathbf{J}^H$. It gives a positive contribution to the stability of the example, hence to its correct classification. The second term is the so-called *noise* term stemming from the crosstalk with the other examples. It is a random quantity that interferes with the correct classification of $\boldsymbol{\xi}^{\nu}$.

For the analysis of the statistical properties of Δ^{ν} it is most convenient to assume that the distribution P_S according to which the examples $\boldsymbol{\xi}^{\mu}$ are chosen is the uniform distribution on the N-sphere.[1] We now decompose all the examples into parts orthogonal and parallel to the teacher vector:

$$\boldsymbol{\xi}^{\mu} = \boldsymbol{\xi}_{\perp}^{\mu} + \boldsymbol{\xi}_{\parallel}^{\mu} \tag{3.4}$$

with $\boldsymbol{\xi}_{\parallel}^{\mu} = \xi_{\parallel}^{\mu} \mathbf{T}$. This gives rise to

$$\Delta^{\nu} = 1 + \xi_{\parallel}^{\nu} \sigma_T^{\nu} \frac{1}{N} \sum_{\mu \neq \nu} \xi_{\parallel}^{\mu} \sigma_T^{\mu} + \frac{1}{N} \sum_{\mu \neq \nu} \boldsymbol{\xi}_{\perp}^{\mu} \boldsymbol{\xi}_{\perp}^{\nu} \sigma_T^{\mu} \sigma_T^{\nu}. \tag{3.5}$$

The orthogonal part is uncorrelated with the classification σ_T^{μ}, so that $\boldsymbol{\xi}_{\perp}^{\mu} \sigma_T^{\mu}$ is a random vector on the $(N-1)$-sphere in the space orthogonal to $\mathbf{T}$. Consequently $\sum_{\mu \neq \nu} \boldsymbol{\xi}_{\perp}^{\mu} \boldsymbol{\xi}_{\perp}^{\nu} \sigma_T^{\mu} \sigma_T^{\nu}$ is the sum of $N(p-1)$ independent random variables, so it

---

[1] For large N only the first and second moment of P_S are important and these coincide with the distribution (1.5), see problem 1.3.

converges to $N\sqrt{\alpha}y$, where y is a normally distributed random variable with zero mean and unit variance.

On the other hand $\xi_{\parallel}^{\mu}\sigma_{T}^{\mu} = |\xi_{\parallel}^{\mu}|$ is the absolute value of a normal random variable x, independent of y. Furthermore, $\sum_{\mu \neq \nu}|\xi_{\parallel}^{\mu}|$ is the sum of the absolute values of $(p-1)$ independent random variables, so it converges to $N\alpha\sqrt{2/\pi}$.

The probability for misclassification of example ξ^{ν} by the Hebbian coupling vector is thus equal to the probability that $\Delta^{\nu} = 1 + \alpha\sqrt{2/\pi}|x| + \sqrt{\alpha}y$ is negative. The training error is hence given by

$$\varepsilon_t = 2\int_0^{\infty} Dx \int_{-\infty}^{-\frac{1}{\sqrt{\alpha}}-\sqrt{\frac{2\alpha}{\pi}}x} Dy = 2\int_0^{\infty} Dx\, H\left(\frac{1}{\sqrt{\alpha}}+\sqrt{\frac{2\alpha}{\pi}}x\right). \quad (3.6)$$

Note that in contrast to the Gibbs rule, where the training error is zero by construction, the Hebb rule does not succeed in learning the training examples perfectly. One might suspect that the generalization error will then always be higher. It turns out, however, that this is not the case.

To evaluate the generalization error ε, we use again the statistical properties of $\xi_{\parallel}^{\mu}$ and note that

$$\frac{\mathbf{J}^H\mathbf{T}}{N} = \frac{1}{N}\sum_{\mu}\frac{\mathbf{T}\xi^{\mu}\sigma_{T}^{\mu}}{\sqrt{N}} = \frac{1}{N}\sum_{\mu}|\xi_{\parallel}^{\mu}| \quad (3.7)$$

is, by virtue of the law of large numbers, a self-averaging quantity equal to $\alpha\sqrt{2/\pi}$. By a similar argument one finds that the length of $\mathbf{J}^H$ is self-averaging and equal to $\sqrt{N\alpha(1+2\alpha/\pi)}$. Since $R = \mathbf{JT}/(|\mathbf{J}||\mathbf{T}|)$ and the generalization error is given in terms of R by (2.3), we find

$$\varepsilon = \frac{1}{\pi}\arccos\sqrt{\frac{2\alpha}{2\alpha+\pi}}. \quad (3.8)$$

To make the comparison with Gibbs learning, it is instructive to determine the small- and large-α behaviour:

$$\varepsilon_t \sim \sqrt{\frac{2\alpha}{\pi}}\exp\left(-\frac{1}{2\alpha}+\frac{1}{\pi}\right)H\left(\sqrt{\frac{2}{\pi}}\right) \quad \text{and} \quad \varepsilon(\alpha) \sim \frac{1}{2}-\frac{\sqrt{2\alpha}}{\pi^{3/2}} \quad \text{for} \quad \alpha \to 0 \quad (3.9)$$

$$\varepsilon_t \sim \varepsilon \sim \frac{1}{\sqrt{2\pi\alpha}} \sim \frac{0.40}{\sqrt{\alpha}} \quad \text{for} \quad \alpha \to \infty. \quad (3.10)$$

One concludes that the generalization error decreases to zero much more slowly than for the Gibbs rule for $\alpha \to \infty$ (cf. problem 2.10). Nevertheless, in a sense, the Hebb rule is doing not much worse than most of the other learning rules for large α since the *difference* between training and generalization error decreases asymptotically as $1/\alpha$. Its generalization performance is hence poor due to the poor ability to learn the training examples correctly!

The situation is quite different for small α: the Hebb rule produces a decrease of the generalization error with α that is faster than for the Gibbs rule. In fact, as we will see below, it achieves the lowest possible initial generalization error.

Being based on the simple principle of coincidence training, the Hebb rule has a wide range of applicability, including most neural architectures and training schemes. It will therefore be used in several of the following chapters. A point of particular importance for hardware implementation is that the Hebb rule is a *local* learning rule: one only needs to know the state at the input and output to calculate the correction on the connecting synapse. Moreover, it is very easy to implement by using the explicit and additive prescription (3.1). New examples can hence be included into the training set without having to reconsider the previous ones.

On the downside, we note that the Hebb rule has a non-zero training error, so it does not learn the available information perfectly. As a result its performance on large training sets is rather poor. We also mention that the Hebb rule fails miserably if the examples of the training set are correlated with each other.

3.2 The perceptron rule

The couplings (3.1) resulting from the Hebb rule can be written in the form

$$\mathbf{J} = \frac{1}{\sqrt{N}} \sum_{\mu} x^{\mu} \boldsymbol{\xi}^{\mu} \sigma_T^{\mu} \tag{3.11}$$

with the *embedding strengths* x^{μ} all equal. Hence all examples of the training set leave the same trace in the couplings and it is this levelling of information which causes the poor performance of the Hebb rule for large α.

An obvious modification to overcome the problem is to *omit* those examples from the superposition (3.1) that are correctly classified anyway. This can be done most easily in a sequential manner. Let $\mathbf{J}^{(\text{old})}$ be the weight vector at some point in the training and let $\boldsymbol{\xi}^{\mu}$ be a new training example. If it is correctly classified, we leave the old weight vector *unchanged*. Otherwise we make a correction identical to that of the Hebb rule, i.e.

$$\mathbf{J}^{(\text{new})} = \begin{cases} \mathbf{J}^{(\text{old})} + \dfrac{1}{\sqrt{N}} \boldsymbol{\xi}^{\mu} \sigma_T^{\mu} & \text{if } \mathbf{J}^{(\text{old})} \boldsymbol{\xi}^{\mu} \sigma_T^{\mu} < 0 \\ \mathbf{J}^{(\text{old})} & \text{otherwise.} \end{cases} \tag{3.12}$$

This is the famous perceptron learning rule which together with the perceptron became very popular during the early 1960s, largely thanks to the pioneering work of F. Rosenblatt [6]. It clearly produces a non-trivial spectrum of embedding strengths x^μ. The striking feature of the perceptron rule is that, when iterated, it converges, i.e. it finds a **J**-vector with zero training error in a *finite* number of steps, whenever such a solution is available. The proof of convergence is given in appendix 3.

The calculation of the generalization error cannot be performed in the same simple way as for the Hebb rule. In fact being a dynamical prescription the perceptron rule is most conveniently analysed in the framework of on-line learning (cf. section 9.2). However, building on the analogy with the Hebb rule, an "off-line" analogue of the perceptron rule may be formulated, for which the generalization properties are discussed in [33].

An interesting aspect of the perceptron rule is that it may easily be modified for the numerical analysis of Gibbs learning. It is not completely trivial to implement Gibbs learning in simulations since it is not straightforward how to pick a vector at random from the version space, which is only an exponentially small fraction of the total **J**-space. By including, in the perceptron rule, a random contribution with zero mean and suitable variance with each update (3.12) of the couplings, one is sure to finally land in the version space at more or less a random position. This procedure was used in the simulations shown in fig. 1.4 with the variance of the random part 50 times the systematic contributions. Of course the convergence of the algorithm is slowed down by this modification but the resulting coupling vectors are to a very good approximation distributed evenly over the version space [34]. In this respect the modified perceptron rule seems to be superior to other methods for simulating Gibbs learning such as random walk [21, 35] or billiard [36] in the version space or randomly augmented training sets [37].

3.3 The pseudo-inverse rule

Any learning rule tries to tally the student and the teacher output. The idea of the pseudo-inverse rule is to circumvent the non-linearity inherent in the neuron activation function and to prescribe the post-synaptic potentials or, equivalently, the stabilities Δ^μ of the student rather than his outputs. Intuitively one would expect a good generalization performance if these stabilities were as large as possible. The corresponding coupling vectors would then lie near the centre of the version space, the boundaries of which are given by $\Delta^\mu = 0$ for at least one μ. Specifically, the pseudo-inverse rule requires that all stabilities should be equal to each other, $\Delta^\mu = \kappa$, with the common value κ for fixed norm $\mathbf{J}^2$ *as large as possible* [38]. In other words, the pseudo-inverse vector is the vector that makes the same angle with all the aligned inputs $\boldsymbol{\xi}^\mu \sigma_T^\mu$, while this angle is at the same time as small as possible.

Geometrically, it is clear that the condition that all angles are equal can only be realized for $p/N = \alpha < 1$. Furthermore, the pseudo-inverse $\mathbf{J}$-vector must lie in the subspace spanned by the examples, i.e. have again the form (3.11). This can be most easily seen as follows. Maximizing the stabilities for constant normalization of the couplings is equivalent to minimizing the norm $\mathbf{J}^2$ for fixed stabilities. Components of $\mathbf{J}$ perpendicular to all examples do not contribute to the stabilities Δ^μ. Since they nevertheless increase the norm $\mathbf{J}^2$ the optimal $\mathbf{J}$ should have no such components.

To find the pseudo-inverse coupling vector we may hence set $\Delta^\mu = \kappa = 1$ for all μ and use the form (3.11) in order to ensure minimal norm of $\mathbf{J}^2$. We can then use simple linear algebra to explicitly construct $\mathbf{J}$. To this end we start with the following system of linear equations:

$$\sum_\nu C_{\mu\nu} x^\nu = 1 \quad \text{for all } \mu \tag{3.13}$$

for the embedding strengths x^μ, where we have introduced the correlation matrix of the examples according to

$$C_{\mu\nu} = \frac{1}{N} \boldsymbol{\xi}^\mu \boldsymbol{\xi}^\nu \sigma_T^\mu \sigma_T^\nu. \tag{3.14}$$

If the vectors $\boldsymbol{\xi}^\mu \sigma_T^\mu$ are linearly independent, as happens with probability 1 for large N and independent $\boldsymbol{\xi}^\mu$, $C_{\mu\nu}$ is non-singular and (3.13) has a unique solution. The corresponding coupling vector is given by

$$\mathbf{J}^{\text{PI}} = \frac{1}{\sqrt{N}} \sum_{\mu,\nu} (C^{-1})_{\mu\nu} \boldsymbol{\xi}^\mu \sigma_T^\mu. \tag{3.15}$$

It may be obtained without recourse to the embedding strengths by using the Moore–Penrose pseudo-inverse of the $N \times p$ matrix formed by the column vectors $\boldsymbol{\xi}^\mu \sigma_T^\mu$ [38, 39], hence the name of this learning rule. It is also referred to as the *projection* rule since $\mathbf{J}^{\text{PI}}\mathbf{S}$ gives the projection of the input $\mathbf{S}$ on the subspace spanned by the examples $\boldsymbol{\xi}^\mu$. Like the perceptron rule, it realizes zero training error. It is very efficient in the case of correlated inputs since (3.15) effectively decorrelates the examples. Note on the other hand that the projection rule is very awkward to implement due to its non-local character. Adding a new example to the training set requires one to calculate and invert the correlation matrix $C_{\mu\nu}$ completely afresh! In this form it is not a likely candidate for biological or technical use.

For $\alpha > 1$ it is impossible to satisfy the condition $\Delta^\mu = \kappa$ for all μ. The best one could try then is to minimize the error between observed and required stabilities. This is realized by the adaline rule.

3.4 The adaline rule

Adaline stands for *adap*tive *lin*ear *ne*uron. It was introduced by Widrow in the early 1960s [40] and commercialized by the sale of a hardware device, the memistor, by what is probably the first neural network company ever, the Memistor Corporation. The output of a linear neuron is just its post-synaptic potential

$$\sigma = \mathbf{J}\boldsymbol{\xi}. \tag{3.16}$$

As a learning rule, Widrow introduced the so-called delta or adaline rule, which goes back to the method of least square error, familiar from statistics. To achieve least square error, one performs gradient descent on the total square error

$$E(\mathbf{J}) = \frac{1}{2} \sum_{\mu} (\mathbf{J}\boldsymbol{\xi}^{\mu} - \sigma_T^{\mu})^2, \tag{3.17}$$

leading to the updating correction

$$\delta \mathbf{J} = -\gamma \frac{\partial E}{\partial \mathbf{J}} = \gamma \sum_{\mu} \delta^{\mu} \boldsymbol{\xi}^{\mu}, \tag{3.18}$$

where we have introduced a learning rate γ. The delta factor $\delta^{\mu} = \mathbf{J}\boldsymbol{\xi}^{\mu} - \sigma_T^{\mu}$, which is the error contributed by example μ, appears as the increment for the embedding strength of example μ. One of the advantages of using such *adaptive* increments, rather than the constant steps $\delta x^{\mu} = 1$ of the perceptron rule, is the rather fast convergence of the algorithm. In fact it can be shown that the quadratic error decreases exponentially as a function of the updates in the learning process, and the characteristic learning time τ has been calculated as a function of the training set size α [41]. Another advantage of the delta rule is that it can be easily generalized to the case of a neuron with a general differentiable activation function and, more importantly, to multilayer architectures, where it takes the form of the well-known back-propagation algorithm (see chapter 13). The adaline rule formulated above has a slight disadvantage, namely that components of the $\mathbf{J}$-vector lying in the subspace orthogonal to the examples do not decay. This feature is avoided in the explicit prescription given by the pseudo-inverse rule. However, one can prove that for $\alpha < 1$ the adaline rule converges to the couplings $\mathbf{J}^{\text{PI}}$ of the projection rule as given by (3.15) [42], provided one starts with a vector that has no component in this subspace. In fact, as such it is nothing but a sequential algorithm to perform the matrix inversion needed for the implementation of the pseudo-inverse rule.

To formulate the adaline rule in a way consistent with the statistical mechanics approach presented in the next chapter, we will restrict ourselves to the case of binary output values $\sigma_T = +1$ or -1, so that (3.17) may be rewritten as

$$E(\mathbf{J}) = \frac{1}{2} \sum_\mu (\mathbf{J}\boldsymbol{\xi}^\mu \sigma_T^\mu - 1)^2. \tag{3.19}$$

In the adaline rule, the length of the $\mathbf{J}$-vector forms an integer part of the set of parameters which have to be optimized. Instead, we consider a vector $\mathbf{J}' = \sqrt{N}\mathbf{J}/|\mathbf{J}|$, which obeys our standard normalization constraint $(\mathbf{J}')^2 = N$, and introduce $|\mathbf{J}|^{-1} = \kappa$ as a new parameter over which a maximization may be performed. Dropping the prime in $\mathbf{J}'$ the cost function takes on the form

$$E(\mathbf{J}) = \frac{1}{2\kappa^2} \sum_\mu (\Delta^\mu - \kappa)^2, \tag{3.20}$$

which we will refer to as the adaline cost function in the sequel. In this form the adaline rule forms a natural generalization of the pseudo-inverse rule to $\alpha > 1$.

3.5 Maximal stability

The pseudo-inverse rule discussed in subsection 3.3 introduces the constraint $\Delta^\mu = \kappa$ for all μ. However, the correct condition for a network with optimal stabilities is

$$\Delta^\mu \geq \kappa > 0 \tag{3.21}$$

with κ, characterizing the *minimal* confidence the student has in his classifications of the training set examples, again *as large as possible*.[2] Analysing, however, the embedding strengths x^μ resulting from the pseudo-inverse rule one realizes that some of them are negative! This means that examples which by chance have large stabilities right from the start are actually *unlearned*. A rather obvious idea to avoid unlearning is to leave examples with $\Delta^\mu > \kappa$ untouched. In this way the *maximally stable network* is produced, the coupling vector $\mathbf{J}^{MS}$ of which has the largest possible distance to all boundaries of the version space.

A straightforward solution to the optimization problem (3.21) goes as follows. For a current weight vector $\mathbf{J}^{(old)}$, we determine the example $\boldsymbol{\xi}^\nu$ with minimal stability, i.e.

$$\Delta^\nu = \min_\mu \Delta^\mu, \tag{3.22}$$

and perform the Hebb learning step $\mathbf{J}^{(new)} = \mathbf{J}^{(old)} + \boldsymbol{\xi}^\nu \sigma_T^\nu/\sqrt{N}$. This so-called *minover* (*min*imal *over*lap) algorithm converges to a solution with $\Delta^\mu > c$ for all μ after a finite number of steps for any given c. Furthermore the maximally stable coupling vector $\mathbf{J}^{MS}$ is generated in the limit $c \to \infty$ [43]. As for the adaline rule

---

[2] This condition is of course only meaningful if we at the same time fix the length of $\mathbf{J}$, for example by choosing it on the N-sphere.

the convergence time τ can be calculated [44], and one finds for large training set size α the asymptotic behaviour $\tau \sim 0.65\alpha^2$ [45].

However, a much more direct and elegant way to solve the optimization problem for the maximally stable coupling vector is to use the decomposition (3.11) and to work from the start with the embedding strengths x^μ. We then find

$$\Delta^\mu = \sum_\nu C_{\mu\nu} x^\nu \quad \text{and} \quad J^2 = \sum_{\mu,\nu} x^\mu C_{\mu\nu} x^\nu \tag{3.23}$$

with the correlation matrix $C_{\mu\nu}$ as defined in (3.14). To determine J^{MS} we have therefore to minimize $f(x^\mu) = \sum_{\mu,\nu} x^\mu C_{\mu\nu} x^\nu$ subject to the constraints $\sum_\nu C_{\nu\mu} x^\nu > 1$ for all μ. This is a standard problem of convex optimization. Since the quadratic cost function is strictly convex the solution is unique and there is a set of necessary and sufficient conditions called the *Kuhn–Tucker conditions* which result from a generalization of the Lagrange method of undetermined multipliers to inequality constraints [46]. In the present problem these conditions require that a solution $\bar{x}^\mu$ of the optimization problem has to satisfy

$$\sum_\nu C_{\mu\nu} \bar{x}^\nu \geq 1, \quad \bar{x}^\mu \geq 0 \quad \text{and} \quad \bar{x}^\mu \left(1 - \sum_\nu C_{\mu\nu} \bar{x}^\nu\right) = 0. \tag{3.24}$$

The first set of these conditions is identical to the constraints. The second ensures that contrary to the pseudo-inverse rule no example is unlearned. The third has the following simple intuitive meaning. If an example ξ^μ has a stability larger than 1, which means that it is by chance correctly classified, it is not necessary to include its Hebbian term into J^{MS} and therefore $x^\mu = 0$. Such an example is called *passive*. On the other hand, if an example ξ^μ requires an explicit contribution in J in order to be classified correctly it is called *active*. In such a case $x^\mu > 0$ but at the same time the maximally stable coupling vector J^{MS} would make the stability Δ^μ *exactly* equal to 1 since a larger value would only reduce the flexibility with respect to the other examples in the training set.

It is now very attractive to design a learning algorithm which exploits this division of the examples into active and passive ones. Such an algorithm would leave the passive examples untouched and use the quick adaline prescription to learn all the active ones to the *same* stability. This so called *adatron* algorithm [47] therefore combines the selectivity of the perceptron rule with the adaptive step size of adaline, as the name suggests. Explicitly, it uses after the calculation of the correlation matrix $C_{\mu\nu}$ the updates

$$\delta x^\mu = \begin{cases} \gamma(1 - \Delta^\mu) & \text{if} \quad \Delta^\mu < 1 \\ -x^\mu & \text{otherwise} \end{cases} \tag{3.25}$$

where again γ denotes the learning rate. The adatron rule clearly produces nonnegative embedding strengths x^μ. Moreover its convergence can be proven in a similar way as for the perceptron rule. For sequential implementation the adatron rule finds the maximally stable coupling vector whenever it exists for $0 < \gamma < 2$ [47]. Furthermore, as in the case of adaline learning the convergence is exponential and very efficient numerical implementations exist [47, 48, 49]. The generalization behaviour of this rule is better than that of all rules discussed before, as will be shown in the next chapter. For these reasons the adatron rule is probably the most frequently used learning rule in numerical investigations of perceptron learning. The notion of maximal stability also plays a crucial role in the theory of support vector machines (see section 14.1).

3.6 The Bayes rule

It is of principal interest to know for a generalization problem whether there is an *optimal way* to use the information about the teacher contained in the classifications of the training set. If so it should give rise to a *lower bound* for the generalization error that cannot be passed by any learning rule. The question then arises how near one can come to this theoretical optimum and whether an explicit learning prescription can be found that saturates the bound. These questions will be investigated in the present section since the Bayes rule is *defined* as the rule which minimizes the generalization error by utilizing the available information in a statistically optimal way.

First of all we have to realize that all the training set can tell us about the teacher is that she has to lie in the version space. In order to find the optimal student, however, we need additional statistical information about *where* in the version space the teacher is more or less likely to be found. This information is given by what is called the *a priori* distribution P_T of the teacher. We consider here only the simplest and most natural situation, by assuming "equal *a priori* probabilities", or more precisely, by specifying that the **T**-vector is chosen at random with uniform probability on the N-sphere. It is then clear that the teacher will occupy any position in the version space with equal probability.

We now proceed to construct the optimal coupling vector $\mathbf{J}^B$ with lowest generalization error. Since the generalization error is a monotonically decreasing function of the overlap R, we need the vector on the N-sphere which on average realizes the largest overlap with the teacher, where the average is now *over the distribution of the teacher*. For a vector $\mathbf{J}$, constructed on the basis of a given training set, this average overlap is given by

$$R = \frac{1}{N} \frac{\int_{\text{VS}} d\mu(\mathbf{T}) \, \mathbf{J} \mathbf{T}}{\int_{\text{VS}} d\mu(\mathbf{T})}. \tag{3.26}$$

The vector $\mathbf{J}$ is fixed in this average and can hence be moved outside of the integration over the version space. Since furthermore its length is fixed, the above expression attains its maximum for a vector pointing along the *centre of mass* of the version space. The Bayes coupling vector is hence given by

$$\mathbf{J}^{\mathrm{B}} \sim \int_{\mathrm{VS}} d\mu(\mathbf{T})\, \mathbf{T}. \qquad (3.27)$$

To determine the generalization error of the Bayes vector $\mathbf{J}^{\mathrm{B}}$ constructed in this way we use the following elegant argument [37]. A simple approximate way to generate $\mathbf{J}^{\mathrm{B}}$ is to sample a large number M of Gibbs vectors $\mathbf{J}^{(i)}$, $i = 1, \ldots, M$, and to form their centre of mass. In fact, in the limit $M \to \infty$ this centre of mass will coincide exactly with the direction of $\mathbf{J}^{\mathrm{B}}$, i.e.

$$\mathbf{J}^{\mathrm{B}} = \lim_{M \to \infty} \sqrt{N}\, \frac{\sum\limits_{i=1}^{M} \mathbf{J}^{(i)}}{\sqrt{\left(\sum\limits_{i=1}^{M} \mathbf{J}^{(i)}\right)^2}}. \qquad (3.28)$$

Using the fact that the overlap between two randomly chosen members of the version space is a self-averaging quantity R as discussed in section 2.3, one finds that the denominator behaves as $\sqrt{MN + M(M-1)RN} \sim M\sqrt{NR}$ for M large. One thus obtains $R_{\mathrm{B}} = \mathbf{J}^{\mathrm{B}}\mathbf{T}/N = \sqrt{R}$ and hence from (2.42) the equation

$$\frac{R_{\mathrm{B}}^2}{\sqrt{1 - R_{\mathrm{B}}^2}} = \frac{\alpha}{\pi} \int Dt\, \frac{\exp\{-\frac{1}{2}R_{\mathrm{B}}^2 t^2\}}{H(-R_{\mathrm{B}}t)} \qquad (3.29)$$

for R_{B} is found.

From this equation one may extract the asymptotic results

$$\varepsilon(\alpha) \sim \frac{1}{2} - \frac{\sqrt{2\alpha}}{\pi^{3/2}} + O(\alpha) \quad \text{for} \quad \alpha \to 0 \qquad (3.30)$$

which is identical to the result obtained for the Hebb rule, cf. (3.9), and

$$\varepsilon(\alpha) \sim \frac{\varepsilon_{\mathrm{Gibbs}}(\alpha)}{\sqrt{2}} \sim \frac{0.442}{\alpha} \quad \text{for} \quad \alpha \to \infty. \qquad (3.31)$$

This result hence gives a lower bound for the asymptotic performance of any rule of perceptron learning.

When optimizing the generalization error according to the above procedure, we made a tacit and innocent looking assumption, namely that the optimal choice $\mathbf{J}^{\mathrm{B}}$ does not depend on the new question that is being posed. In fact, a truly Bayesian optimal procedure goes as follows. Upon presenting a new example, we let every member of the version space give its classification, and then we follow the majority

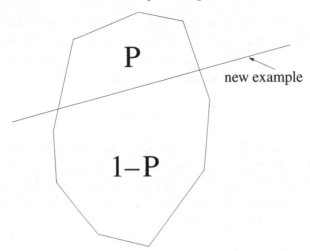

Fig. 3.1. Schematic representation of the version space. Upon presentation of a new example, it is divided into two regions with relative sizes P and $1 - P$.

vote. In this way the probability of error is indeed minimized. It is instructive to visualize this procedure, cf. fig. 3.1. The version space is represented schematically as the enclosed region. A new example will divide the version space into two subsets, corresponding respectively to a $+1$ and -1 classification of the example. Since the teacher is evenly distributed in the version space the classification which has lowest probability of error is obviously that of the majority region. So any member in this region will be Bayes optimal for the particular example under consideration. Now consider another example, characterized by another line dividing the version space. Again, the Bayes rule prescribes following the new majority decision, but this consists of another subregion of the version space. It is now clear that, as more and more examples are considered, it becomes doubtful whether one can identify one single point in the version space that always lies in the majority region. In fact, there is no such point in general; see fig. 3.2 for a simple example [36]. One of the remarkable features however of the thermodynamic limit is that, at least for the simple case of the perceptron, the centre of mass of the version space does have this property with probability 1. This is in turn the reason why Bayesian learning can be implemented without modifying the architecture of the perceptron. This is no longer true when one considers multilayer networks.

The geometric point of view presented above also allows us to find a simple bound relating the Bayes and Gibbs generalization errors [50]. Consider again the two subsets of the version space, corresponding to a $+1$ or -1 classification of a randomly chosen new example $\mathbf{S}$ shown in fig. 3.1, and let us call their respective fractions of the version space P and $1 - P$. A student from the version space will

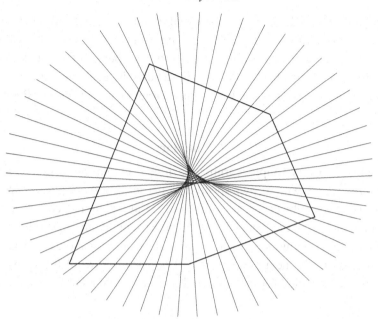

Fig. 3.2. The set of lines which divide a polygon, representing the version space, into two regions of equal size do not cross through the same point. Hence there is no single point which, for all possible lines, lies in the region with largest size.

give the wrong answer to the question under consideration whenever the teacher happens to lie in the other subset. In the Gibbs scenario, one samples at random a student from the version space. Since the teacher is also equally likely to lie anywhere in the version space, we find that the Gibbs generalization error is equal to $2P(1-P)$. In the Bayes rule, one follows the majority rule, which will be wrong if the teacher happens to lie in the minority region. Hence the Bayes generalization error is given by $\min(P, 1-P)$. Note that P is unknown, and is in fact a random variable depending on the question under consideration. However, one may use the following inequalities, which are valid for any $P \in [0, 1]$

$$\min(P, 1-P) \le 2P(1-P) \le 2\min(P, 1-P). \qquad (3.32)$$

We conclude that the Gibbs generalization error is always larger than the Bayes error (as it should be) but smaller than twice the Bayes error.

It is finally tempting to use the above argument to derive a bound for the generalization error of a *worst case* scenario. What about an "anti-Bayes" rule in which one follows the minority decision? Here the generalization error should be $\max(P, 1-P)$. In writing down this result, we overlooked a detail: when the minority region is empty, $\min(P, 1-P) = 0$, one cannot select a student in the version space with this wrong classification (since there is none). So in fact the generalization error of the worst case is equal to $\max(P, 1 - P)$ when $P \neq 0$ and zero when $P = 0$. Unfortunately, this explicit result does not allow us to compare it with the Bayes or Gibbs error if the probability distribution of P is unknown; see however problem 3.8. In chapter 10, we will see that the generalization error of the worst student in the version space is not much larger than the Gibbs or Bayes error.

3.7 Summary

The perceptron is a very simple learning machine. Yet one can formulate a variety of learning rules, each with its own specific properties. For those who are interested in the history of the subject, we recommend [51] in which a selection of reprints can be found, including the works of Hebb and Rosenblatt amongst others.

We derived the training and generalization error only for the case of Hebb and Bayes learning. In the next chapter, it will be shown how all the rules may be discussed within a unified formalism based on a statistical mechanics approach.

3.8 Problems

3.1 Write a sequence of 100 numbers $S_i = +1$ or $S_i = -1$, $i = 1, \ldots, 100$. Train a 3-input perceptron to predict the next digit, say S_i, on the basis of the 3 previous ones. Include a bias term by including a fourth input with fixed activation $+1$. The output of the perceptron is $\text{sgn}(J_1 S_{i-1} + J_2 S_{i-2} + J_3 S_{i-3} + J_4)$. Use the Hebb rule applied to the first 50 examples to construct the **J**-vector. Test whether the network is able to out-guess you on the remaining examples. In particular try to make the sequence as random as possible (without using a computer, of course). Does the network nevertheless predict more than half of the remaining 50 outputs correctly? (See [52] for more details.)

3.2 Consider learning from a set of p *mutually orthogonal* examples $\boldsymbol{\xi}^\mu$, $\mu = 1, \ldots, p$, with $p < N$. Show that Hebb learning, the pseudo-inverse rule, and Bayes learning coincide. The training error is zero and the overlap $R^H = R^{PI} = R^B = \sqrt{2\alpha/\pi}$. The version space is reduced to the N-dimensional analogue of a quadrant. Show that the typical overlap q of two vectors chosen at random in the version space is given by $q = 2\alpha/\pi$ in agreement with the fact that $q = R = (R^B)^2$ for Gibbs learning.
(Hint: Use the examples as part of an orthogonal coordinate system.)

3.3 Convince yourself of the fact that using orthogonal examples is the best one can do to learn as fast as possible. Do you see how to proceed for $\alpha > 1$?

3.4 Suppose that the version space consists of the set of vectors **J** which have an overlap larger than $\sqrt{R}$ with a direction $\mathbf{J}^B$. Show that two Gibbs students have the typical overlap $q = R$. Show that the minimal overlap between two students of the version space is given by $2R - 1$. What does this argument predict for the asymptotic behaviour of the generalization error of the worst student versus the Gibbs student?

3.5 Consider again the high–low game introduced in problem 1.4. Calculate the generalization error for Hebb learning and for Bayes learning. Verify that the Gibbs and Bayes generalization errors satisfy the bounds derived in section 3.6.

3.6 To show explicitly that a majority of Gibbs students $\mathbf{J}^{(i)}$ classify a new example in the same way as the centre of mass of the version space, verify that, for $M \to \infty$,

$$\mathrm{sgn}\left(\sum_{i=1}^{M} \mathrm{sgn}(\mathbf{J}^{(i)}\boldsymbol{\xi})\right) = \mathrm{sgn}\left(\sum_{i=1}^{M} \mathbf{J}^{(i)}\boldsymbol{\xi}\right). \tag{3.33}$$

3.7 Consider a learning scenario in which both teacher and student are perceptrons with the same *continuous* and invertible activation function $g(x)$, i.e. the outputs

$$\sigma = g\left(\frac{1}{\sqrt{N}}\sum_i J_i\xi_i\right) \quad \text{and} \quad \sigma_T = g\left(\frac{1}{\sqrt{N}}\sum_i T_i\xi_i\right) \tag{3.34}$$

are real numbers (which are usually confined to the interval $(-1, 1)$, a popular choice being $g(x) = \tanh(x)$). Defining the generalization error by

$$\varepsilon = \frac{1}{4}(\sigma - \sigma_T)^2 \tag{3.35}$$

verify that the pseudo-inverse rule

$$J_i = \frac{1}{\sqrt{N}}\sum_{\mu,\nu} g^{-1}(\sigma_T^\mu)(C^{-1})_{\mu\nu}\xi_i^\nu \tag{3.36}$$

with the correlation matrix C as defined in (3.14) realizes $\varepsilon = 0$ for all $\alpha > 1$.

3.8 Show that the probability density $\mathrm{Prob}(P)$ of the reduction P of the version space volume upon presentation of a new example $\boldsymbol{\xi}$ is given by

$$\mathrm{Prob}(P) = 2\int Dt\, H\left(\sqrt{\frac{R}{1-R}}t\right)\delta\left(P - H\left(\sqrt{\frac{R}{1-R}}t\right)\right), \tag{3.37}$$

where R is the typical overlap of two vectors of the version space. Verify that

Prob$(P) = 2P$ for $R = 1/2$, that Prob$(P = 1) = 0$ for $R < 1/2$ and that Prob(P) has an integrable divergence at $P = 1$ for $R > 1/2$. (See [12] for a short and elegant proof.)

4

Augmented Statistical Mechanics Formulation

The generalization performance of some of the learning rules introduced in the previous chapter could be characterized either by using simple arguments from statistics as in the case of the Hebb rule, or by exploiting our results on Gibbs learning obtained in chapter 2 as in the case of the Bayes rule. Neither of these attempts is successful, however, in determining the generalization error of the remaining learning rules.

In this chapter we will introduce several modifications of the central statistical mechanics method introduced in chapter 2 which will allow us to analyse the generalization behaviour of these remaining rules. The main observation is that all these learning rules can be interpreted as prescriptions to *minimize* appropriately chosen *cost functions*. Generalizing the concept of Gibbs learning to non-zero training error will pave the way to studying such minimization problems in a unified fashion.

Before embarking on these general considerations, however, we will discuss in the first section of this chapter how learning rules aiming at maximal stabilities are most conveniently analysed.

The main results of this chapter concerning the generalization error of the various rules are summarized in fig. 4.3 and table 4.1.

4.1 Maximal stabilities

A minor extension of the statistical mechanics formalism introduced in chapter 2 is sufficient to analyse the generalization performance of the adatron and the pseudo-inverse rule. The common feature of these two rules is that they search for couplings with *maximal stabilities*, formalized by the maximization of the stability parameter κ. The coupling vector aimed for is hence *unique* quite in contrast to, e.g., the Gibbs rule. It is this uniqueness which makes the statistical mechanics analysis rather straightforward.

49

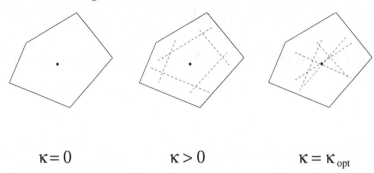

$$\kappa = 0 \qquad\qquad \kappa > 0 \qquad\qquad \kappa = \kappa_{\text{opt}}$$

Fig. 4.1. Schematic plot of the part of the version space ensuring stabilities larger than κ. With increasing value of κ this region gets smaller and smaller and finally shrinks to the point $\mathbf{J}^{\text{MS}}$ denoted by the dot, implying $q = 1$ for $\kappa = \kappa_{\text{opt}}$. Note that only part of the lines in the figure are active constraints as discussed in section 3.5.

Let us first consider the maximally stable coupling vector produced by the adatron rule. Obviously the indicator function $\chi(\mathbf{J})$ characterizing coupling vectors satisfying (3.21), i.e. which make all stabilities larger than or equal to a given κ, is

$$\chi(\mathbf{J}) = \prod_{\mu=1}^{p} \theta\left(\text{sgn}\left(\frac{1}{\sqrt{N}}\mathbf{T}\boldsymbol{\xi}^{\mu}\right)\left(\frac{1}{\sqrt{N}}\mathbf{J}\boldsymbol{\xi}^{\mu} - \kappa\right)\right). \tag{4.1}$$

This is only a minor modification of (2.13) and the resulting saddle point equations for the order parameters R and q can be directly read off (A2.34) and (A2.35). They are of the form

$$\frac{q - R^2}{1 - q} = \frac{\alpha}{\pi} \int Dt\, H\left(\frac{Rt}{\sqrt{q - R^2}}\right) \exp\left\{-\frac{(\kappa - \sqrt{q}t)^2}{1 - q}\right\}\left[H\left(\frac{\kappa - \sqrt{q}t}{\sqrt{1 - q}}\right)\right]^{-2} \tag{4.2}$$

$$\frac{R\sqrt{q - R^2}}{\sqrt{q}\sqrt{1 - q}} = \frac{\alpha}{\pi} \int Dt\, \exp\left\{-\frac{(\kappa - \sqrt{q}t)^2}{2(1 - q)} - \frac{R^2 t^2}{2(q - R^2)}\right\}\left[H\left(\frac{\kappa - \sqrt{q}t}{\sqrt{1 - q}}\right)\right]^{-1}. \tag{4.3}$$

Note that we need both equations since the introduction of κ has broken the symmetry between teacher and student, implying $q \neq R$.

We now have to find the maximal value of κ for which a solution of the coupling vector still exists. As is evident from fig. 4.1 increasing κ from 0 to κ_{opt} will be accompanied by an increase of q from R to 1. Indeed, since q gives the typical overlap between two coupling vectors $\mathbf{J}^{(1)}$ and $\mathbf{J}^{(2)}$ ensuring stabilities larger than κ, the uniqueness of the solution $\mathbf{J}^{\text{MS}}$ at $\kappa = \kappa_{\text{opt}}$ implies $q = 1$ at this point. The properties of the maximally stable coupling vector are hence given by (4.2) and

(4.3) *in the limit* $q \to 1$. Using the asymptotic expansion (A1.6) of the H-function we find

$$1 - R^2 = 2\alpha \int_{-\infty}^{\kappa_{\text{opt}}} Dt\, H\left(-\frac{Rt}{\sqrt{1-R^2}}\right)(\kappa_{\text{opt}} - t)^2, \tag{4.4}$$

$$R = \frac{\alpha}{\sqrt{2\pi(1-R^2)}} \int_{-\infty}^{\kappa_{\text{opt}}} Dt\, \exp\left(-\frac{R^2 t^2}{2(1-R^2)}\right)(\kappa_{\text{opt}} - t). \tag{4.5}$$

These two equations determine $\kappa_{\text{opt}}(\alpha)$ and $R(\alpha)$. From the latter we easily obtain the generalization error ε as a function of α by using (2.3). Comparing the behaviour of $\varepsilon(\alpha)$ that results from the numerical solution of these equations with the generalization error of Gibbs learning one realizes that the maximally stable vector $\mathbf{J}^{\text{MS}}$ determined by the adatron rule gives a lower value of the generalization error for all values of α (cf. fig. 4.3). This seems reasonable since $\mathbf{J}^{\text{MS}}$ lies near the centre of the version space as shown schematically in fig. 4.1.

The asymptotic behaviour for $\alpha \to \infty$ can be extracted by noting that $\alpha \sqrt{1-R^2}$ and $\kappa/\sqrt{1-R^2}$ remain finite in this limit. One finds

$$\varepsilon(\alpha) \sim \frac{c}{\alpha \int_{-\infty}^{1} du\, (1-u)e^{-u^2/2c}} \sim \frac{0.5005}{\alpha} \quad \text{for} \quad \alpha \to \infty \tag{4.6}$$

with the constant c determined by the transcendental equation

$$\sqrt{\frac{c}{2\pi}} = \frac{\int_{-\infty}^{1} du\, (1-u)^2 H(-u/\sqrt{c})}{\int_{-\infty}^{1} du\, (1-u)e^{-u^2/2c}}. \tag{4.7}$$

The limit $q \to 1$ may be employed analogously to derive the generalization performance of the pseudo-inverse rule (cf. problem 4.8). The resulting saddle point equations assume the simple form

$$1 - R^2 = \alpha\left(\kappa^2 + 1 - 2\sqrt{\frac{2}{\pi}}\kappa R\right), \tag{4.8}$$

$$R = \sqrt{\frac{2}{\pi}}\alpha\kappa. \tag{4.9}$$

These equations can be easily solved and one finds for R

$$R = \sqrt{\frac{2\alpha(1-\alpha)}{\pi - 2\alpha}}. \tag{4.10}$$

The resulting generalization behaviour is shown by the long-dashed line in fig. 4.3. Note the remarkable behaviour of the generalization error as a function of α. It goes through a local minimum at $\alpha = 0.62$ and *increases back* to the random guessing value $\varepsilon = 0.5$ for $\alpha = 1$. This non-monotonic behaviour is termed *over-fitting* because of its similarity with the analogous phenomenon observed in polynomial interpolation. In the present case it results from the insistence on a "wrong concept" when training the system. Indeed the real stabilities of the examples with respect to the teacher are not all identical and forcing the student to obey this prescription destroys his generalization ability. In particular, near $\alpha = 1$ it forces $\mathbf{J}^{\text{PI}}$ to grow indefinitely in size while becoming perpendicular to all the examples, thus leading to a complete loss of performance.

4.2 Gibbs learning at non-zero temperature

In order to analyse the generalization performance of the remaining learning rules introduced in the previous chapter we need another generalization of our statistical mechanics method. As a convenient starting point we discuss in the present section a general form of Gibbs learning.

Gibbs learning as introduced in chapter 2 characterizes the generalization performance of a typical compatible student by averaging over the version space comprising all vectors $\mathbf{J}$ that realize zero training error. On the other hand our analysis of the Hebb rule has revealed that appreciable generalization is possible even with non-zero training error. There are interesting situations in which perfect learning is either *impossible* (see chapters 5 and 6) or *too expensive* in the sense that practically the same quality of generalization can be achieved before zero training error has actually been reached. Under these circumstances it is interesting to know the typical generalization behaviour of a student with given *non-zero* training error ε_t. Let us see how the approach of statistical mechanics may be adapted to this more general situation.

For a particular learning situation specified by a teacher vector $\mathbf{T}$ and a set of inputs $\boldsymbol{\xi}^\mu$ the training error ε_t was defined in chapter 1 as the fraction of disagreements between teacher and student on the examples $\boldsymbol{\xi}^\mu$, i.e.

$$\varepsilon_t(\mathbf{J}) = \frac{1}{p} \sum_{\mu=1}^{p} \theta(-\Delta^\mu), \tag{4.11}$$

where the stability Δ^μ is defined in (3.2). The central quantity in the analysis of compatible students was the version space volume (cf. (2.14))

$$\Omega(\boldsymbol{\xi}^\mu, \mathbf{T}) = \int d\mu(\mathbf{J}) \prod_{\mu=1}^{p} \theta(\Delta^\mu). \tag{4.12}$$

It is clear that in order to include coupling vectors $\mathbf{J}$ with non-zero training error into the analysis we have to replace the indicator function $\chi(\mathbf{J})$ defined in (2.13) by a function weighting the different $\mathbf{J}$-vectors according to their training error ε_t

in a smooth manner. The choice advocated by statistical mechanics[1] is

$$\chi(\mathbf{J}) \mapsto \exp(-\beta E(\mathbf{J})) \tag{4.13}$$

where

$$E(\mathbf{J}) = \sum_{\mu} \theta(-\Delta^{\mu}) = N\alpha\varepsilon_t(\mathbf{J}) \tag{4.14}$$

and β is a free parameter. It implies that the probability of a student vector $\mathbf{J}$ being chosen on the basis of his performance on the training examples is given by

$$P(\mathbf{J}) \sim \exp(-\beta E(\mathbf{J})), \tag{4.15}$$

hence also couplings with $\varepsilon_t > 0$ are taken into account. Surely, their chance of being realized decreases rapidly with increasing ε_t.

Let us shortly illustrate why the replacement (4.13) serves the required purpose. Consider the average of some function $g(\mathbf{J})$ which depends on $\mathbf{J}$ only through the training error $\varepsilon_t(\mathbf{J})$. This average may be written as

$$\int d\mu(\mathbf{J}) \exp(-\beta E(\mathbf{J})) \, g(\mathbf{J}) = \int_0^1 d\varepsilon_t \, \Omega(\varepsilon_t) \exp(-\beta\alpha N\varepsilon_t) \, g(\varepsilon_t) \tag{4.16}$$

where

$$\Omega(\varepsilon_t) = \int d\mu(\mathbf{J}) \, \delta\left(\varepsilon_t - \frac{1}{p}\sum_{\mu=1}^{p} \theta(-\Delta^{\mu})\right) \tag{4.17}$$

describes the part of $\mathbf{J}$-space giving rise to training error ε_t. As in section 2.2 it can be shown that the entropy $S(\varepsilon_t) = \ln \Omega(\varepsilon_t)$ is extensive and may hence be written as $S(\varepsilon_t) = Ns(\varepsilon_t)$ with $s(\varepsilon_t) = O(1)$ for $N \to \infty$. The integral (4.16) therefore assumes the form

$$\int_0^1 d\varepsilon_t \exp(N[s(\varepsilon_t) - \beta\alpha\varepsilon_t]) \, g(\varepsilon_t) \tag{4.18}$$

and for large N the average of $g(\mathbf{J})$ is dominated by coupling vectors $\mathbf{J}$ with the *typical* training error ε_t that maximizes the exponent in (4.18), and which is hence the solution of $ds/d\varepsilon_t = \beta\alpha$. Consequently, by appropriately choosing the free parameter β one may concentrate the whole average on student vectors with a particular training error ε_t. As β increases, the corresponding typical training error decreases. The version space analysis of chapter 2 is eventually recovered for $\beta \to \infty$.

The observation that the temperature selects a specific training error, and hence a specific value of E is, of course, just an illustration of the equivalence

---

[1] For an argument based on statistics, see [53].

between a canonical and a micro-canonical description, well known from statistical mechanics. $E(\mathbf{J})$ as defined in (4.14) plays the role of *energy* and β that of the inverse temperature, $T = 1/\beta$. The evaluation of the phase space volume $\Omega(\varepsilon; \boldsymbol{\xi}^\mu, \mathbf{T})$ as the basis of the micro-canonical approach used in chapter 2 is thus replaced by the calculation of the so-called *partition function*

$$Z(\beta, \boldsymbol{\xi}^\mu, \mathbf{T}) = \int d\mu(\mathbf{J}) \exp(-\beta E(\mathbf{J})) \tag{4.19}$$

normalizing the canonical distribution (4.15). The central quantity of the canonical approach becomes the so-called *free energy*

$$F(\beta, \boldsymbol{\xi}^\mu, \mathbf{T}) = -T \ln Z(\beta, \boldsymbol{\xi}^\mu, \mathbf{T}), \tag{4.20}$$

which is extensive and therefore assumed to be self-averaging for large N. The corresponding free energy density

$$f(\beta, \alpha) = \lim_{N\to\infty} \frac{1}{N} \langle\!\langle F(\beta, \boldsymbol{\xi}^\mu, \mathbf{T}) \rangle\!\rangle = -T \lim_{N\to\infty} \frac{1}{N} \langle\!\langle \ln Z(\beta, \boldsymbol{\xi}^\mu, \mathbf{T}) \rangle\!\rangle \tag{4.21}$$

may be calculated by a minor modification of the formalism discussed in appendix 2. Since

$$\exp(-\beta E(\mathbf{J})) = \exp\left(-\beta \sum_\mu \theta(-\Delta^\mu)\right) \tag{4.22}$$
$$= \prod_\mu [e^{-\beta} + (1 - e^{-\beta})\theta(\Delta^\mu)]$$

this modification reduces to the replacement

$$\theta(\Delta) \mapsto \left[e^{-\beta} + (1 - e^{-\beta})\theta(\Delta)\right] \tag{4.23}$$

in (A2.5). The final results can then be read off (A2.33)–(A2.35) as

$$f(\beta, \alpha) = -\operatorname*{extr}_{q,R}\left[\frac{1}{2\beta}\ln(1-q) + \frac{q - R^2}{2\beta(1-q)}\right.$$
$$\left. + \frac{2\alpha}{\beta} \int Dt\, H\left(-\frac{Rt}{\sqrt{q-R^2}}\right) \ln\left[e^{-\beta} + (1 - e^{-\beta})H\left(-\sqrt{\frac{q}{1-q}}t\right)\right]\right], \tag{4.24}$$

with the corresponding saddle point equations

$$\frac{q - R^2}{1 - q} = \frac{\alpha}{\pi} \int Dt\, H\left(-\frac{Rt}{\sqrt{q-R^2}}\right) \frac{\exp\left\{-\frac{q}{1-q}t^2\right\}}{\left[\frac{1}{e^\beta - 1} + H\left(-\sqrt{\frac{q}{1-q}}t\right)\right]^2} \tag{4.25}$$

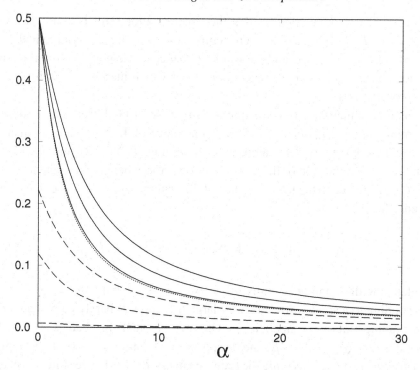

Fig. 4.2. Generalization error (full) and training error (dashed) as functions of the training set size α for Gibbs learning at temperature $T = 0.2, 0.5$ and 0.8 (from bottom to top). For comparison the generalization error for $T = 0$ is shown as a dotted line.

and

$$\frac{R\sqrt{q-R^2}}{\sqrt{q}\sqrt{1-q}} = \frac{\alpha}{\pi} \int Dt \; \frac{\exp\left\{-\frac{t^2}{2}\left(\frac{R^2}{q-R^2} + \frac{q}{1-q}\right)\right\}}{\frac{1}{e^\beta-1} + H\left(-\sqrt{\frac{q}{1-q}}t\right)} \tag{4.26}$$

fixing the order parameters R and q. Again R denotes the typical teacher–student overlap, determining the corresponding generalization error ε through (2.3), while q corresponds to the typical overlap between two students. Note that $R \neq q$ due to the absence of teacher–student symmetry.

The relation between the free energy, the internal energy $\alpha\varepsilon_t$, and the entropy s can of course be written as usual: $f = \min_{\varepsilon_t}[\alpha\varepsilon_t - Ts(\varepsilon_t)]$. The *typical* training error then follows from the standard relation

$$\varepsilon_t = \frac{1}{\alpha}\frac{\partial(\beta f(\beta, \alpha))}{\partial\beta}. \tag{4.27}$$

In fig. 4.2 the training and generalization error are shown for different values of T

as a function of α. One observes that the generalization error is almost as small for moderate $T > 0$ as it is for zero-temperature learning. Asymptotically the behaviour remains $\varepsilon \sim 1/\alpha$ and the whole influence of the non-zero training error boils down to a temperature dependent prefactor which increases with increasing T (cf. problem 4.5).

Let us finally mention an interesting limiting case of Gibbs learning. Consider the training energy $E(\mathbf{J}) = N\alpha\varepsilon_t$ for a given choice of $\mathbf{J}$. It is a random quantity due to the randomness of the examples $\boldsymbol{\xi}^{\mu}$. Its average is $N\alpha\varepsilon(\mathbf{J})$ since $\langle\!\langle\varepsilon_t(\mathbf{J})\rangle\!\rangle = \varepsilon(\mathbf{J})$ by the very definition of the generalization error, whereas the fluctuations are $\delta E = O(\sqrt{\alpha N})$ due to the independence of the training examples. The free energy can hence be written as

$$-\beta F = \left\langle\!\!\left\langle \ln \int d\mu(\mathbf{J}) \exp(-\beta\alpha N\varepsilon(\mathbf{J}) - \beta\delta E) \right\rangle\!\!\right\rangle. \qquad (4.28)$$

Consider now the combined limits $\alpha \to \infty$, $T \to \infty$ with $\beta\alpha = \tilde{\alpha} = O(1)$ corresponding to a spoiled student (very large training set) barely paying attention to the training (infinite temperature). One realizes that the second term in the exponent is $O(\beta\sqrt{\alpha}) = O(\sqrt{\beta})$ and disappears[2] in the limit $\beta \to 0$. In this regime called *high-temperature learning* the training energy $E(\mathbf{J})$ is hence simply replaced by its average, and training and generalization error coincide. No dependence on the randomness of the training examples remains and the calculations are reminiscent of those from the annealed approximation. This limit is a valuable first line of attack for problems in which a complete replica treatment is technically rather involved. Note that it is less trivial than the usual high-temperature limit of statistical mechanics, which is entirely dominated by the entropic term so that the most disordered configurations prevail. In high-temperature learning there remains an interesting interplay between energy and entropy since α and T diverge at the same rate.

4.3 General statistical mechanics formulation

We are now ready to demonstrate that for most of the learning rules introduced in the previous chapter an analytical calculation of the learning and generalization error is possible within the statistical mechanics framework. The main point is the observation that the learning rules are equivalent to selecting a student vector which gives the *minimum* value of an appropriately chosen *cost function* which we will call the *learning error* $E(\mathbf{J})$.

[2] A systematic expansion in this fluctuation term is described in [21].

For random examples chosen independently of each other, it is most natural to use a learning error of the additive form

$$E(\mathbf{J}) = \sum_{\mu} V(\Delta^{\mu}),\qquad(4.29)$$

with the stabilities Δ^{μ} defined in (3.2). The cost function (4.14) used in Gibbs learning forms a special case of (4.29).

The learning error introduced above is extensive in the number p of examples, which itself is chosen proportional to the dimensionality N of the input space. We saw in finite-temperature Gibbs learning that within the statistical mechanics analysis this error plays the role of the *energy*, with which by happy coincidence it shares the same abbreviation E. The generalization error will be determined by the competition of this energy with the entropic term, namely the number of **J**-vectors which realize a given value of the learning error.

Our aim is to calculate the generalization performance as a function of the training set size α for different choices of the *potential V*. Similarly to the analysis of general Gibbs learning of the last section this can be achieved by introducing the partition function associated with the error E:

$$Z = \int d\mu(\mathbf{J})\,e^{-\beta E(\mathbf{J})}.\qquad(4.30)$$

The partition function is a random variable through its dependence on the randomly chosen training examples and teacher couplings. Again the corresponding free energy $F = Nf = -T \ln Z$ is an extensive quantity, which is expected to be self-averaging in the thermodynamic limit. Hence F can be evaluated by averaging over the examples and the teacher. The required replica technique follows very closely the line of calculation for the finite-temperature Gibbs case, with the only modification that $\theta(-\Delta)$ is replaced by $V(\Delta)$. Under the assumption of replica symmetry one finds that

$$f(\beta, \alpha) = -\operatorname*{extr}_{q,R}\left[\frac{1}{2\beta}\ln(1-q) + \frac{q-R^2}{2\beta(1-q)} + \frac{2\alpha}{\beta}\int Dt\,H\left(-\frac{Rt}{\sqrt{q-R^2}}\right)\right.$$

$$\left. \times \ln \int \frac{d\Delta}{\sqrt{2\pi(1-q)}}\exp\left(-\beta V(\Delta) - \frac{(\Delta - \sqrt{q}t)^2}{2(1-q)}\right)\right].\qquad(4.31)$$

The order parameters q and R have their usual meaning and are determined from the extremum conditions corresponding to (4.31). The generalization error is then obtained by inserting the value of R into (2.3).

The only coupling vectors **J** that contribute substantially to the partition function Z defined in (4.30) are those for which the learning error $E(\mathbf{J})$ is only of order $1/\beta$ larger than the minimal possible value E_{min}. It is hence clear that with increasing β both the partition function and the free energy will be dominated by vectors **J** with smaller and smaller values of $E(\mathbf{J})$. Eventually, i.e. in the limit $\beta \to \infty$, it will therefore be possible to extract the properties of the optimal coupling vector minimizing the cost function from (4.31).

From an algorithmic point of view, those cost functions $E(\mathbf{J})$ which possess a *unique minimum* are of particular interest. Indeed, if this is the case, the minimum may be found by a standard gradient descent algorithm. The Hebb rule will shortly be seen to be one example of such a situation. In such a case, the limit $\beta \to \infty$ will be accompanied by $q \to 1$ since the different solutions **J** all have to converge to the same minimum. One observes from the saddle point equations corresponding to (4.31) that $\beta \to \infty$ and $q \to 1$ are compatible if we take $x = \beta(1 - q)$ to be finite. Replacing the extremum condition for q by one for x and applying a saddle point argument to the Δ-integral, the free energy density in this limit reduces to

$$f(T = 0, \alpha) = e_{min}(\alpha)$$

$$= -\operatorname*{extr}_{x,R} \left[\frac{1 - R^2}{2x} - 2\alpha \int Dt\, H\left(-\frac{Rt}{\sqrt{1 - R^2}}\right) \min_{\Delta} \left(V(\Delta) + \frac{(\Delta - t)^2}{2x}\right) \right],$$

$$(4.32)$$

where $E_{min} = N e_{min}$ is the minimum of the learning error $E(\mathbf{J})$.

For a given potential $V(\Delta)$ the generalization performance of the **J**-vector minimizing V can hence be obtained by the following two steps:

(1) Find the function $\Delta_0(t, x)$ which minimizes

$$V(\Delta) + \frac{(\Delta - t)^2}{2x}. \tag{4.33}$$

(2) Determine the values of R and x as a function of α from the saddle point equations corresponding to (4.32), which are of the form

$$1 - R^2 = 2\alpha \int Dt\, (\Delta_0(t, x) - t)^2\, H\left(-\frac{Rt}{\sqrt{1 - R^2}}\right) \tag{4.34}$$

$$R = \frac{2\alpha}{\sqrt{2\pi(1 - R^2)}} \int Dt\, \Delta_0(t, x) \exp\left(-\frac{R^2 t^2}{2(1 - R^2)}\right). \tag{4.35}$$

It is important to remember that the above simplification of the free energy and the corresponding saddle point expressions requires a cost function with a unique minimum. If the minimum is *degenerate*, as e.g. in the case of Gibbs learning characterized by $V(\Delta) = \theta(-\Delta)$, the limit $\beta \to \infty$ will not imply $q \to 1$ and no substantial simplification of (4.31) is possible. Some cost functions may have a degenerate minimum for $\alpha < \alpha_c$ and a unique one for $\alpha > \alpha_c$, as e.g. the adaline rule discussed in the next section. If one approaches α_c from below, the transition is signalled by $q \to 1$. If on the other hand one starts with large values of α then approaching α_c from above will show up by $x \to \infty$ because q remains smaller than 1 even for $\beta \to \infty$ (see problem 4.11).

4.4 Learning rules revisited

The above formalism can be applied to the various learning rules introduced before. As a particularly simple example Hebb learning gives a useful illustration. It corresponds to the specific choice

$$V(\Delta) = -\Delta, \tag{4.36}$$

for which the minimum of the cost function $E(\mathbf{J})$ can be found explicitly, namely

$$\mathbf{J} \sim \sum_\mu \xi^\mu \sigma_T^\mu, \tag{4.37}$$

which is precisely the Hebb rule. From (4.33)–(4.35) one obtains

$$\Delta_0(t, x) = t + x \tag{4.38}$$

and

$$R = \sqrt{\frac{2\alpha}{2\alpha + \pi}} \tag{4.39}$$

$$x = \sqrt{\frac{\pi}{2} \frac{R}{\alpha}}, \tag{4.40}$$

which agrees with (3.8).

Gibbs learning uses the training error as cost function, i.e.

$$V(\Delta) = \theta(-\Delta), \tag{4.41}$$

so that the corresponding error function $E(\mathbf{J})$ just counts the total number of misclassifications. Obviously (4.31) reduces to (4.24) in this case.

As a combination of Hebb and Gibbs learning the perceptron rule performs a correction to $\mathbf{J}$ identical to that of the Hebb rule but only if the example under consideration is misclassified, i.e. when $\Delta < 0$. Therefore the perceptron rule corresponds to the choice of potential[3]

$$V(\Delta) = -\Delta \theta(-\Delta). \tag{4.42}$$

---

[3] The original perceptron rule, discussed in the previous chapter, is an on-line algorithm which will be discussed in more detail in chapter 9.

As a natural generalization one may require Δ to be larger than a minimum stability κ in order to be accepted as error-free, which gives rise to the potential

$$V(\Delta) = (\kappa - \Delta)\,\theta(\kappa - \Delta). \tag{4.43}$$

The analysis of the generalization behaviour of this learning rule, though straightforward within the formalism introduced in the previous section, requires one to distinguish different intervals of α. Since the results are not particularly revealing we omit here a detailed discussion, which can be found in [33].

Adaline learning is defined by a least square error goal of the form

$$V(\Delta) = \frac{1}{2\kappa^2}(\Delta - \kappa)^2. \tag{4.44}$$

As discussed in section 3.4 this rule gives for $\alpha < 1$ the coupling vector of the pseudo-inverse rule, the generalization behaviour of which has already been discussed in section 4.1. The analysis of adaline learning for $\alpha > 1$ can now be accomplished as follows. From (4.44) we get

$$\Delta_0(t, x) = \frac{t + x/\kappa}{1 + x/\kappa^2}, \tag{4.45}$$

so that the integral in the expression (4.32) for the ground state energy may be performed analytically and we find, including the extremization in κ,

$$e_{\min}(\alpha) = -\operatorname*{extr}_{x, R, \kappa}\left[\frac{1 - R^2}{2x} - \frac{\alpha}{2(\kappa^2 + x)}\left(\kappa^2 + 1 - 2\sqrt{\frac{2}{\pi}}\kappa R\right)\right]. \tag{4.46}$$

The extremum conditions give rise to the following three equations:

$$1 - R^2 = \alpha\left(\frac{x}{\kappa^2 + x}\right)^2\left(\kappa^2 + 1 - 2\sqrt{\frac{2}{\pi}}\kappa R\right), \tag{4.47}$$

$$R = \sqrt{\frac{2}{\pi}}\frac{x}{\kappa^2 + x}\alpha\kappa, \tag{4.48}$$

$$1 - R^2 = \alpha\frac{x^2}{\kappa^2 + x}\left(1 - \sqrt{\frac{2}{\pi}}\frac{R}{\kappa}\right). \tag{4.49}$$

For $\alpha > 1$ these equations admit the unique solution

$$\kappa = \sqrt{\frac{\pi(\alpha - 1)}{\pi + 2\alpha - 4}} \qquad R = \sqrt{\frac{2(\alpha - 1)}{\pi + 2\alpha - 4}} \qquad x = \frac{\pi}{\pi + 2\alpha - 4}. \tag{4.50}$$

The result for $R(\alpha)$ specifies the decay of the generalization error and is included in fig. 4.3. The asymptotic behaviour is given by

$$\varepsilon(\alpha) \sim \sqrt{\frac{\pi - 2}{2\pi^2\alpha}}, \tag{4.51}$$

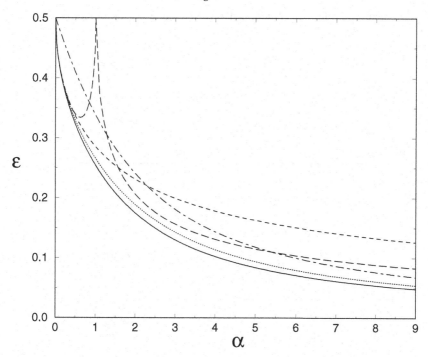

Fig. 4.3. Generalization error ε as a function of the training set size α for the Hebb rule (dashed), Gibbs learning at zero temperature (dashed–dotted), the adaline/pseudo-inverse rule (long-dashed), the maximally stable vector resulting e.g. from the adatron rule (dotted) and the Bayes rule (full). The asymptotic behaviours for $\alpha \to \infty$ are listed in table 4.1.

which obeys the same power law as for the Hebb rule. To make contact with the results for the pseudo-inverse rule, i.e. the case $\alpha < 1$, we have simply to remember that in this case the minimum of the cost function (4.44) is degenerate and κ has to be determined as the largest possible value which still allows zero training error. Consequently the extremum condition for κ in (4.46) has to be replaced by $x \to \infty$, expressing the emergence of a degenerate ground state. In this way we recover (4.8) and (4.9) from (4.47) and (4.48).

Since the adatron rule leaves examples with large stabilities untouched and uses a quadratic cost function similar to adaline learning for the rest, the appropriate potential is

$$V(\Delta) = \frac{1}{2}(\Delta - \kappa)^2 \theta(\kappa - \Delta). \qquad (4.52)$$

Problem 4.11 shows how the results (4.4) and (4.5) can be re-derived from this cost function.

learning rule	potential $V(\Delta)$	large-α asymptotics of ε
Hebb	$-\Delta$	$\dfrac{1}{\sqrt{2\pi\alpha}}$
Gibbs ($T = 0$)	$\theta(-\Delta)$	$\dfrac{0.625}{\alpha}$
adaline	$\dfrac{1}{2\kappa^2}(\Delta - \kappa)^2$	$\sqrt{\dfrac{\pi - 2}{2\pi^2\alpha}}$
adatron	$\frac{1}{2}(\Delta - \kappa)^2\theta(\kappa - \Delta)$	$\dfrac{0.5005}{\alpha}$
Bayes		$\dfrac{0.442}{\alpha}$

Table 4.1. *Potential of the cost function and asymptotic behaviour of the generalization error ε for large values of the training set size α for various learning rules. The generalization performances for smaller values of α are shown in fig. 4.3.*

This completes the analysis of the learning rules introduced in section 3. The results are summarized in table 4.1 and fig. 4.3.

After reviewing potentials which correspond to known learning algorithms one may wonder whether any interesting new choices are available. To guide us in this search, we remember that the minimal generalization error is achieved by the Bayes student who lies at the centre of the version space. It thus looks promising to consider cost functions based on potentials, defined within the version space, which "repel" the students from the border of this space. To achieve this, we may focus on potentials $V(\Delta)$ which are infinite outside the version space, i.e. for $\Delta < 0$, and monotonically decreasing functions of Δ for $\Delta > 0$. Monotonicity is included because it guarantees that $E(\mathbf{J})$ is a convex function on the N-sphere. Consequently there is a unique minimum, which may be found through gradient descent in the version space. A detailed analytic study of power law potentials $V(\Delta) = -\Delta^s/s$ with $s \leq 1$ can be found in [54]. For $s = -1$ the generalization error of the perceptron which minimizes the corresponding cost function $E(\mathbf{J})$ lies at most a few per cent above the Bayes result for all values of α.

4.5 The optimal potential

Two natural questions have remained unanswered so far: first, is there an optimal choice of the potential $V(\Delta)$ and second, does the resulting generalization error saturate the lower bound resulting from the Bayes rule? A variational calculation allows us to answer both questions affirmatively [55, 56]. Let us define the quantities

$$F(t, x) = \Delta^0(t, x) - t = -xV'\left(\Delta^0(t, x)\right), \tag{4.53}$$

$$X = 2H\left(-\frac{Rt}{\sqrt{1 - R^2}}\right), \tag{4.54}$$

$$Y = \sqrt{\frac{2}{\pi}} \exp\left(-\frac{R^2 t^2}{2(1 - R^2)}\right), \tag{4.55}$$

where Δ^0 is defined through (4.33). From (4.34) and (4.35), one obtains

$$R^2 = \alpha \frac{\langle YF \rangle^2}{\langle XF^2 \rangle} = \alpha \frac{\langle (Y^2/X)(XF/Y) \rangle^2}{\langle (Y^2/X)(XF/Y)^2 \rangle}, \tag{4.56}$$

where the average is with respect to the Gaussian measure Dt. It is easy to verify, e.g. on the basis of the Schwartz inequality, that $\langle u v \rangle^2 \leq \langle u \rangle \langle u v^2 \rangle$ for any function $u > 0$, with the equality sign attained only for v constant with respect to the variables over which the average is being taken. It follows that the r.h.s. of (4.56), and hence also the value of R, is maximal for the choice $F^* = CY/X$, where C is a constant independent of t. Its value follows immediately from dividing (4.34) by (4.35): $C = \sqrt{1 - R^2}/R$. The r.h.s. of (4.56) then simplifies to $\alpha \langle Y^2/X \rangle$. By a change of variables $t = u\sqrt{1 - R^2}$, one thus finds that (4.56) is equivalent to (3.29), the equation for the Bayes rule! Hence, through the explicit form of F^*, we have identified a cost function whose unique minimum reproduces the Bayes generalization behaviour.

This result sounds exciting, since we are able to reproduce the lowest possible generalization error through gradient descent. There are however some reasons for caution. First, the potential is specific to the teacher–student perceptron scenario with random examples. Second, even though one can construct the optimal potential explicitly, it does not have a simple form. In particular, a more detailed analysis [55] reveals that the potential is infinite for negative stabilities, and hence one has to start the gradient descent procedure while already inside the version space (which may, e.g., be achieved by a prior application of the adatron algorithm). Third, the optimal potential depends on α, i.e. its form changes with the size of the training set. This feature is expected to be rather generic since the optimal strategy will in general depend on the amount of information already obtained. Note also that the optimal cost function depends on R, and hence in order to use it in a simulation we have first to calculate $R(\alpha)$ analytically and then to use the result in the simulation, thereby relying on the self-averaging character of R.

4.6 Summary

In this chapter it was shown that the question how a student perceptron can learn from a teacher perceptron may be discussed in great detail within the context of a statistical mechanics analysis. The basic feature is the competition between an entropic term, namely the number of students with a given generalization error, and the learning error E, which quantifies how well a student is doing on the training set. Different learning algorithms correspond to different choices of this learning error and the statistical mechanics approach has demonstrated its great flexibility when dealing with different learning rules. All results could be obtained from minor modifications of the central Gardner technique introduced in chapter 2.

The simplest rule, Hebb learning, treats all the training examples in exactly the same way all along the training process. This rule performs optimally on small training sets, with a generalization error decreasing as $(0.5 - \varepsilon(\alpha)) \sim \sqrt{\alpha}$ for α small. For large α its inability to learn the training set perfectly compromises its generalization ability and results in a slow $\varepsilon \sim 1/\sqrt{\alpha}$ decay of the generalization error. Most of the more sophisticated learning rules achieve $\varepsilon \sim 1/\alpha$ asymptotically with different prefactors.

To boost performance in the presence of larger training sets and to realize optimal learning, the student needs to incorporate two new elements in his strategy, namely self-confidence and surprise; see [57] for a nice discussion. The element of surprise justifies the use of distinct weights (i.e. embedding strength) for different examples for a given value of α. The basic rule is that more attention should be given to examples classified by the teacher in a way that the student finds surprising. Self-confidence refers to the experience that the student acquires for a given amount of training. Its effect is clearly seen from the fact that the optimal algorithm (or potential) is a function of α. In practice, the use of this element will of course require a procedure of self-evaluation.

We close with a short review of some relevant references. The generalization error for the Hebb rule was first derived in [29]. The adaline and adatron rules were discussed in [58], and the perceptron rule in [33]. Finite-temperature Gibbs learning was considered in [30], while the high-temperature limit was introduced in [21]. The Bayes result was derived in [59], while the centre of mass argument was given in [37]. A detailed discussion for a general choice of the potential V is to be found in [54]. The saturation of the Bayes bound by an optimal potential was shown in [55].

4.7 Problems

4.1 Derive (2.41) from (4.24). Show that (4.31) reduces to (4.24) for Gibbs learning.

4.2 Consider the potential corresponding to Hebb learning in the version space

$$V(\Delta) = \begin{cases} \infty & \Delta < 0 \\ -\Delta & \Delta \geq 0. \end{cases} \tag{4.57}$$

Calculate the generalization error from (4.33)–(4.35) and show that it decays asymptotically as $1/\alpha$. Do the same for anti-Hebb learning in the version space ($V(\Delta) = \Delta$ for $\Delta \geq 0$). What is the asymptotic behaviour for $\alpha \to \infty$ in this case?

4.3 Calculate the free energy for learning with a general cost function (4.29) in the annealed approximation. To this end consider a vector $\mathbf{J}$ with given overlap R with the teacher and show that the probability distribution for the stability Δ of an example is given by

$$P_R(\Delta) = 2 \frac{\exp(-\Delta^2/2)}{\sqrt{2\pi}} H\left(-\frac{R\Delta}{\sqrt{1-R^2}}\right). \tag{4.58}$$

The annealed free energy density may then be written as (cf. (2.23))

$$\beta f^{\text{ann}}(\beta, \alpha) = -\max_R \left[\ln(1-R^2) + \alpha \ln \int d\Delta \exp(-\beta V(\Delta)) P_R(\Delta) \right]. \tag{4.59}$$

4.4 Starting with the expression (4.11) for the training error $\varepsilon_t(\mathbf{J})$ of a student with coupling vector $\mathbf{J}$ the average training and generalization error of the Gibbs ensemble at temperature T are defined by

$$\varepsilon_t(\alpha, \beta) = \left\langle\!\!\left\langle \frac{1}{Z} \int d\mu(\mathbf{J}) \varepsilon_t(\mathbf{J}) \exp(-\beta N \alpha \varepsilon_t(\mathbf{J})) \right\rangle\!\!\right\rangle \tag{4.60}$$

and (cf. (1.8))

$$\varepsilon(\alpha, \beta) = \left\langle\!\!\left\langle \frac{1}{Z} \int d\mu(\mathbf{J}) \langle\!\langle \varepsilon_t(\mathbf{J}) \rangle\!\rangle_S \exp(-\beta N \alpha \varepsilon_t(\mathbf{J})) \right\rangle\!\!\right\rangle \tag{4.61}$$

respectively. Show that for all values of α and β one has always $\varepsilon_t \leq \varepsilon$. Show also that for high-temperature learning equality holds.
(Hint: See appendix 1 of [21] for an elegant proof.)

4.5 Show that the large-α behaviour of the generalization error of Gibbs learning with $T > 0$ is of the form $\varepsilon \sim C(T)/\alpha$ and determine $C(T)$.

4.6 Show that the optimal potential discussed in section 4.5 reduces to the Hebb form in the limit $\alpha \to 0$.

4.7 Use the adaline cost function (4.44) and calculate the free energy (4.31) for general α and β by subsequently evaluating the Δ- and t-integrals. Show that the entropy tends to $-\infty$ for $\beta \to \infty$ irrespective of the value of α. How do you reconcile this result with the fact that $q(\beta \to \infty) < 1$ for $\alpha < 1$?

4.8 Perform the statistical mechanics analysis for the pseudo-inverse rule by using the indicator function

$$\chi(\mathbf{J}) = \prod_{\mu} \delta(\Delta^{\mu} - \kappa) \qquad (4.62)$$

instead of (2.13). Show that the resulting saddle point equations reduce to (4.8) and (4.9) for $q \to 1$.

(Hint: Note that the change in the indicator function just amounts to omitting the λ_{μ}^{a}-integrals in the analysis of appendix 2.)

4.9 A useful method to improve the generalization ability in practical applications is to allow the *student* to reject difficult questions in the test phase. Calculate the generalization error

$$\varepsilon(R, \Lambda) = \text{Prob}\left((\mathbf{TS})(\mathbf{JS}) < 0 \,\middle|\, \frac{\mathbf{JS}}{\sqrt{N}} > \Lambda\right) \qquad (4.63)$$

for test examples $\mathbf{S}$ that are at least a distance $\Lambda > 0$ away from the decision boundary of the student. Show that for $R \to 1$ one finds

$$\varepsilon(R, \Lambda) \sim \frac{1}{\sqrt{\pi}} \frac{\sqrt{1-R}}{\Lambda} \exp\left(-\frac{\Lambda^2}{4(1-R)}\right), \qquad (4.64)$$

i.e. an exponentially fast decrease of the generalization error. See [60] for a further discussion.

4.10 Complementary to the previous discussion, consider the case in which all examples $\boldsymbol{\xi}^{\mu}$ of the training set are at least a distance $\Lambda > 0$ away from the decision boundary of the *teacher* [61].

(a) Show first that an example distribution of the form

$$P(\boldsymbol{\xi}) = \frac{1}{(2\pi)^{N/2}} \exp\left(-\frac{\boldsymbol{\xi}^2}{2}\right) f\left(\frac{\mathbf{T}\boldsymbol{\xi}}{\sqrt{N}}\right) \qquad (4.65)$$

with $\int Duf(u) = 1$ gives rise to the following expression for the replica symmetric entropy:

$$s = \operatorname*{extr}_{q,R}\left[\frac{1}{2}\ln(1-q) + \frac{q-R^2}{2(1-q)}\right.$$
$$\left. + 2\alpha \int_0^\infty Duf(u) \int Dt \ln H\left(-\frac{\sqrt{q-R^2}t + Ru}{\sqrt{1-q}}\right)\right].$$

(b) Using

$$f(u) = \frac{\theta(|u|-\Lambda)}{2H(\Lambda)}, \tag{4.66}$$

which implies that the teacher restricts herself to examples she feels sufficiently confident about, verify that the initial decrease of the generalization error of the student is improved.

(c) Show that this strategy is however very bad for the final stages of learning since it results in the extremely slow decrease $\varepsilon \sim 1/\sqrt{\ln\alpha}$ of the generalization error for large α.

Teaching easy questions thus appears to be a sensible strategy in the early stages of learning, but should be abandoned at a more advanced level in order not to withhold from the student the finer points which are needed to reach a full understanding.[4] This approach can be further refined by using a varying threshold $\Lambda(\alpha)$ where the optimal dependence on α may be determined variationally [61].

4.11 Use the cost function (4.52) of the adatron rule and show that the solution for $\Delta_0(x, t)$ is given by

$$\Delta_0(x, t) = \begin{cases} \dfrac{t + \kappa x}{1 + x} & t \leq \kappa \\[2mm] t & t \geq \kappa. \end{cases} \tag{4.67}$$

By inserting this result into (4.34) and (4.35) and considering the limit $x \to \infty$ corresponding to choosing the optimal κ, reproduce the results (4.4) and (4.5).

4.12 Alternatively to (4.44) adaline learning may be described by the cost function

$$V(\Delta) = \frac{1}{2}(\Delta - 1)^2 \tag{4.68}$$

if the norm of the coupling vector is included as a parameter over which

---

[4] cf. e.g. the organization of this book.

E is to be minimized. Omitting the spherical constraint and introducing an additional order parameter

$$Q = \frac{1}{N} \sum_i J_i^2, \tag{4.69}$$

re-derive the results for the adaline rule obtained in section 4.4.

4.13 Show by using the methods of appendix 4 that in the case of learning by minimizing a cost function with potential $V(\Delta)$ the condition for the local stability of the replica symmetric saddle point may be written in the form

$$\alpha \int Dt\, 2H\left(-\frac{Rt}{\sqrt{1-R^2}}\right)\left[\frac{\partial \Delta_0(t,x)}{\partial t} - 1\right]^2 < 1, \tag{4.70}$$

where $\Delta_0(t, x)$ is defined in (4.33) (see also (A6.24)).

5

Noisy Teachers

As a rule teachers are unreliable. From time to time they mix up questions or answer absentmindedly. How much can a student network learn about a target rule if some of the examples in the training set are corrupted by random noise? What is the optimal strategy for the student in this more complicated situation?

To analyse these questions in detail for the two-perceptron scenario is the aim of the present chapter. Let us emphasize that quite generally a certain robustness with respect to random influences is an indispensable requirement for any information processing system, both in biological and in technical contexts. If learning from examples were possible only for perfectly error-free training sets it would be of no practical interest. In fact, since the noise blurring the correct classifications of the teacher may usually be assumed to be independent of the examples, one expects that it will remain possible to infer the rule, probably at the expense of a larger training set.

A general feature of noisy generalization tasks is that the training set is no longer generated by a rule that can be implemented by the student. The problem is said to be *unrealizable*. A simple example is a training set containing the same input with different outputs, which is quite possible for noisy teachers. This means that for large enough training sets no student exists who is able to reproduce all classifications and the version space becomes *empty*. For large networks this transition occurs at a sharp threshold α_c of the training set size. Above this threshold the training error ε_t of the student is always larger than zero and the question arises whether it is really necessary or advantageous to insist on zero training error below the threshold.

5.1 Sources of noise

We will now investigate these problems in detail for the paradigmatic setup of a teacher and a student perceptron. As before **T** and **J** are the coupling vectors of teacher and student perceptron respectively, and $\boldsymbol{\xi}^\mu$ denotes the inputs of the training set chosen at random according to the distribution (1.5). However, the corresponding outputs are now given by

$$\sigma'^\mu_T = \eta^\mu \, \text{sgn}\left(\frac{1}{\sqrt{N}} \mathbf{T}'^\mu \boldsymbol{\xi}'^\mu\right).$$ (5.1)

Several sources of noise have been incorporated into this expression. The possibility that the couplings of the teacher herself are fluctuating from example to example around the pure values $\mathbf{T}$ has been accounted for by the replacement $\mathbf{T} \mapsto \mathbf{T}'^\mu$. An appropriate distribution for the T'^μ_i is

$$P(T'^\mu_i) = \frac{1}{\sqrt{2\pi\sigma^2_w}} \exp\left(-\frac{(T'^\mu_i - T_i)^2}{2\sigma^2_w}\right),$$ (5.2)

where σ_w denotes the strength of the fluctuations. This type of noise is called *weight noise*.

Alternatively the errors in the training set may arise because the teacher receives corrupted inputs $\boldsymbol{\xi}'^\mu$ instead of the original $\boldsymbol{\xi}^\mu$. The generic probability distribution for this kind of *input noise* is given by

$$P(\xi'^\mu_i) = \frac{1}{\sqrt{2\pi\sigma^2_{\text{in}}}} \exp\left(-\frac{(\xi'^\mu_i - \xi^\mu_i)^2}{2\sigma^2_{\text{in}}}\right),$$ (5.3)

where again σ_{in} characterizes the noise strength. The effect of input noise is for large input dimension N identical to that of weight noise because in both cases the local field of the teacher is Gaussian distributed around the error-free value $\mathbf{T}\boldsymbol{\xi}^\mu/\sqrt{N}$. Both types of noise therefore particularly affect examples which are near to the decision boundary of the teacher.

A qualitatively different mechanism to blur the examples of the training set is described by the parameters η^μ with distribution

$$P(\eta^\mu) = \frac{1+a}{2} \delta(\eta^\mu - 1) + \frac{1-a}{2} \delta(\eta^\mu + 1).$$ (5.4)

In this case a fraction $(1-a)/2$ of all classifications is inverted, irrespective of how "confident" the teacher is. It will turn out that this type of *output noise* has a quite different influence on the generalization behaviour of the student.

At this point we have to note that in the case of noisy examples there are two ways to characterize the degree to which the student is able to approximate the teacher. We may either ask for the probability that the student gives for a randomly chosen input a different output than the teacher. Or we may be interested in the probability that there is a difference between the *error-free* classifications of the teacher and those of the student. The first quantity is called the *prediction error* ε_p

and the latter is the generalization error ε. Only in the case of noiseless learning do both error measures coincide. Clearly, if the student is able to decipher the target rule the generalization error ε will tend to zero for large training set sizes. The prediction error ε_p, however, will always be larger than a certain residual error ε_r characterizing the noise corrupting the teacher classifications.

Both the generalization and the prediction error are simple functions of the teacher–student overlap R which, even in the presence of noise, remains a self-averaging quantity. The generalization error is again given by (2.3), i.e. $\varepsilon = \arccos R/\pi$. The prediction error can be obtained by a similar argument. For the case of input and weight noise we get from its definition

$$\varepsilon_p = \langle\!\langle \theta(-\sigma_T'\sigma)\rangle\!\rangle_{\mathbf{S},\text{noise}} = \left\langle\!\!\left\langle \theta\left(-\frac{1}{\sqrt{N}}\sum_i T_i' S_i' \frac{1}{\sqrt{N}}\sum_i J_i S_i\right)\right\rangle\!\!\right\rangle_{\mathbf{S},\text{noise}}, \quad (5.5)$$

where the average is now over the test example $\mathbf{S}$ and the noise. As in (2.17) we introduce the auxiliary variables

$$\lambda = \frac{\mathbf{JS}}{\sqrt{N}} \quad \text{and} \quad u' = \frac{\mathbf{T'S'}}{\sqrt{N}}, \quad (5.6)$$

which for large N are Gaussian random variables with moments

$$\langle\!\langle \lambda \rangle\!\rangle = \langle\!\langle u' \rangle\!\rangle = 0, \quad (5.7)$$
$$\langle\!\langle \lambda^2 \rangle\!\rangle = 1,$$
$$\langle\!\langle u'^2 \rangle\!\rangle = (1 + \sigma_{\text{in}}^2)(1 + \sigma_{\text{w}}^2),$$
$$\langle\!\langle \lambda u' \rangle\!\rangle = R.$$

Replacing the disorder average in (5.5) by the average over u' and λ and using (2.22) we find for input and weight noise

$$\varepsilon_p = \frac{1}{\pi} \arccos(\gamma R), \quad (5.8)$$

where

$$\gamma = \frac{1}{\sqrt{(1 + \sigma_{\text{in}}^2)(1 + \sigma_{\text{w}}^2)}} \quad (5.9)$$

is an appropriate parameter describing the noise strength. The residual error ε_r, which remains even if the student has learned the error-free classification of the teacher perfectly, results from this expression for $R = 1$, i.e.

$$\varepsilon_r = \frac{1}{\pi} \arccos \gamma. \quad (5.10)$$

In the case of output noise we get similarly

$$\varepsilon_p = \langle\!\langle\theta(-\sigma_T'\sigma)\rangle\!\rangle_{\text{S,noise}} \tag{5.11}$$

$$= \frac{1+a}{2}\langle\!\langle\theta(-\sigma_T\sigma)\rangle\!\rangle_{\text{S}} + \frac{1-a}{2}\langle\!\langle\theta(\sigma_T\sigma)\rangle\!\rangle_{\text{S}}$$

$$= \frac{1}{\pi}\left(\frac{1+a}{2}\arccos R + \frac{1-a}{2}\arccos(-R)\right)$$

$$= \frac{1-a}{2} + \frac{a}{\pi}\arccos R.$$

The residual error is of course given by

$$\varepsilon_r = \frac{1-a}{2}. \tag{5.12}$$

Hence, in the presence of noise the central quantity to characterize the generalization performance is still the teacher–student overlap R. In order to calculate it as a function of the training set size α and the parameters of the noise we may use a straightforward generalization of the methods introduced in appendix 2.

5.2 Trying perfect learning

To begin with we investigate the generalization behaviour of a student perceptron that irrespective of the noise present in the training set tries to reproduce all example classifications exactly. A suitable learning rule to do this is to use zero-temperature Gibbs learning, which characterizes the performance of a typical student from the version space.

Let us first consider the case of weight or input noise. Including the average over the noise as specified by the probability distributions (5.2) and (5.3) into the pattern average (A2.10) we find that all that changes in the subsequent calculations is the replacement $R \mapsto \gamma R$ in the energetic part (A2.19). Consequently the saddle point equations (A2.34), (A2.35) for the two order parameters R and q are modified to

$$\frac{q-R^2}{1-q} = \frac{\alpha}{\pi}\int Dt\, H\left(-\frac{\gamma Rt}{\sqrt{q-\gamma^2 R^2}}\right)\exp\left\{-\frac{q}{1-q}t^2\right\}\left[H\left(-\sqrt{\frac{q}{1-q}}t\right)\right]^{-2} \tag{5.13}$$

and

$$\frac{R\sqrt{q-\gamma^2 R^2}}{\sqrt{q}\sqrt{1-q}} = \gamma\frac{\alpha}{\pi}\int Dt\, \exp\left\{-\frac{t^2}{2}\left(\frac{\gamma^2 R^2}{q-\gamma^2 R^2} + \frac{q}{1-q}\right)\right\}\left[H\left(-\sqrt{\frac{q}{1-q}}t\right)\right]^{-1}. \tag{5.14}$$

Clearly the solution $q = R$ is lost, reflecting the absence of symmetry between teacher and student. In fact for $\gamma < 1$ one has always $q > R$ and there is a critical training set size α_c at which $q \to 1$ with $R = R_c < 1$. Taking the limit $q \to 1$ in the above saddle point equations by using the asymptotic behaviour (A1.6) of the H-function one finds after some integration

$$\frac{\gamma}{R_c}\sqrt{1 - \gamma^2 R_c^2} = \arccos(\gamma R_c) \tag{5.15}$$

and

$$\frac{1}{\alpha_c} = \frac{1}{\pi}\arccos(\gamma R_c) = \varepsilon_p(R_c), \tag{5.16}$$

from which R_c and α_c may be easily determined numerically.

A qualitatively similar behaviour results for the case of output noise. Now the presence of the η-variables gives rise to the replacement $\prod_a \theta(u\lambda^a) \mapsto \langle\langle\prod_a \theta(\eta u \lambda^a)\rangle\rangle_\eta$ in the expression (A2.19) for the energetic part and the saddle point equations assume the form

$$\frac{q - R^2}{1 - q} = \frac{\alpha}{\pi}\int Dt \left[\frac{1 - a}{2} + aH\left(-\frac{Rt}{\sqrt{q - R^2}}\right)\right]\frac{\exp\{-\frac{q}{1-q}t^2\}}{H^2(-\sqrt{\frac{q}{1-q}}t)} \tag{5.17}$$

and

$$\frac{R\sqrt{q - R^2}}{\sqrt{q}\sqrt{1 - q}} = a\frac{\alpha}{\pi}\int Dt\frac{\exp\{-\frac{t^2}{2}(\frac{R^2}{q-R^2} + \frac{q}{1-q})\}}{H(-\sqrt{\frac{q}{1-q}}t)}. \tag{5.18}$$

Again $q > R$ for $a < 1$, and taking the limit $q \to 1$ as above we arrive at the following equations determining α_c and R_c:

$$\frac{\sqrt{1 - R_c^2}}{R_c} = \pi\frac{1 - a}{2a} + \arccos R_c \tag{5.19}$$

and

$$\frac{1}{\alpha_c} = \frac{a}{\pi}\frac{\sqrt{1 - R_c^2}}{R_c} = \varepsilon_p(R_c). \tag{5.20}$$

It is intuitive that the critical training set size α_c is reached when the product of prediction error and training set size approaches 1. The dependence of α_c on γ is shown in fig. 5.1 for both types of noise.

For $\gamma \to 1$ and $a \to 1$ respectively the intensity of the noise tends to zero (cf. (5.9)) and accordingly $\alpha_c \to \infty$. The value of α_c for output noise is always smaller than that for weight or input noise. This is in accordance with the fact that output noise introduces some "gross errors" into the training set whereas weight and input

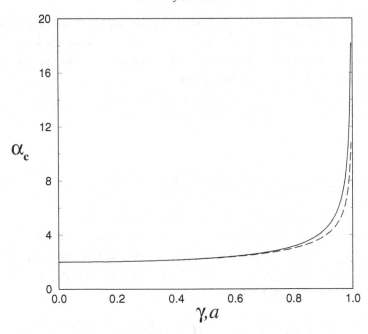

Fig. 5.1. Critical training set size α_c above which no student can be found who reproduces all examples perfectly. Results for input or weight noise of intensity γ defined in (5.9) (full line) and output noise characterized by strength a (cf. (5.4)) (dashed line).

noise only give rise to misclassifications at the decision boundary of the teacher and result in an "almost realizable" problem for the student.[1]

In order to investigate the generalization behaviour for $\alpha > \alpha_c$ we cannot use the above methods resting on averages over the version space because the latter is empty. Nevertheless it is still possible to study the performance of the student who *minimizes* the training error ε_t by using the canonical phase space analysis introduced in sections 4.2 and 4.3 with the training error as cost function. The minimum of ε_t is found by taking the zero-temperature limit $\beta \to \infty$, which is accompanied by $q \to 1$ giving rise to the new order parameter $x = \beta(1 - q)$. The replica symmetric calculations are again straightforward modifications of those performed in chapter 4 and will not be discussed in detail here. They result in the case of input and weight noise in the saddle point equations

$$1 - R^2 = 2\alpha \int_{-\sqrt{2x}}^{0} Dt\, t^2 H\left(-\frac{\gamma Rt}{\sqrt{q - \gamma^2 R^2}}\right) \qquad (5.21)$$

---

[1] Note that the two parameters γ and a measuring the noise intensities are not directly comparable with each other. One could instead compare situations with noise intensities which give rise to the same *fraction* of errors in the training set. Again the value of α_c for output noise would be smaller than the one for input or weight noise.

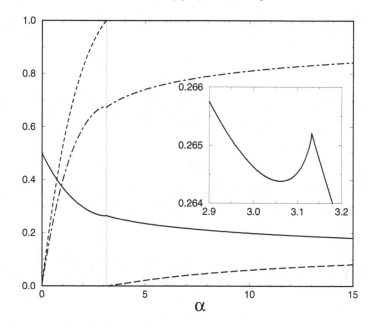

Fig. 5.2. Generalization (full) and training error (long-dashed) together with the order parameters R (dashed–dotted) and q (dashed) as functions of the training set size α for $T = 0$ Gibbs learning in the presence of input or weight noise of intensity $\gamma = 0.8$. The vertical dotted line marks the critical training set size α_c. The inset shows an enlarged part of the $\varepsilon(\alpha)$-curve around α_c displaying the over-fitting that precedes criticality.

and

$$\frac{R}{\sqrt{1 - \gamma^2 R^2}} = \gamma \frac{\alpha}{\pi} \left(1 - \exp\left(-\frac{x}{1 - \gamma^2 R^2} \right) \right), \qquad (5.22)$$

which fix the order parameters R and x, and the expression

$$\varepsilon_t = \frac{1}{\pi} \arccos(\gamma R) - \frac{1 - R^2}{2\alpha x} + 2 \int_{-\sqrt{2x}}^0 Dt\, H\left(-\frac{\gamma R t}{\sqrt{q - \gamma^2 R^2}} \right) \left(\frac{t^2}{2x} - 1 \right), \qquad (5.23)$$

which gives the typical training error ε_t as a function of R and x. Note that for $x = \infty$ equations (5.15) and (5.16) for R_c and α_c are reproduced; this is as it should be since for $\alpha < \alpha_c$ the minimum of ε_t is not unique and q remains smaller than 1 even if $\beta \to \infty$. The results of the numerical solution of (5.13), (5.14), (5.21) and (5.22) are shown in fig. 5.2 and give a complete picture of the generalization behaviour in the presence of weight and input noise.

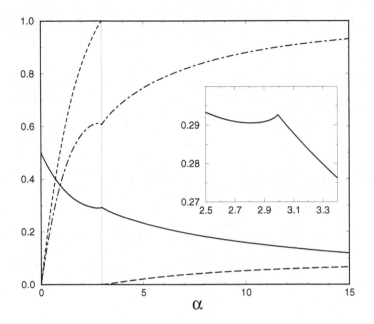

Fig. 5.3. Generalization (full) and training error (long-dashed) together with the order parameters R (dashed–dotted) and q (dashed) as functions of the training set size α for $T = 0$ Gibbs learning in the presence of output noise of strength $a = 0.8$. The vertical dotted line marks the critical training set size α_c. The inset shows an enlarged part of the $\varepsilon(\alpha)$-curve around α_c displaying the over-fitting that precedes criticality.

Equivalent calculations for output noise give rise to

$$1 - R^2 = 2\alpha \int_{-\sqrt{2x}}^{0} Dt\, t^2 \left[\frac{1-a}{2} + a\, H\left(-\frac{Rt}{\sqrt{q - R^2}} \right) \right] \qquad (5.24)$$

and

$$\frac{R}{\sqrt{1 - R^2}} = a\, \frac{\alpha}{\pi} \left(1 - \exp\left(-\frac{x}{1 - R^2} \right) \right) \qquad (5.25)$$

as the saddle point equations for the order parameters R and x, and

$$\varepsilon_t = \frac{1-a}{2} + \frac{a}{\pi} \arccos R - \frac{1 - R^2}{2\alpha x}$$
$$+ 2 \int_{-\sqrt{2x}}^{0} Dt \left[\frac{1-a}{2} + a H\left(-\frac{Rt}{\sqrt{q - R^2}} \right) \right] \left(\frac{t^2}{2x} - 1 \right) \qquad (5.26)$$

as the expression for the typical training error. For $x = \infty$ we again recover (5.19) and (5.20) determining R_c and α_c. Figure 5.3 gives the complete information on the generalization performance of zero-temperature Gibbs learning in the presence of output noise. Qualitatively the behaviour is similar to the case of input or weight noise.

It is finally interesting to investigate the asymptotic behaviour of the error measures for $\alpha \to \infty$. Remarkably, for all kinds of noise considered an asymptotic analysis of the saddle point equations gives $R \to 1$, implying $\varepsilon \to 0$ for $\alpha \to \infty$. This means that the student is able to perfectly decipher the rule behind the examples even if these are corrupted by random noise. Using the asymptotic behaviour of the order parameters in the expression for the training and prediction error one finds that both converge to the respective residual error for large training set sizes as expected.

The detailed dependence of the generalization error for large α is, however, different for weight or input noise on the one hand and output noise on the other hand. In the former case one finds from (5.21) and (5.22)

$$\varepsilon \sim \sqrt{\frac{2}{3\pi}} \left(\frac{1-\gamma^2}{\gamma^2}\right)^{3/8} \alpha^{-1/4}, \tag{5.27}$$

which is much slower than the decay $\varepsilon \sim 0.625/\alpha$ found in (2.50) for Gibbs learning from an error-free example set. On the other hand for output noise (5.24) and (5.25) yield the asymptotic result

$$\varepsilon \sim \frac{C(a)}{\alpha}, \tag{5.28}$$

where the dependence of the prefactor C on the noise parameter a has to be determined numerically. One finds $C \to 0.625$ in the zero noise limit $a \to 1$ and $C \to \infty$ for $a \to 0$. It is remarkable that, unlike weight or input noise, output noise does not change the qualitative character of the asymptotic decay of the generalization error but just increases the prefactor. The reason for this is the same which made α_c rather small for output noise: for large training sets the corrupted examples are typically so inconsistent with the rest of the set that it is easy for the student to detect them as being "obvious nonsense". In the case of weight or input noise the situation is quite different. If ε is already rather small the student particularly needs reliable classifications of examples near the decision boundary of the teacher to make further progress and these are notoriously difficult to get in the presence of input or weight noise.

From both fig. 5.2 and 5.3 we can moreover realize a typical feature of zero-temperature learning. Slightly below the critical training set size α_c the generalization error stops decreasing and even increases as can be clearly seen in the insets. This is another example of over-fitting where the student tries to imitate the teacher perfectly but uses the wrong concept. In trying to reproduce the noisy training set exactly the student spoils his understanding of the rule. One may therefore suspect that a noisy student who also below α_c uses a learning rule with non-zero training error may be able to avoid over-fitting and could consequently be more successful in grasping the rule hidden in the examples. Whether this is really true will be investigated in the next section.

To complete the $T = 0$ analysis we have finally to note that for $\alpha > \alpha_c$ a technical complication shows up that we have ignored so far. It turns out that the replica symmetric saddle point (A2.28) we have been using throughout becomes unstable [30] and the results (5.21)–(5.28) have to be considered as mere approximations. From related problems it is, however, known that these approximations are quite good [62] so we will not discuss here which modifications occur if replica symmetry breaking is included.

5.3 Learning with errors

In a situation where the training set is free of noise it is reasonable to try to reproduce *all* classifications exactly in order to approximate the target rule as well as possible. On the other hand if the training set contains mistakes we have seen in the previous section that insisting on zero training error can be misleading. In this case it may be more advisable for the student to "imitate" the teacher even in her errors, i.e. to use a learning rule that gives non-zero training error from the start and hence does not reproduce the training set exactly. A simple way to do this is given by Gibbs learning at non-zero temperature $T > 0$ as introduced in section 4.2 to characterize the typical performance of a student perceptron with given training error ε_t.

Let us briefly discuss what happens in this case by again using variants of the statistical mechanics treatment. We will only consider the case of output noise explicitly; the analogous discussion of weight and input noise is relegated to problem 5.1. Using a straightforward generalization of (4.25) and (4.26) the order parameters follow from

$$\frac{q - R^2}{1 - q} = \frac{\alpha}{\pi} \int Dt \left[\frac{1-a}{2} + a\, H\left(-\frac{Rt}{\sqrt{q-R^2}}\right) \right] \frac{\exp\left\{-\frac{q}{1-q}t^2\right\}}{\left[\frac{1}{e^\beta - 1} + H\left(-\sqrt{\frac{q}{1-q}}t\right)\right]^2}$$

$$(5.29)$$

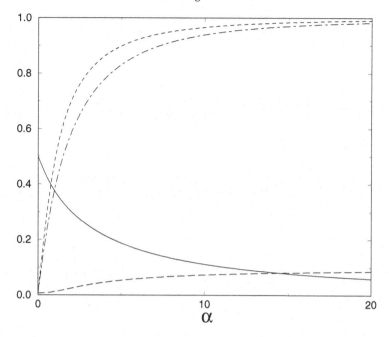

Fig. 5.4. Generalization (full) and training error (long-dashed) together with the order parameters R (dashed–dotted) and q (dashed) as functions of the training set size α for Gibbs learning with temperature $T = 0.2$ in the presence of output noise with parameter $a = 0.8$.

and

$$\frac{R\sqrt{q - R^2}}{\sqrt{q}\sqrt{1 - q}} = a\frac{\alpha}{\pi} \int Dt \, \frac{\exp\{-\frac{t^2}{2}(\frac{R^2}{q - R^2} + \frac{q}{1-q})\}}{\left[\frac{1}{e^\beta - 1} + H\left(-\sqrt{\frac{q}{1-q}}t\right)\right]}, \tag{5.30}$$

whereas the typical training error results from (4.27) as

$$\varepsilon_t = 2 \int Dt \left[\frac{1-a}{2} + a\, H\left(-\frac{Rt}{\sqrt{q - R^2}}\right)\right] \frac{H\left(\sqrt{\frac{q}{1-q}}t\right)}{1 + (e^\beta - 1)H\left(-\sqrt{\frac{q}{1-q}}t\right)}. \tag{5.31}$$

The results of a numerical solution of these equations are shown in fig. 5.4. The main differences from the corresponding behaviour for $T = 0$ as displayed in fig. 5.3 are that $q < 1$ for all values of α and $\varepsilon_t > 0$ from the start. Note also that there is no over-fitting since R and consequently ε are monotonic functions of α.

The generalization behaviour for $T > 0$ is compared with that at $T = 0$ in fig. 5.5. It is clearly seen that in the presence of noise in the training data a non-zero temperature in the learning rule is advantageous for learning from examples.

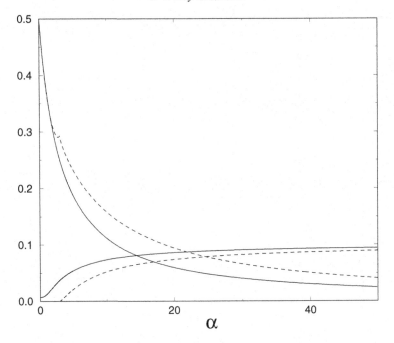

Fig. 5.5. Generalization and training error as functions of the training set size α for $T = 0$ (dashed) and $T = 0.2$ (full) Gibbs learning in the presence of output noise with parameter $a = 0.8$.

A larger training error allows a smaller generalization error since it enables the student to ignore those classifications of the training set which are probably due to the noise and therefore misleading in his task of reproducing the pure target rule. The difference between ε for $T = 0$ and $T > 0$ displayed in fig. 5.5 is asymptotically due to different prefactors of the $1/\alpha$ behaviour since even in the absence of noise the same asymptotics holds.

Remarkably, in the case of input and weight noise Gibbs learning with general temperature $T > 0$ still does not qualitatively alter the, in this case very slow, asymptotic decrease of the generalization error (cf. problem 5.2). Here a more substantial improvement would have been desirable. In the next section we will investigate whether more can be gained by *tuning* the training error or equivalently the learning temperature to the intensity of the noise present in the training set.

5.4 Refinements

The optimal performance of a student in learning from examples clearly depends on the overall information he gets. In the previous section we have seen that if this information includes, besides the training set per se, a hint that some of the teacher's classifications are unreliable he can improve by using a learning rule with non-zero training error. If in addition he also happens to know the *type* and *intensity* of the noise that corrupted the training set a further improvement is possible. The question what he can optimally gain from the available information is a typical problem of mathematical statistics and the answer is most elegantly derived in the framework of Bayesian density estimation [59, 12]. Although the improvements which may be obtained are often too small to matter in practical applications, the lower bounds for the generalization error that follow are of principal interest.

We will discuss the question of optimal performance here only briefly and in a rather qualitative manner. Let us consider the case of output noise. The clue lies in the relation between the order parameters R and q describing the similarity between teacher and student and between two students respectively. If there is no noise at all we found in chapter 2 that Gibbs learning is characterized by $q = R$. This symmetry between teacher and students is in general lost in the presence of noise. If the learning temperature of the student is very high we find $q < R$ and the student overestimates the error rate of the teacher. On the other hand for rather low temperature we have $q > R$, the student takes the teacher too seriously and risks over-fitting. It turns out that the optimal T is characterized by $q = R$ in which case the training error of the student is exactly equal to the fraction of wrong classifications in the training set. From (5.29) and (5.30) we infer that the symmetry between teacher and student is restored if

$$\beta = \ln \frac{1 + a}{1 - a}. \tag{5.32}$$

This gives indeed the optimal temperature the student should choose if he knows that the training set is blurred by output noise with parameter a [59]. For $a = 0.8$ the curve for $\varepsilon(\alpha)$ which results for the corresponding value $\beta \cong 2.2$ from the numerical solution of the saddle point equation is hardly distinguishable from the curve for $\beta = 5$ given in fig. 5.4. Asymptotically again only the prefactor is slightly reduced.

More can be gained in the case of input or weight noise. If the student knows that the examples are corrupted by such noise he may use a modified cost function that changes the asymptotic decay of the generalization error from $\varepsilon \sim \alpha^{-1/4}$ to $\varepsilon \sim \alpha^{-1/2}$; see [12] for details.

Let us finally note that there is also a technical advantage resulting from $R = q$. In this case we can use for the calculations the $n \to 1$ version of the replica trick, already utilized in section 2.3, which is not affected by problems of replica symmetry breaking.

5.5 Summary

Learning a rule from examples was found to be possible even when the training set classifications are corrupted by various types of random noise. For any noise type and intensity there is a critical size α_c of the training set beyond which the version space becomes empty and any learning rule has a non-zero training error. Nevertheless, since the noise is uncorrelated with the examples the student is able to filter it out and hence succeeds in approximating the pure teacher to any desired accuracy.

The detailed generalization behaviour can be analysed in the two-perceptron scenario by using the statistical mechanics techniques developed in chapters 2 and 4. Two general types of noise effect may be distinguished. Either the local field of the teacher is disturbed (as a result of input or weight noise) giving rise to erroneous classifications of inputs near her decision boundary or the teacher outputs are simply flipped at random with a given rate (output noise) resulting in "gross errors" completely at variance with the underlying rule.

At the beginning of the generalization process, i.e. for small α, inputs with large local field of the teacher are important and correspondingly output noise is more harmful. This shows up in a smaller value of α_c for comparable noise strengths. The asymptotic decay of the generalization error for large values of α, on the other hand, is determined by inputs near the decision boundary of the teacher. Now input or weight noise is more difficult for the student to cope with and the $1/\alpha$ decay of noise-free learning is changed into the much slower $1/\alpha^{1/4}$ behaviour in this case. Remarkably, for output noise the $1/\alpha$ law persists with just a larger prefactor.

The generalization behaviour can be improved by using learning rules with non-zero training error from the start. In fact, trying perfect learning for $\alpha < \alpha_c$ results in over-fitting that can be overcome by a non-zero training error as for instance in Gibbs learning with $T > 0$. The training errors allow the student to ignore those classifications of the training set which are most probably due to the noise and hence misleading in the attempt to reproduce the pure target rule. For output noise the optimal choice of the training error further reduces the prefactor of the asymptotic $\varepsilon(\alpha)$-dependence. In the case of input or weight noise even a crossover to a $1/\alpha^{1/2}$ decay is possible.

Learning from noisy data is a prototype of what is called an *unrealizable* learning problem since no student vector $\mathbf{J}$ exists that is able to reproduce all classifications. Several other unrealizable situations have been studied, including a teacher with a threshold $\theta \neq 0$ or with a non-monotonic activation function (e.g. the "reversed wedge" perceptron, cf. section 7.3) [63], and situations in which teacher and student differ in their architecture, as for instance an Ising student $\mathbf{J}_i = \pm 1$ trying to learn from a spherical teacher [21], or in their degree of dilution, i.e. fraction of non-zero couplings [12, 64]. All these scenarios share some important features. First, merely from the definition of an unrealizable problem, there is a critical size α_c of the training set above which the version space is empty, i.e. $\varepsilon_t(\alpha) > 0$ if $\alpha > \alpha_c$. Then, in all these cases one observes that trying perfect learning sooner or later fails by resulting in $\partial\varepsilon/\partial\alpha > 0$ and thus in over-fitting. Trying to learn from a reversed wedge teacher, e.g. by using the maximally stable student vector $\mathbf{J}^{MS}$ that results from the adatron algorithm, may yield a generalization error larger than 0.5 [63]! Therefore in unrealizable situations it is usually advantageous to use learning rules with non-zero training error; in fact high-temperature learning as introduced in section 4.2 performs remarkably well (see problem 5.4). Finally, when analysing an unrealizable learning problem in the statistical mechanics framework one should be aware that replica symmetry breaking is likely to occur.

Besides trying to imitate an unrealizable target function as well as possible it may also be desirable to simply *detect* that a problem is unrealizable. For a perceptron this is done by an algorithm introduced in [65] which learns a target function if possible and indicates non-linear-separability otherwise.

The first investigation of learning from examples in the presence of weight and input noise using the methods of statistical mechanics was done in [66] and [30]. The idea that a non-zero training error might improve generalization was already used in [67]. A detailed Bayesian analysis of the student's optimal strategy in the presence of different types of noise was developed in [59] and [12].

5.6 Problems

5.1 Consider Gibbs learning with $T > 0$ for the case of a training set corrupted by input and/or weight noise. Show that the typical training error is given by

$$\varepsilon_t = 2 \int Dt\, H\left(-\frac{\gamma Rt}{\sqrt{q - \gamma^2 R^2}}\right) \frac{H\left(\sqrt{\frac{q}{1-q}}t\right)}{1 + (e^\beta - 1)H\left(-\sqrt{\frac{q}{1-q}}t\right)}, \tag{5.33}$$

where the order parameters R and q are fixed by the saddle point equations

$$\frac{q - R^2}{1 - q} = \frac{\alpha}{\pi} \int Dt\, H\left(-\frac{\gamma Rt}{\sqrt{q - \gamma^2 R^2}}\right) \frac{\exp\left\{-\frac{q}{1-q}t^2\right\}}{\left[\frac{1}{e^\beta - 1} + H\left(-\sqrt{\frac{q}{1-q}}t\right)\right]^2} \tag{5.34}$$

and

$$\frac{R\sqrt{q - \gamma^2 R^2}}{\sqrt{q}\sqrt{1-q}} = \gamma\frac{\alpha}{\pi} \int Dt\, \frac{\exp\left\{-\frac{t^2}{2}\left(\frac{\gamma^2 R^2}{q - \gamma^2 R^2} + \frac{q}{1-q}\right)\right\}}{\left[\frac{1}{e^\beta - 1} + H\left(-\sqrt{\frac{q}{1-q}}t\right)\right]}. \tag{5.35}$$

Determine the dependence of R, q, ε and ε_t on α for $\gamma = 0.8$ from a numerical solution of these equations and compare with the performance of zero-temperature Gibbs learning as specified by fig. 5.2.

5.2 Show by an asymptotic analysis of (5.34) and (5.35) that also for $T > 0$ the asymptotic behaviour of $\varepsilon(\alpha)$ for $\alpha \to \infty$ remains $\varepsilon \sim \alpha^{-1/4}$ as in the case $T = 0$ (cf. (5.27)).

5.3 Read the review [12]!

5.4 Consider a teacher perceptron with threshold θ, i.e. $\sigma_T^\mu = \text{sgn}(\mathbf{T}\boldsymbol{\xi}^\mu + \theta)$, and a student without threshold. Analyse this unrealizable generalization problem within the framework of high-temperature learning. Is the decay to the asymptotic value of the generalization error monotonic? Characterize the problem in the limits $\theta \to 0$ and $\theta \to \infty$.

5.5 A rule which slowly changes in time (i.e. with α) in general poses an unrealizable problem to the student. In order to adapt to this more complicated situation Hebb learning may be modified to "learning within bounds" [68]. The rule is that Hebb learning is applied to the components of $\mathbf{J}$ as long as they lie within a given interval. Any correction that leads outside of these bounds is just not performed. Convince yourself that such a network works as a palimpsest, namely the information of earlier examples is gradually erased in favour of the newer ones. See [69] for a nice analytical discussion and [70, 71] for related problems.

6

The Storage Problem

There is an important extreme case of learning from a noisy source as discussed in the previous chapter which deserves special consideration. It concerns the situation of an *extremely noisy* teacher in which the added noise is so strong that it completely dominates the teacher's output. The task for the student is then to reproduce a mapping with no correlations between input and output so that the notion of a teacher actually becomes obsolete. The central question is *how many* input–output pairs can typically be implemented by an appropriate choice of the couplings **J**. This is the so-called *storage problem*. Its investigation yields a measure for the *flexibility* of the network under consideration with respect to the implementation of different mappings between input and output.

The reason why we include a discussion of this case in the present book, which is mainly devoted to the generalization behaviour of networks, is threefold. Firstly, there is a historical point: in the physics community the storage properties of neural networks were discussed before emphasis was laid on their ability to learn from examples, and several important concepts have been introduced in connection with these earlier investigations. Secondly, in several situations the storage problem is somewhat simpler to analyse and therefore forms a suitable starting point for the more complicated investigation of the generalization performance. Thirdly, we will see in chapter 10 that the flexibility of a network architecture with respect to the implementation of different input–output relations also gives useful information on its generalization behaviour.

6.1 The storage capacity

Let us briefly come back to the world of attractor neural networks introduced in chapter 1. In these systems every neuron is connected with every other neuron and for a pattern $\boldsymbol{\xi}^\mu$ of neuron activity to be a stationary point of the dynamics

$$S_i(t+1) = \text{sgn}\left(\sum_j J_{ij} S_j(t)\right) \tag{6.1}$$

it is necessary to ensure

$$\xi_i^\mu \sum_j J_{ij}\xi_j^\mu \geq 0 \qquad \text{for all} \quad i = 1, \ldots, N. \tag{6.2}$$

For the attractor properties of the patterns it is in fact advantageous to enforce the stronger condition

$$\frac{1}{\sqrt{N}}\xi_i^\mu \sum_j J_{ij}\xi_j^\mu \geq \kappa \qquad \text{for all} \quad i = 1, \ldots, N, \tag{6.3}$$

with the *stability parameter* $\kappa > 0$. For symmetric couplings large values of κ correspond to deep minima of $H(\mathbf{S})$ at the pattern. Asymmetric synaptic matrices can also give rise to an attractor dynamics and again large values of κ can roughly be associated with large basins of attraction of the patterns.

From (6.2) and (6.3) respectively one sees that if there are no constraints between the different J_{ij}'s the storage problem for an attractor neural network is equivalent to a set of storage problems for N independent perceptrons.[1] The storage properties of a perceptron are hence intimately connected with the performance of attractor neural networks when used as associative memories. It is likewise clear that (6.2) and (6.3) are very similar to the learning problem for a noisy teacher with output noise characterized by $a = 0$ (cf. (5.1) and (5.4)).

The storage problem for a perceptron $\mathbf{J}$ is hence defined by a stability parameter $\kappa \geq 0$ and a set of p random input–output pairs $\{\boldsymbol{\xi}^\mu, \sigma^\mu\}$ with $\mu = 1, \ldots, p$ where the components of the inputs and the outputs are all independent random variables. As before we will assume that they all derive from a distribution with zero mean and unit variance. The aim is to determine the maximal value p_c of p for which typically all the input–output mappings can be implemented by the perceptron in the sense that there exists a coupling vector $\mathbf{J}$ such that

$$\frac{1}{\sqrt{N}}\sigma^\mu \mathbf{J}\boldsymbol{\xi}^\mu \geq \kappa \qquad \text{for all} \quad \mu = 1, \ldots, p. \tag{6.4}$$

Posed as a learning problem in the sense of the last chapter the problem is hence to determine the maximal size of the training set for which the training error is still zero when learning from an extremely noisy teacher. As in the generalization problem we will find that $p_c = O(N)$ in the limit $N \to \infty$ and accordingly $\alpha_c = p_c/N$ is called the *storage capacity* of the network.

---

[1] The weak correlations which occur because the output of one perceptron is part of the input of all the other perceptrons turn out to be negligible in the limit $N \to \infty$.

An elegant and flexible statistical mechanics approach to this problem was introduced by Elizabeth Gardner in her famous paper [24]. It sets out with the volume in phase space of couplings **J** which fulfil (6.4):

$$\Omega(\boldsymbol{\xi}^\mu, \sigma^\mu) = \int d\mu(\mathbf{J}) \prod_{\mu=1}^{p} \theta\left(\frac{\sigma^\mu}{\sqrt{N}} \mathbf{J}\boldsymbol{\xi}^\mu - \kappa\right). \tag{6.5}$$

This volume is a random quantity due to the random choice of the $\boldsymbol{\xi}^\mu$ and σ^μ. Its *typical* value can be obtained from the quenched entropy

$$s = \frac{1}{N} \langle\!\langle \ln \Omega(\boldsymbol{\xi}^\mu, \sigma^\mu) \rangle\!\rangle. \tag{6.6}$$

For the calculation of this average again the replica trick is used. The detailed calculation is very similar to those of section 2.3 and appendix 2 respectively. After averaging over the inputs one introduces the order parameter matrix

$$q^{ab} = \frac{1}{N} \sum_i J_i^a J_i^b \quad \text{with} \quad a < b \tag{6.7}$$

describing the typical overlap between two solutions J_i^a and J_i^b to (6.4). Similarly to (A2.17) we then find

$$\langle\!\langle \Omega^n \rangle\!\rangle = \int \prod_a \frac{d\hat{k}^a}{4\pi} \int \prod_{a<b} \frac{dq^{ab}\, d\hat{q}^{ab}}{2\pi/N}$$

$$\times \exp\left(N\left[\frac{i}{2} \sum_a \hat{k}^a + i \sum_{a<b} q^{ab}\hat{q}^{ab} + G_S(\hat{k}^a, \hat{q}^{ab}) + \alpha G_E(q^{ab}) \right] \right) \tag{6.8}$$

with the entropic part

$$G_S(\hat{k}^a, \hat{q}^{ab}) = \ln \int \prod_a \frac{dJ^a}{\sqrt{2\pi e}} \exp\left(-\frac{i}{2} \sum_a \hat{k}^a (J^a)^2 - i \sum_{a<b} \hat{q}^{ab} J^a J^b \right) \tag{6.9}$$

and the energetic part

$$G_E(q^{ab}) = \int_\kappa^\infty \prod_a d\lambda^a \int \prod_a \frac{d\hat{\lambda}_a}{2\pi}$$

$$\times \prod_a \exp\left(i \sum_a \lambda^a \hat{\lambda}^a - \frac{1}{2} \sum_a (\hat{\lambda}^a)^2 - \frac{1}{2} \sum_{(a,b)} \hat{\lambda}^a \hat{\lambda}^b q^{ab} \right). \tag{6.10}$$

Assuming replica symmetry $q^{ab} = q$, $\hat{q}^{ab} = \hat{q}$, $\hat{k}^a = \hat{k}$ and eliminating $\hat{k}$ and $\hat{q}$ by using the respective saddle point equations these expressions simplify to

$$G_S = n\left(\frac{1}{2} \ln(1-q) + \frac{q}{2(1-q)} \right) + O(n^2) \tag{6.11}$$

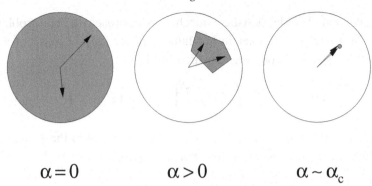

$$\alpha = 0 \qquad\qquad \alpha > 0 \qquad\qquad \alpha \sim \alpha_c$$

Fig. 6.1. Schematic plot of the solution volume Ω (shaded) for different values of α. Also shown are two possible coupling vectors $\mathbf{J}^1$ and $\mathbf{J}^2$, the typical overlap of which is described by q. When α approaches the storage capacity α_c one finds $q \to 1$ and $\Omega \to 0$.

and

$$G_E = n \int Dt \ln H\left(\frac{\kappa - \sqrt{q}t}{\sqrt{1-q}}\right) + O(n^2), \tag{6.12}$$

giving rise to the final expression for the quenched entropy

$$s(\alpha) = \underset{q}{\text{extr}}\left[\frac{1}{2}\ln(1-q) + \frac{q}{2(1-q)} + \alpha \int Dt \ln H\left(\frac{\kappa - \sqrt{q}t}{\sqrt{1-q}}\right)\right]. \tag{6.13}$$

The corresponding saddle point equation determining q follows as

$$\frac{q}{1-q} = \frac{\alpha}{\pi} \int Dt \exp\left(-\frac{(\kappa - \sqrt{q}t)^2}{1-q}\right)\left[H\left(\frac{\kappa - \sqrt{q}t}{\sqrt{1-q}}\right)\right]^{-2}. \tag{6.14}$$

From this equation we can determine the typical overlap q between two different solutions to (6.4) as a function of the storage ratio α. For $\alpha = 0$ we find $q = 0$ since all vectors $\mathbf{J}$ from the N-sphere are admissible solutions. With increasing α the typical solution volume shrinks, implying an increasing value of q. Eventually, the critical storage capacity α_c is reached when $q \to 1$. In this limit two different solutions to (6.4) become practically identical and accordingly the typical volume of solutions vanishes (see fig. 6.1) as follows also from (6.13). Using the asymptotic form of the H-function as given in (A1.6) we get in this limit from (6.14)

$$\frac{1}{\alpha_c} = \int_{-\infty}^{\kappa} Dt\,(\kappa - t)^2. \tag{6.15}$$

The dependence of the storage capacity α_c on the stability parameter κ is shown in fig. 6.2. For $\kappa = 0$ we get $\alpha_c = 2$ in accordance with the findings of section 5.2, see in particular fig. 5.1 for $a = 0$. As expected, α_c decreases with increasing κ,

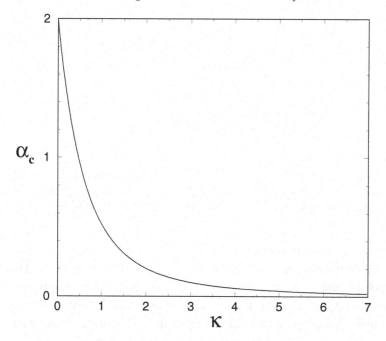

Fig. 6.2. Storage capacity α_c of a perceptron as a function of the stability parameter κ defined in (6.4).

implying for attractor neural nets a tradeoff between storage capacity and basin of attraction.

6.2 Counting dichotomies: the Cover analysis

The result $\alpha_c = 2$ for $\kappa = 0$ can also be obtained in a completely different way which highlights the geometrical aspect of the storage problem. It was derived by Cover as early as 1965 [72], but the mathematical results behind it are apparently much older [73, 74].

The idea is as follows. Consider p points in an N-dimensional Euclidean space which are coloured black or white. The colouring is called a *dichotomy* if a hyperplane through the origin exists which separates the points in the sense that all black points lie on one side of the plane and all white points on the other side. Figure 6.3 shows two simple examples for $N = 2$ and $p = 3$. If one takes the coordinates of the points as N-dimensional input vectors and their colours as coding their outputs $\sigma^\mu = \pm 1$ it is clear that a perceptron coupling vector **J** normal to the separating hyperplane would implement the corresponding input–output relation since its scalar product with all white points would have the same sign

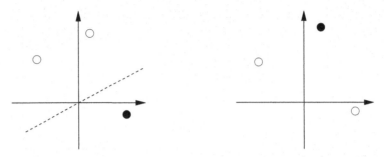

Fig. 6.3. Two different colourings of three points in two dimensions. The left example shows a dichotomy together with a possible separating hyperplane. In the right example no line through the origin exists which separates black points from white ones.

and its scalar product with all black points the other one.[2] In the following we will determine the number of dichotomies $C(p, N)$ of p points in N dimensions. The probability that a *random* colouring is a dichotomy is then simply given by the ratio between $C(p, N)$ and the total number of different possible colourings, 2^p.

The remarkable property behind this analysis is that under rather weak conditions the number $C(p, N)$ does indeed only depend on p and N and not on the *detailed position* of the points. This property is specific to the perceptron and, as we will see in chapter 12, will foil the attempt to use similar techniques for an exact analysis of multilayer networks. The only necessary and rather reasonable condition we have to ensure for the present analysis of the perceptron is that the points are in what is called *general position*, which means that the elements of any subset of N or fewer points are linearly independent. Note that points generated at random from a continuous probability distribution satisfy this condition with probability 1.

The actual calculation of $C(p, N)$ proceeds by induction. Of course

$$C(1, N) = 2 \quad \text{and} \quad C(p, 1) = 2 \tag{6.16}$$

since one point can always be "separated" irrespective of its colour and since the only "hyperplane" available in one dimension is the origin itself. Next assume that we know $C(p, N)$ and want to determine $C(p + 1, N)$. Clearly $C(p + 1, N) \geq C(p, N)$ since every dichotomy of p points gives rise to at least one dichotomy of $p + 1$ points as well. To find it we have just to colour the new point with the colour "of its side" (see fig. 6.4a).

In fact, sometimes even two new dichotomies may arise from an old one, namely exactly in the case where there is a separating hyperplane of the parent dichotomy

---

[2] This is precisely the reason why the input–output mappings a perceptron can realize are called *linearly separable*. Note also that the condition that the hyperplane should go through the origin corresponds to the absence of a threshold, $\theta = 0$, for the perceptron.

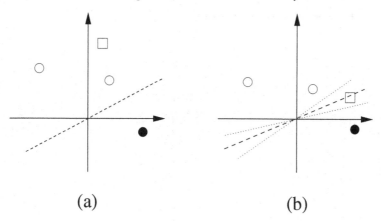

(a) (b)

Fig. 6.4. Change of the number of dichotomies $C(p, N)$ by adding a new point (square). (a) The new point *must* be coloured white, and the number of dichotomies does not increase. (b) There is a hyperplane through the new point separating the old points. Therefore by slightly rotating this hyperplane (dotted lines) both colourings of the new point are linearly separable, and the number of dichotomies hence increases by 1.

of p points which goes through the new point. Then by a slight rotation of the hyperplane to either side of the new point both colourings of the new point are possible (fig. 6.4b). Note that due to the general position of the points this rotation can be made such that no other point crosses the hyperplane. But how many dichotomies of p points in N dimensions are induced by hyperplanes through the origin and *one additional point P*? By projecting all points onto the hyperplane perpendicular to the line connecting the origin and P, one realizes that these are exactly $C(p, N - 1)$. Requiring the hyperplane to go through P just reduces the available dimensions by 1. We hence find

$$C(p + 1, N) = C(p, N) + C(p, N - 1) \qquad (6.17)$$

since all the $C(p, N)$ dichotomies of p points give rise to one dichotomy of $p + 1$ points and $C(p, N - 1)$ of them contribute an additional one. This neat recursion relation is the crucial step of the calculation. With the help of the boundary conditions (6.16) it is now not too difficult to derive the following expression for the number $C(p, N)$ of dichotomies of p points in N dimensions

$$C(p, N) = 2 \sum_{i=0}^{N-1} \binom{p-1}{i}. \qquad (6.18)$$

In fig. 6.5 we have used (6.18) to plot the probability $C(p, N)/2^p$ for a random colouring to be a dichotomy as a function of $\alpha = p/N$ for different values of N.

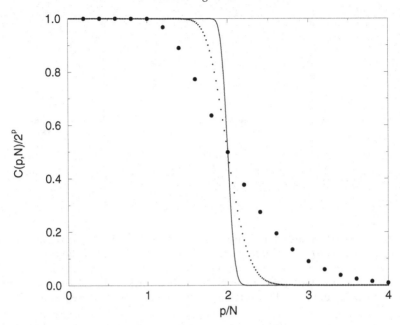

Fig. 6.5. Probability for a random colouring of p points in N dimensions to be a dichotomy as a function of p/N for $N = 5$ (large dots), $N = 50$ (small dots) and $N = 500$ (line) as determined by (6.18).

One clearly sees that for large N there is a sharp transition from probability 1 to probability 0 at $\alpha_c = 2$ in accordance with the findings of the previous section.

The approaches of Cover and Gardner to the storage problem of the perceptron are rather complementary. The first one *counts* the number of different implementable mappings whereas the second one *measures* the variability for realizing *one particular* mapping. The Cover method yields results for all values of N and is able to detect subtle differences far beyond the resolution of the saddle point reasoning of the Gardner method. Note e.g. that from (6.18) it follows that $C(p, N)/2^p = 1$ exactly if $p \leq N$ whereas $C(p, N)/2^p - 1 = O(e^{-N})$ for $N < p < 2N$. This tiny difference does not show up in the Gardner calculation where $\alpha = 1$ is in no sense special.

Moreover the Cover approach does not rely on a technique as mathematically dubious as the replica method. On the other hand it is not very flexible. Several attempts to generalize the method to $\kappa > 0$ or to other types of networks have all failed so far. The big advantage of the Gardner approach is that it is widely applicable and allows several interesting modifications. Being a statistical mechanics technique, however, it always needs the limit $N \to \infty$.

6.3 Galilean pastiche: the Ising perceptron

Simplicio: I have a nice problem to apply your methods for determining the storage capacity to. Let us again consider a perceptron with the storage condition (6.4) but now with the additional constraint that all components of the coupling vector must be either plus or minus one,

$$J_i = \pm 1. \tag{6.19}$$

The result for the storage capacity for this system will show how much the restriction of the **J**-components to technically easily manageable values does influence the performance of the network. This seems good to know, particularly for possible hardware realizations.

Salviati: This is indeed a nice problem. Let us call it the *Ising*[3] perceptron to distinguish it from the *spherical* perceptron with continuous couplings studied before.

Simplicio: I do not see a way to use the Cover method for analysing the Ising perceptron since it relies on the possibility of a *continuous* change of the direction of **J** (cf. fig. 6.4). It therefore seems better to employ the Gardner approach.

Salviati: You are right again. There is no known way to derive a recursion relation like (6.17) for the Ising perceptron. On the other hand you will find the application of the Gardner method highly instructive!

Simplicio: In fact the calculation is very similar to that done in section 6.1. Concentrating again on the typical value of the solution volume $\Omega(\xi^\mu, \sigma^\mu)$ all I have to do is to use the replacement

$$\int d\mu(\mathbf{J}) \mapsto \sum_{\{J_i = \pm 1\}} \tag{6.20}$$

reflecting the discrete nature of the Ising couplings. Consequently there is no change at all in the energetic part (6.10) whereas for the entropic part I get instead of (6.9)

$$G_S(\hat{q}^{ab}) = \ln \sum_{\{J^a = \pm 1\}} \exp\left(-i \sum_{a<b} \hat{q}^{ab} J^a J^b\right). \tag{6.21}$$

This gives rise to the following expression for the replicated phase space volume:

$$\langle\!\langle \Omega^n \rangle\!\rangle = \int \prod_{a<b} \frac{dq^{ab}\, d\hat{q}^{ab}}{2\pi/N} \exp\left(N\left[i \sum_{a<b} q^{ab}\hat{q}^{ab} + G_S(\hat{q}^{ab}) + \alpha G_E(q^{ab})\right]\right). \tag{6.22}$$

---

[3] The Ising model, named after Ernst Ising, is a famous model for a ferromagnet in statistical mechanics where the individual microscopic magnetic moments are represented by binary variables $S_i = \pm 1$.

The saddle point method allows me to calculate the integrals over q^{ab} and $\hat{q}^{ab}$ for $N \to \infty$. Unfortunately the conjugated order parameters $\hat{q}^{ab}$ cannot be eliminated analytically at this stage as was possible for the spherical perceptron. Nevertheless, using the replica symmetric ansatz

$$q^{ab} = q \qquad \text{and} \qquad -i\hat{q}^{ab} = \hat{q} \tag{6.23}$$

the expression for G_S simplifies to

$$
\begin{aligned}
G_S(\hat{q}^{ab}) &= \ln \sum_{\{J^a = \pm 1\}} \exp\left(\hat{q} \sum_{a<b} J^a J^b \right) \\
&= \ln \sum_{\{J^a = \pm 1\}} \exp\left(\frac{\hat{q}}{2} \sum_{a,b} J^a J^b - n\frac{\hat{q}}{2} \right) \\
&= -n\frac{\hat{q}}{2} + \ln \int Dz \sum_{\{J^a = \pm 1\}} \exp\left(\sqrt{\hat{q}}z \sum_a J^a \right) \\
&= -n\frac{\hat{q}}{2} + n \int Dz \ln 2 \cosh(\sqrt{\hat{q}}z) + O(n^2) \tag{6.24}
\end{aligned}
$$

and I therefore finally find for the quenched entropy

$$s(\alpha) = \operatorname*{extr}_{q,\hat{q}} \left[-\frac{\hat{q}}{2}(1-q) + \int Dz \ln 2 \cosh(\sqrt{\hat{q}}z) + \alpha \int Dt \ln H\left(\frac{\kappa - \sqrt{q}t}{\sqrt{1-q}} \right) \right]. \tag{6.25}$$

The corresponding saddle point equations are

$$q = \int Dz \tanh^2(\sqrt{\hat{q}}z) \tag{6.26}$$

$$\hat{q} = \frac{\alpha}{2\pi(1-q)} \int Dt \exp\left(-\frac{(\kappa - \sqrt{q}t)^2}{1-q} \right) \left[H\left(\frac{\kappa - \sqrt{q}t}{\sqrt{1-q}} \right) \right]^{-2}. \tag{6.27}$$

For $\kappa = 0$ I find from the numerical solution of these equations that q approaches 1 for $\alpha \cong 1.27$. This is a quite reasonable value for α_c. It is smaller than 2, as it should be because the Ising perceptron is a special case of the spherical perceptron. On the other hand it shows that the restriction to binary synapses is not very severe for the storage capacity.

Salviati: Your calculations look rather convincing. In fact concentrating on the case $\kappa = 0$ from the saddle point equation for $\hat{q}$ you may get $\hat{q} \sim \alpha/(2\pi(1-q)^2)$ in the limit $q \to 1$. Using this the right hand side of (6.25) may be written in the form $(\sqrt{\alpha/\pi} - \alpha/2)/(1-q)$. In order to have a sound limit $q \to 1$ you must therefore have $\alpha \to \alpha_c = 4/\pi$, which is rather near to your numerical value for α_c.

Simplicio: Good, so we are done.

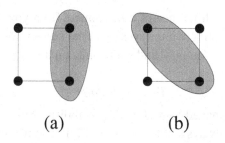

(a)   (b)

Fig. 6.6. Schematic plot of a portion of the Gardner sphere comprising four corners of the N-dimensional hypercube corresponding to possible coupling vectors for the Ising perceptron. The solution space for the spherical perceptron is shown in grey. It is always convex and therefore also connected. (a) The two solutions for the Ising perceptron contained in the general solution volume are connected by a link of the hypercube. (b) There is no way along the edges of the hypercube from one Ising solution to the other one without leaving the solution volume. The solution space for the Ising perceptron is hence *not* necessarily connected, which might render the replica symmetric saddle point unstable.

Salviati: Not really. Let me draw your attention to the following problem. Your result $\alpha_c \cong 1.27$ means that by properly choosing the couplings J_i we can (with probability 1 for large N) implement any mapping of $1.27N$ inputs $\boldsymbol{\xi}^\mu$ to binary outputs σ^μ. This implies that we can code $1.27N$ bits in the structure of the network. But this very structure is already fixed by N bits, namely the binary values of the J_i's! Consequently values for α_c which are larger than 1 are impossible.[4]

Simplicio: But this problem should also show up in my replica calculation. I do not find an error!

Salviati: Your calculations are correct *within the replica symmetric ansatz.* But the use of the replica symmetric saddle point must always be accompanied by the analysis of its stability. For the spherical perceptron this analysis shows that the replica symmetric (RS) saddle point is stable for all $\alpha < \alpha_c$ [24, 25, 75]. This is in accordance with the fact that the solution space is convex as shortly discussed already at the end of chapter 2. For the Ising perceptron this is not necessarily the case; see fig. 6.6 for a qualitative illustration.

In fact this figure suggests the following reasoning. In order to find an Ising solution of the storage problem, the solution volume Ω of the spherical case should include at least one of the 2^N corners of the N-dimensional hypercube. If we assume that there are no correlations between these corners and the spherical solution volume we expect that Ising solutions will exist with high probability as long as $\Omega > 2^{-N}$. A numerical investigation of (6.13) reveals that $\Omega \cong 2^{-N}$ for $\alpha \cong 0.85$ with $q \cong 0.5$. So 0.85 looks like a good approximate candidate for α_c.

---

[4] The same upper bound $\alpha_c \leq 1$ results from an annealed calculation of the solution volume, see problem 6.11.

In order to clarify the difference of this estimate from your RS result $\alpha \cong 1.27$ it should therefore be instructive to investigate the stability of the RS saddle point for the Ising perceptron. You may find some hints on how to do this in appendix 4.

Two weeks later

Simplicio: I finally managed to perform the stability analysis. You are right, the RS saddle point is not always stable. For $\kappa = 0$ I find an instability for $\alpha > \alpha_{AT} \cong 1.015$. Hence my result $\alpha_c = 4/\pi$ is meaningless since it derives from the RS ansatz in a region where this ansatz is not valid. On the other hand, the stability analysis seems of no great help for determining the correct value of α_c. We know already that α_c must be smaller than 1 and hence belongs to the region in which RS is correct!

Salviati: Your stability analysis was very useful since it demonstrated that replica symmetry breaking (RSB) *is* important for the Ising perceptron. However, we still do not know that RS is correct for all $\alpha < \alpha_{AT}$! The *local* stability is a necessary condition for the reliability of the RS ansatz but it is not sufficient. The exponent of the integrand in (6.22) may have several maxima which are all locally stable. Nevertheless for $N \to \infty$ only the *global* maximum contributes significantly to the integral.

Simplicio: This is true of course. In fact what you suggest is that the transition to RSB might be similar to a first order phase transition as studied in statistical mechanics rather than to a second order transition characterized by the local instability of the old phase. But how can I check whether in my problem there are other maxima than the RS one for $\alpha < \alpha_{AT}$?

Salviati: To this end you have to describe a *disconnected* solution space. In this case there must be at least two different values for the order parameters q^{ab}, one describing the typical overlap of two solutions belonging to the same patch of the solution space and one characterizing the typical overlap of two solutions from different patches. Fortunately, there have already been other statistical mechanics investigations of disordered systems which ran into similar problems [76]. From this experience it is known that the proper way to test the *global* stability of a RS saddle point is to determine the replicated solution volume using the ansatz of *one-step replica symmetry breaking* (RSB) and to compare the result with the RS calculation to find the correct extremum.

Simplicio: And there is really no way to use the Cover method?

Salviati: Unfortunately not. But appendix 5 offers you a safe guide to the one-step RSB result for the Ising perceptron.

Another two weeks later

Simplicio: The result I finally find for the entropy using the one-step RSB ansatz is

$$s(\alpha) = \operatorname*{extr}_{q_0, \hat{q}_0, q_1, \hat{q}_1, m} \left[\frac{m}{2}(q_0 \hat{q}_0 - q_1 \hat{q}_1) - \frac{\hat{q}_1}{2}(1 - q_1) \right. \tag{6.28}$$

$$+ \frac{1}{m} \int Dz_0 \ln \int Dz_1 [2 \cosh(\sqrt{\hat{q}_0} z_0 + \sqrt{\hat{q}_1 - \hat{q}_0} z_1)]^m$$

$$\left. + \frac{\alpha}{m} \int Dt_0 \ln \int Dt_1 H^m \left(-\frac{\sqrt{q_0} t_0 + \sqrt{q_1 - q_0} t_1}{\sqrt{1 - q_1}} \right) \right].$$

It is quite hard to find solutions to the corresponding five saddle point equations, even numerically.

Salviati: Your result is correct and fortunately you do not need detailed solutions for all five order parameters to determine the storage capacity. The parameter q_1 describes the typical overlap between two solutions from the same connected part of the solution space. For $\alpha \to \alpha_c$ we expect that these individual patches shrink to points and accordingly that $q_1 \to 1$. Since the different points are distributed over the sphere the value of q_0 will remain less than 1 even at α_c. It should therefore be possible to extract the value of α_c by considering the limit $q_1 \to 1$ in the saddle point equations corresponding to (6.28).

Simplicio: For $q_1 \to 1$ I find $\hat{q}_1 \sim 1/\sqrt{1 - q_1} \to \infty$ and the saddle point equation for m takes on the form

$$0 = -\frac{m \hat{q}_0}{2}(1 - q_0) + \frac{1}{m} \int Dz \ln 2 \cosh(\sqrt{m \hat{q}_0} z) + \frac{\alpha_c}{m} \int Dt \ln H \left(-\frac{\sqrt{q_0} t}{\sqrt{1 - q_0}} \right). \tag{6.29}$$

Salviati: Good, but substituting now $\hat{q}_0 \mapsto \hat{q}/m^2$ and $q_0 \mapsto q$ and comparing with (6.25) you realize that this saddle point equation for m can be written in the simple form

$$s^{RS}(\alpha_c) = 0. \tag{6.30}$$

The superscript RS is now necessary to distinguish the replica symmetric expression (6.25) for the entropy from the result (6.28) in one-step RSB. The result (6.30) is called the *zero-entropy condition* and is indeed the correct way to determine the storage capacity for neural networks with discrete couplings. We will use it from now on at various times.

Simplicio: So all the complicated calculations beyond the RS expression of the entropy were superfluous! It is quite plausible to identify the value α_{ZE} of α at which the (RS) entropy vanishes with the storage capacity α_c. After all $s(\alpha_{ZE}) = 0$

simply means that for $\alpha > \alpha_{ZE}$ there are only sub-exponentially many solutions **J** to the storage problem left. So, typically none will be found!

Salviati: The zero-entropy criterion does indeed seem rather natural. Nevertheless, its detailed origin is quite subtle as you have seen. In fact, the complete story has still more surprises in store [43]. As for your argument for identifying α_{ZE} and α_c, note that it is impossible to characterize the solution space for $\alpha > \alpha_{ZE}$ within the framework of RS. Your small excursion into the world beyond RS was hence very useful, even if the procedure it justified only uses RS results in the end. Moreover your new expertise in breaking the replica symmetry will come in handy later in the study of multilayer neural nets.

But coming back to the Ising perceptron, what is the value of α_c after all?

Simplicio: Looking numerically for the root of (6.30) with q and $\hat{q}$ determined by (6.26) and (6.27) I find $\alpha_c \cong 0.83$ with $q \cong 0.5$. This is quite near to your estimate 0.85.

Salviati: Your result is in accordance with results from exact numerical calculations [77, 78] and therefore believed to be correct. Although there exists for related systems such as the random energy model [79, 76] a proof that the result in one-step RSB is already the exact one, this is to date not known for the Ising perceptron. Finally, although your result is markedly different from the naive RS result $4/\pi$ it still shows the impressive robustness of the storage abilities. It is a big step to cut back the values of the couplings from real numbers to just 1 and -1; nevertheless the storage capacity just decreases to roughly 40%. Incidentally, if one allows three values $J_i = -1, 0, 1$ for the couplings the result for α_c increases back to $\alpha_c = 1.17$ [80].

6.4 The distribution of stabilities

Prior to learning, when the couplings **J** are still completely unrelated to the inputs ξ^μ, the distribution of stabilities

$$\Delta^\mu = \frac{1}{\sqrt{N}}\sigma^\mu \mathbf{J}\xi^\mu \tag{6.31}$$

is Gaussian

$$P(\Delta) = \frac{1}{\sqrt{2\pi}} \exp(-\Delta^2/2) \tag{6.32}$$

by the central limit theorem. Hence half of the inputs will have positive and half of them negative stabilities initially. From the analysis of section 6.1 we know that for all $\kappa > 0$ it is possible to find couplings **J** for which all stabilities are larger than κ if $\alpha < \alpha_c(\kappa)$. It is interesting to know what the distribution of stabilities looks like *after* such a learning process. The calculation of this distribution can be done by an instructive modification of the replica method [81, 26].

After averaging over the inputs $\boldsymbol{\xi}^\mu$ all indices μ are equivalent to each other and without loss of generality we may use the stability of the first input, $\mu = 1$, for the definition of $P(\Delta)$ after learning

$$P(\Delta) = \left\langle\!\!\left\langle \frac{\int d\mu(\mathbf{J}) \prod_{\mu=1}^p \theta\left(\frac{\sigma^\mu}{\sqrt{N}}\mathbf{J}\boldsymbol{\xi}^\mu - \kappa\right) \delta\left(\frac{\sigma^1}{\sqrt{N}}\mathbf{J}\boldsymbol{\xi}^1 - \Delta\right)}{\int d\mu(\mathbf{J}) \prod_{\mu=1}^p \theta\left(\frac{\sigma^\mu}{\sqrt{N}}\mathbf{J}\boldsymbol{\xi}^\mu - \kappa\right)} \right\rangle\!\!\right\rangle. \tag{6.33}$$

This definition includes the average over all coupling vectors $\mathbf{J}$ which successfully implement the desired input–output mappings as well as the average over the random inputs. The problem in performing this latter average is that both numerator and denominator in (6.33) depend on the $\boldsymbol{\xi}^\mu$ and that one must not average them separately. To circumvent this difficulty we rewrite (6.33) by introducing replicas in the form

$$P(\Delta) = \lim_{n\to 0} \left\langle\!\!\left\langle \int \prod_a d\mu(\mathbf{J}^a) \prod_{\mu,a} \theta\left(\frac{\sigma^\mu}{\sqrt{N}}\mathbf{J}^a\boldsymbol{\xi}^\mu - \kappa\right) \delta\left(\frac{\sigma^1}{\sqrt{N}}\mathbf{J}^1\boldsymbol{\xi}^1 - \Delta\right) \right\rangle\!\!\right\rangle. \tag{6.34}$$

Note that besides the first input index $\mu = 1$ the first replica index $a = 1$ now also plays a special role. The equivalence of (6.34) with (6.33) can be most easily realized by noting that the integrals over $\mathbf{J}^2, \ldots, \mathbf{J}^n$ in (6.34) are the same and give just one integral to power $(n-1)$ which in the limit $n \to 0$ gives rise to the denominator in (6.33).

The input average can now be found as usual. To this end we rewrite the expression for $P(\Delta)$ as

$$P(\Delta) = \theta(\Delta - \kappa) \lim_{n\to 0} \left\langle\!\!\left\langle \int \prod_a d\mu(\mathbf{J}^a) \delta\left(\frac{\sigma^1}{\sqrt{N}}\mathbf{J}^1\boldsymbol{\xi}^1 - \Delta\right) \right.\right.$$
$$\left.\left. \times \prod_{a>1} \theta\left(\frac{\sigma^1}{\sqrt{N}}\mathbf{J}^a\boldsymbol{\xi}^1 - \kappa\right) \prod_{\mu>1,a} \theta\left(\frac{\sigma^\mu}{\sqrt{N}}\mathbf{J}^a\boldsymbol{\xi}^\mu - \kappa\right) \right\rangle\!\!\right\rangle \tag{6.35}$$

and introduce integral representations for the δ- and θ-functions. This gives rise to (cf. (A2.9))

$$P(\Delta) = \theta(\Delta - \kappa) \lim_{n \to 0} \int \prod_a d\mu(\mathbf{J}^a) \int \frac{d\hat{\lambda}_1^1}{2\pi} \int_\kappa^\infty \prod_{a>1} \frac{d\lambda_1^a}{2\pi} \int d\hat{\lambda}_1^a$$

$$\times \int_\kappa^\infty \prod_{a,\mu>1} \frac{d\lambda_\mu^a}{2\pi} \int \prod_{a,\mu>1} d\hat{\lambda}_\mu^a \exp\left(i\Delta\hat{\lambda}_1^1 + i \sum_{a>1} \lambda_1^a \hat{\lambda}_1^a + i \sum_{\mu>1,a} \lambda_\mu^a \hat{\lambda}_\mu^a \right)$$

$$\times \left\langle\!\!\left\langle \exp\left(-\frac{i}{\sqrt{N}} \sum_{a,\mu} \hat{\lambda}_\mu^a \mathbf{J}^a \boldsymbol{\xi}^\mu \right) \right\rangle\!\!\right\rangle. \tag{6.36}$$

After averaging over $\boldsymbol{\xi}^\mu$ we introduce the usual order parameters and end up with

$$P(\Delta) = \theta(\Delta - \kappa) \lim_{n \to 0} \int \prod_a \frac{d\hat{k}^a}{4\pi} \int \prod_{a<b} \frac{dq^{ab} d\hat{q}^{ab}}{2\pi/N} \int \frac{d\hat{\lambda}_1^1}{2\pi} \int_\kappa^\infty \prod_{a>1} \frac{d\lambda_1^a}{2\pi} \int d\hat{\lambda}_1^a$$

$$\times \exp\left(i\Delta\hat{\lambda}_1^1 + i \sum_{a>1} \lambda_1^a \hat{\lambda}_1^a - \frac{1}{2} \sum_a (\hat{\lambda}_1^a)^2 - \frac{1}{2} \sum_{(a,b)} \hat{\lambda}_1^a \hat{\lambda}_1^b q^{ab} \right)$$

$$\times \exp\left(N\frac{i}{2} \sum_a \hat{k}^a + Ni \sum_{a<b} q^{ab} \hat{q}^{ab} + NG_S(\hat{k}^a, \hat{q}^{ab}) + (\alpha N - 1) G_E(q^{ab}) \right) \tag{6.37}$$

where $G_S(\hat{k}^a, \hat{q}^{ab})$ and $G_E(q^{ab})$ are exactly the same as given by (6.9) and (6.10) respectively. The order parameter integrals in this expression can be calculated by the saddle point method and the corresponding saddle point equations are of course also the same as in section 6.1. Note that in the subsequent limit $n \to 0$ the exponent in the last line of (6.37) disappears. Nevertheless it is very important since it fixes the values of the order parameters which appear also in the remaining terms (cf. also (A1.21)).

Assuming replica symmetry we find after manipulations which are by now standard to the reader

$$P(\Delta) = \theta(\Delta - \kappa) \lim_{n \to 0} \int Dt \int \frac{d\hat{\lambda}^1}{2\pi} \int_\kappa^\infty \prod_{a>1} \frac{d\lambda^a}{2\pi} \int d\hat{\lambda}^a$$

$$\times \exp\left(i\Delta\hat{\lambda}^1 + i \sum_{a>1} \lambda_1^a \hat{\lambda}_1^a - \frac{1-q}{2} \sum_a (\hat{\lambda}^a)^2 - i\sqrt{q}\, t \sum_a \hat{\lambda}^a \right).$$

The integrals over $\hat{\lambda}^2, \ldots, \hat{\lambda}^n$ are all identical and give rise to one integral to power

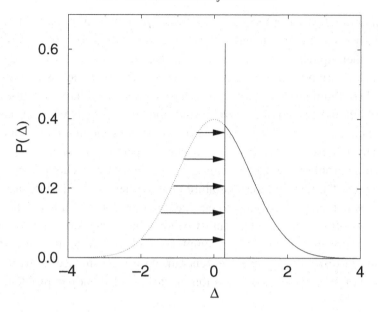

Fig. 6.7. Distribution of stabilities $P(\Delta)$ as given by (6.39) for $\alpha = 1.0$ and $\kappa = 0.3$. The part of the initial Gaussian distribution (6.32) corresponding to stabilities larger than κ remains unmodified by the learning process, and all stabilities smaller than κ are shifted to the δ-peak at $\Delta = \kappa$. The height of this peak in the figure is equal to the prefactor of the δ-function in (6.39).

$(n - 1)$. Taking the limit $n \to 0$ we finally get

$$P(\Delta) = \theta(\Delta - \kappa)\frac{1}{\sqrt{2\pi(1 - q)}} \int Dt \exp\left(-\frac{(\Delta - \sqrt{q}t)^2}{2(1 - q)}\right)\left[H\left(\frac{\kappa - \sqrt{q}t}{\sqrt{1 - q}}\right)\right]^{-1}$$
(6.38)

where q is determined by (6.14). We hence eventually recover the average of a quotient we started from in (6.33) with t now in some way playing the role of the quenched disorder.

The expression for $P(\Delta)$ is particularly instructive at the storage capacity, i.e. for $\alpha = \alpha_c$. As discussed in section 6.1 we then have $q \to 1$, which simplifies (6.38) to

$$P(\Delta) = \theta(\Delta - \kappa)\frac{1}{\sqrt{2\pi}} \exp(-\Delta^2/2) + H(-\kappa)\,\delta(\Delta - \kappa).$$
(6.39)

Comparing this result with the distribution of stabilities before learning as given by (6.32) one realizes that the Gaussian distribution of stabilities larger than κ remains whereas all stabilities which were initially smaller than κ are shifted by the learning process to *exactly* the required stability border (see fig. 6.7). This is clearly an optimal way to reach $\Delta^\mu \geq \kappa$ for all μ since shifting stabilities which were initially smaller than κ to values beyond κ would decrease the flexibility with respect to other inputs. In fact, the distribution (6.39) perfectly mirrors the strategy of the adatron learning rule as discussed in section 3.5. Nevertheless we emphasize that the rule of thumb to leave untouched those inputs which have stabilities larger than κ from the start is not quite correct since the sets of inputs which produce the Gaussian tail at $\Delta > \kappa$ before and after learning are in general *not* the same.

The analysis described in this section may be performed analogously for the generalization problem, i.e. for learning a rule defined by a teacher perceptron, see problem 6.16. The distribution of stabilities may then be used to determine the *confidence* which may be assigned to the classifications of the student. This refines the characterization of the learning ability beyond the average estimate provided by the generalization error alone [82]. A simple example of how to use this additional information in order to improve the generalization performance is given by the prescription of rejecting difficult questions as discussed already in problem 4.9.

6.5 Beyond the storage capacity

Let us finally shortly discuss the main features of the storage problem for the case in which the number of input–output mappings exceeds $\alpha_c N$. By definition of the storage capacity it is then impossible to implement all mappings and the question of the *minimal* possible fraction of errors $\varepsilon_{\min}$ naturally arises. This quantity may be calculated by methods similar to those employed in section 4.3 with the number of wrong classifications playing the role of the energy and considering the zero-temperature limit $\beta \to \infty$ in order to concentrate on those coupling vectors $\mathbf{J}$ that minimize the error [25]. The calculation is, of course, also analogous to the determination of the training error for a noisy teacher problem as discussed in section 5.3. We therefore only quote the result (cf. problem 6.14). Within replica symmetry one finds [25]

$$\varepsilon_{\min} = \operatorname*{extr}_x \left[H(\sqrt{2x} - \kappa) + \frac{1}{2x} \int_{\kappa - \sqrt{2x}}^{\kappa} Dt\, (\kappa - t)^2 - \frac{1}{2\alpha x} \right]. \qquad (6.40)$$

Using the corresponding saddle point equation for x

$$\frac{1}{\alpha} = \int_{\kappa - \sqrt{2x}}^{\kappa} Dt\, (\kappa - t)^2, \qquad (6.41)$$

which fixes x for given values of α and κ, (6.40) simplifies to

$$\varepsilon_{\min} = H(\sqrt{2x} - \kappa). \qquad (6.42)$$

For $\alpha \to \alpha_c(\kappa)$ we find $x \to \infty$ and correspondingly $\varepsilon_{\min} \to 0$ as it should do.

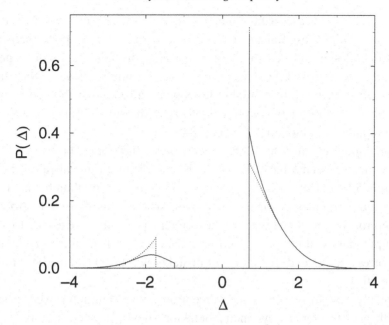

Fig. 6.8. Distribution of stabilities $P(\Delta)$ for a perceptron above saturation ($\alpha = 1.0$, $\kappa = 0.7$). The dotted line gives the replica symmetric expression (6.43), the full line is the result in one-step replica symmetry breaking as determined in [62]. The gap in the distribution is typical for a cost function just *counting* errors; the jump at the left border of the gap renders replica symmetry unstable [75, 83].

It is also instructive to determine the distribution of stabilities $P(\Delta)$ above saturation. Analogously to the previous section we get, again assuming replica symmetry to hold,

$$P(\Delta) = \theta(\kappa - \sqrt{2x} - \Delta)\,\frac{1}{\sqrt{2\pi}}\,\exp(-\Delta^2/2)$$

$$+ \,(H(\kappa - \sqrt{2x}) - H(\kappa))\,\delta(\Delta - \kappa) + \theta(\Delta - \kappa)\,\frac{1}{\sqrt{2\pi}}\,\exp(-\Delta^2/2), \quad (6.43)$$

where x is again determined by (6.41). The distribution now has three parts as shown in fig. 6.8. It is Gaussian for $\Delta > \kappa$ and has a δ-peak at $\Delta = \kappa$ as in the case $\alpha < \alpha_c$. However, additionally a Gaussian tail of stabilities *smaller* than κ appears that comprises the input–output pairs the network was unable to implement. The integral over this part of wrong stabilities of course yields back the result (6.42) for the fraction of errors.

Note that there is a marked gap in the stability distribution, implying that the errors that occur are really "gross" errors. This is due to the cost function used, which only *counts* the number of mistakes but does not pay attention to how severe the errors are in the sense of how much their stabilities differ from the required threshold κ. Other cost functions, e.g. those corresponding to the perceptron and adatron rules introduced in chapter 3, *weigh* the mistakes with respect to the difference of their stabilities from κ. Correspondingly, above α_c they favour couplings which give rise to more, but less severe, mistakes. A thorough analysis of the behaviour of different cost functions above the storage capacity within the replica symmetric assumption is given in [84].

As a final grain of salt it has to be noted that for the storage problem above α_c replica symmetry is unstable [25, 75], as is typical for an unrealizable situation (cf. section 5.5). This is in accordance with our rule of thumb that replica symmetry breaking may occur if the solution space is disconnected. Above α_c the perceptron has to make errors and different possibilities exist as to which input–output pairs will not be correctly implemented. It is intuitive that coupling vectors corresponding to different sets of mistakes will in general not be connected with each other.

Fortunately, investigations of the perceptron above saturation using a saddle point with one-step replica symmetry breaking show that some results, such as the minimal fraction of errors, are not markedly modified by replica symmetry breaking (RSB) [85, 62]. On the other hand, the distribution of stabilities is reshaped to a certain extent as shown in fig. 6.8.

A careful analysis shows that the discontinuous jump of $P(\Delta)$ at the beginning of the gap is the formal reason for the instability of the saddle point [75]. It can then be shown that *any finite* level of RSB will yield such a discontinuous jump and will in turn also be unstable [83]. Consequently, the ambitious proposal of an analysis using the *full* continuous Parisi scheme of RSB [86, 17] has been put forward [87]. The necessary calculations are rather complicated and indicate that a gap in the distribution of stabilities remains with $P(\Delta)$ tending to zero continuously at the left border of the gap [88, 89].

6.6 Problems

6.1 Figure 6.9 was generated as follows: $p = 250$ points in a space of dimension $N = 200$ were generated at random by choosing their individual coordinates independently of each other as Gaussian random numbers with zero mean and unit variance. Also the points were coloured black and white independently of each other with equal probability. The left part of the figure shows a projection of the points onto a randomly chosen two-dimensional plane. The right part shows *the same* set of points but now seen from a suitably chosen direction. What is the maximal possible distance between black and white points one can obtain in this way? Could one also find a projection where

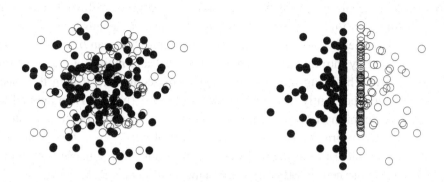

Fig. 6.9. Projection of 250 random points in 200 dimensions with random colourings onto two different two-dimensional planes.

all the points lie above one hyperplane through the origin? Are there such directions for all N and p?

6.2 Show that the result of Cover (6.18) on the number of dichotomies allows the following dual formulation: p hyperplanes in general position divide the N-dimensional space into $C(p, N)$ regions.

6.3 Show that all curves of fig. 6.5 intersect at the point $(2, 0.5)$.

6.4 Consider the result (6.18) for the number of dichotomies in the thermodynamic limit $N \to \infty$ with $p = \alpha N$. Using Stirling's formula to approximate the binomial and transforming the sum to an integral show by a saddle point argument that

$$\frac{1}{N} \ln C(p, N) \begin{cases} = \alpha \ln 2 & \text{for} \quad \alpha \leq 2 \\ \leq \alpha \ln \alpha - (\alpha - 1) \ln(\alpha - 1) & \text{for} \quad \alpha > 2, \end{cases} \tag{6.44}$$

implying that for $\alpha < 2$ almost all dichotomies are linearly separable whereas for $\alpha > 2$ only an exponentially small fraction of them are.

6.5 A threshold θ of a perceptron can be interpreted as an additional component of the coupling vector $\mathbf{J}$ attached to a *constant* component $S_0 = 1$ of all input vectors. Using this interpretation show that the number of colourings of p points in general position in N-dimensional space which can be separated by a hyperplane not necessarily going through the origin is given by $C(p, N + 1)$. Give an explicit example for $p = 4$ and $N = 2$ which is *not* linearly separable.

6.6 Consider the storage problem for a spherical perceptron with sign-constraint couplings. In this case the learning process can only change the *strengths* of the synapses but not alter their *signs*. This constraint can be conveniently formulated by introducing N numbers $\varepsilon_i = \pm 1$ and requiring $\varepsilon_i J_i \geq 0$ for all i. Show by using the Gardner method of section 6.2 that in this case $\alpha_c = 1$ independently of the realization of the ε_i. (Note: When applied to attractor neural networks this result implies, e.g., that it is possible to store and retrieve information with a network made of *purely excitatory* synapses. It is also related to the neurophysiological finding that synapses emerging from the same neuron often have the same sign (Dale's Rule). See [90, 91] for more details.)

6.7 Re-derive the result of the previous problem by using the Cover approach [92]. Show also that by prescribing the signs of a fraction s of synapses only the result for the storage capacity is $\alpha_c = 2 - s$ [93].

6.8 Determine the critical storage capacity of an attractor neural network with symmetric couplings $J_{ij} = J_{ji}$. (Note: This is a hard one, which to our knowledge has not been solved so far. If you find the solution do not forget to notify us!)

6.9 Generalize the results (6.13) and (6.15) to *biased* inputs and outputs, i.e. to distributions of the form

$$P_\xi(\boldsymbol{\xi}) = \prod_i \left(\frac{1 + m_{\text{in}}}{2} \delta(\xi_i - 1) + \frac{1 - m_{\text{in}}}{2} \delta(\xi_i + 1) \right)$$

$$P_\sigma(\sigma) = \frac{1 + m_{\text{out}}}{2} \delta(\sigma - 1) + \frac{1 - m_{\text{out}}}{2} \delta(\sigma + 1)$$

and a perceptron with a *threshold* θ as in (1.1).

6.10 Show that the replica symmetric saddle point in the Gardner calculation for the storage problem of the spherical perceptron as described in section 6.1 becomes unstable when $\kappa < 0$.

6.11 Show that the annealed calculation for the storage problem of the Ising perceptron using $\ln\langle\!\langle \Omega \rangle\!\rangle$ instead of $\langle\!\langle \ln \Omega \rangle\!\rangle$ gives $\alpha_c = 1$ for $\kappa = 0$. Prove that this is a rigorous upper bound for the true α_c.

6.12 Show by using the zero-entropy criterion that the storage capacity for a perceptron with couplings $J_i = 0, 1$ is given by $\alpha_c(\kappa = 0) = 0.59$ [94].

6.13 Consider a perceptron with *fixed* couplings J_i generated independently at random and study the storage problem for *learning by dilution*. This means that the only modification allowed during learning is the removal of a fraction $(1 - c)$ of the couplings.

(a) Show that $\alpha_c(c=0) = \alpha_c(c=1) = 0$.

(b) Introducing the dilution parameters $c_i = 0, 1$, show that the quenched entropy

$$s(c) = \lim_{N \to \infty} \frac{1}{N} \left\langle\!\!\left\langle \sum_{\{c_i\}} \prod_\mu \theta\left(\frac{\sigma^\mu}{\sqrt{N}} \sum_i c_i J_i \xi_i^\mu - \kappa\right) \delta\left(\sum_i c_i, cN\right) \right\rangle\!\!\right\rangle \tag{6.45}$$

with the Kronecker symbol $\delta(m, n)$ defined in (A1.13) is in replica symmetry given by

$$s(c) = \operatorname*{extr}_{\hat{k},\hat{q},q,\hat{Q},Q} \left[\frac{c\hat{k}}{2} + \frac{q\hat{q}}{2} - \frac{Q\hat{Q}}{2} + \alpha \int Dt \ln H\left(\frac{\kappa + \sqrt{q}t}{\sqrt{Q-q}}\right) \right.$$
$$\left. + \left\langle\!\!\left\langle \int Dz \ln\left(1 + \exp\left(\sqrt{\hat{q}}|J|z + \frac{J^2}{2}(\hat{Q} - \hat{q}) - \frac{\hat{k}}{2}\right)\right) \right\rangle\!\!\right\rangle \right],$$

where the remaining average is over the distribution of the coupling components J_i and we have introduced the order parameters

$$q = \frac{1}{N} \sum_i J_i^2 c_i^a c_i^b \quad \text{and} \quad Q = \frac{1}{N} \sum_i J_i^2 c_i^a. \tag{6.46}$$

(c) For a distribution $P(J)$ which only allows the values $J_i = \pm 1$, show that $\alpha_c(c) \leq 0.59$ for all c by mapping the problem onto the previous one.

For a detailed analysis with references on the possible neurophysiological relevance of this learning scenario see [95].

6.14 Verify (6.40) by calculating the minimal fraction of misclassified inputs in the storage problem of a spherical perceptron for $\alpha > \alpha_c(\kappa)$.

6.15 Show by using the techniques of section 6.4 that the distribution of stabilities for learning rules minimizing a potential $V(\Delta)$ is given by

$$P(\Delta) = \int Dt \, \delta(\Delta - \Delta_0(x, t)), \tag{6.47}$$

where $\Delta_0(x, t)$ is the minimum of $V(\Delta) + (\Delta - t)^2/2x$.

6.16 Generalize the previous result to supervised learning by showing that for zero-temperature learning with learning error $E = \sum_\mu V(\Delta^\mu)$, the distribution $P(\Delta)$ of the stabilities is given by

$$P(\Delta) = \int Dt \delta(\Delta - \Delta_0(t, x))2H\left(-\frac{Rt}{\sqrt{1-R^2}}\right), \tag{6.48}$$

where $\Delta_0(t, x)$ is again the minimum of $V(\Delta) + (\Delta - t)^2/2x$ and R denotes the teacher–student overlap. In particular derive the result for Hebb learning and verify that the training error is given by $\varepsilon_t = \int_{-\infty}^{0} d\Delta P(\Delta)$.

7

Discontinuous Learning

So far we have been considering learning scenarios in which generalization shows up as a gradual process of improvement with the generalization error ε decreasing continuously from its initial pure guessing value $\varepsilon = 0.5$ to the asymptotic limit $\varepsilon = 0$. In the present chapter we study systems which display a quite different behaviour with *sudden* changes of the generalization ability taking place during the learning process. The reason for this new feature is the presence of *discrete* degrees of freedom among the parameters, which are adapted during the learning process. As we will see, discontinuous learning is a rather subtle consequence of this discreteness and methods of statistical mechanics are well suited to describe the situation. In particular the abrupt changes which occur in the generalization process can be described as first order phase transitions well studied in statistical physics.

7.1 Smooth networks

The learning scenarios discussed so far have been described in the framework of statistical mechanics as a continuous shift of the balance between energetic and entropic terms. In the case of perfect learning the energy describes how difficult it is for the student vector to stay in the version space (see (2.13)). For independent examples it is naturally given as a sum over the training set and scales for large α as $e \sim \alpha \varepsilon$ since the generalization error ε gives the probability of error and hence of an additional cost when a new example is presented. The entropy on the other hand, being defined as the logarithm of the available phase space volume Ω, measures the diversity of different couplings that realize the same training error. If the couplings $\mathbf{J}$ of the system are *continuous* Ω is an N-dimensional volume with linear extension ε since the generalization error gives the geodesic distance between teacher and student. We therefore find $\Omega \sim \varepsilon^N$ and the scaling of the entropy per coupling is correspondingly given by $s \sim \ln \varepsilon$.

109

The balance between energy and entropy is mathematically described by the extremum condition in ε for the sum of energetic and entropic terms. For small α couplings with large *a priori* measure dominate the version space and the entropic part is the decisive one. With increasing α this balance is shifted more and more towards the energetic part and for large α most couplings have been eliminated from the version space with only those with small values of e remaining. Using the asymptotics of energy and entropy discussed above we find by minimizing their sum that

$$0 \sim \frac{\partial}{\partial \varepsilon}(\ln \varepsilon - \alpha \varepsilon) = \frac{1}{\varepsilon} - \alpha, \tag{7.1}$$

resulting in the ubiquitous $1/\alpha$ decay of the generalization error ε for large training set size α. Different learning rules just give rise to different prefactors to this asymptotic law. Similar results are obtained also for the more general case of learning rules including students with non-zero training error by introducing a temperature and the extremum condition for the associated free energy, see section 4.3.

In fact in view of (7.1) one expects for all learning scenarios with

$$\lim_{\varepsilon \to \varepsilon_{\min}} \frac{\partial s}{\partial \varepsilon} = \infty \tag{7.2}$$

a smooth convergence of the generalization error to its minimal value with diverging training set size α.

These statements can be made somewhat more quantitative in the case of differentiable activation functions $g(x)$ (cf. problem 3.7). The training and generalization error are then differentiable functions of the coupling vectors and their asymptotic behaviour may be inferred from Taylor expansions around their minimal values [21, 12].

If, however, the coupling space of the network under consideration is not continuous, the behaviour of the entropy for small generalization error can be quite different. A simple example is provided by the *Ising perceptron*, the coupling components J_i of which are confined to the values ± 1. Its storage properties have already been studied in section 6.3. Simple combinatorial arguments show that the entropy of the couplings **J** which realize a specific overlap R with a teacher Ising perceptron **T** is given by (see problem 7.2)

$$s(R) = -\frac{1+R}{2}\ln\frac{1+R}{2} - \frac{1-R}{2}\ln\frac{1-R}{2}, \tag{7.3}$$

which by using $\varepsilon = \arccos R/\pi$ gives rise to

$$s(\varepsilon) \sim -\frac{\pi^2}{2}\varepsilon^2 \ln \varepsilon \tag{7.4}$$

for $\varepsilon \to 0$. The minimization of the sum of energy and entropy now results asymptotically in

$$0 \sim -\pi^2 \varepsilon \ln \varepsilon - \alpha, \tag{7.5}$$

to be contrasted with (7.1). For large α this equation has no solution, indicating that the minimum of f does not lie inside the interval of allowed values of ε but at the boundary. In this case a continuous decrease of the generalization error with increasing training set size is not to be expected.

The difference in the behaviour of the entropy for systems with continuous and discrete degrees of freedom respectively is related to the fact that in the latter case the entropy of the actual state can never be negative. For a system with discrete phase space the "volume" Ω is a natural number counting the different microscopic ways to realize a given macroscopic state. Consequently the minimal value of Ω is, at least for the realizable case, equal to 1 and the corresponding entropy is 0.

7.2 The Ising perceptron

From the considerations in the previous section we expect that the asymptotic properties of the learning process will be modified in the case of networks with discrete couplings. A nice example is given by an Ising perceptron learning classifications provided by another Ising perceptron; in the following we analyse this example in some detail.

The statistical mechanics calculation of the quenched entropy is again a variation of the general method of appendix 2. In fact the energetic part $G_E(q^{ab}, R^a)$ is not at all sensitive to the nature of the couplings $\mathbf{J}$ and is hence again given by (A2.19). For the entropic part one finds from (A2.18) by replacing the integral by a sum and omitting the spherical constraint

$$G_S(\hat{q}^{ab}, \hat{R}^a) = \ln \sum_{\{J^a = \pm 1\}} \exp\left(-i \sum_{a<b} \hat{q}^{ab} J^a J^b - i \sum_a \hat{R}^a J^a\right), \tag{7.6}$$

which coincides with (6.21) for $R = 0$ as it should. Assuming replica symmetry and anticipating imaginary saddle point values we use $-i\hat{q}^{ab} = \hat{q}$ and $-i\hat{R}^a = \hat{R}$ to get after analogous manipulation to that used in (6.24)

$$G_S(\hat{q}, \hat{R}) = -\frac{n\hat{q}}{2} + n \int Dz \ln 2 \cosh(\sqrt{\hat{q}}\, z + \hat{R}) + O(n^2), \tag{7.7}$$

which gives rise to the following result for the quenched entropy

$$
s = \underset{q,\hat{q},R,\hat{R}}{\text{extr}} \left[\frac{\hat{q}}{2}(q-1) - \hat{R}R + \int Dz \ln 2 \cosh(\sqrt{\hat{q}}\, z + \hat{R}) \right.
$$

$$
\left. + 2\alpha \int Dt\, H\!\left(-\frac{Rt}{\sqrt{q-R^2}}\right) \ln H\!\left(-\sqrt{\frac{q}{1-q}}\, t\right) \right]. \quad (7.8)
$$

In order to find the dependence of the order parameters on the training set size α we have to determine the extremum of s with respect to these parameters. Note that contrary to the case of the spherical perceptron the conjugated order parameters cannot be eliminated analytically. Nevertheless, the saddle point equations corresponding to (7.8) can again be simplified due to the teacher–student symmetry, giving rise to the solution $q = R$ and $\hat{q} = \hat{R}$. After a transformation of the integration variables the remaining equations assume the form

$$
R = \int Dz \tanh(\sqrt{\hat{R}}\, z + \hat{R}) \quad (7.9)
$$

$$
\hat{R}\sqrt{1-R} = \frac{\alpha}{\pi} \int Dt\, \frac{\exp(-Rt^2/2)}{H(\sqrt{R}t)}. \quad (7.10)
$$

To find the extremum in (7.8) these equations have to be solved numerically and the corresponding results for the quenched entropy *have to be compared with its values at the boundary $R = 0$ and $R = 1$.* The results of this procedure are shown in fig. 7.1.

As can be clearly seen the solution of (7.9), (7.10) does indeed not always give the maximum of the entropy. This is the case for $\alpha < \alpha_d \cong 1.245$ only whereas for larger values of α the boundary value $s(R = 1) = 0$ gives the maximum of s. The discontinuous jump of the value of R maximizing s is clearly seen in the plot of the entropy as a function of R for different values of α as shown in the inset. There is hence a *discontinuous* transition to the state of *perfect generalization* characterized by $R = 1$, $\varepsilon = 0$ at a finite value $\alpha_d \cong 1.245$ of α which shows up as a *first order phase transition* in the statistical mechanics analysis of the problem. If a large Ising perceptron classifies $1.245N$ random inputs in the same way as a teacher perceptron of the same architecture it will therefore do so (with probability 1) for *all* the 2^N possible inputs!

The above expressions rely on the assumption of replica symmetry and from our experience with the storage problem of the Ising perceptron discussed in section 6.3 we might expect replica symmetry to be broken. In fact the results shown as dotted lines in fig. 7.1 are locally stable but globally unstable with respect to replica symmetry breaking as can be inferred from a solution in one-step RSB. As in (6.30) the transition to the RSB state is signalled by a vanishing

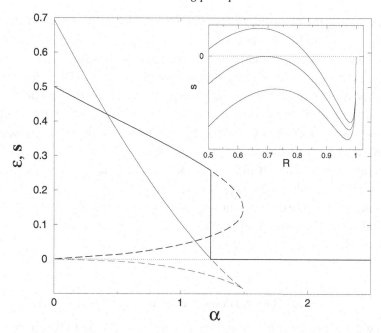

Fig. 7.1. Generalization error (thick line) and quenched entropy (thin line) as a function of the training set size α for an Ising student perceptron learning a classification provided by an Ising teacher. The dashed parts of the lines correspond to unstable solutions. The inset shows the quenched entropy as a function of the teacher–student overlap R for $\alpha = 1.2$, $\alpha_d = 1.245$ and $\alpha = 1.3$ (from top to bottom).

replica symmetric entropy and this zero-entropy criterion is a useful tool to determine the point of the discontinuous transition to perfect learning without having to perform the more involved RSB calculations. Note also that in the generalization problem the zero-entropy criterion has a very intuitive meaning. As a consequence of $s(R = 1) = 0$ perfect generalization sets in at the point where coupling vectors realizing the poorly generalizing phase become exponentially rare. Since this is also exactly the point where RSB occurs the discontinuous transition takes us from the abyss of RSB to the safe region at $R = 1$ and the whole generalization process can be analysed within a replica symmetric framework.

Discontinuous learning of the described type is as a rule always present when at least some of the adjustable parameters have a discrete nature. Examples include systems with finite synaptic depth [96] and dilution parameters [97]. Another interesting case is given by multilayer networks where the binary internal representations serve as discrete degrees of freedom and may result in a cascade of first order transitions in the generalization behaviour (see chapter 12). In the next section we discuss the reversed wedge perceptron, which in this respect may serve as a toy model for multilayer nets.

Let us finally emphasize that these discontinuous transitions are not at all a trivial consequence of the discrete nature of the phase space. There is, of course, a minimal possible non-zero value $R_{min} = 1 - 2/N$ for the overlap between two Ising vectors $\mathbf{J}$ and $\mathbf{T}$, but $R_{min} \to 0$ for $N \to \infty$. The value $R \cong 0.695$ of the teacher–student overlap at which the discontinuous transition takes place in the Ising scenario has a very different explanation. The clue is that there are extremely few coupling vectors with an overlap R close to 1, in fact so few of them that they are eliminated in the early stages of the learning process. Therefore a band of negative entropy quickly develops around $R = 1$ (cf. problem 7.2 and the inset of fig. 7.1) and the final transition takes place when this band merges with the negative entropy band developing around $R = 0$.

7.3 The reversed wedge perceptron

The reversed wedge perceptron classifies inputs $\boldsymbol{\xi}^{\mu}$ according to their projection λ onto the coupling vector $\mathbf{J}$ just as the usual perceptron does, but the simple sign function between local field and output is replaced by

$$\sigma = \text{sgn}((\lambda - \gamma)\lambda(\lambda + \gamma)). \tag{7.11}$$

The most remarkable feature of this activation function is that it is *non-monotonic*, see fig. 7.2. As a result inputs which are classified by $\sigma = +1$ may have stabilities either larger than γ or in the interval $(-\gamma, 0)$ and a similar ambiguity holds, of course, for inputs classified as -1. The state of the reversed wedge perceptron is hence characterized by additional discrete degrees of freedom, which may be called *internal representation* of each input, specifying the internal realization of the classification. As a consequence two reversed wedge perceptrons of the same kind, i.e. with the same parameter γ, may give the same output for all examples of a certain set but nevertheless differ in the internal organization of the classifications.[1]

The reversed wedge perceptron looks rather artificial and in fact there seems to be no biological indication that neurons with non-monotonic activation functions exist. However, the occurrence of an internal representation, which is the hallmark of multilayer networks (see chapters 12 and 13), gives rise to some new and interesting storage and generalization properties which are worth studying in some detail. Since the reversed wedge perceptron is on the other hand not much more

---

[1] By rewriting (7.11) as $\sigma = \text{sgn}(\lambda - \gamma)\,\text{sgn}(\lambda)\,\text{sgn}(\lambda + \gamma)$ one can map the reversed wedge perceptron onto a parity machine whose output is the product of the outputs of three perceptrons with parallel hyperplanes. The internal representation is then specified by the classifications of the constituent perceptrons.

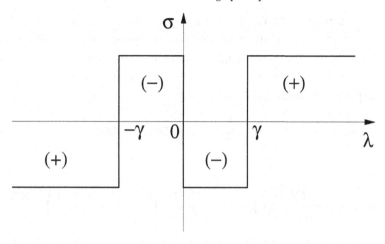

Fig. 7.2. Non-monotonic activation function of the reversed wedge perceptron. There are two types of inputs realizing positive output, those with local field larger than γ (internal representation "+") and those with local field between $-\gamma$ and 0 (internal representation "$-$").

difficult to analyse than the simple perceptron it may serve as a nice toy model for the more complex multilayer nets.

The similarity with multilayer networks shows up already when investigating the storage problem for a reversed wedge perceptron. The replica symmetric result for the storage capacity is rather large, cf. problem 7.6. However, replica symmetry is broken and the result for α_c is markedly reduced in one-step replica symmetry breaking. In fact it is easy to convince oneself that the existence of different internal representations for the examples implies that the Gardner volume may no longer be connected. As already discussed this may entail the breakdown of replica symmetry.

As for the generalization abilities we will first consider the simple realizable case in which a reversed wedge perceptron with continuous coupling vector $\mathbf{J}$ is trying to infer the continuous coupling vector $\mathbf{T}$ of another reversed wedge perceptron with the same wedge parameter γ from labelled examples. In order to use our statistical mechanics methods resting on the calculation of the typical teacher–student overlap R we have first to realize that the simple relation (2.3) between ε and R no longer holds. In fact, using the statistical properties (2.19) of the local fields of teacher and student we find instead

$$\varepsilon = 2 \left(\int_{-\gamma}^{0} Du + \int_{\gamma}^{\infty} Du \right) \left[H\left(\frac{Ru + \gamma}{\sqrt{1 - R^2}} \right) - H\left(\frac{Ru}{\sqrt{1 - R^2}} \right) + H\left(\frac{Ru - \gamma}{\sqrt{1 - R^2}} \right) \right],$$

$$(7.12)$$

which of course reduces to (2.3) for both $\gamma = 0$ and $\gamma \to \infty$. Performing the statistical mechanics analysis as detailed in appendix 2, assuming replica symmetry, which, for the generalization problem, can be shown to be reliable, and using the teacher–student symmetry giving rise to $R = q$ we end up with the following expression for the quenched entropy

$$s = \max_R \left[\frac{1}{2} \ln(1 - R) + \frac{R}{2} + 2\alpha \int Dt \, H_\gamma(t) \ln H_\gamma(t) \right], \tag{7.13}$$

with

$$H_\gamma(t) = H \left(\frac{\sqrt{R}\,t + \gamma}{\sqrt{1 - R}} \right) - H \left(\frac{\sqrt{R}\,t}{\sqrt{1 - R}} \right) + H \left(\frac{\sqrt{R}\,t - \gamma}{\sqrt{1 - R}} \right). \tag{7.14}$$

Solving the self-consistent equation corresponding to (7.13) numerically one finds that for all values of $\gamma < \gamma_c \cong 1.6$ there is an interval of α-values for which *two local maxima* of the entropy exist. This gives rise to the generic generalization behaviour shown in fig. 7.3. For small values of α the system starts in a phase with poor generalization ability in which the generalization error decays only slowly. This phase is characterized by a large misfit between the internal representations of teacher and student despite the agreement on the final classification of the inputs. With increasing α the entropy of this phase decreases more rapidly than that of the well generalizing phase and correspondingly there is at a certain value α_d of α a *discontinuous* transition to the well generalizing phase characterized by a large similarity between the internal representations of teacher and student. The final decay of the generalization error then follows the usual $1/\alpha$ behaviour. We therefore find that the existence of discrete degrees of freedom, which are in the present case the internal representations, again results in a discontinuous transition in the learning process. Since contrary to the case of the Ising perceptron discussed before there are also continuous variables smooth learning takes place both before and after the discontinuous jump. Note also that in this more general case the zero-entropy criterion cannot be used to locate the transition.

An interesting special situation occurs for $\gamma = \gamma_c = \sqrt{2 \ln 2}$. For this parameter value, the reversed wedge classification σ, given by (7.11), implies the following symmetry property for a randomly chosen example ξ on the N-sphere

$$\left\langle\!\!\left\langle \frac{\mathbf{J}\xi \, \sigma}{\sqrt{N}} \right\rangle\!\!\right\rangle = 0. \tag{7.15}$$

As we will see in chapter 8, this property results in a very specific behaviour including retarded learning, of which we see here a first example. Indeed, in this case one finds that $R = 0$ is a solution to the saddle point equation corresponding to (7.13) *for all* α. Consequently the poorly generalizing phase is characterized by a

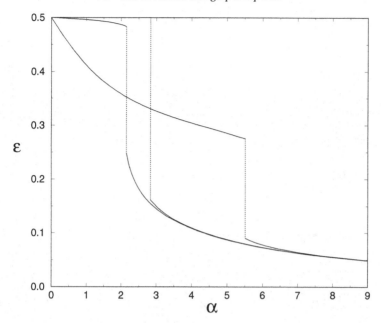

Fig. 7.3. Generalization error of a reversed wedge perceptron learning from examples labelled by another reversed wedge perceptron with the same parameter γ as a function of α for $\gamma = 1.5$, $\gamma = \gamma_c = \sqrt{2 \ln 2} \sim 1.177$ and $\gamma = 0.4$ (from left to right).

constant value $\varepsilon = 0.5$ of the generalization error. On the other hand one finds from (7.13) that this phase is characterized by $s = -\alpha \ln 2$. In the initial learning phase the version space is hence bisected by every new example, and this corresponds to an optimal reduction of its volume; nevertheless the student gains no information at all about the teacher due to the large misfit in internal representations! Only later is there a sudden "Eureka"-like transition putting the student on the right track and starting a final stage of continuous learning.

This discontinuous transition is even more dramatic in the case of reversed wedge perceptrons with Ising couplings, i.e. $T_i = \pm 1$ and $J_i = \pm 1$. One then finds that for $\gamma = \gamma_c$ the generalization error remains at its initial value $\varepsilon = 0.5$ for all $\alpha < 1$ and then jumps discontinuously to $\varepsilon = 0$ at $\alpha_d = 1$. There is hence a transition from learning nothing at all to perfect generalization!

This remarkable behaviour may already be anticipated from the annealed approximation. Figure 7.4 shows the annealed entropy as a function of ε for this situation (compare with fig. 2.2 for the spherical perceptron). The cusp at $\varepsilon = 0.5$ arises because of $\partial \varepsilon / \partial R(R = 0, \gamma = \gamma_c) = 0$ as can be easily verified from (7.12). This ensures that s has for all values of α a local maximum at $\varepsilon = 0.5$ with value $s(R = 0) = (1 - \alpha) \ln 2$. Hence student vectors with $R = 0$ dominate the phase

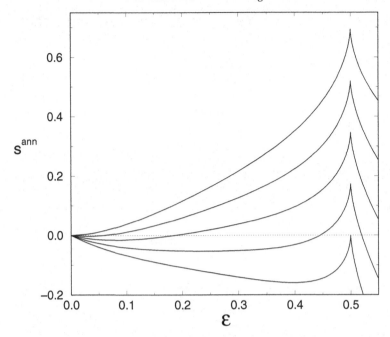

Fig. 7.4. Annealed entropy of an Ising reversed wedge perceptron as a function of the generalization error ε for training set sizes $\alpha = 0, 0.25, 0.5, 0.75$ and 1 (from top to bottom). The cusp at $\varepsilon = 0.5$ is specific to the critical wedge parameter $\gamma_c = \sqrt{2\ln 2}$.

space up to the point $\alpha_d = 1$ at which $s(R = 0)$ becomes negative and the transition to perfect generalization ($\varepsilon = 0$) takes place. Note that the value $\alpha_d = 1$ has to be compared with $\alpha_d = 1.245$ for the Ising perceptron. It is in fact the smallest possible threshold for which a transition to perfect generalization is possible: the teacher has N unknown binary couplings and hence at least N bits are necessary to pin them down. It is remarkable that the reversed wedge Ising perceptron can saturate this information theoretical bound. A similar optimality characterizes the storage properties of this special architecture, see problem 7.8.

7.4 The dynamics of discontinuous learning

From the results of the last sections it may appear that discontinuous learning is extremely attractive for applications. Indeed on crossing a critical training set size α_d a marked improvement in the generalization ability sets in, sometimes even to a state of perfect generalization.

Unfortunately, it turns out that the learning process itself, i.e. the determination of the appropriate coupling vector **J** on the basis of examples, is as a rule an extremely hard problem. There are two main approaches to address this issue. Either learning is done directly in the discrete coupling space and discrete analogues of learning rules minimizing a given cost function as studied in section 4.4 are used. Or one starts with the results of teaching a continuous network with the same examples and tries to find a suitable mapping to a discrete coupling vector. Both approaches have been studied in some detail for the Ising perceptron.

The generic experience when using the first approach is that the minimization procedures get trapped in metastable states which although local minima of the cost function are far from the wanted solution. Using more sophisticated algorithms to escape from such metastable states as, e.g., simulated annealing [98] does not give rise to significant improvements. This is related to the freezing of the system already at $T > 0$ into a disordered, glassy state (see problem 7.4) with a non-ergodic behaviour and critical slowing down of the dynamics [99]. As a result minimization procedures in general fail to find the appropriate coupling vectors. Note that the dynamical freezing of the system occurs in the replica symmetric phase, so that learning already becomes practically impossible *well before* the discontinuous transition.

For small system sizes N one can use exact enumeration methods supplemented by branch-and-bound techniques to solve the minimization problem exactly [78, 100]. Approaching the problem from this side one likewise realizes that learning in the Ising perceptron is a hard combinatorial problem. In fact it has been shown to be an NP-complete problem of algorithmic complexity [101] which roughly means that no numerical procedure is known at present which solves it in a time growing only like a power of its size[2] N. Therefore this approach is limited to very small system sizes ($N \lesssim 35$).

The second method of learning in a discrete coupling space builds on our experience with continuous couplings, for which several learning rules work rather well (see chapter 3). An obvious way to get an Ising vector from a continuous one is to just keep the sign of its components; this is referred to as *clipping*. By an interesting modification of the phase space method introduced in section 6.4 one can calculate the fraction of correctly predicted Ising couplings by clipping the results of different learning rules for continuous couplings [102]. For the storage problem one finds, e.g., that clipping the maximally stable network resulting from the adatron rule gives 90% correct Ising couplings at $\alpha = 0.1$ and still 80% at $\alpha = \alpha_c$. On the other hand for the generalization problem it is not difficult to show (cf. problem 7.10) that clipping may improve the teacher–student overlap only if $R > 0.77$, which roughly corresponds to more than 88% correctly predicted couplings already.

---

[2] Strictly speaking this characterizes the worst case only and it may well be that a *typical* learning problem is much easier to solve. The numerical experience to date, however, seems to indicate that even the typical case is hard. See also section 14.2.

As a simple example for the second strategy we consider the performance of the clipped Hebb rule when learning an Ising teacher $\mathbf{T}$. Without loss of generality we may assume $T_i = +1$. The coupling vector of the clipped Hebb rule is then according to (3.1) given by

$$J_i = \text{sgn}\left(\frac{1}{\sqrt{N}} \sum_\mu \xi_i^\mu \sigma_T^\mu\right) = \text{sgn}\left(\frac{1}{\sqrt{N}} \sum_\mu \xi_i^\mu \, \text{sgn}\left(\frac{1}{\sqrt{N}} \sum_j \xi_j^\mu\right)\right). \quad (7.16)$$

We introduce the auxiliary variables $y_i^\mu = \xi_i^\mu \, \text{sgn}(\sum_j \xi_j^\mu / \sqrt{N})$ and $Y_i = \sum_\mu y_i^\mu / \sqrt{N}$ and first determine the probability that y_i^μ is $+1$:

$$\text{Prob}(y_i^\mu = 1) = \text{Prob}\left(\xi_i^\mu = 1 \text{ and } \frac{1}{\sqrt{N}} \sum_j \xi_j^\mu > 0\right)$$

$$+ \text{Prob}\left(\xi_i^\mu = -1 \text{ and } \frac{1}{\sqrt{N}} \sum_j \xi_j^\mu < 0\right)$$

$$= \frac{1}{2} \text{Prob}\left(\frac{1}{\sqrt{N}} \sum_{j \neq i} \xi_j^\mu > -\frac{1}{\sqrt{N}}\right) + \frac{1}{2} \text{Prob}\left(\frac{1}{\sqrt{N}} \sum_{j \neq i} \xi_j^\mu < \frac{1}{\sqrt{N}}\right)$$

$$= \text{Prob}\left(\frac{1}{\sqrt{N}} \sum_{j \neq i} \xi_j^\mu > -\frac{1}{\sqrt{N}}\right). \quad (7.17)$$

Now $\sum_{j \neq i} \xi_j^\mu / \sqrt{N}$ is Gaussian distributed with zero mean and unit variance and hence

$$\text{Prob}\left(\frac{1}{\sqrt{N}} \sum_{j \neq i} \xi_j^\mu > -\frac{1}{\sqrt{N}}\right) = \int_{-1/\sqrt{N}}^\infty Dz \sim \frac{1}{2} + \frac{1}{\sqrt{2\pi N}} \quad (7.18)$$

for large N, implying $\langle\langle y_i^\mu \rangle\rangle = 2/\sqrt{2\pi N}$ and $\langle\langle (y_i^\mu)^2 \rangle\rangle = 1$. Therefore Y_i is a Gaussian variable as well with average value $2\alpha/\sqrt{2\pi}$ and variance α. This gives finally for the teacher–student overlap

$$R = \frac{1}{N} \sum_i J_i = \langle\langle J_i \rangle\rangle = \text{Prob}(Y_i > 0) - \text{Prob}(Y_i < 0)$$

$$= 1 - 2H\left(\sqrt{\frac{2\alpha}{\pi}}\right). \quad (7.19)$$

For large α we hence find

$$1 - R \sim \frac{1}{\sqrt{\alpha}} \exp\left(-\frac{\alpha}{\pi}\right), \quad (7.20)$$

indicating an *exponential* decay of the generalization error for large α. This exponential decay may be interpreted as an approximation of the discontinuous transition for the optimal coupling vector by a continuous one: the clipped Hebb vector cannot realize the discontinuous drop to perfect generalization and mimics it by a very fast asymptotic decay of the generalization error.

Learning in discrete coupling spaces is usually a very difficult problem. Both approaches discussed above have their advantages and their disadvantages. The best results so far have been obtained by combining them. On the one hand one may reduce the number of couplings that have to be enumerated by fixing those which are correctly predicted by some clipping procedure [103]; on the other hand approximate results obtained by clipping a continuous coupling vector may provide useful bounds for branch-and-bound algorithms.

7.5 Summary

In this chapter we investigated learning scenarios displaying "Eureka"-like discontinuous transitions characterized by an abrupt drop in the generalization error ε at specific values of the training set size α. The basic prerequisite for such transitions is the presence of discrete degrees of freedom to be adjusted during learning. When *all* degrees of freedom are discrete the discontinuous jump usually immediately reaches the state of perfect generalization characterized by $R = 1$ and $\varepsilon = 0$. The student is then an almost perfect copy of the teacher, differing in at most a non-extensive fraction of couplings. If *some* of the adjustable parameters are discrete and others are continuous the generalization process shows phases of gradual improvement interrupted by discontinuous jumps. In both cases the reason for the discontinuous transitions lies in the peculiarities of the entropy for systems with discrete degrees of freedom.

From the point of view of statistical mechanics discontinuous learning is a quite natural phenomenon since it corresponds to a first order phase transition. Such discontinuous transitions are more difficult to analyse using other approaches to machine learning and have been the object of a long-standing debate in psychology (see e.g. [104]). From the practical point of view, the attractive features of discontinuous learning are diminished by the complexity of carrying through a learning process in a discrete coupling space.

Let us again close with a short guide to the literature. A first hint about the occurrence of discontinuous learning in the Ising perceptron scenario came from numerical investigations reported in [27]. Soon afterwards a thorough statistical mechanics analysis of this problem was given in [105]. The storage properties of the reversed wedge perceptron were analysed in [106], and its generalization behaviour was investigated in [107]. The peculiarities of the reversed wedge perceptron with Ising couplings were first studied in [108]. The complications of the learning dynamics in a discrete coupling space were elucidated in [99].

7.6 Problems

7.1 Verify by using (2.3) and (2.41) that for the basic learning scenario discussed in chapter 2 the asymptotic behaviour of the entropy for large α is indeed given by $s \sim \ln \varepsilon$.

7.2 Consider the case in which both teacher and student are Ising perceptrons, i.e. $J_i = \pm 1$ and $T_i = \pm 1$.

    (a) Show that before learning the number of students with generalization error ε scales like

$$\Omega_0(\varepsilon) \sim \exp\left(N\left[-\frac{1 - \cos \pi \varepsilon}{2} \ln \frac{1 - \cos \pi \varepsilon}{2}\right.\right.$$
$$\left.\left. - \frac{1 + \cos \pi \varepsilon}{2} \ln \frac{1 + \cos \pi \varepsilon}{2}\right]\right). \qquad (7.21)$$

    (Hint: Explicitly count the number of ways to realize an overlap R with a given Ising vector **T**.)

    (b) Replacing (2.5) by this expression calculate the generalization error within the annealed approximation and show that it predicts a discontinuous transition to perfect generalization at $\alpha \cong 1.45$.

7.3 Re-derive the saddle point equations (7.9), (7.10) and the corresponding expression for the quenched entropy by exploiting the teacher–student symmetry from the start and using the $n \to 1$ replica trick as in section 2.3.

7.4 Consider Gibbs learning with $T > 0$ for the Ising scenario discussed in section 7.2 and show that the discontinuous transition to perfect generalization still takes place. In fact it even remains in the limiting case of high-temperature learning! Note that from the point of view of statistical mechanics it is quite remarkable that a system already "freezes" into a zero-entropy state at non-zero temperature.

7.5 Consider the unrealizable problem in which an Ising student is trying to learn from a continuous teacher, i.e. $J_i = \pm 1$ and **T** is a real vector satisfying the spherical constraint $\mathbf{T}^2 = N$.

    (a) Show that the generalization error is bounded from below by the residual error $\varepsilon_r = \arccos(\sqrt{2/\pi})/\pi \cong 0.206$. Explain this result by locating the Ising vector closest to **T**.

    (b) Calculate the asymptotics of the generalization error for large α using either high-temperature learning or the annealed approximation and verify that they yield $\varepsilon - \varepsilon_r \sim \alpha^{-2}$.

Consult [21] for a complete statistical mechanics solution that includes replica symmetry breaking and shows that the asymptotic approach of ε towards ε_r is slower than predicted in (b).

7.6 Calculate the storage capacity of the reversed wedge perceptron within the replica symmetric ansatz. Show that the maximal value is obtained for $\gamma \cong 1.224$ and is given by $\alpha_c^{RS} \cong 10.5$ [106].

7.7 Consider two reversed wedge perceptrons with the same value γ of the wedge parameter. Consider the probability P that, for the same classification of a new random example, the internal representations are nevertheless different. Show that it is given by

$$P = 8 \int_\gamma^\infty Du \left[H\left(\frac{Ru}{\sqrt{1-R^2}} \right) - H\left(\frac{\gamma + Ru}{\sqrt{1-R^2}} \right) \right]. \tag{7.22}$$

What is the maximal value of P at $R = 0$? Does the maximum occur at $\gamma = \gamma_c = \sqrt{2\ln 2}$?

7.8 Show that the reversed wedge Ising perceptron with optimal wedge parameter $\gamma = \sqrt{2\ln 2}$ saturates the information theoretic bound $\alpha_c = 1$ for the storage capacity.
(Hint: Try to use the annealed calculation in order to keep the algebra as simple as possible.)

7.9 Consider an Ising teacher vector $\mathbf{T}$ and a real valued student vector $\mathbf{J}$ with $\mathbf{J}^2 = N$ and $\mathbf{JT}/N = R$. Show that, assuming cylindrical symmetry of the distribution of $\mathbf{J}$ around $\mathbf{T}$, the overlap $\tilde{R}$ of the clipped student vector $\tilde{\mathbf{J}}$ with components $\tilde{J}_i = \text{sgn}\, J_i$ is on average larger than R only if $R > R_c \cong 0.77$.
(Hint: Note $T_i \,\text{sgn}\, J_i = \text{sgn}(T_i J_i)$ since $T_i = \pm 1$ and use the self-averaging nature of R.)

7.10 Generalizing the last problem consider a transformed vector $\tilde{\mathbf{J}}$, with components $\tilde{J}_i = f(J_i)$. Assuming that the student vector $\mathbf{J}$ with continuous components has a self-averaging overlap R with an Ising teacher vector $\mathbf{T}$, show that the overlap $\tilde{R}$ of $\tilde{\mathbf{J}}$ with $\mathbf{T}$ is given by [109]

$$\tilde{R} = \frac{\langle f(x) \rangle}{\sqrt{\langle f^2(x) \rangle}} \tag{7.23}$$

where $\langle g(x) \rangle = \int_{-\infty}^{+\infty} P(x)g(x)\,dx$, and $P(x)$ is the probability density for $x = J_j T_j$. Using the cylindrical symmetry of the distribution of $\mathbf{J}$ around the teacher vector $\mathbf{T}$, show that $P(x)$ is given by

$$P(x) = \frac{1}{\sqrt{2\pi(1-R^2)}} \exp\left(-\frac{1}{2} \frac{(x-R)^2}{1-R^2} \right). \tag{7.24}$$

Verify that one recovers the clipping result (7.19) for $f(x) = \text{sgn}(x)$. Show that a maximal increase of the overlap is realized for the transformation function $f = f_{\text{opt}}$

$$f_{\text{opt}}(x) = \tanh\left(\frac{R}{1 - R^2}x\right). \tag{7.25}$$

8

Unsupervised Learning

In the preceding chapters we investigated in detail the scenario of a student perceptron learning from a teacher perceptron. This is a typical example of what is commonly referred to as *supervised* learning. But we all gratefully acknowledge that learning from examples does not always require the presence of a teacher!

However, what is it that can be learned besides some specific classification of examples provided by a teacher? The key observation is that learning from unclassified examples is possible if their distribution has some underlying *structure*. The main issue in *unsupervised* learning is then to extract these intrinsic features from a set of examples alone. This problem is central to many pattern recognition and data compression tasks with a variety of important applications [110].

Far from attempting to review the many existing approaches to unsupervised learning, we will show in the present chapter how statistical mechanics methods introduced before can be applied to some special scenarios of unsupervised learning closely related to the teacher–student perceptron problem. This will illustrate on the one hand how statistical mechanics can be used for the analysis of unsupervised situations, while on the other hand we will gain new understanding of the supervised problem by reformulating it as a special case of an unsupervised one.

8.1 Supervised versus unsupervised learning

Consider a set of p examples drawn at random from some probability distribution P. The aim of unsupervised learning is to extract information on P on the basis of the examples. For simplicity, and in order to preserve the continuity with the supervised problems discussed so far, we assume that the examples may be represented by N-dimensional vectors $\boldsymbol{\xi} = \{\xi_i, i = 1, \ldots, N\}$ lying on the surface of the N-sphere, i.e. $\boldsymbol{\xi}^2 = N$.

We will restrict ourselves to the study of data point distributions with very weak structure only. More precisely, the input distribution is assumed to have only *one* symmetry-breaking direction while being uniform in the high dimensional subspace orthogonal to this direction. Let us denote the special symmetry-breaking direction by a vector $\mathbf{B}$ with $\mathbf{B}^2 = N$. The non-uniformity of the probability distribution with respect to this direction will show up in the distribution $P^*(h)$ of the aligning field

$$h = \frac{\mathbf{B}\boldsymbol{\xi}}{\sqrt{N}} \tag{8.1}$$

of the examples along this direction $\mathbf{B}$. Recall that for any direction perpendicular to $\mathbf{B}$, the alignment would be a Gaussian variable with zero mean and unit variance. It is therefore convenient to characterize the non-uniformity of the example distribution by the deviation of $P^*(h)$ from a Gaussian distribution, which we specify by introducing the potential V^* according to

$$P^*(h) = \frac{1}{\sqrt{2\pi}} \exp\left(-\frac{h^2}{2} - V^*(h)\right). \tag{8.2}$$

Here the normalization constant has been absorbed into the definition of V^*. From (8.2) we easily find for the distribution $P(\boldsymbol{\xi}|\mathbf{B})$ of the examples given a realization of the symmetry-breaking direction $\mathbf{B}$

$$P(\boldsymbol{\xi}|\mathbf{B}) = \frac{1}{(2\pi)^{N/2}} \exp(-\boldsymbol{\xi}^2/2) \exp(-V^*(h)). \tag{8.3}$$

To uncover the structure of this probability distribution we introduce a vector $\mathbf{J}$ which, with the help of a learning rule, is determined solely on the basis of the examples and serves as an estimate for the unknown direction $\mathbf{B}$. We are therefore interested in maximizing the overlap $R = \mathbf{J}\mathbf{B}/N$. Building on our experience with the supervised case, the formulation of the problem within the context of statistical mechanics is now straightforward. We will characterize the learning rule by an energy function as in section 4.3, whose general form is

$$E(\mathbf{J}) = \sum_{\mu=1}^{p} V(\lambda^\mu), \tag{8.4}$$

where the student alignment λ^μ is given by

$$\lambda^\mu = \frac{\mathbf{J}\boldsymbol{\xi}^\mu}{\sqrt{N}}, \tag{8.5}$$

and the learning process is equivalent to searching for the minimum of $E(\mathbf{J})$. Assuming that the free energy

$$F(\beta) = -\frac{1}{\beta}\langle\langle \ln Z \rangle\rangle, \tag{8.6}$$

deriving from the partition function

$$Z = \int d\mu(\mathbf{J}) \, e^{-\beta E(\mathbf{J})} \tag{8.7}$$

is self-averaging in the thermodynamic limit, the average over the inputs can be performed with the techniques of appendix 2. The properties of the $\mathbf{J}$-vector which minimizes the cost $E(\mathbf{J})$ are, as usual, inferred from the zero-temperature limit

$$e_0(\alpha) = \lim_{\beta \to \infty} f(\alpha, \beta). \tag{8.8}$$

Many learning rules for the supervised problem discussed in section 4.4 have an unsupervised counterpart which may easily be obtained by replacing the stability $\Delta = \mathbf{J}\boldsymbol{\xi}\sigma_T/\sqrt{N}$ by the alignment λ. A simple example is the unsupervised Hebb rule defined by the potential

$$V(\lambda) = -\lambda, \tag{8.9}$$

which as estimate for the symmetry-breaking direction $\mathbf{B}$ obviously generates a vector $\mathbf{J}^H \sim \sum_\mu \boldsymbol{\xi}^\mu$ pointing along the centre of mass of the examples.

Another popular choice is

$$V(\lambda) = -\lambda^2 \tag{8.10}$$

corresponding to Oja's rule [111, 112]. Clearly the purpose here is to maximize the second moment of the alignment. This is of particular interest in examples for which the first moment is equal to zero: the second moment is then equal to the variance, so that the $\mathbf{J}$-vector that minimizes the energy function, gives the orientation along which the data scatter most. In fact, the direction of maximal variance is also called the first *principal component* of the distribution. Principal component analysis is one of the basic and most frequently used algorithms for data analysis [110]. Furthermore, if the distribution of the alignment is Gaussian, maximal variance is identical to maximal information. In other words, the direction which has the largest variance is also the direction that contains the maximum of information about the examples. The infomax principle, introduced by Linsker [113], stipulates that these directions are the best choice if one wants to compress information with minimum loss.

Before switching to the detailed analysis of unsupervised learning, it is gratifying to realize that several variants of the teacher–student perceptron scenario discussed before can be transformed into an unsupervised problem. To illustrate this, we return to our basic supervised scenario of a student perceptron learning from a teacher perceptron. The main observation is that learning rules and cost functions are in this case constructed on the basis of the *aligned* examples $\text{sgn}(\mathbf{T}\boldsymbol{\xi}^\mu)\boldsymbol{\xi}^\mu$. Since the *raw* examples $\boldsymbol{\xi}^\mu$ are chosen at random, the aligned ones

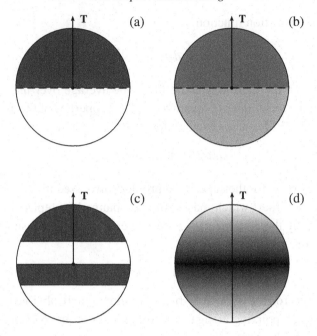

Fig. 8.1. Some examples of non-uniform distributions corresponding to supervised problems: (a) teacher–student perceptron, (b) the same but with output noise on the teacher, (c)
the reversed wedge perceptron, and (d) the Gaussian scenario. To get the right perspective,
one has to imagine that the shading represents the density of examples lying on the *surface*
of a high dimensional N-sphere. The density of examples for the projection onto the
2-d plane of the page is a bi-Gaussian modulated by $\exp(-V^*(h))$; see fig. 2.1 for such
representation for case (a).

are uniformly distributed on the upper hemisphere, with **T** playing the role of the
"north pole" (see fig. 8.1a). We can thus view this problem as a particular case of
an unsupervised learning problem: p examples are sampled independently from
a uniform distribution on half of the N-sphere and the task is to approximate the
direction of the north pole, which is the only symmetry-breaking direction of this
distribution. The alignment distribution $P^*(h)$ is in this case given by

$$P^*(h) = \frac{2}{\sqrt{2\pi}} \exp(-h^2/2)\theta(h). \tag{8.11}$$

Some other cases, whose "unsupervised" versions are of interest for comparison
with previous results, are the perceptron teacher with output noise, see (5.4) and
fig. 8.1b,

$$P^*(h) = \frac{1}{\sqrt{2\pi}} \exp(-h^2/2)[(1+a)\theta(h) + (1-a)\theta(-h)], \tag{8.12}$$

the teacher perceptron with weight noise, cf. (5.2),

$$P^*(h) = \frac{2}{\sqrt{2\pi}} \exp(-h^2/2) \left[\left(1 - H\left(\frac{h}{\sigma_w}\right)\right)\theta(h) + H\left(\frac{h}{\sigma_w}\right)\theta(-h) \right], \quad (8.13)$$

and the reversed wedge perceptron, cf. (7.11) and fig. 8.1c,

$$P^*(h) = \frac{2}{\sqrt{2\pi}} \exp(-h^2/2)[\theta(h-\gamma) + \theta(h+\gamma)\theta(-h)]. \quad (8.14)$$

We also mention the so-called Gaussian scenario, see fig. 8.1d,

$$P^*(h) = \sqrt{\frac{2(1+a)}{\pi}} \exp\left(-\frac{(1+a)h^2}{2}\right), \quad (8.15)$$

for which full analytic results can be obtained [114].

Note that, whereas it is natural to assume that a general unsupervised problem is given by a smooth distribution $P^*(h)$, unsupervised scenarios equivalent to supervised problems are usually characterized by a non-smooth distribution, cf. the occurrence of the Heaviside function θ in (8.11), (8.12) and (8.14). Furthermore, some distributions have a special symmetries, for example a vanishing first moment $\langle\langle h \rangle\rangle = 0$, as e.g. (8.14) for $\gamma = \sqrt{2\ln 2}$ and (8.15). As we will see below, these different features induce qualitative differences in the observed learning behaviour.

8.2 The deceptions of randomness

It may come as a surprise that we will start our study of unsupervised learning with examples that have no structure, i.e. that are chosen from a completely uniform distribution. We do so because it reveals one of the serious pitfalls of unsupervised learning, namely that it may discover structures that appear by chance in the realizations of randomness. In fact, as we will see shortly, this order by chance leads, when competing with a genuine non-random structure, to the phenomenon of retarded learning.

Consider then a set of p examples $\boldsymbol{\xi}$ which are uniformly distributed on the N-sphere. We would like to investigate whether this set is clustered along a preferential direction. A reasonable guess of this direction is the one pointing along the centre of mass

$$\mathbf{J}^H = C \sum_{\mu=1}^{p} \boldsymbol{\xi}^\mu, \quad (8.16)$$

where the constant C is chosen such that $|\mathbf{J}^H|^2 = N$. This choice corresponds to unsupervised Hebb learning (8.9). To illustrate how this construction can be misleading, we determine the alignment of $\mathbf{J}^H$ with any vector $\boldsymbol{\xi}^\nu$ of the data set.

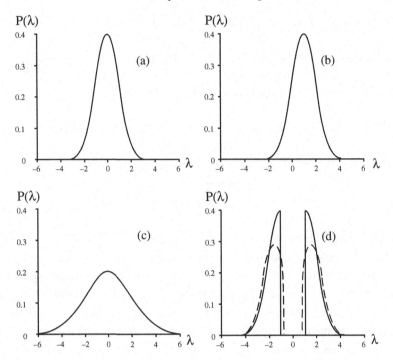

Fig. 8.2. Alignment distributions for random and independent examples with the **J**-vector minimizing $E(\mathbf{J})$, cf. (8.4), with $\alpha = 1$, for (a) $V = 0$, (b) $V = -\lambda$, (c) $V = -\lambda^2$ and (d) $V = -|\lambda|$ (with the dashed line corresponding to the one-step RSB result).

In the limit $N \to \infty$, $p \to \infty$ with $\alpha = p/N$ fixed, this is easily done by separating out the contribution of $\boldsymbol{\xi}^\nu$ to $\mathbf{J}^H$. One finds that the resulting alignment λ is a Gaussian random variable with unit dispersion as for an uncorrelated vector **J** (see fig. 8.2a) but now with *non-zero mean* equal to $1/\sqrt{\alpha}$, cf. fig. 8.2b. This result creates the false impression that the data points are generated from a non-uniform probability distribution with a preferential orientation along the centre of mass. The observed structure however is just the product of chance, even though it will appear, in the above described limit, with probability 1 and be perfectly reproducible![1]

This failure to realize the *absence* of structure is not restricted to the Hebb rule. In fact, for the case of completely random examples considered in this section, the investigation of a general cost function $E(\mathbf{J})$ along the lines of (8.6)–(8.8) is just a minor modification of the standard procedure of appendix 2. Due to the absence of a teacher and hence of the order parameter R it is even simpler than before and is identical to a *capacity* calculation for a cost function, with the standard case

[1] More precisely, for another choice of p random and independent examples, one will find a $\mathbf{J}^H$-vector which points in another direction, but the distribution of the alignments along this direction will again be given by the same shifted Gaussian.

discussed in chapter 6 corresponding to $V(\lambda) = \theta(-\lambda)$. Omitting the details we give the result of a replica symmetric calculation of the free energy density

$$f(\alpha, \beta) = - \underset{q}{\mathrm{extr}} \left[\frac{q}{2\beta(1-q)} + \frac{1}{2\beta} \ln(1-q) \right.$$

$$\left. + \frac{\alpha}{\beta} \int Dt \ln \int \frac{d\lambda}{\sqrt{2\pi(1-q)}} \exp\left(-\beta V(\lambda) - \frac{(\lambda - \sqrt{q}t)^2}{2(1-q)} \right) \right]. \quad (8.17)$$

This result is identical to (4.31) if one sets $R = 0$ in the latter equation. This is not surprising since, for a teacher who is forced to lie in the subspace orthogonal to $\mathbf{J}$, an extra factor σ_T does not affect the statistical properties of the examples when they are chosen at random.

Taking the zero-temperature limit $\beta \to \infty$ according to (8.8) we find from (8.17)

$$e_0(\alpha) = - \underset{x}{\mathrm{extr}} \left[\frac{1}{2x} - \alpha \int Dt \underset{\lambda}{\min} \left(V(\lambda) + \frac{(\lambda - t)^2)}{2x} \right) \right]. \quad (8.18)$$

For $V(\lambda) = \theta(-\lambda)$ this is equivalent to (6.40) as it should be.

Moreover the expression for the distribution $P(\lambda)$ of the alignment between the vector $\mathbf{J}^*$ that minimizes E, and the data points $\boldsymbol{\xi}^\mu$ that enter in the construction of E, is again very similar to the one given in section 6.4 for the capacity problem, see also problem 8.1,

$$P(\lambda) = \int Dt \, \delta(\lambda - \lambda_0(t, x)), \quad (8.19)$$

where $\lambda_0(t, x)$ is the function of t and x that minimizes the expression in the exponent of the λ-integral in (8.17) and x is the function of α that extremizes the ground state energy (8.18). Either by a direct calculation or by applying a cavity argument, one verifies that $\lambda_0(t, x)$ has the following simple meaning (cf. problem 8.1). Let t be the normally distributed alignment of a random new example with the vector $\mathbf{J}$. $\lambda_0(t, x)$ is the alignment of this example with the vector $\mathbf{J}'$ that minimizes the cost function $E(\mathbf{J})$ including the new example. In other words $\lambda_0(t, x) - t$ is the adjustment of the alignment upon learning the new example. It is a function of the initial alignment t and of α through the dependence on x.

For the unsupervised Hebb rule, $V(\lambda) = -\lambda$, one finds $\lambda_0(t, x) = t + x$ and $x = 1/\sqrt{\alpha}$, and hence recovers the result cited before. This specific choice of V reflects the intention to find a direction along which the overlap λ is as large as possible. Maximal variance learning characterized by the potential (8.10), on the other hand, gives rise to a $P(\lambda)$ that is indeed a broadened Gaussian with zero mean and dispersion $\langle \lambda^2 \rangle = (1+\sqrt{\alpha})^2/\alpha$, see fig. 8.2c, so again one finds what one is looking for. As another variant, one which does not correspond to any specific algorithm, but will be important in later discussions, we consider a potential which penalizes the overlap according to its absolute value

$$V(\lambda) = -|\lambda|.$$

(8.20)

The corresponding overlap distribution reads, cf. fig. 8.2d,

$$P(\lambda) = \begin{cases} \dfrac{1}{\sqrt{2\pi}}e^{-\frac{1}{2}(\lambda+x)^2} & \lambda \leq -x \\[2mm] 0 & -x < \lambda < x \\[2mm] \dfrac{1}{\sqrt{2\pi}}e^{-\frac{1}{2}(\lambda-x)^2} & \lambda \geq x \end{cases}$$

(8.21)

with $x = 1/\sqrt{\alpha}$.

This result contains two minor surprises. Firstly, the overlap distribution possesses a genuine gap of width $2/\sqrt{\alpha}$. There are no data points whatsoever in the band $-x < \lambda < x$, which occupies a finite fraction of the total surface of the sphere. One concludes that the data points, even though they are sampled from a uniform distribution on the sphere, are highly structured when viewed from the special direction $\mathbf{J}^*$. There is of course a close analogy to the storage problem, cf. chapter 6 and in particular problem 6.1, where we succeeded in confining randomly chosen points on the N-sphere to a half sphere up to the capacity limit $\alpha = 2$. In fact, the band $-x < \lambda < x$ corresponds for $\alpha = 2$ to a fraction $1 - 2H(1/\sqrt{2}) \approx 0.52$ of the total surface of the sphere, very similar to the factor $1/2$ in the capacity problem.

Secondly, it turns out that the de Almeida–Thouless (AT) condition for the stability of the replica symmetric point is violated. This condition is of the form (see problem 4.13 and appendix 6)

$$\alpha \int Dt \left[\frac{\partial \lambda_0(t, x)}{\partial t} - 1 \right]^2 < 1,$$

(8.22)

where x is again taken at the extremum of (8.18). The results of a one-step replica symmetry-breaking calculation (cf. appendix 5) are included in fig. 8.2d. One observes that the width of the gap is slightly reduced. The fact that replica symmetry breaking occurs indicates that the energy function corresponding to (8.20) has a large number of minima, revealing the underlying glassy structure appearing at finite α in the realizations of a uniform distribution.

This concludes our discussion of unsupervised learning of structureless distributions. The fact that the realizations of randomness are typically less symmetric than the corresponding distributions is of course well known. A well documented example is the trajectory of a random walker [115]. Our point here, however, is that when applying algorithms that specifically search for some type of structure, one should be able to identify and isolate the contribution which appears by chance.

8.3 Learning a symmetry-breaking direction

Let us now study a genuine problem in unsupervised learning, namely the detection of a symmetry-breaking direction of the example distribution. To this end we return to the calculation of the free energy, as defined in (8.6), but now with an average performed over examples which have a non-uniform distribution (8.3) along a single symmetry-breaking direction **B**, and are uniform in the orthogonal subspace. The average over the example distribution can again be performed with minor modifications of the standard calculation of appendix 2. Assuming replica symmetry one finds for the free energy density

$$
f(\alpha, \beta) = - \underset{q,R}{\text{extr}} \left[\frac{q - R^2}{2\beta(1 - q)} + \frac{1}{2\beta} \ln(1 - q) + \frac{\alpha}{\beta} \int Dt_1 \int D^* t_2 \right.
$$

$$
\left. \times \ln \int \frac{d\lambda}{\sqrt{2\pi(1 - q)}} \exp\left(-\beta V(\lambda) - \frac{(\lambda - Rt_2 - \sqrt{q - R^2}t_1)^2}{2(1 - q)}\right)\right], \quad (8.23)
$$

where $D^*t := dt \, P^*(t)$. Here R is the overlap between a typical vector **J** and the symmetry-breaking direction **B** whereas q denotes the typical overlap between two different vectors **J**. The above result reduces to (4.31) for P^* given by (8.11), in agreement with the discussion of the previous section. Note also that (8.17) is recovered for the choice $V^* = 0$, corresponding to purely random examples with no preferential direction.

The zero-temperature limit $\beta \to \infty$ is of particular interest. If the cost function has a unique minimum q tends to 1 with $x = \beta(1 - q)$ finite. Then we obtain from (8.8)

$$
e_0(\alpha) = - \underset{x,R}{\text{extr}} \left[\frac{1 - R^2}{2x} - \alpha \int Dt_1 \int D^* t_2 \min_\lambda \left(V(\lambda) + \frac{(\lambda - t)^2}{2x}\right)\right], \quad (8.24)
$$

with $t = Rt_2 + \sqrt{1 - R^2}t_1$.

The above results allow us to study in detail how various algorithms, corresponding to various choices of V, are able to detect and identify the non-random structure, characterized by V^*, that is present along the direction **B**. In addition to the distribution of the alignment $P(\lambda)$ the quantity of interest is now the overlap $R = \mathbf{JB}/N$. A full detailed study can only be performed in some special cases, such as the Gaussian scenario [114]. Note that for the latter case, the distribution is perfectly symmetric so that the solution of the saddle point equation will be degenerate, including both the values R and $-R$. Another problem which appears in this case is that the centre of mass of the examples is, in the thermodynamic limit, exactly equal to zero. To avoid these complications, we will implicitly assume below that perfectly symmetric distributions are the limiting case of distributions with a small bias which is taken to zero after all the calculations have been performed.

In what follows we will focus on the Gibbs learning algorithm and its relation to the optimal one maximizing the overlap R. Let us first define what Gibbs learning means for an unsupervised problem. Since we do not have the sharp distinction between compatible and incompatible students, we have to discuss instead how likely it is for a given vector $\mathbf{J}$ to be the symmetry-breaking orientation. Given a set of examples $\boldsymbol{\xi}^{\mu}$, the corresponding distribution is the so-called posterior probability density, and will be denoted as $P(\mathbf{J}|\boldsymbol{\xi}^{\mu})$. In the supervised problem, this posterior probability has a rather simple form, since it is zero outside the version space, and uniform inside. The Gibbs algorithm, which selects a teacher at random from the version space, thus corresponds to a sampling from this posterior distribution.

The posterior distribution for the unsupervised problem can be obtained by Bayes' theorem [116]. For simplicity we again assume that the prior probability P_0 for $\mathbf{J}$ is uniform on the N-sphere. Using the independence of the examples and the specific form of the density generating the examples, cf. (8.3), one finds

$$P(\mathbf{J}|\boldsymbol{\xi}^{\mu}) = \mathcal{N} \prod_{\mu=1}^{p} P(\boldsymbol{\xi}^{\mu}|\mathbf{J}) P_0(\mathbf{J})$$

$$= \mathcal{N}' \delta(\mathbf{J}^2 - N) \exp\left(-\sum_{\mu=1}^{p} V^*(\lambda^{\mu})\right), \tag{8.25}$$

where $\mathcal{N}$ and $\mathcal{N}'$ are normalization constants. Gibbs learning corresponds to sampling from this distribution. One concludes by comparison with (8.4) and (8.7) that it can be realized by choosing the potential $V = V^*$ and setting the "temperature" equal to 1, $\beta = 1$. The free energy may be further simplified by anticipating that, due to the complete symmetry between $\mathbf{B}$ and the Gibbs student $\mathbf{J}$, one has $R = q$. Using the orthogonal transformation of variables

$$\begin{aligned} t &= \sqrt{R}\, t_2 + \sqrt{1-R}\, t_1 & t_1 &= \sqrt{1-R}\, t - \sqrt{R}\, t' \\ t' &= \sqrt{1-R}\, t_2 - \sqrt{R}\, t_1 & t_2 &= \sqrt{R}\, t + \sqrt{1-R}\, t' \end{aligned} \tag{8.26}$$

implying $Dt\, Dt' = Dt_1 Dt_2$ and setting

$$\lambda = \sqrt{R}\, t + \sqrt{1-R}\, t'', \tag{8.27}$$

the free energy (8.23) acquires the form

$$f(\alpha, \beta = 1) = -\operatorname*{extr}_{R}\left[\frac{R}{2} + \frac{1}{2}\ln(1-R) + \alpha \int Dt\, X(\sqrt{R}, t) \ln X(\sqrt{R}, t)\right] \tag{8.28}$$

with

$$X(R, t) = \int Dt' \exp\left(-V^*(R t + \sqrt{1 - R^2}\, t')\right), \qquad (8.29)$$

obeying the normalization condition

$$\int Dt\, X(R, t) = 1. \qquad (8.30)$$

$$(8.31)$$

Upon defining

$$Y(R, t) = \int Dt'\, t' \exp\left(-V^*(R t + \sqrt{1 - R^2}\, t')\right) = \frac{\sqrt{1 - R^2}}{R} \frac{\partial X(R, t)}{\partial t}, \qquad (8.32)$$

the saddle point equation for R obtained from (8.28) may be written after partial integration as

$$R = \alpha \int Dt\, \frac{Y^2(\sqrt{R}, t)}{X(\sqrt{R}, t)}. \qquad (8.33)$$

This completes the analysis of the Gibbs rule. For the supervised case with V^* given by (8.11), (8.33) reduces to (2.42) (see also (4.56), noting that the latter equation gives the Bayes overlap $R_B = \sqrt{R}$).

At this point, we note that to apply the Gibbs algorithm one needs to know the potential V^* in advance. In the supervised case, (8.11), with $V^* = \infty$ outside the version space and constant inside, this knowledge is also used but it is hidden by the fact that sampling from the version space appears to be quite natural. Problem 8.6 reveals the surprising fact that the knowledge of V^* can actually be acquired, at least in the thermodynamic limit, at no extra cost in α.

Next we address *optimal* learning, defined as the rule that realizes the maximum overlap. One can repeat the general argument given in 3.6, to conclude that the maximal average overlap R is achieved by the centre of mass of the posterior probability. Indeed the average overlap of a vector $\mathbf{J}$ which is constructed on the basis of a given set of training examples with the symmetry-breaking direction $\mathbf{B}$ is given by

$$\left\langle \frac{\mathbf{JB}}{N} \right\rangle = \int d\mathbf{B}\, P(\mathbf{B}|\boldsymbol{\xi}^\mu) \frac{\mathbf{JB}}{N}. \qquad (8.34)$$

Since $\mathbf{J}$ is independent of the integration variables, it can be moved outside the integration, and the maximum is reached for the centre of mass of the posterior distribution

$$\mathbf{J}^B \sim \int d\mathbf{B}\, P(\mathbf{B}|\boldsymbol{\xi}^\mu) \mathbf{B} \qquad (8.35)$$

with the normalization constant chosen such that $(\mathbf{J}^B)^2 = N$. One can also repeat the argument in 3.6 that links the resulting overlap R_B with the Gibbs overlap R, yielding $R_B = \sqrt{R}$. By combination with (8.33) one thus obtains the overlap for the optimal rule.

A general explicit solution of (8.33) for R, and hence for R_B, is not available, but one may derive analytic results for small and large α. We quote here only the results for the optimal overlap R_B. Focusing first on the small-α behaviour, one readily sees that the integral on the r.h.s. of (8.33) converges to $\alpha \langle\!\langle h \rangle\!\rangle^2$ in the limit $R \to 0$, where $\langle\!\langle h \rangle\!\rangle = \int dh\, P^*(h)\, h$. For $\langle\!\langle h \rangle\!\rangle \neq 0$ it follows that $R_B(\alpha) = \sqrt{\alpha \langle\!\langle h \rangle\!\rangle^2}$ for asymptotically small α. Incidentally, this result coincides with the small-α result obtained by the unsupervised Hebb rule, cf. problem 8.9. If, on the other hand, $\langle\!\langle h \rangle\!\rangle = 0$, one readily verifies that $R = 0$ is always a solution of (8.33). To study the appearance of non-zero solutions through a second order phase transition, one verifies that the first term in the expansion of the r.h.s. of (8.33) is $\alpha(1 - \langle\!\langle h^2 \rangle\!\rangle)^2 R$. The crossing of the coefficient of R through the value 1 signals the appearance of a non-zero solution for R. One concludes that $R_B(\alpha) = 0$ in a finite interval $[0, \alpha_r]$, where $\alpha_r = (1 - \langle\!\langle h^2 \rangle\!\rangle)^{-2}$. This phenomenon has been termed *retarded learning* [117, 118, 108]. In supervised problems, this initial phase is quite remarkable, since the learned examples can be memorized perfectly, i.e. the training error is zero, while the underlying rule is not discovered at all, i.e. the generalization error is equal to $1/2$; see for example the reversed wedge perceptron, discussed in section 7.3, for $\gamma = \gamma_c = \sqrt{2 \ln 2}$. Learning starts above the threshold α_r. As an example of retarded learning in a truly unsupervised problem, we mention the explicit results for the overlap obtained for the Gaussian scenario (8.15):

$$R_B(\alpha) = 0 \qquad\qquad \text{if} \quad \alpha < \alpha_r,$$

$$R_B(\alpha) = \sqrt{\frac{\alpha - \alpha_r}{\alpha - \sqrt{\alpha_r}}} \qquad \text{if} \quad \alpha > \alpha_r, \qquad\qquad (8.36)$$

where $\alpha_r = (1 + 1/a)^2$.

The perturbative analysis given above cannot predict or rule out the appearance of first order phase transitions. A more detailed analysis is needed. It turns out that first order transitions are quite common. They may appear both before and after the threshold of the second order phase transition; for an example see [119].

Let us now turn to the large-α behaviour. For smooth example distributions, one finds

$$1 - R_B(\alpha) \sim \left(2\alpha \int dh \left[\frac{dV^*(h)}{dh} \right]^2 P^*(h) \right)^{-1}, \qquad\qquad (8.37)$$

i.e. a $1/\alpha$ decay of R, provided the integral converges. As expected, a more pronounced structure in the example distribution (large $dV^*(h)/dh$) facilitates optimal learning.

When the distribution has discontinuities, i.e. in the presence of singular derivatives $dV^*(h)/dh$, the divergence of the integral signals a change in the asymptotic law. For simplicity, we restrict ourselves to a particularly interesting special case: assume that $P^*(h) = 0$ for $h < h_1$, $P^*(h)$ is smooth for $h > h_1$ and $\lim_{h \to +h_1} P^*(h) = \Delta P^* > 0$, a situation which typically occurs in supervised problems, cf. (8.11). By closer inspection one then finds that in the region of t- and t'-values which, for $R \to 1$, contribute notably to the integral in (8.33), $\exp[-V^*(\tau)]$, with $\tau = Rt + \sqrt{1 - R^2}t'$, can be replaced by $\exp[-V^*(h_1)]\theta(\tau - h_1)$. This yields the leading order asymptotics

$$1 - R_B(\alpha) = \pi \left(\alpha \, \Delta P^* \int Dt \, \frac{e^{-t^2/2}}{H(t)} \right)^{-2}. \tag{8.38}$$

This α^{-2} decay with similar coefficients is also found for other discontinuities of the same type.

The asymptotic behaviour for a smooth distribution thus differs markedly from that of a non-smooth distribution. In fact, we have already encountered this feature in our discussion of the noisy teacher: weight noise is equivalent to an unsupervised problem with a smooth distribution while output noise corresponds to the non-smooth case; see (8.12) and (8.13) as well as problems 8.3 and 8.5. The interpretation is quite clear: the existence of a sharp boundary in the distribution of examples makes it easier to reconstruct the symmetry-breaking direction which is orthogonal to the boundary. Therefore the asymptotic approach to the solution is faster.

8.4 Clustering through competitive learning

As the word implies, clustering is about grouping data points into different sets. Often, the task is unsupervised, i.e. there are no external guidelines on how to perform the separation into different clusters. In fact, this separation will serve different purposes, depending on the problem at hand. It can, e.g., be used to compress data: all the examples which fall in a given cluster are represented by a single point. In other cases, one hopes that the different clusters will allow different states of the system to be identified. Here the clustering corresponds to a genuine learning process since it extracts information about the state of the system from the examples. In both these instances, we expect the number of clusters to be much smaller than the number of data points.

We will first consider the simplest situation, corresponding to clustering into two different sets, each characterized by a cluster axis $\mathbf{J}_m$, $m = 1, 2$. The problem is

now to find these two directions such that the data points are separated in some
optimal way in two classes. Since one expects that the deceptions of randomness
will also affect these types of algorithm, we first focus in this section on the case of
examples chosen at random. To preserve continuity with the previous discussions,
we consider directional clustering, i.e. we take the examples on the N-sphere and
investigate their directional clustering properties.

Since directional clustering is only concerned with angles, the quantities of
importance will be the alignments λ of the examples with the cluster axes $\mathbf{J}_m$.
Building on our experience with the single $\mathbf{J}$ case, it is natural to define the optimal
directions as the minima of an energy function $E(\mathbf{J}_1, \mathbf{J}_2)$ of the form

$$E(\mathbf{J}_1, \mathbf{J}_2) = \sum_{\mu=1}^{p} V(\lambda_1^\mu, \lambda_2^\mu), \tag{8.39}$$

with

$$\lambda_1^\mu = \frac{\mathbf{J}_1 \boldsymbol{\xi}^\mu}{\sqrt{N}}, \qquad \lambda_2^\mu = \frac{\mathbf{J}_2 \boldsymbol{\xi}^\mu}{\sqrt{N}}. \tag{8.40}$$

Note that the numbering of the clusters is interchangeable, hence we will assume
that the potential reflects this symmetry, $V(\lambda_1, \lambda_2) = V(\lambda_2, \lambda_1)$. Furthermore,
in the applications we will deal with below, the potential has the specific form
$V(\lambda_1, \lambda_2) = V_+(\lambda_+) + V_-(\lambda_-)$ where $\lambda_+ = (\lambda_1 + \lambda_2)/\sqrt{2}$ and $\lambda_- = (\lambda_1 - \lambda_2)/\sqrt{2}$.
This form will simplify the discussion and make the comparison with the results
obtained in the previous sections possible. We introduce the partition function

$$Z = \int d\mu(\mathbf{J}_1) \int d\mu(\mathbf{J}_2)\, e^{-\beta E(\mathbf{J}_1, \mathbf{J}_2)} \tag{8.41}$$

and calculate the corresponding free energy F, which is expected to be self-
averaging in the limit $N \to \infty$, $p \to \infty$ with $\alpha = p/N$ finite. Adopting an
RS ansatz and restricting for simplicity to the zero-temperature result [120], we
obtain for a uniform distribution of examples

$$e_0(\alpha) = -\operatorname*{extr}_{Q, x_+, x_-} \left[\frac{1}{2x_+} - \alpha \int Dt_+ \min_{\lambda_+} \left(V_+(\lambda_+) + \frac{(\lambda_+/\sqrt{1+Q} - t_+)^2}{2x_+} \right) \right.$$
$$\left. + \frac{1}{2x_-} - \alpha \int Dt_- \min_{\lambda_-} \left(V_-(\lambda_-) + \frac{(\lambda_-/\sqrt{1-Q} - t_-)^2}{2x_-} \right) \right], \tag{8.42}$$

where $Q = (\mathbf{J}_1 \mathbf{J}_2)/N$ has the meaning of the overlap between the cluster axes.

It is convenient to determine the extremum of e_0 in two steps. First one fixes
the value of Q and extremizes with respect to x_+ and x_-. Comparing with
(8.18) this corresponds to finding the vectors $\mathbf{J}_+ = (\mathbf{J}_1 + \mathbf{J}_2)/\sqrt{2(1 + Q)}$ and

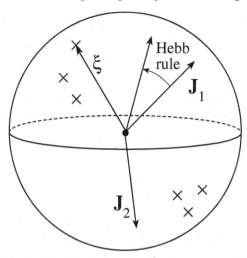

Fig. 8.3. A simple example for clustering through competitive learning. A set of points, represented by the six crosses, clusters into two subsets of three crosses each. This structure can be detected without a teacher. Consider two perceptrons, represented by their coupling vectors $\mathbf{J}_1$ and $\mathbf{J}_2$. Upon presentation of an example $\boldsymbol{\xi}$, the synaptic vector of the perceptron with larger overlap with the example (the "winner"), will, upon application of the Hebb rule, move closer to $\boldsymbol{\xi}$. By iterating this algorithm, the two synaptic vectors will hopefully converge to positions located more or less at the centres of the two clusters.

$\mathbf{J}_- = (\mathbf{J}_1 - \mathbf{J}_2)/\sqrt{2(1-Q)}$ which minimize $V_+(\lambda_+\sqrt{1+Q})$ and $V_-(\lambda_-\sqrt{1-Q})$ respectively. These two minimization procedures are of exactly the same type as the ones encountered in the problem with a single symmetry-breaking orientation. In a second step one minimizes the resulting total cost with respect to Q, and in this way determines the optimal angle between $\mathbf{J}_1$ and $\mathbf{J}_2$.

The distribution $P(\lambda_1, \lambda_2)$ of alignments is given by

$$P(\lambda_1, \lambda_2) = \int Dt_+ \int Dt_- \, \delta(\lambda_1 - \lambda_1^0) \, \delta(\lambda_2 - \lambda_2^0), \qquad (8.43)$$

where $\lambda_+^0 = (\lambda_1^0 + \lambda_2^0)/\sqrt{2}$ and $\lambda_-^0 = (\lambda_1^0 - \lambda_2^0)/\sqrt{2}$ are the functions of Q, x_+, x_-, t_+, and t_- minimizing the expressions between the large brackets in (8.42).

Let us apply this result to competitive learning [3], one of the standard clustering algorithms, also known under the name of the K-means algorithm [121]. In a practical application, the algorithm runs as follows, see also fig. 8.3. Consider a randomly chosen example $\boldsymbol{\xi}$. Identify the nearest cluster centre, say $\mathbf{J}_1$. In directional clustering, this is the direction $\mathbf{J}_1$ which makes the smallest angle with $\boldsymbol{\xi}$. It is called the winner. Update the winner by moving it closer to the example under consideration. This is done using the familiar Hebb rule. If only the winner is updated, one talks about "winner takes all".[2] Note that competitive learning can be implemented very naturally in a neural network comprising linear perceptrons, with outputs linked to each other by inhibitory connections. The perceptron with largest output wins, suppresses the other perceptrons, and adapts its weights according to the Hebb rule. The important observation for us is that this algorithm is equivalent to the minimization of an energy function with the potential

$$V(\lambda_1, \lambda_2) = -\lambda_1 \theta(\lambda_1 - \lambda_2) - \lambda_2 \theta(\lambda_2 - \lambda_1) \tag{8.44}$$

$$= -\frac{\lambda_1 + \lambda_2}{2} - \frac{|\lambda_1 - \lambda_2|}{2}. \tag{8.45}$$

Indeed, the Heaviside function in (8.44) guarantees that the performance of a particular $\mathbf{J}$-vector is only determined by the alignments of the examples with which it makes the smallest angle. Furthermore the relative importance of these examples in determining the performance of a particular $\mathbf{J}$ is precisely of the Hebbian type. Indeed, one recognizes the Hebbian contributions $-\lambda_m$, $m = 1, 2$, multiplied by a θ-function which "classifies" the example as belonging either to cluster 1 or 2, depending on which overlap λ_i^μ is largest. Alternatively, in (8.45) we have written the potential as the sum of a purely Hebbian term (along the direction of $\mathbf{J}_1 + \mathbf{J}_2$), $V_+(\lambda) = -\lambda_+/\sqrt{2}$, and a maximal absolute value term (following the direction of $\mathbf{J}_1 - \mathbf{J}_2$), $V_-(\lambda) = -|\lambda_-|/\sqrt{2}$. Both these single $\mathbf{J}$ potentials were discussed in the previous section, and we can build on the corresponding results.

Let us first consider the overlap distribution. For random orientations of $\mathbf{J}_m$, $m = 1, 2$, this distribution is bi-normal. Due to the potential contribution of the Hebb type along $\lambda = \lambda_1 + \lambda_2$, one observes that the distribution is shifted along this line over a distance equal to $1/\sqrt{\alpha}$. Furthermore, the maximal absolute value potential acting along $\lambda = \lambda_1 - \lambda_2$ results in the overlap distribution being cut in half and shifted apart along this direction, cf. fig. 8.4. The width of this gap decreases as $2/\sqrt{\alpha}$. Only in the limit $\alpha \to \infty$ will the overlap distribution in the $\lambda_1 - \lambda_2$ plane return to the bi-normal form characteristic of random examples. The overlap Q is found to be

$$Q(\alpha) = -\frac{2\sqrt{\frac{\alpha}{2\pi}}(1 + \sqrt{\frac{\alpha}{2\pi}})}{1 + 2\sqrt{\frac{\alpha}{2\pi}}(1 + \sqrt{\frac{\alpha}{2\pi}})}. \tag{8.46}$$

We conclude that the angle between the cluster centres increases from $\pi/2$ at $\alpha = 0$ to π for $\alpha \to \infty$. As in the single $\mathbf{J}$ case, the maximal absolute value contribution to the potential leads to a discontinuity in the overlap structure and,

---

[2] In more sophisticated prescriptions, like the Kohonen algorithm, one also updates other vectors which are related to the winner (for example through their spatial location), see e.g. [38].

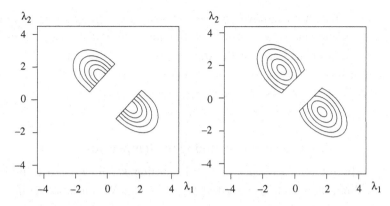

Fig. 8.4. Contour lines of the distribution of alignment $P(\lambda_1, \lambda_2)$, for competitive learning applied to random examples, as predicted in replica symmetry (left hand side) and one-step replica symmetry breaking (right hand side) for $\alpha = 1$.

as a result, replica symmetry is broken. We have therefore included the results of a one-step RSB calculation in fig. 8.4. It turns out that the corrections due to RSB for the free energy and for Q are quite small, whereas the overlap distribution and the gap between the two clusters are modified similarly to fig. 8.2d. Figure 8.4 clearly illustrates again the deceptive structure which is found when one applies a clustering algorithm to a random distribution of examples: one observes two clearly separated clusters when viewing the examples from the special directions which competitive learning will pick out.

We finally turn to the application of competitive learning to non-uniformly distributed examples. For simplicity we focus on the probability density

$$P(\boldsymbol{\xi}) = \frac{1}{2} \prod_{i=1}^{N} \frac{\exp\left[-\frac{1}{2}(\xi_i - \rho B_i/\sqrt{N})^2\right]}{\sqrt{2\pi}} + \frac{1}{2} \prod_{i=1}^{N} \frac{\exp\left[-\frac{1}{2}(\xi_i + \rho B_i/\sqrt{N})^2\right]}{\sqrt{2\pi}},$$

(8.47)

where $\mathbf{B}$ is a vector whose length is normalized to $\sqrt{N}$. Since the inputs have a preferential alignment h equal to $+\rho$ or $-\rho$ with the structure-generating vector $\mathbf{B}$, we expect that the cluster axes will reflect this structure. Furthermore, since the calculations and analytic expressions are relatively tedious, whereas the results are a natural generalization of those found for the single $\mathbf{J}$ case, we will be very brief. It is found that there exists a critical value α_r below which $R_- = (\mathbf{J}_1 - \mathbf{J}_2)\mathbf{B}/N$ is exactly zero and all the statistical properties are identical to those for random inputs. In other words, the underlying non-random structure of the data points is not discovered at all! Within RS one finds $\alpha_r = \pi/2\rho^4$, whereas one-step RSB predicts a somewhat smaller value $\alpha_r \approx 1.13/\rho^4$. For $\alpha > \alpha_r$, the overlap R_- becomes different from zero and in fact converges to 1 for $\alpha \to \infty$.

We conclude that the deceptive structure, revealed by competitive learning in the subspace orthogonal to the symmetry-breaking direction, again completely dominates below a critical size of the training set. As in the single $\mathbf{J}$ case, this retarded learning is unavoidable, i.e. it is impossible to identify the directions of cluster centres below a critical value α_r.

8.5 Clustering by tuning the temperature

One of the difficult issues in unsupervised learning schemes is to estimate the accuracy to which the examples have to be scrutinized. We did not encounter this problem in the previous discussion on clustering since we decided from the outset to work with two cluster centres and limited our analysis to the ground state $T = 0$. But various algorithms, including the well-known adaptive resonance theory [122], have been devised in which the number of "active" cluster centres adjusts itself to a pre-set accuracy threshold. As the accuracy requirement is increased, existing clusters break up into finer ones, thereby revealing the underlying hierarchical structure of the example set. Here we discuss another approach [123], which is closer in spirit to statistical mechanics, and controls the number of cluster centres by varying the analogue of an inverse temperature β. We assume that each of the examples $\boldsymbol{\xi}^\mu$, $\mu = 1, \ldots, p$ is associated with a single cluster chosen from the set of M available clusters with corresponding cluster centres $\mathbf{J}_m$, $m = 1, \ldots, M$. The cost of attributing a particular example $\boldsymbol{\xi}^\mu$ to a cluster m will be denoted by $V_m(\boldsymbol{\xi}^\mu)$. For simplicity, we only consider a squared-distance cost $V_m(\boldsymbol{\xi}^\mu) = (\boldsymbol{\xi}^\mu - \mathbf{J}_m)^2$. Furthermore, we define the quantity X_m^μ which identifies the cluster to which example μ is attributed, namely $X_m^\mu = 1$ if $\boldsymbol{\xi}^\mu$ is associated to the mth cluster, and 0 otherwise. Note that only representations of the form

$$X_m^\mu = \delta(m, m^\mu) \tag{8.48}$$

are allowed, with X_m^μ taking the value 1 for a single m only, for any value of μ, $\mu = 1, \ldots, p$. For a given choice of the assignments $\{X_m^\mu\}$ and the cluster centres $\{\mathbf{J}_m\}$, we conclude that the total cost is given by

$$E(\{\mathbf{J}_m\}, \{X_m^\mu\}) = \sum_{\mu, m} X_m^\mu (\boldsymbol{\xi}^\mu - \mathbf{J}_m)^2. \tag{8.49}$$

We will accept such a choice according to a Boltzmann factor

$$\text{Prob}(\{\mathbf{J}_m\}, \{X_m^\mu\}) \sim e^{-\beta E(\{\mathbf{J}_m\}, \{X_m^\mu\})}, \tag{8.50}$$

where, as usual, the inverse temperature β controls the competition between the cost and the entropy. As β is raised, the locations of the cluster centres and the assignments will change as the importance of minimizing the cost becomes more stringent. To make the connection with the preceding discussion in this chapter, we note that when ξ^μ and $\mathbf{J}_m$ lie on the N-sphere, the cost (8.49) corresponds, apart from a trivial constant, to that for a Hebbian potential $V(\lambda) = -\lambda$. In particular for a given choice of the attribution variables X_m^μ, the minimum of the cost E is reached for

$$\mathbf{J}_m = \sum_\mu X_m^\mu \xi^\mu \tag{8.51}$$

so that each cluster centre is the centre of mass of the examples that are attributed to it. This is of course a consequence of using the quadratic cost function or, in neural network parlance, the result of the Hebb learning rule. On the other hand, the fact that we attribute each example to exactly one cluster centre implies that there will also be a kind of competition between those centres. The difference with competitive learning as discussed in the previous section is that an example is not automatically attributed to the cluster centre that is nearest to it. In fact, the basic quantity is now the entropy which arises from all the permutations of the examples which are possible without changing the value of E. These include in particular the permutations of all the examples belonging to a given cluster. As a result, the entropy favours clusters of large size. The competition with the cost E, which is lower for smaller clusters focused around each centre, leads to a non-trivial rearrangement of these centres as the temperature β^{-1} is tuned.

To investigate the implications of the Boltzmann sampling (8.50) on the location of the cluster centres, we define a free energy depending on the cluster centres by

$$F(\{\mathbf{J}_m\}) = -\frac{1}{\beta} \ln \sum_{\{X_m^\mu\}} e^{-\beta E(\{\mathbf{J}_m\}, \{X_m^\mu\})}. \tag{8.52}$$

From (8.48) we find for general f_m^μ the identity

$$\sum_{\{X_m^\mu\}} e^{\sum_{\mu,m} f_m^\mu X_m^\mu} = \sum_{m^1=1}^{M} \cdots \sum_{m^p=1}^{M} e^{\sum_\mu f_{m\mu}^\mu} = \prod_{\mu=1}^{p} \left(\sum_{m=1}^{M} e^{f_m^\mu} \right) \tag{8.53}$$

which allows us to simplify expression (8.52) for the free energy by eliminating the attribution variables X_m^μ to yield

$$F(\{\mathbf{J}_m\}) = -\frac{1}{\beta} \sum_\mu \ln \sum_m \exp\left(-\beta(\xi^\mu - \mathbf{J}_m)^2\right). \tag{8.54}$$

In the thermodynamic limit $p \to \infty$, $N \to \infty$ with $\alpha = p/N$ finite, one can again argue that the intensive free energy density F/N is self-averaging and evaluate it using the replica technique (see [124] for such a calculation with two cluster centres). Here we follow [123] and consider the simpler self-averaging limit $p \to$

∞ with N finite. It illustrates an essential new feature of interest, while it can be analysed by an elementary calculation.

In the high-temperature limit $\beta = 0$, we find that all the cluster centres coincide and point to the centre of mass of the entire example set,

$$\mathbf{J}_m \sim \frac{1}{p} \sum_\mu \xi^\mu \tag{8.55}$$

for all m. For simplicity of notation, we locate the origin at this centre of mass. We expect that upon decreasing the temperature, this unique cluster will split into smaller ones at some critical value β_c. By differentiating (8.54) with respect to $\mathbf{J}_m$, we find that an extremum of the free energy is reached when

$$\sum_\mu \frac{(\xi^\mu - \mathbf{J}_m) \exp(-\beta (\xi^\mu - \mathbf{J}_m)^2)}{\sum_k \exp(-\beta (\xi^\mu - \mathbf{J}_k)^2)} = 0. \tag{8.56}$$

From an expansion of this expression including the first order correction terms in β and linear terms in $\mathbf{J}_m$ one finds

$$(1 - 2\beta \mathbf{C})\mathbf{J}_m + \frac{1}{M} \sum_k 2\beta \mathbf{C} \mathbf{J}_k = 0, \tag{8.57}$$

where $\mathbf{C}$ is the covariance matrix of the example set,

$$\mathbf{C} = \frac{1}{p} \sum_\mu \xi^\mu \xi^\mu. \tag{8.58}$$

The stability of the solution $\mathbf{J}_m = \mathbf{0}$ is, upon decreasing the temperature, compromised by the appearance of negative eigenvalues for the matrix formed by the coefficients in (8.57). Writing $\lambda_{\max}$ for the largest eigenvalue of $\mathbf{C}$, we conclude that the critical value of β is given by

$$\beta_c = \frac{1}{2\lambda_{\max}}. \tag{8.59}$$

Hence it is determined, as expected, by the variance along the largest principal axis of the example distribution, and the first cluster splitting occurs along this direction. In the limit $p \to \infty$, this splitting corresponds to a genuine second order phase transition. Further splitting is expected to occur as one further decreases the temperature.

As a simple illustration consider the one-dimensional example distribution

$$P(\xi) = \frac{\delta(\xi - 1) + \delta(\xi - 3)}{4} + \frac{\delta(\xi + 2)}{2}. \tag{8.60}$$

The matrix $\mathbf{C}$ reduces to a scalar variable $C = 9/2$, and hence the critical value

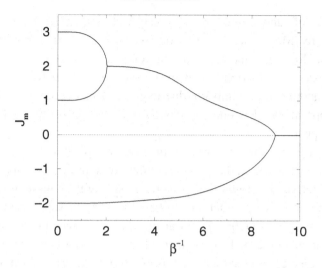

Fig. 8.5. Solutions $\mathbf{J}_m$ with $m = 1, 2, 3$ of (8.56) for the distribution (8.60) plotted as a function of β^{-1}.

is $\beta_c = 1/9$. In fig. 8.5, we have plotted the solutions of the full non-linear problem (8.56). One clearly observes a second order phase transition at $\beta_c = 1/9$, corresponding to the break-up of the centre of mass of all examples into an upper and a lower cluster, followed by a second transition at $\beta \approx 1/2$, in which the upper cluster splits further.

Finally, we comment on the observation made in the previous sections about the masking of a genuine structure by one produced by chance. Why is the direction of largest variance not suppressed by the randomness? The reason is simple: we are considering the limit $p \to \infty$ with N finite and hence $\alpha = \infty$. In fact, an analysis for α finite [124] does reveal the competition between genuine structure and randomness. One observes the appearance of a clustering phase along a random direction, for α below a critical threshold value and at sufficiently low temperature.

8.6 Discussion

We illustrated in this chapter how clustering techniques can be discussed within the context of statistical mechanics, allowing their properties and performance to be quantified on a set of uniformly and non-uniformly distributed high dimensional examples.

The first lesson is that one risks finding what one is searching for. If the number of examples is of the same order as the dimension of the example space the realizations of randomness are extremely rich and incorporate virtually any type of structure. Moreover, this order by chance is perfectly reproducible in the thermodynamic limit. Competitive learning for example will reveal a reproducible and sharp cluster-like distribution of examples, even when these examples are generated at random from a uniform distribution. A nice feature of the statistical mechanics approach is that one can characterize the properties of the order by chance that appears.

The second lesson is that the structure inherent in typical realizations of random data can mask a genuine underlying structure. In some cases, this leads to the appearance of retarded learning: below a critical size of the data set no information at all about the underlying structure can be extracted. Unsupervised learning by examples then sets in through a phase transition which can be first or second order. One of the benefits of the analysis presented here is that one can show that retarded learning is in some cases unavoidable. It is no use then trying to beat it.

The third point is that retarded learning appears because of symmetries which the non-uniform distribution shares with the random distribution. This symmetry may be rather obvious (such as symmetry under reflection, rotation or permutation), but it may also be hidden. For example, retarded learning is present when the average overlap of the examples along the symmetry-breaking direction is zero, $\langle\langle h \rangle\rangle = 0$, but the distribution of the overlap need not be an even function. One can speculate that these symmetries are the most serious and unavoidable limitations encountered in learning by examples. It has been known for some time that hidden symmetries are indeed a source of trouble in the process of learning by examples. The explicit analysis of simple scenarios by statistical mechanics allows one to understand and characterize the types of symmetries involved and the price one has to pay for them in terms of the size of the training set.

Finally, statistical mechanics provides a novel interpretation of the breaking up of an example set into finer and finer clusters as the result of successive phase transitions taking place as a temperature-like parameter is reduced. In fact the application of this type of ideas appears to be quite successful in real-world data, see for example [125].

We finally give a short guide to some of the relevant literature. Early references to unsupervised learning using techniques from statistical mechanics are [123, 112, 126, 118, 117]. Competitive learning was first studied in [120]. The general discussion of the problem with a single symmetry-breaking direction, including the relation between supervised and unsupervised learning, is given in [127]. For an example of retarded learning in supervised learning, see [108], while a discussion about supervised learning on non-uniformly distributed examples is to be found in [128]. A rigorous proof for the existence of retarded learning is given in [129].

8.7 Problems

8.1 Verify the interpretation of $\lambda_0(t, x)$ and the resulting formula for its probability density (8.19), on the one hand by a direct calculation analogous to that carried out for the capacity problem in section 6.4, and on the other hand by the application of the cavity method of appendix 6.

8.2 Calculate the distribution of alignments obtained for random examples by applying *minimal* variance learning

$$V(\lambda) = \lambda^2. \tag{8.61}$$

Do you expect replica symmetry to be broken?

8.3 By combining (8.12) with (8.33), calculate the Gibbs overlap of the student perceptron learning from a teacher perceptron with output noise and show that it is identical to the Gibbs overlap at optimal temperature, cf. (5.29) with $R = q$ and $\beta = \ln((1 + a)/(1 - a))$.

8.4 Similarly, by combining (8.14) with (8.33), reproduce the results for the reversed wedge perceptron obtained in section 7.3.

8.5 Verify that the asymptotic behaviour of the generalization error for the Gibbs student learning from a teacher perceptron with weight noise is in agreement with the discussion about learning at the optimal temperature in section 5.4. Why can learning at the optimal temperature not saturate the Bayes limit in this case?

8.6 Consult [130] and verify that, in the limit $N \to \infty$, one can determine P^* exactly by using a subset of p' examples, with $p' \to \infty$ but $\alpha' = p'/N \to 0$. Hence, finding the symmetry-breaking orientation itself, which requires $p \sim N$, is more costly than finding P^*.

8.7 Unsupervised Gibbs learning as defined in section 8.3 is in fact the analogue of the zero-temperature Gibbs learning from the supervised case. So why do we have to take $\beta = 1$?

8.8 Starting from (8.24), find the saddle point equations for R and x. Show that an optimal potential exists, which yields an overlap equal to the Bayes overlap $R_B = \sqrt{R}$, with the Gibbs overlap given in (8.33), see also section 4.5.

8.9 Show that the overlap R for the zero-temperature unsupervised Hebb rule applied to examples with a single symmetry-breaking orientation is given by, cf. (8.24),

$$R = \langle h \rangle \sqrt{\frac{\alpha}{1 + \alpha \langle h \rangle^2}}. \tag{8.62}$$

Show that this result is identical to the optimal overlap R_B for $\alpha \to 0$.

8.10 Consider maximal variance competitive learning, defined by the potential

$$V(\lambda_1, \lambda_2) = -\lambda_1(1 + \gamma(\lambda_1 - \lambda_2)) - \lambda_2(1 + \gamma(\lambda_2 - \lambda_1))$$
$$= -(\lambda_1 + \lambda_2) - \gamma(\lambda_1 - \lambda_2)^2. \tag{8.63}$$

Show that for random examples Q is given by

$$Q = \begin{cases} -1 + \dfrac{\alpha}{8\gamma^2(1 + \sqrt{\alpha})^4} & \alpha \le \alpha_- \text{ or } \alpha > \alpha_+ \\ 1 & \alpha_- \le \alpha \le \alpha_+, \end{cases} \tag{8.64}$$

where α_+ and α_- are defined as the positive real roots of the equation $4\gamma(1 + \sqrt{\alpha})^2 - \sqrt{\alpha} = 0$. These roots do not exist for $\gamma > 1/16$. In this case the first line in (8.64) holds for all values of α, and $Q(\alpha)$ attains its maximal value (< 1) at $\alpha = 1$. Note that in contrast to what happens for competitive learning, Q is now non-monotonic in α. Show that the distribution of the alignment is given by

$$P(\lambda_1, \lambda_2) = \frac{1 + \sqrt{\alpha}}{2\pi\sqrt{\alpha}} \exp\left(-\frac{1}{2}\left(\frac{\lambda_1 + \lambda_2}{\sqrt{2(1 + Q)}} - \frac{1}{\sqrt{\alpha}}\right)^2\right.$$
$$\left. - \frac{1}{2}\left(\frac{1 + \sqrt{\alpha}}{\sqrt{\alpha}}\frac{\lambda_1 - \lambda_2}{\sqrt{2(1 - Q)}}\right)^2\right). \tag{8.65}$$

8.11 Consider again maximal variance competitive learning as defined in the previous problem, but now applied to non-random examples characterized by (8.47). Show that $\alpha_r = 1/\rho^4$.

9

On-line Learning

So far we have focused on the performance of various learning rules as a function of the size of the training set with examples which are all selected before training starts and remain available during the whole training period. However, in both real life and many practical situations, the training examples come and go with time. Learning then has to proceed *on-line*, using only the training example which is available at any particular time. This is to be contrasted with the previous scenario, called *off-line* or batch learning, in which all the training examples are available at all times.

For the Hebb rule, the off-line and on-line scenario coincide: each example provides an additive contribution to the synaptic vector, which is independent of the other examples. We mentioned already in chapter 3 that this rule performs rather badly for large training sets, precisely because it treats all the learning examples in exactly the same way. The purpose of this chapter is to introduce more advanced or alternative on-line learning rules, and to compare their performance with that of their off-line versions.

9.1 Stochastic gradient descent

In an on-line scenario, the training examples $\left(\boldsymbol{\xi}^{\mu}, \sigma_T^{\mu}\right)$ are presented once and in a sequential order and the coupling vector $\mathbf{J}$ is updated at each time step using information from this single example only. Denoting the coupling vector which has been constructed on the basis of the examples *preceding* example μ by $\mathbf{J} = \mathbf{J}^{\mu}$, on-line learning is defined by the updating rule

$$\mathbf{J}^{\mu+1} = \mathbf{J}^{\mu} + \frac{1}{\sqrt{N}} F^{\mu} \boldsymbol{\xi}^{\mu}, \tag{9.1}$$

where F^{μ} is called the *learning amplitude*. The prefactor $1/\sqrt{N}$ has been introduced into (9.1) to obtain a vector $\mathbf{J}$ which has, in the thermodynamic limit, a normalization $\mathbf{J}^2 \sim N$.

149

The explicit form of F, and in particular the variables on which it may depend, will be discussed in more detail below when we introduce more specific learning rules. Its meaning can be clarified from the following explicit solution of (9.1) when starting from *tabula rasa* $\mathbf{J}^0 = \mathbf{0}$

$$\mathbf{J}^{\nu+1} = \frac{1}{\sqrt{N}} \sum_{\mu=1}^{\nu} F^\mu \boldsymbol{\xi}^\mu, \tag{9.2}$$

so that $F^\mu \sigma_T^\mu$ is the on-line analogue of the embedding strength x^μ discussed in the context of off-line learning cf. (3.11). Note however that F^μ will in general depend on the vector $\mathbf{J}^\mu$, which is constructed on the basis of the examples preceding μ. Hence the embedding strength is history dependent and the statistical equivalence of all examples that characterize off-line learning is lost in on-line learning.

Another interpretation of F^μ may be obtained by multiplying both sides of (9.1) by $\boldsymbol{\xi}^\mu$ to find

$$F^\mu = \lambda^\mu - t^\mu, \tag{9.3}$$

where

$$t^\mu = \frac{\mathbf{J}^\mu \boldsymbol{\xi}^\mu}{\sqrt{N}} \tag{9.4}$$

and

$$\lambda^\mu = \frac{\mathbf{J}^{\mu+1} \boldsymbol{\xi}^\mu}{\sqrt{N}} \tag{9.5}$$

are the alignments *before* and *after* the learning step using example μ, respectively. In other words, F^μ is the amplitude of the realignment of the synaptic vector with $\boldsymbol{\xi}^\mu$ upon presentation of this example.

Turning to the dynamical evolution of the $\mathbf{J}$-vector as implied by the on-line prescription (9.1), we will in the following measure time simply by counting the number of examples and thus describe learning as a motion in coupling space as a function of the time variable μ. From (9.1) or (9.2) and the fact that the examples are chosen at random, it follows that this motion is stochastic. However, one again expects that the "order parameters"

$$\rho^\mu = \frac{\mathbf{J}^\mu \mathbf{T}}{N} \quad \text{and} \quad Q^\mu = \frac{\mathbf{J}^\mu \mathbf{J}^\mu}{N} \tag{9.6}$$

are self-averaging in the thermodynamic limit. We give here a heuristic derivation of this fact, which, at the same time, provides the equations of motion for those quantities. For a rigorous treatment, see [131].

Multiplying (9.1) by the teacher vector $\mathbf{T}$, one finds

$$N(\rho^{\mu+1} - \rho^\mu) = F^\mu \frac{\mathbf{T}\boldsymbol{\xi}^\mu}{\sqrt{N}} \tag{9.7}$$

and by iteration

$$N\frac{\rho^{\mu+l} - \rho^\mu}{l} = \frac{1}{l}\sum_{i=0}^{l-1} F^{\mu+i}\frac{\mathbf{T}\boldsymbol{\xi}^{\mu+i}}{\sqrt{N}}. \tag{9.8}$$

Bearing in mind the thermodynamic limit $N \to \infty$, $p \to \infty$ with $\alpha = p/N$ finite, we now consider the limit $l \to \infty$, but with $l/N = d\alpha \to 0$. In this limit, α plays the role of a continuous time variable, with (9.8) prescribing the small change of $\rho_\mu = \rho(\alpha)$ during a small increment $d\alpha$ of time. The r.h.s. of (9.8) is the sum of a large number of random variables. We will assume that the correlations which appear due to the dependence of F^μ on previous examples are weak, so that we can invoke the law of large numbers. We conclude that the r.h.s. is self-averaging, i.e. equal to the average to be taken with respect to the training examples. Consequently, the l.h.s. is also self-averaging and clearly equal to the derivative of ρ with respect to time α. We may thus write

$$\frac{d\rho}{d\alpha} = \langle Fu \rangle, \tag{9.9}$$

where

$$u = \frac{\mathbf{T}\boldsymbol{\xi}}{\sqrt{N}} \tag{9.10}$$

is the local field of the teacher and the average is with respect to a randomly chosen example $\boldsymbol{\xi}$.

In the same way, by taking the square on both sides of (9.1), and passing to the limit as described above, one finds for $Q^\mu = Q(\alpha)$

$$\frac{dQ}{d\alpha} = \langle F(F + 2t) \rangle. \tag{9.11}$$

We stress again that the aligning field t

$$t = \frac{\mathbf{J}\boldsymbol{\xi}}{\sqrt{N}} \tag{9.12}$$

is that of a *new* example $\boldsymbol{\xi}$ whereas the vector $\mathbf{J}$ is constructed on the basis of preceding examples. Hence $\boldsymbol{\xi}$ is *uncorrelated* with $\mathbf{J}$. It is this absence of correlations which makes the mathematical analysis of on-line learning much easier than the analysis of its off-line analogues.

The expressions (9.9) and (9.11) are the basic equations describing on-line learning in the perceptron. The averages appearing in these equations may be performed once the training rule, i.e. the form of F, is specified. It then remains to find the explicit solutions $\rho(\alpha)$ and $Q(\alpha)$ of the resulting evolution equations. The properly normalized overlap between teacher and student related to the generalization error follows as the ratio $R = \rho/\sqrt{Q}$.

In chapter 4, we studied the generalization performance of students $\mathbf{J}$ who minimize various global cost functions $E(\mathbf{J}) = \sum_\mu V\left(t^\mu \sigma_T^\mu\right)$. The on-line equivalent of these learning rules involves the *local* cost $V\left(t^\mu \sigma_T^\mu\right)$ at the time when example μ is presented. The natural analogue for the minimization of the total cost by a decrease of the local cost is called *stochastic gradient descent*, and is defined by a learning amplitude

$$F^\mu = -\eta V'(t^\mu \sigma_T^\mu)\sigma_T^\mu \tag{9.13}$$

or, in the continuous time limit,

$$F = F(t, \mathrm{sgn}(u)) = -\eta V'(t\,\mathrm{sgn}(u))\,\mathrm{sgn}(u) \tag{9.14}$$

where η is called the *learning rate*. Using (9.14) in (9.9) and (9.11) a variety of on-line learning scenarios may be investigated.

9.2 Specific examples

To perform the averages in (9.9) and (9.11), it is very helpful to remember, see (2.19), that u and $t/\sqrt{Q}$ are correlated Gaussian random variables with zero mean and with second moments

$$\langle u^2 \rangle = 1, \qquad \left\langle \frac{t^2}{Q} \right\rangle = 1, \qquad \left\langle u\frac{t}{\sqrt{Q}} \right\rangle = \frac{\rho}{\sqrt{Q}} = R. \tag{9.15}$$

Furthermore, since the example $\boldsymbol{\xi}$ only appears in these equations in the form of u and t, the average over $\boldsymbol{\xi}$ is reduced to an average over these correlated Gaussian variables.

With this simplification in mind, we first turn to Hebb learning, where we have $V(t) = -t$, and hence $F = \eta\,\mathrm{sgn}(u)$. Using the Gaussian properties of t and u one easily finds that

$$\frac{d\rho}{d\alpha} = \eta\sqrt{\frac{2}{\pi}},$$

$$\frac{dQ}{d\alpha} = \eta^2 + 2\eta\rho\sqrt{\frac{2}{\pi}}. \tag{9.16}$$

Hence, with $\rho(0) = Q(0) = 0$, one obtains

$$\rho(\alpha) = \eta\sqrt{\frac{2}{\pi}}\alpha \tag{9.17}$$

and

$$Q(\alpha) = \eta^2 \left(\alpha + \frac{2}{\pi} \alpha^2 \right), \tag{9.18}$$

which reproduces the result found in (3.8) which is of course independent of the value of η.

The various other choices of $V(t)$ discussed in the context of off-line learning can be treated in a similar way. We focus on two cases of interest which give surprising results. First we turn to the perceptron algorithm. Since it was originally formulated as an on-line algorithm by Rosenblatt, a discussion of its properties is in order. The perceptron algorithm corresponds to the choice $V(t) = -t\theta(-t)$, so that

$$F = \eta\theta(-tu)\,\text{sgn}(u). \tag{9.19}$$

The calculations leading to the equations for ρ, Q and ultimately to R are straightforward, since they just involve Gaussian integrals (cf. problem 9.1). One finds

$$\frac{d\rho}{d\alpha} = \frac{\eta}{\sqrt{2\pi}} \left(1 - \frac{\rho}{\sqrt{Q}} \right) \tag{9.20}$$

$$\frac{dQ}{d\alpha} = \frac{\eta^2}{\pi} \arccos \frac{\rho}{\sqrt{Q}} + \sqrt{\frac{2}{\pi}} \eta (\rho - \sqrt{Q})$$

and therefore

$$\frac{dR}{d\alpha} = \frac{\eta(1 - R^2)}{\sqrt{2\pi Q}} - \frac{R\eta^2}{2\pi Q} \arccos R. \tag{9.21}$$

In fig. 9.1, we have plotted the generalization error $\varepsilon = (\arccos R)/\pi$, obtained from a numerical solution of (9.21) together with the result (3.8) for the Hebb rule. Note that (9.20) has as steady state solutions the line $\rho = \sqrt{Q}$, corresponding to $R = 1$. From the asymptotic approach of R to this fixed point we obtain the following asymptotic behaviour of the corresponding generalization error:

$$\varepsilon(\alpha) \sim \left(\frac{2}{3} \right)^{1/3} \pi^{-1} \alpha^{-1/3}. \tag{9.22}$$

This result is surprisingly bad. Indeed the simplest and most basic of the on-line algorithms, namely the Hebb rule, has a faster asymptotic decay ($\sim \alpha^{-1/2}$). This observation is however somewhat misleading since it turns out that the $\alpha^{-1/3}$ behaviour of the perceptron algorithm persists for quite general distributions of the examples [132], while on the other hand the Hebb rule generically fails to converge to a zero asymptotic generalization error for a non-uniform distribution of examples, cf. problem 9.18. What appears to go wrong as far as the perceptron

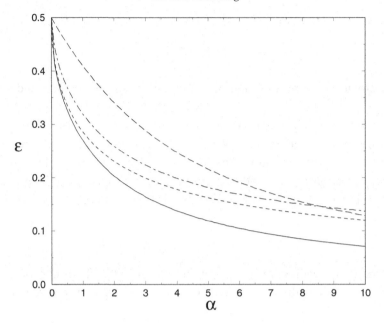

Fig. 9.1. Generalization error ε as a function of the training set size α in different on-line scenarios. Shown are the results for the Hebb rule (dashed), which is identical to what is shown in fig. 4.3, for the perceptron rule ($\eta = 1$, dashed–dotted), the adatron rule ($\eta = 1$, long-dashed), and the optimal on-line rule discussed in section 9.3 (full).

algorithm is concerned is that its performance is very sensitive to the learning amplitude. In fact by decreasing η with the size of the training set α in an appropriate way, cf. problem 9.4, one can achieve an asymptotic decay $\varepsilon(\alpha) \sim \alpha^{-1}$, which is comparable to that of off-line algorithms. Such a change of the learning rate with α is called *annealing*, in analogy to the procedure of slowly decreasing the temperature in a thermodynamic system in order to locate its ground state. Note finally that in real applications, the perceptron algorithm is usually operating with a positive stability κ resulting in an $\varepsilon \sim \alpha^{-1/2}$ asymptotic decay, even for a constant learning rate, as long as $\kappa > 0$ (cf. problem 9.2).

We next turn to adatron learning at zero stability $\kappa = 0$, discussed in section 4.4. It has $V(t) = t^2\theta(-t)/2$ and hence $F = -\eta t \theta(-tu) = \eta|t|\theta(-tu)\,\mathrm{sgn}\,u$. The Gaussian integrals are straightforward again. We only quote the final resulting equation for R, which has the nice feature of being decoupled from the Q-variable:

$$\frac{dR}{d\alpha} = -\frac{\eta^2 R \arccos R}{2\pi} + \frac{\eta}{\pi}(1 - R^2)^{3/2} + \frac{\eta^2 R^2\sqrt{1 - R^2}}{2\pi}. \qquad (9.23)$$

The corresponding generalization error, obtained from a numerical solution of (9.23), is included in fig. 9.1. To extract the asymptotic behaviour for $\alpha \to \infty$, we expand the r.h.s. of (9.23) around $R = 1$ to leading order

$$\frac{dR}{d\alpha} = \left(-\frac{\eta^2}{3} + \eta\right) \frac{2\sqrt{2}}{\pi}(1 - R)^{3/2}, \tag{9.24}$$

implying for the generalization error

$$\varepsilon(\alpha) \sim \frac{3}{\eta(3 - \eta)} \frac{1}{\alpha}. \tag{9.25}$$

This result is surprisingly good: it displays the $1/\alpha$ behaviour typical of most *off-line* algorithms. In particular, it means that the on-line algorithm performs as well as the students who lie in the version space.

The relatively simple form of (9.23) allows the effect of the learning rate η to be discussed in detail. $R = 1$ is always a fixed point, but it becomes unstable when the learning rate η exceeds the critical value $\eta_c = 3$, as is immediately clear from (9.24). A more detailed analysis, cf. problem 9.6, reveals that there is another stable fixed point $R < 1$, appearing for $\eta > 3$. The solution $R = 1$ loses its stability by a bifurcation at $\eta = \eta_c$ and is replaced by the $R < 1$ solution for $\eta > \eta_c$. We conclude that for too large a learning rate $\eta > \eta_c$ the on-line rule fails to learn perfectly, even with an infinite training set! This feature is a well-known and documented weakness of on-line learning [133].

9.3 Optimal on-line learning

The remarkable results for the on-line adatron algorithm raise the question about the best possible on-line performance. Since the generalization error is a monotonically decreasing function of R, we will seek to maximize the average of $dR/d\alpha$, which, from (9.9) and (9.11), is given by

$$\frac{dR}{d\alpha} = \frac{\langle 2QFu - \rho F(F + 2t)\rangle}{2Q^{3/2}}. \tag{9.26}$$

At first sight, one is tempted to maximize the quadratic expression in F inside the averaging bracket, by choosing

$$F = -t + \frac{Qu}{\rho}. \tag{9.27}$$

However, the local field u of the teacher is not known to the student! The learning amplitude F should only depend on the quantities available to the student such as t and σ_T. By first averaging in (9.26) over the unavailable degrees of freedom, those on which F cannot depend, one finds that u is replaced by its average value constrained by the values of t and $\sigma_T = \text{sgn}(u)$. Optimizing then with respect to the choice of F yields instead of (9.27)

$$F_{\text{opt}} = -t + \frac{Q}{\rho} \langle u \rangle \big|_{t,\sigma_T} \tag{9.28}$$

with an obvious notation for the conditional average. Note that F_{opt} depends on Q and R. Being self-averaging order parameters, however, their appropriate values are available to the student for almost all realizations of the learning process. In fact, for the optimal algorithm presented here, one has the additional property that for the initial conditions $\sqrt{Q(0)} = R(0) = 0$ one finds $\sqrt{Q(\alpha)} = R(\alpha)$ for all α, see problem 9.8. Hence the values of $\sqrt{Q} = R$ are obtained from the length of $\mathbf{J}$, cf. (9.6). Inserting (9.28) in (9.26), we obtain the optimal increase of the overlap

$$\frac{dR}{d\alpha} = R\frac{\langle F_{\text{opt}}^2 \rangle}{2Q}, \tag{9.29}$$

where the remaining average is with respect to t and σ_T. From the fact that $t/\sqrt{Q}$ and u are Gaussian variables with correlations as given in (9.15), we find

$$P(t, \sigma_T) = \int du\, P(t, u)\, \theta(u\,\sigma_T)$$

$$= \frac{\exp(-t^2/2Q)}{\sqrt{2\pi Q}} H\left(-\frac{R}{\sqrt{1-R^2}}\frac{t}{\sqrt{Q}}\sigma_T\right). \tag{9.30}$$

Hence one gets by application of Bayes' theorem [116]

$$P(u|t, \sigma_T) = \frac{P(t, u, \sigma_T)}{P(t, \sigma_T)}$$

$$= \theta(u\,\sigma_T)\frac{\exp\left(-\left(u - \frac{R}{\sqrt{Q}}t\right)^2/2(1-R^2)\right)}{\sqrt{2\pi(1-R^2)}\,H\left(-\frac{R}{\sqrt{1-R^2}}\frac{t}{\sqrt{Q}}\sigma_T\right)}, \tag{9.31}$$

and for the conditional average of u follows

$$\langle u \rangle\big|_{t,\sigma_T} = \int du\, u\, P(u|t, \sigma_T)$$

$$= \sigma_T\frac{\sqrt{1-R^2}}{\sqrt{2\pi}}\frac{\exp\left(-\frac{R^2}{2(1-R^2)}\frac{t^2}{Q}\right)}{H\left(-\frac{R}{\sqrt{1-R^2}}\frac{t}{\sqrt{Q}}\sigma_T\right)} + R\frac{t}{\sqrt{Q}}. \tag{9.32}$$

The optimal learning amplitude is hence of the form

$$F_{\text{opt}} = \frac{\sigma_T}{\sqrt{2\pi}}\frac{\sqrt{Q(1-R^2)}}{R}\frac{\exp\left(-\frac{R^2}{2(1-R^2)}\frac{t^2}{Q}\right)}{H\left(-\frac{R}{\sqrt{1-R^2}}\frac{t}{\sqrt{Q}}\sigma_T\right)}. \tag{9.33}$$

The r.h.s. of (9.29) may now be computed explicitly. With the change of variable $x = -R t \, \sigma_T / \sqrt{(1 - R^2)Q}$, one finally obtains

$$\frac{dR}{d\alpha} = \frac{(1 - R^2)^{3/2}}{2\pi R^2} \int Dx \, \frac{e^{-x^2/2R^2}}{H(x)}. \tag{9.34}$$

A numerical solution of this equation is included in fig. 9.1. As expected it is below all other curves for the generalization error for all α. The small and large α behaviour are quite interesting. For small α one finds

$$R(\alpha) \approx \sqrt{\frac{2\alpha}{\pi}}, \tag{9.35}$$

which is identical to the off-line Bayes and Hebb result. This might have been anticipated since for small example sets Hebb learning is Bayes optimal, cf. (3.9) and (3.30). For $\alpha \to \infty$ on the other hand we have

$$R(\alpha) \sim 1 - \frac{1}{\alpha^2} \frac{2\pi^2}{\left(\int Dx \, e^{-x^2/2} \, (H(x))^{-1} \right)^2}, \tag{9.36}$$

which is identical to the off-line Bayes result, with the replacement of α by $\alpha/2$, cf. (3.29) and (3.31). In other words, optimal on-line learning needs only twice as many examples to equal off-line Bayes performance asymptotically for $\alpha \to \infty$ and is therefore surprisingly effective.

The connection between optimal on-line and off-line learning in fact runs much deeper. Using the definitions (4.54) and (4.55) we may rewrite F_{opt} as

$$F_{\text{opt}} = \frac{\sigma_T \sqrt{Q(1 - R^2)}}{R} \frac{Y(R, \sigma_T t/\sqrt{Q})}{X(R, \sigma_T t/\sqrt{Q})}. \tag{9.37}$$

For $Q = 1$, which corresponds to the normalization convention used in the off-line case, we conclude that $F_{\text{opt}}(R, t) = \sigma_T F^*(R, t\sigma_T)$, where F^* is the optimal value of the learning amplitude for off-line learning as determined in section 4.5. The extra factor σ_T comes from the incorporation of this factor into the definition for t and Δ used in section 4.5. So it appears that, in the optimal case, the alignments are the same! But one has to keep in mind the basic difference between on- and off-line learning, which also explains the difference in performance. In off-line learning there exists a complete permutation symmetry in the statistical properties of the examples. Hence the above optimal alignment is realized for all of them, while in on-line learning it is realized only for the last example that is presented. Note also that the corresponding optimal potentials are not the same: while in on-line learning F is related to the derivative of the potential with respect to the alignment t before learning, cf. (9.14), it is expressed in off-line learning in terms of the derivative with respect to the alignment after learning, cf. (4.53).

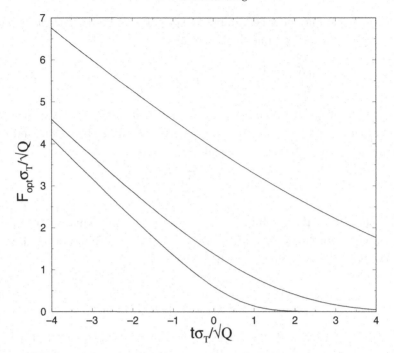

Fig. 9.2. The alignment amplitude $F_{opt}\sigma_T/\sqrt{Q}$ as a function of $t\sigma_T/\sqrt{Q}$, with, from top to bottom, the values of the overlap $R = 0.2, 0.5, 0.9$ respectively.

We close with an interpretation of the observed optimal alignment F_{opt}. Note that it is, as expected, proportional to σ_T, since the correction should be such that it gives the correct sign for the example under consideration. Focusing on the amplitude $F_{opt}\sigma_T$ of the correction, we observe that it is a very specific function of R and $t\sigma_T$. The sign of $t\sigma_T$ tells us whether the existing synaptic vector **J** classifies a new example $\boldsymbol{\xi}$ in agreement (+ sign) or disagreement (− sign) with the teacher. Furthermore, it is quite natural to interpret the absolute value of $t\sigma_T$ as the conviction with which the student comes up with his classification. One expects that a reasonable learning algorithm will prescribe a lesser correction of the synaptic vector for an example that is already correctly reproduced. However, a significant correction should be applied when there is an error, and the more so if the wrong classification is made with great conviction. This behaviour is indeed observed for the optimal potential, see fig. 9.2.

The change of $F_{opt}\sigma_T$ as function of the parameter R may be explained in a similar vein, but in order to keep the right perspective, we need to take into account the change in modulus of **J**. Hence one considers the normalized amplitude $F_{opt}\sigma_T/\sqrt{Q}$ as a function of the normalized alignment $t\sigma_T/\sqrt{Q}$. For $R \to 0$, F_{opt}

converges to a constant, i.e. Hebb learning is optimal. As learning proceeds and R gets closer to 1, the student gains confidence and the corrections will become smaller, and especially so for the correctly reproduced examples, see again fig. 9.2. In the limit $R \to 1$ (9.33) converges to the adatron result $F_{\mathrm{opt}} \approx -t\theta(-t\sigma_T)$.

9.4 Perceptron with a smooth transfer function

One of the disadvantages of the perceptron with binary output values is that one cannot perform a local gradient descent directly on the *output error*. This very standard algorithm is rooted in the tradition of statistics in the context of least square error approximations and appears under the name "back-propagation" as one of the most popular training rules in neural networks, cf. [10]. In order to discuss this algorithm from the point of view of statistical mechanics we now consider a perceptron with a continuous output $\sigma = g(\mathbf{J}\boldsymbol{\xi}/\sqrt{N})$ as introduced in problem 3.7. We again restrict ourselves to the simple scenario in which this perceptron is trained by a teacher $\mathbf{T}$, $\mathbf{T}^2 = N$, with the same transfer function. The quadratic error is defined as

$$V\left(\frac{\mathbf{J}\boldsymbol{\xi}^{\mu}}{\sqrt{N}}\right) = \frac{1}{2}\left[g\left(\frac{\mathbf{J}\boldsymbol{\xi}^{\mu}}{\sqrt{N}}\right) - g\left(\frac{\mathbf{T}\boldsymbol{\xi}^{\mu}}{\sqrt{N}}\right)\right]^2, \tag{9.38}$$

and a gradient descent correction is given by (cf. (9.1) and (9.13))

$$\mathbf{J}^{\mu+1} = \mathbf{J}^{\mu} + \frac{1}{\sqrt{N}}F^{\mu}\boldsymbol{\xi}^{\mu} \tag{9.39}$$

with

$$F^{\mu} = -\eta\left[g(t^{\mu}) - g(u_{\mu})\right]g'(t^{\mu}). \tag{9.40}$$

Since the transfer function is typically chosen to be a monotonically increasing function of its argument, we note that knowing the output of the teacher now implies that the aligning field u_{μ} is available. Proceeding in exactly the same way as before, one may again derive a set of two equations for the order parameters ρ and Q, cf. (9.9) and (9.11). Furthermore the averages appearing in these equations can be evaluated explicitly for the specific choice $g(x) = 1 - 2H(x)$, with $g'(x) = 2\exp(-x^2/2)/\sqrt{2\pi}$. One finds, after lengthy but straightforward calculations [134],

$$\frac{d\rho}{d\alpha} = \frac{2}{\pi}\frac{\eta}{1+Q}\left[\frac{1+Q-\rho^2}{\sqrt{2(1+Q)-\rho^2}} - \frac{\rho}{\sqrt{1+2Q}}\right] \tag{9.41}$$

$$\frac{dQ}{d\alpha} = \frac{4}{\pi}\frac{\eta}{1+Q}\left[\frac{\rho}{\sqrt{2(1+Q)-\rho^2}} - \frac{Q}{\sqrt{1+2Q}}\right]$$

$$+ \frac{4}{\pi^2} \frac{\eta^2}{\sqrt{1+2Q}} \left[\arcsin \frac{Q}{1+3Q} + \arcsin \frac{1+2Q-2\rho^2}{2(1+2Q-\rho^2)} \right.$$

$$\left. - \arcsin \frac{\rho}{\sqrt{2(1+2Q-\rho^2)(1+3Q)}} \right]. \tag{9.42}$$

Without going into the details of the analysis, we mention that this example again illustrates the crucial importance of the learning rate η. For small η, the student vector will smoothly move in the direction of the teacher until a zero quadratic error is achieved corresponding to $\rho = 1$, $Q = 1$. The speed of this approach is controlled by varying η. However, there exists a critical learning rate $\eta_c = \pi\sqrt{5/3} \approx 4.06$, above which the fixed point $\rho = 1$, $Q = 1$ loses its stability. Indeed, by linearizing the r.h.s. of (9.41) and (9.42) around this fixed point one finds that the eigenvalues of the resulting 2×2 matrix are

$$\gamma_1 = 4 \frac{\sqrt{5}}{3} \frac{\eta}{\eta_c} \left(\frac{\eta}{\eta_c} - 1 \right), \tag{9.43}$$

$$\gamma_2 = -2\sqrt{5} \frac{\eta}{9\eta_c}. \tag{9.44}$$

Since γ_1 becomes positive for $\eta > \eta_c$, the corresponding fixed point becomes unstable and a fixed point with imperfect learning takes over. Furthermore, beyond another critical value $\eta = \pi/\sin(1/3) \approx 9/24$, one finds that no stable fixed points exist and one has $\rho, Q \to \infty$ in the limit $\alpha \to \infty$. Finally, there exists an optimal learning rate η_{opt}, namely $\eta_{opt} = 2\eta_c/3 \approx 2.704$, yielding the fastest asymptotic decay of the quadratic error for $\alpha \to \infty$. These results are quite similar to those for the adatron learning of the perceptron with a sign threshold function.

9.5 Queries

The rather slow algebraic decay of the generalization error for large training set sizes common to many off- and on-line learning rules studied so far has a very simple reason. Already in the example on ranking numbers in the introductory chapter 1, we realized that by using random examples it is very hard to get information about the couplings connected with the most insignificant bits of the input. Quite generally one expects that in the later stages of the learning process, with the student almost parallel with the teacher, most of the new examples do not convey much information since their corresponding hyperplane rarely cuts the existing small version space. This can also be seen explicitly from the behaviour of the information gain $\Delta I(\alpha)$ shown for Gibbs learning in fig. 2.3: for $\alpha \to \infty$ it converges to zero proportionally to ε, rendering learning boring and slow.

It is hence tempting to modify the learning scenario to avoid the presentation of largely redundant examples and to realize in this way a more constant flow of information to the student. In fact, assuming an information gain $\Delta I = \partial s/\partial \alpha$ tending to a constant for $\alpha \to \infty$ and an entropy $s \sim \ln \varepsilon$, as typical for smooth networks (cf. section 7.1), we find asymptotically

$$\frac{\partial s}{\partial \alpha} = \frac{\partial s}{\partial \varepsilon}\frac{\partial \varepsilon}{\partial \alpha} \sim \frac{1}{\varepsilon}\frac{\partial \varepsilon}{\partial \alpha} \to \text{const.}, \tag{9.45}$$

implying an *exponential* decay of the generalization error for large α. The fastest such decay is realized by the situation in which every input label received from the teacher conveys the maximal possible information of one bit.

To achieve an information flow that outperforms the one for random examples, a learning strategy is needed in which the distribution of examples is correlated with the actual state of the learning process. In other words, the student is allowed to *pose* special questions, so-called *queries*, which are most helpful at a particular moment in the learning process. Such a prescription is intrinsically on-line and can thus be studied by the techniques introduced in this chapter.

A simple and appealing idea [135] is to choose a new example $\boldsymbol{\xi}$ at random from the subspace *perpendicular* to the present student vector $\mathbf{J}$,

$$\frac{\mathbf{J}\boldsymbol{\xi}}{\sqrt{N}} = 0, \tag{9.46}$$

i.e. the student asks for the classification of inputs he is at the moment most uncertain about ($t = 0$). The explicit analysis is particularly easy for the Hebb rule. Using (9.46) and $F = \text{sgn}(u)$ in (9.11) we immediately get

$$\frac{dQ}{d\alpha} = 1, \tag{9.47}$$

which together with $Q(0) = 0$ gives $Q = \alpha$. Similarly (9.9) yields

$$\frac{d\rho}{d\alpha} = \langle |u| \rangle. \tag{9.48}$$

To calculate the remaining average we note that the angle between teacher and student vector is given by $\theta = \theta(\alpha) = \arccos(\rho(\alpha)/\sqrt{\alpha})$. Therefore the projection of the teacher vector onto the subspace spanned by the example has length $\sqrt{N} \sin \theta$ and correspondingly u is a Gaussian random variable with zero mean and variance $\sin^2 \theta$, i.e.

$$P(u) = \frac{1}{\sqrt{2\pi} \sin \theta} \exp\left(-\frac{u^2}{2 \sin^2 \theta}\right). \tag{9.49}$$

On taking the average we find as the evolution equation for the overlap

$$\frac{d\rho}{d\alpha} = \sqrt{\frac{2}{\pi}}\sqrt{1 - \frac{\rho^2}{\alpha}}. \tag{9.50}$$

This differential equation has to be solved numerically and from the solution $\rho(\alpha)$ we can determine the generalization error as usual via $\varepsilon = \theta/\pi$. The solution shows that ε is for all values of α smaller than for independently chosen examples. For small α the asymptotic behaviour is the same in both cases, which is reasonable; for large α one finds that the generalization error for queries is half that of learning from unselected examples.

It is reassuring to find that for the special case of the Hebb rule, learning with queries is superior to learning from random examples. However the improvement is found to be rather modest. Indeed, as discussed above we expect for a constant flow of information a generalization error which decreases exponentially with the size of the training set. The Hebb rule is hence not able to fully exploit the advantages of query learning. Even more surprisingly, more sophisticated learning rules like the perceptron or the adatron rule do not perform better! Since they differ from the Hebb rule only in the t-dependence of the learning rate while $t = 0$ for query learning, we get the same asymptotic decay as for the Hebb rule. Hence for these learning rules the query performance is even worse than learning from unselected examples! The apparent reason is that although every new example gives by itself a non-vanishing amount of information about the teacher, it significantly interferes with and destroys the information accumulated in previous examples by the on-line character of the learning process.

There are two ways to improve the performance under these circumstances. The first one is to stick to an on-line prescription but to let the learning amplitude depend on the training set size α. The second one is to resort to off-line learning from queries, i.e. new examples are generated at random perpendicular to the student and when they have been added to the training set the *whole* set is re-learned.

Let us start with the first possibility and consider on-line learning from queries using the optimal amplitude derived in section 9.3. Using $t = 0$ we get from (9.33) the form relevant for query learning

$$F_{\text{opt}}^{\text{query}} = \frac{\sigma_T}{\sqrt{2\pi}} \frac{2\sqrt{(1 - R^2)Q}}{R}. \tag{9.51}$$

From (9.29) we immediately conclude that

$$\frac{dR}{d\alpha} = \frac{1}{\pi} \frac{1 - R^2}{R} \tag{9.52}$$

with solution

$$R(\alpha) = \sqrt{1 - \exp\left(-\frac{2\alpha}{\pi}\right)}, \tag{9.53}$$

giving rise to $\varepsilon \sim \exp(-\alpha/\pi)$ for large α. We hence indeed obtain an exponential decay of the generalization error in an on-line query scenario if we appropriately reduce the learning amplitude. In fact using the result for R in (9.51) we see that the learning rate also decreases exponentially in α. Strong reduction of the influence of later inputs on the couplings is hence necessary in on-line query learning in order not to spoil what has already been accomplished.

A mathematical description of the second alternative, which we call off-line query learning, is not straightforward since it is difficult to allow the quenched average over the examples $\boldsymbol{\xi}$ to depend on the dynamical variables $\mathbf{J}$. To sidestep this complication we replace the correlation between examples and student vector by a technically simpler scenario in which the examples are correlated with the teacher vector. We expect similar results at least for large α when $\mathbf{J}$ and $\mathbf{T}$ are almost parallel with each other. Comparison with numerical simulations shows, however, that also the intermediate phases of learning are already accurately characterized.

Let us hence assume that the distribution of examples is given by

$$P(\boldsymbol{\xi}^{\mu}) = \frac{1}{(2\pi)^{N/2}} \exp\left(-\frac{(\boldsymbol{\xi}^{\mu})^2}{2}\right) f_{\mu}\left(\frac{\mathbf{T}\boldsymbol{\xi}^{\mu}}{\sqrt{N}}\right) \tag{9.54}$$

with

$$f_{\mu}(u) = \frac{1}{\sin\theta_{\mu}} \exp\left(-\frac{u^2}{2}\cot^2\theta_{\mu}\right). \tag{9.55}$$

This special form of $f_{\mu}(u)$ is used since it gives rise to the same distribution (9.49) for the aligning field u of the teacher as queries do. Nevertheless not all examples drawn from (9.54) are perpendicular to the student. Note also that f_{μ} depends on the μ through its dependence on θ_{μ}, which, for the time being, we need not specify further.

The general statistical mechanics analysis then proceeds similarly to appendix 2 (cf. also problem 4.10a) and we recover (A2.16) with the replacement $Du_{\mu} \mapsto Du_{\mu} f_{\mu}(u_{\mu})$. The main new feature at this point is that the distribution of u_{μ} depends explicitly on μ. We hence cannot replace the average over all u_{μ} by just one to power αN but instead get

$$\int \prod_{\mu} du_{\mu} \prod_{\mu} P_{\mu}(u_{\mu}) \prod_{\mu} F(u_{\mu}) = \prod_{\mu} \int du\, P_{\mu}(u) F(u)$$

$$= \exp\left(\sum_{\mu} \ln \int du\, P_{\mu}(u) F(u)\right). \tag{9.56}$$

Therefore the energetic part in the calculation acquires the form

$$G_E(q^{ab}, R^a) = \frac{1}{N} \sum_\mu \int Du \, f_\mu(u) \dots \qquad (9.57)$$

where the dots indicate that the rest of the expression is exactly the same as in (A2.19). For $N \to \infty$ we now invoke the replacement

$$\frac{1}{N} \sum_{\mu=1}^{\alpha N} \dots f_\mu(u) \dots \mapsto \int_0^\alpha d\alpha' \dots f_{\alpha'}(u) \dots \qquad (9.58)$$

and using (9.55) finally get for the quenched entropy (cf. (A2.33))

$$s = \underset{q,R}{\text{extr}} \left[\frac{1}{2} \ln(1-q) + \frac{q - R^2}{2(1-q)} \right.$$
$$\left. + 2 \int_0^\alpha d\alpha' \int Dt \, H\left(\frac{R \sin\theta(\alpha')}{\sqrt{q - R^2}} t \right) \ln H\left(\sqrt{\frac{q - R^2 \cos^2\theta(\alpha')}{1-q}} \, t \right) \right]. \qquad (9.59)$$

The saddle point equations corresponding to this expression allow us to determine $R(\alpha)$ and $q(\alpha)$ if $\theta(\alpha')$ is known for all $\alpha' < \alpha$. We now make the crucial assumption $\theta(\alpha') = \arccos R(\alpha')$ which transforms the saddle point equations into a closed set of integral equations for $R(\alpha)$ and $q(\alpha)$. Note that this assumption is non-trivial and could not have been introduced earlier in the calculation where θ, being a parameter of the distribution of the quenched variables, must not carry a replica index while R must not depend on μ in order to decouple the energetic and entropic integrals.

It is quite appealing that off-line learning of queries gives rise to order parameter equations which are non-local in α. Solving them numerically or investigating the asymptotic form for large α one can show that for $\alpha \to \infty$ the information gain indeed approaches a non-zero limit with the generalization error decreasing exponentially. For the case of the Ising perceptron discussed in section 7.2 one may use the zero-entropy criterion to show that the first order transition to perfect generalization occurs for query learning already at $\alpha \cong 1.17$, to be compared with $\alpha \cong 1.24$ for unselected examples.

The prescription for selecting queries discussed above relies on the simple geometrical interpretation of perceptron classifications. In the case of more complicated learning machines, it might be non-trivial to find a criterion according to which queries should be generated. In this case it is advantageous to use the properties of the system itself. The idea is to consider an *ensemble* of students receiving the same inputs and to choose as queries those inputs for which there is *maximal disagreement* between the students. If the number of students becomes very large this clearly produces queries which always bisect the version space. But even with only two students this algorithm of *query by committee* works rather well and gives rise to an exponential decrease of the generalization error. The price to pay, on the other hand, is that it becomes increasingly hard to find a new query. After all, the probability of finding an input on which the two students disagree is for Gibbs learning proportional to the generalization error itself and hence decreases quickly with α. Query by committee is hence advantageous if it is cheap to generate new inputs but costly to receive their respective teacher classifications.

Learning from queries is in general very efficient. As a final caveat we note that since queries are *selected* it may happen that the effective probability distribution of queries is rather different from the original distribution of inputs, which is after all used to determine the generalization error. It is then possible that although the version space volume decreases rapidly with α the generalization error decays only slowly. As a simple example, consider perceptron learning from examples which are perpendicular to the teacher. In the optimal case the version space may be bisected by each new example; nevertheless no alignment between teacher and student vector builds up (see also the discussion of the reversed wedge perceptron with critical wedge parameter in section 7.3).

9.6 Unsupervised on-line learning

Other important features of on-line learning are revealed in the on-line version of the unsupervised problem discussed in chapter 8, to which we turn now. One can repeat the steps of section 9.1 with the following minor modifications. The basic equations (9.9) and (9.11) remain valid, but the learning amplitude F is now given by

$$F = -\eta V'(t), \tag{9.60}$$

since no teacher classification σ_T is provided. Furthermore, using the same notation as in the unsupervised case, the alignment u is replaced by

$$h = \frac{\mathbf{B}\boldsymbol{\xi}}{\sqrt{N}} \tag{9.61}$$

where $\mathbf{B}$ is the symmetry-breaking direction. The major difference from the previous sections is that the examples $\boldsymbol{\xi}$ are now sampled from a non-uniform distribution. The probability for the alignment is no longer normal, but given by $P^*(h) = \exp(-h^2/2 - V^*(h))/\sqrt{2\pi}$, cf. (8.3).

To calculate the averages in (9.9) and (9.11), we need the joint probability distribution $P(t, h)$. Since the distribution $P^*(h)$ is given explicitly, the form of the conditional probability $P(t|h)$ can be inferred from the following arguments (for an explicit calculation, see problem 9.15). We expect that upon applying a specific on-line algorithm, the vector $\mathbf{J}$ will, after a training set of size α, attain a specific self-averaging overlap R with $\mathbf{B}$. Hence $\mathbf{J} = R\mathbf{B} + \mathbf{J}_\perp$, where $\mathbf{J}_\perp$ is the component of $\mathbf{J}$ orthogonal to $\mathbf{B}$. Therefore

$$t = \frac{\mathbf{J}\boldsymbol{\xi}}{\sqrt{N}} = Rh + \frac{\mathbf{J}_\perp\boldsymbol{\xi}}{\sqrt{N}}. \tag{9.62}$$

Since there is no symmetry breaking in the $(N-1)$-dimensional subspace orthogonal to $\mathbf{B}$, the vectors $\mathbf{J}_\perp$ and $\boldsymbol{\xi}$ are uniformly distributed in this subspace. Furthermore, $J_\perp^2 = (1 - R^2)N$ and $\boldsymbol{\xi}^2 = N$, and it follows that $\mathbf{J}_\perp\boldsymbol{\xi}/\sqrt{N}$ is a Gaussian random variable with zero mean and variance $(1 - R^2)$. We conclude from (9.62) that $P(t|h)$ is a Gaussian distribution with average $\langle t|h \rangle = Rh$ and variance $1 - R^2$. Together with the known distribution $P^*(h)$, this completes our knowledge of the joint distribution $P(t, h) = P(t|h)P^*(h)$. The averages in (9.9) and (9.11) (note the change in notation with h instead of u) may thus be calculated once the choice of the symmetry-breaking P^* and the learning rule F have been specified.

Rather than applying these results to some specific cases, we focus here, for reasons of greater theoretical appeal, on the optimal choice of the learning amplitude. The discussion of section 9.3 may be repeated with the result

$$F_{\text{opt}} = -t + \frac{\sqrt{Q}}{R}\langle h \rangle\big|_t \tag{9.63}$$

and

$$\frac{dR}{d\alpha} = R\frac{\langle F_{\text{opt}}^2 \rangle}{2Q}, \tag{9.64}$$

the remaining average being over t. Calculating the averages leads to the following closed evolution equation for R:

$$\frac{dR^2}{d\alpha} = (1 - R^2)\int Dx \frac{Y^2(R, x)}{X(R, x)} \tag{9.65}$$

where $Y(R, x)$ and $X(R, x)$ are defined as in (8.29) and (8.32). Note the surprising analogy in form with the equation for the Bayes overlap in off-line learning, cf. (8.33).

Before turning to a more general discussion of (9.65), we mention some special cases of interest. For $P^*(h) = 2\exp(-h^2/2)\theta(h)/\sqrt{2\pi}$, cf. (8.11), corresponding to the supervised teacher–student perceptron learning, we recover the results of section 9.3. For the Gaussian scenario, $P^*(h) = \exp(-(1 + a)h^2/2)/\sqrt{2\pi/(1 + a)}$, cf. (8.15), one finds

$$\frac{dR}{d\alpha} = \frac{a^2 R(1 - R^2)^2}{2(1 + a)(1 + a - aR^2)}. \tag{9.66}$$

This result reveals a disturbing feature of on-line learning. For the case under consideration, the symmetry-breaking direction cannot be learned on-line from scratch: $R(\alpha = 0) = 0$ implies $R(\alpha) \equiv 0$, for all α. This example is probably the simplest illustration of what has been called the problem of "plateaus" in on-line learning. This name refers to regions in the learning curve $\varepsilon(\alpha)$ which are essentially flat. The fact that these plateaus are not infinitely long in real applications has to do with finite size effects. Indeed, remember that (9.66) is the result obtained in the thermodynamic limit. On the other hand, $R = 0$ is an unstable fixed point, and hence any small initial deviation will be amplified. In systems of finite dimension N small fluctuations of order $1/\sqrt{N}$ are to be expected. One can therefore argue that the length of these plateaus scales as $\ln N$ (see also problem 9.16). For a more detailed analysis, one needs to calculate the finite size corrections to the equation obeyed by R, see [136].

Having explained the escape from the marginal fixed point, we can turn to the asymptotic behaviour for $\alpha \to \infty$. From (9.66), one finds $R(\alpha) \sim 1 - (1 + a)/(2a^2\alpha)$, which is *identical* to the result from off-line learning, cf. (8.36). In other words, on-line learning is as efficient as off-line learning for α asymptotically large (provided of course one has escaped from the $R = 0$ fixed point).

We now turn to a more general discussion, which will establish the conditions under which the specific features observed in the Gaussian scenario will appear. The asymptotic properties of $R(\alpha)$ for α small and α large may be extracted directly from (9.65). The calculations are akin to those for the off-line case, because the off-line and on-line formulas resemble each other, cf. (8.33) and (9.65) respectively.

For small α with $R \approx 0$ the r.h.s. of (9.65) converges to $\langle h^2 \rangle$, and hence $R \sim \sqrt{\langle h^2 \rangle \alpha}$, which is identical to Hebb and off-line Bayes learning. For $\langle h \rangle = 0$ however one concludes $R(\alpha = 0) = 0$ and therefore we find $R(\alpha) = 0$ for all α. The appearance of a plateau is thus not restricted to the Gaussian distribution: any kind of on-line learning from scratch is impossible for a distribution that possesses the symmetry $\langle h \rangle = 0$. For an example derived from a supervised learning scenario, see problem 9.14.

For the large α result, one finds from (9.65)

$$R(\alpha) \approx 1 - \left[2\alpha \int \left[\frac{dV^*(h)}{dh} \right]^2 P^*(h)\, dh \right]^{-1} \tag{9.67}$$

provided the integral in the r.h.s. of (9.67) converges. This result harbours a number of surprises. First, (9.67) is identical to the off-line Bayes result, cf. (8.37)! Hence, the observation made in the Gaussian case that on-line learning performs asymptotically as well as off-line learning appears to be quite general. But how can this observation be reconciled with the results that we derived in, for example, section 9.3 for supervised learning, where it was found that off-line learning needs only half as many examples asymptotically? Furthermore, we note that the $1/\alpha$ approach of R to 1, observed in (9.67), translates for supervised problems into a rather slow decay of the generalization error as $\varepsilon \sim \alpha^{-1/2}$, in contrast to the $1/\alpha$ decay reported before. The point is that supervised learning scenarios that are characterized by a sharp decision boundary in the classification lead to a potential V^* with a singular derivative, invalidating the above asymptotic analysis. As a notable exception we cite the case of a teacher with noisy weights discussed in chapter 5, cf. (8.13). The resulting blurring of the decision boundary makes the recognition of such a teacher indeed more difficult, with an $\varepsilon \sim \alpha^{-1/2}$ behaviour as a result, cf. section 5.4 and problem 8.5.

To make the connection with the supervised learning scenarios, we now turn to the case of a singular derivative $dV^*(h)/dh$. For simplicity, we restrict ourselves to the special case that $P^*(h) = 0$ for $h < h_0$ while $P^*(h)$ jumps to a finite value $\Delta P^* > 0$ at $h = h_0$ and is smooth for $h > h_0$. After some algebra one concludes from (9.65) that the leading order asymptotics is now given by

$$R(\alpha) = 1 - 4\pi \left(\alpha \, \Delta P^* \int Dt \, \frac{e^{-t^2/2}}{H(t)} \right)^{-2}. \tag{9.68}$$

The α^{-2} approach of R to 1 agrees with the familiar $1/\alpha$ decay of the generalization error. More precisely, we see by comparison of (9.68) with (8.38) that Bayes off-line uses the examples "twice as efficiently" as the optimal on-line rule discussed here, $R^{\text{off-line}}(\alpha) = R^{\text{on-line}}(2\alpha)$. This corroborates and generalizes the observation made in section 9.3 for the specific student–teacher perceptron scenario.

Since problems characterized by a smooth distribution are more difficult to learn than those with a sharp decision boundary, one could argue that the asymptotic difference between on-line and off-line Bayes becomes more pronounced as the learning task becomes easier. This point of view is confirmed by the study of an even more singular distribution, namely one with a delta peak, e.g. $P^*(h) = \delta(h - h_0)$. Off-line Bayes now reaches $R = 1$ at the finite value $\alpha = 1$, while the approach of R to 1 is only exponential in the limit $\alpha \to \infty$ for on-line learning (cf. problem 9.17).

9.7 The natural gradient

The efficiency of on-line learning as discussed in the previous sections is quite astonishing. We therefore finally discuss a rather surprising connection between this performance and a geometric approach to statistics.

We follow the Bayesian point of view and consider the learning process as a continual reshaping of the probability distribution for the parameters $\mathbf{J}$. The main observation is then that the gradient descent performed in the space of couplings $\mathbf{J}$ is most efficient for the learning process if it reduces the *distance* between the actual and the desired probability distribution of the couplings as much as possible. It turns out that this cannot be realized in general by measuring distances in $\mathbf{J}$-space using the Euclidean metric $|\mathbf{J}|^2 = \sum_i J_i^2$ but that one has to use the more general concept of a Riemannian metric

$$d\mathbf{J}^2 = \sum_{i,j} g_{ij}(\mathbf{J}) \, dJ_i \, dJ_j \tag{9.69}$$

with a metric tensor g_{ij} depending on the location $\mathbf{J}$ [137]. Moreover, there appears to be only one metric which satisfies the fundamental requirement of invariance under a change of the $\mathbf{J}$ variables, namely the so-called *Fisher matrix*

$$g_{ij}(\mathbf{J}) = \left\langle \frac{\partial \ln P_{\mathbf{J}}}{\partial J_i} \frac{\partial \ln P_{\mathbf{J}}}{\partial J_j} \right\rangle, \tag{9.70}$$

where the average is with respect to $P_{\mathbf{J}}$ itself.

Consider once again a function $V(\mathbf{J})$ and let us ask for the direction of steepest descent. This is the direction $d\mathbf{J}$ such that the decrease $V(\mathbf{J} + d\mathbf{J}) - V(\mathbf{J}) \approx d\mathbf{J} \cdot \nabla V(\mathbf{J})$ is maximal for a fixed value of $d\mathbf{J}^2$, given by (9.69). Introducing a Lagrange multiplier, it is straightforward to show that the direction of steepest descent is $-\mathbf{g}^{-1} \cdot \nabla V =: -\widetilde{\nabla} V$. For the metric (9.70) this direction is called the *natural gradient* [137].

In this perspective, stochastic gradient descent (9.1), (9.13) is replaced by

$$\mathbf{J}^{\mu+1} = \mathbf{J}^\mu - \frac{\eta}{\sqrt{N}} \widetilde{\nabla} V = \mathbf{J}^\mu + \frac{1}{\sqrt{N}} F^\mu \mathbf{g}^{-1}(\mathbf{J}^\mu) \boldsymbol{\xi}^\mu. \tag{9.71}$$

The advantage of this formulation is its independence of the choice of variables: the learning process is such that it moves the probability distribution for the unknown parameters closer to their true distribution, whatever parameterization is being used.

In section 10.5, we will come back to the performance of the natural gradient on-line learning rule and compare it with the so-called Cramér–Rao bound. It will be concluded that the natural gradient is optimal for smooth distributions in the limit of large α. In this way, the remarkable observation made in this chapter that optimal on-line learning can actually saturate the optimal off-line performance for $\alpha \to \infty$ receives a much broader basis for the case of smooth distributions.

9.8 Discussion

Apart from the practical interest and biological relevance of on-line learning, its theoretical description as presented in this chapter reveals two other major bonuses of this type of learning. The first is that the analysis of on-line learning appears to be much less technically involved than that of its off-line analogue. Its basic properties are, at least in the thermodynamic limit, described by a set of ordinary differential equations. The second bonus is that on-line learning can perform surprisingly well when compared with the computationally much more demanding off-line schemes. The optimal performances are in fact identical for small training sets (small α), and the asymptotic optimal performances for large training sets ($\alpha \to \infty$) are also identical if the problem under consideration is "difficult", e.g. if it is characterized by a smooth distribution of inputs. For "easier" problems such as the supervised teacher–student perceptron scenario, on-line learning needs asymptotically twice as many learning examples to reach the same performance as off-line learning.

The theoretical analysis also highlights two other important features of the on-line procedure, namely the crucial role of the learning rate η and the appearance of plateaus. Both effects are determined by the structure of the fixed points, attractors and repellors, of the order parameter dynamics. To speed up the learning process, an adequately large η is needed. But beyond a critical value $\eta > \eta_c$, the attractor corresponding to the correct or optimal solution (e.g. the teacher synaptic vector) may disappear, and perfect learning is no longer possible. The problem of plateaus on the other hand is related to the existence of saddle points, which in turn are due to symmetries in the underlying problem or in the architecture. The dynamics has to escape from these fixed points along their unstable manifold. This however may take a very long time because typical initial conditions lie very close to, and in the thermodynamic limit in fact on top of, the stable manifolds. As a result, one observes plateaus in the learning curve. We have encountered a similar feature in off-line learning under the name of retarded learning. But remember that off-line learning presents, in this respect at least, a definite advantage over on-line learning, since we found that, beyond a critical value $\alpha > \alpha_c$, one can, when using a proper learning rule, escape from the symmetry-induced paralysis. In on-line learning on the other hand, the escape from the stable manifold of the saddles is a finite size effect, so that, strictly speaking, on-line learning may completely fail to learn in the thermodynamic limit.

We finally mention that we will return to on-line learning in multilayer architectures in chapter 13, where its relative technical simplicity and its connection to real applications provide a supplementary stimulus for its analysis.

We end with a brief review of the literature. The possibility of a description in terms of ordinary differential equations was first observed in [135]. Soon afterwards, the (at that time) surprising result that the optimal asymptotic performance of on-line learning is the same (modulo a factor 2 in the size of the training set) as for off-line, was recognized in [138]. On-line learning for the perceptron and adatron rules was discussed in [139]. For a detailed analysis of the role of the learning rate, see [140]. On-line learning is quite efficient in dealing with problems that change with time; for examples see [141, 142]. Query learning was first considered in [135], and the exponential decay of the generalization error in an optimal on-line scenario was derived in [143]. The method of studying off-line learning from queries was developed in [144], and query by committee was introduced and analysed in [35]. For a discussion of on-line learning of an unlearnable rule, see [145]. On-line learning for the unsupervised scenario was discussed in [136, 112, 146], and the fact that the asymptotic performances of on- and off-line learning are identical for smooth problems is described in [137, 146, 147]. Numerical evidence that the natural gradient tends to avoid plateaus can be found in [148]. For a more recent review of several on-line learning algorithms and a discussion of more complicated dynamical effects, see [149]. For the analysis of an on-line algorithm which can be applied to a non-smooth cost function, see [150]. Regarding problems with discrete degrees of freedom, it has been proved that on-line learning is impossible if one forces the rule to operate with a finite number of discrete states [151]. Fluctuations are important for the escape from the symmetric plateaus. An early study of the fluctuations appearing in the finite N case can be found in [136].

9.9 Problems

9.1 Show that

$$\langle \theta(-tu) \rangle = \frac{1}{\pi} \arccos \frac{\rho}{\sqrt{Q}}, \tag{9.72}$$

$$\langle t\theta(-tu)\, \mathrm{sgn}\ u \rangle = \frac{\rho - \sqrt{Q}}{\sqrt{2\pi}}, \tag{9.73}$$

$$\langle \theta(-tu)|u| \rangle = \frac{\sqrt{Q} - \rho}{\sqrt{2\pi Q}}, \tag{9.74}$$

where the average is with respect to the Gaussian correlated variables obeying (9.15), and reproduce the results (9.20) and (9.21).

9.2 Repeat the calculations for the perceptron algorithm with stability κ,

$$V(t) = -(t - \kappa)\theta(-(t - \kappa)).$$

Show that for $\kappa > 0$, the asymptotic behaviour of the generalization error is (cf. (9.22))

$$\varepsilon(\alpha) \sim \sqrt{\frac{\frac{1}{2} - H(\kappa)}{(1 - e^{-\kappa^2})\pi\alpha}}.$$

9.3 Consider adatron learning with $\eta = 2$. Show that for this choice of the learning rate, the normalization of the **J**-vector is automatically preserved (i.e. $dQ/d\alpha = 0$).

9.4 The results (9.9) and (9.11) are also valid for the case of a general α-dependent rate $\eta = \eta(\alpha)$ in F, cf. (9.8). Consider on-line perceptron learning. Show that the asymptotically optimal choice

$$\eta_{\text{opt}}(\alpha) \sim \frac{2\sqrt{2\pi Q}}{\alpha} \tag{9.75}$$

leads to a correspondingly fast decrease of the generalization error

$$\varepsilon(\alpha) \sim \frac{4}{\pi\alpha}. \tag{9.76}$$

(Hint: Choose $\eta(\alpha) = K(\alpha)\sqrt{Q(\alpha)}$, which leads to a closed equation in R; then optimize with respect to $K(\alpha)$).

9.5 Repeat the calculations for on-line adatron learning with an optimized learning rate $\eta_{\text{opt}}(\alpha)$. Show that $\lim_{\alpha \to \infty} \eta_{\text{opt}}(\alpha) = 3/2$, with $\varepsilon \sim 4/3\alpha$, just as for a constant (optimal) learning rate. Surprisingly, the on-line perceptron rule with optimized learning rate performs asymptotically better than the adatron rule, cf. problem 9.4 (for more details, see [149]).

9.6 The fixed point solutions for adatron learning are the solutions of the following equation, cf. (9.23):

$$\eta\left(R \arccos R - R^2\sqrt{1 - R^2}\right) = 2(1 - R^2)^{3/2}.$$

Show that there is a bifurcation at $\eta_c = 3$, with the appearance of a second solution $R < 1$ for $\eta > \eta_c$. Prove its stability.

9.7 Replace the on-line learning rule (9.1) by

$$\mathbf{J}^{\mu+1} = \frac{\sqrt{N}}{\sqrt{(\mathbf{J}^\mu + \frac{1}{\sqrt{N}}F^\mu)^2}}\left(\mathbf{J}^\mu + \frac{1}{\sqrt{N}}F^\mu\xi^\mu\right), \tag{9.77}$$

which has the advantage of preserving the normalization $|\mathbf{J}^\mu|^2 = N$, so that one directly obtains a closed equation for the overlap R. Reproduce the result (9.34) for the optimal choice of F. In general the results produced by the above norm-preserving learning rule are not identical to those obtained from (9.1). Indeed, with (9.1) the contribution of a new example will be larger or smaller than with (9.77) depending on whether the size of $\mathbf{J}$ happens to be small or large, respectively. Hence the dynamics of the size of $\mathbf{J}$ as a function of α in (9.1) corresponds in fact to a self-regulated annealing of the learning rate.

9.8 Show that for optimal on-line learning the evolution equation for Q reads

$$\frac{d\sqrt{Q}}{d\alpha} = \frac{\langle F_{\text{opt}}^2 \rangle}{2\sqrt{Q}}. \tag{9.78}$$

By comparison with the equation (9.29) for R one concludes that R and $\sqrt{Q}$ coincide if their initial conditions are the same.

9.9 Consider gradient descent in a quadratic potential $V(y) = y^2/2$,

$$\frac{dy}{d\alpha} = -\eta V'(y) = -\eta y, \tag{9.79}$$

and adopt the discretized approximation

$$y^{\mu+1} - y^\mu = -\eta y^\mu. \tag{9.80}$$

Show that $y = 0$ is a stable fixed point for $\eta < \eta_c = 2$, but loses its stability for $\eta > \eta_c$.

9.10 Investigate off-line learning from queries for the high–low game introduced in problem 1.4 and show that the generalization error decays exponentially with the training set size α. What is the information gain per example?

9.11 The probability distribution for queries in perceptron learning should quite generally be of the form

$$P(\xi) = \frac{1}{(2\pi)^{N/2}} \exp\left(-\frac{\xi^2}{2}\right) f\left(\frac{\mathbf{J}\xi}{\sqrt{QN}}\right) \tag{9.81}$$

with $\int Dt f(t) = 1$. Show that the evolution equation for the overlap $R(\alpha)$ using the optimal potential introduced in section 9.3 is then given by

$$\frac{dR}{d\alpha} = \frac{1}{4\pi} \frac{1 - R^2}{R} \int Dt f(t) \exp\left(-\frac{R^2 t}{1 - R^2}\right)$$

$$\times \left[\frac{1}{H(Rt/\sqrt{1 - R^2})} + \frac{1}{H(-Rt/\sqrt{1 - R^2})}\right]. \tag{9.82}$$

Verify by a variational argument that the choice $f(t) = \sqrt{2\pi}\,\delta(t)$ used in section 9.5 in fact maximizes $dR/d\alpha$ and is hence the best selection criterion for queries in optimal perceptron learning.

9.12 On several occasions in previous chapters we have argued that an example $\boldsymbol{\xi}$ drawn at random and independently of a coupling vector $\mathbf{J}$ is for $N \to \infty$ orthogonal to $\mathbf{J}$ with probability 1. So what is the difference between queries fulfilling $\mathbf{J}\boldsymbol{\xi} = 0$ and ordinary examples?

9.13 Apply the result for unsupervised on-line learning, (9.65), to the case of a teacher with output noise.

9.14 Consider the unsupervised version of the student reversed wedge perceptron learning from a teacher reversed wedge perceptron, cf. (8.14). Derive the evolution equation for optimal on-line learning. Explain the existence of an unstable fixed point at $R = 0$ for the width of the wedge given by $\gamma = \sqrt{2\ln 2}$.

9.15 Using the techniques of appendix 1, verify that

$$P(t|h) = \mathcal{N} \int d\boldsymbol{\xi} \int d\mathbf{J}\, P(\boldsymbol{\xi}|\mathbf{B})\, \delta(\mathbf{J}^2 - N)\delta(\mathbf{J}\mathbf{B} - NR)$$

$$\times \delta\left(\frac{\mathbf{B}\boldsymbol{\xi}}{\sqrt{N}} - h\right)\delta\left(\frac{\mathbf{J}\boldsymbol{\xi}}{\sqrt{N}} - t\right)$$

$$= \frac{1}{\sqrt{2\pi(1 - R^2)}}\exp\left(-\frac{(t - hR)^2}{2(1 - R^2)}\right) \tag{9.83}$$

where $\mathcal{N}$ is a normalization constant ensuring $\int P(t|h)\,dt = 1$.

9.16 Consider equation (9.66) describing on-line learning from a Gaussian distribution in the limit $R \to 0$,

$$\frac{dR}{d\alpha} = \frac{a^2 R}{2(1 + a)^2}. \tag{9.84}$$

To model the finite size effects take the initial condition $R(0)$ to be a Gaussian random variable with average equal to 0 and second moment proportional to N^{-1}. This implies that the statistics of the length of the initial plateau scales as $\alpha \sim (1+a)^2 \ln N/a^2$. Perform simulations for unsupervised Hebb learning ($F^\mu = \eta$) from a Gaussian distribution for N finite and verify whether this provides a good approximation.

9.17 Consider an example distribution with a delta function singularity, $P^*(h) = \delta(h - h_0)$. Show that the evolution equation for the overlap in optimal on-line learning is given by

$$\frac{dR^2}{d\alpha} = (1 - R^2)\left(R^2 + h_0^2(1 - R^2)\right),\tag{9.85}$$

and that consequently the approach of R to 1 is exponential in the limit $\alpha \to \infty$. Show that off-line Bayes learning reaches $R = 1$ at the finite value $\alpha = 1$.

9.18 Consider Hebb learning of a student perceptron from a teacher perceptron using examples generated from a non-uniform distribution. Show that in order to achieve a zero asymptotic generalization error the teacher has to be an eigenvector of the covariance matrix of the examples, see e.g. [152].

10

Making Contact with Statistics

The generalization problem is a variant of the basic problem in (mathematical) statistics: fitting the parameter values of a model on the basis of a training set with the aim of achieving good prediction on new examples. In this setting, neural networks are just a fancy type of non-linear parametric estimation, with the synaptic vector $\mathbf{J}$ as the basic set of parameters which have to be estimated. Yet statistics and statistical mechanics differ widely both in general philosophy and the tool box available. In this chapter, we will review two important results from statistics, namely the Vapnik–Chervonenkis bound and the Cramér–Rao inequality, and compare them with results obtained from statistical mechanics.

10.1 Convergence of frequencies to probabilities

In the introductory chapter 1 we mentioned the relation between the problem of generalization and one of the building blocks of statistics, namely the convergence of frequencies to probabilities. In this chapter we will further clarify and quantify this issue. We start by reformulating the convergence of frequencies to probabilities in a setting that makes its relation to the learning problem particularly clear. Consider functions f, defined on a domain Ω, and taking the values $+1$ or -1

$$
\begin{aligned}
f : \quad & \Omega \to \{+1, -1\} \\
& \boldsymbol{\xi} \to f(\boldsymbol{\xi}).
\end{aligned}
$$

(10.1)

These functions provide all possible binary classifications of the example space Ω. We select one of these functions, say the function f_T, as the so-called teacher function. In the context of learning, we are interested in the "error" probability ε_f, defined as the probability that f and f_T give a different classification for a randomly chosen example, $\boldsymbol{\xi} \in \Omega$. This generalization error tells us how well or rather how badly the function f predicts the outputs of the teacher f_T.

To evaluate ε_f, it is quite natural to *test* the function f on a set of p examples. Indeed, one expects that the frequency of errors v_f^p observed on this sample will be close to the error probability ε_f when the size of the test set is large enough. This is the first basic link between generalization and statistics: quantifying the convergence of the frequency of wrong answers to the actual error probability.

In fact, to evaluate the quantity ε_f for a *particular* function f without an exhaustive comparison over all the possible input patterns, we can invoke the law of large numbers to conclude that the observed error frequency v_f^p converges to the true probability ε_f in the limit of an infinite number of independent trials, $p \to \infty$. The Hoeffding inequality [153] gives an idea of how fast this convergence takes place with increasing test size p:

$$\text{Prob}\big(|v_f^p - \varepsilon_f| > \delta\big) \leq 2e^{-2\delta^2 p}. \tag{10.2}$$

Roughly speaking, one concludes that the convergence of frequency to probability goes as $1/\sqrt{p}$, which is actually the familiar type of convergence associated with the central limit theorem.

Apart from assessing the performance of a particular function f, there is a second basic ingredient needed in the context of generalization: one tries to match the outcomes of a teacher f_T by selecting the best possible "student" function f. A natural way to do so is to work with a whole class of candidate functions $\mathcal{F}$, rather than with a single function, and to select a function on the basis of its performance on a given test set. The class of functions under consideration is called the rule or hypothesis space. For example, $\mathcal{F}$ could correspond to the class of functions that can be implemented by a specific neural network architecture.

It is now tempting to invoke the Hoeffding inequality again and to claim that the true and observed probabilities of error for the selected function will be close to each other. This inequality, however, no longer applies, because the examples have been used to *select* f and hence there exist correlations between the test set and the selected function: the test set has in fact become a *training* set, and v_f^p is a training error, which we denoted in the introduction by ε_t. To illustrate the failure of the Hoeffding inequality by a concrete example, consider a rule space which contains all the binary classifications. We select all the functions that match f_T perfectly on a given test set, so that their test or training error is exactly zero. These very same functions however realize all the possible classifications on the other examples, so that there is, in this case, no correlation at all between training error and true error.

The correct way to proceed then is to *bound* the maximum deviation between frequencies and corresponding probabilities for the *whole class* $\mathcal{F}$ of functions or, more precisely, to establish a bound for the probability

$$\text{Prob}\left(\max_{f \in \mathcal{F}} |v_f^p - \varepsilon_f| > \delta\right). \tag{10.3}$$

In doing so we do not select any particular function, and hence we have no problem with the appearance of correlations with the test set. For this reason we may also stick to our notation v_f^p, which has the meaning of a test error rather than a training error ε_t. The price to pay is that we are de facto investigating the *worst possible case*: the bound (10.3) has to apply to every function, in particular to the one that we select, but also to the one for which the convergence is worst.

If the class $\mathcal{F}$ is finite, say it contains F elements, such a bound can easily be derived from the Hoeffding inequality. Indeed, the inequality in (10.3) will be obeyed if it applies to at least one of the functions $f \in \mathcal{F}$. Since the probability of the occurrence of a union of events is at most the sum of the probabilities of each event separately, we conclude that

$$\text{Prob}\left(\max_{f \in \mathcal{F}} |v_f^p - \varepsilon_f| > \delta\right) \le 2Fe^{-2\delta^2 p}, \tag{10.4}$$

and we say that the error frequencies converge *uniformly* to their corresponding error probabilities. As an example, consider the class of functions which can be implemented by a network with N binary weights. A special case is the class of Ising perceptrons discussed in sections 6.3 and 7.2. In this case one can apply the above result with $F = 2^N$. In the limit p and $N \to \infty$, with a fixed value of the ratio $\alpha = p/N$, one concludes that with probability 1, none of the observed frequencies differ from their corresponding error probability by more than the accuracy threshold $\delta_{\text{th}} = \sqrt{\ln 2/(2\alpha)}$. Note that this result is independent of the teacher f_T.

10.2 Sauer's lemma

From the above derivation, it would appear that not much can be said about the uniform convergence of frequencies to probabilities for a class $\mathcal{F}$ of functions with an infinite number of elements. On the other hand, one expects that there exist such classes the "classification diversity" of which is nevertheless very limited. To quantify this classification diversity we consider the number $\Delta(\{\xi^\mu\})$ of different classifications which may be induced by all the functions $f \in \mathcal{F}$ on the example set $\{\xi^1, \ldots, \xi^p\}$. We then define the so-called *growth function*

$$\Delta(p) = \max_{\{\xi^\mu\}} \Delta(\{\xi^\mu\}), \tag{10.5}$$

giving the maximum number of different classifications which can be induced by the functions $f \in \mathcal{F}$ on p examples.

To get a first idea of what this function may look like, consider the class of functions for which at most d input patterns are classified as $+1$. If the number of elements in Ω is infinite, there is an infinite number of such functions. Clearly, every possible classification can be induced when $p \leq d$. On the other hand, for $p > d$ one can only perform all those classifications in which the number of $+1$'s is not larger than d. Consequently one finds

$$\Delta(p) = \begin{cases} 2^p & \text{for } p \leq d \\ \sum_{l=0}^{d} \binom{p}{l} & \text{for } p \geq d. \end{cases} \tag{10.6}$$

An estimate of how the number of classifications is limited for $p > d > 1$ is provided by the following bounds [154]:

$$\sum_{l=0}^{d} \binom{p}{l} \leq 1.5 \frac{p^d}{d!} \leq \left(\frac{ep}{d}\right)^d. \tag{10.7}$$

Therefore, instead of the exponentially large number of classifications 2^p, only a polynomially large number of them is realized for $p > d$.

It was proved by Vapnik and Chervonenkis [168] and independently by Sauer [156] that this behaviour of $\Delta(p)$ is in fact rather general. For every class of functions $\mathcal{F}$, there exists a unique integer number d_{VC}, called the *Vapnik–Chervonenkis (VC) dimension* (which is possibly equal to ∞), such that for $p \leq d_{VC}$, all the 2^p classifications can be implemented (for at least one choice of the p examples), while for $p > d_{VC}$, this is no longer the case. Moreover the above example, with the growth function (10.6), gives the largest number of classifications which may arise for all the cases with a VC dimension $d_{VC} = d$. Consequently, given a knowledge of the VC dimension, one concludes that (cf. equation (10.7))

$$\Delta(p) \begin{cases} = 2^p & \text{for } p \leq d_{VC} \\ \leq \sum_{l=0}^{d_{VC}} \binom{p}{l} \leq \left(\frac{ep}{d_{VC}}\right)^{d_{VC}} & \text{for } p > d_{VC}. \end{cases} \tag{10.8}$$

The proof of this so-called Sauer lemma is very similar in spirit to Cover's derivation of the number of dichotomies for hyperplanes, cf. section 6.2, with the missing classifications for $p > d_{VC}$ arising by a cascade effect starting from a single missing classification at $p = d_{VC} + 1$ [156].

The VC dimension is thus a way to identify classes of functions with a limited scheme of classifications. Several classes of interest with a finite VC dimension have been identified: rectangles and half-planes (equivalent to perceptrons without threshold) in R^N, Boolean functions, general neural networks and so on [157, 158]. The effect of the limitation in classification diversity expressed by (10.8) on the generalization ability is quantified by the following theorem.

10.3 The Vapnik–Chervonenkis theorem

For classes with a finite VC dimension, Vapnik and Chervonenkis [168] were able to derive an upper bound for the probability that any of the frequencies v_f^p differs by more than δ from its corresponding "true" frequency ε_f, for all $f \in \mathcal{F}$. Their original bound was subsequently refined by several authors [155, 159, 160] to

$$\text{Prob}\left(\max_{f \in \mathcal{F}} |v_f^p - \varepsilon_f| > \delta\right) \le c_1 \, \Delta(2p) \, e^{-\delta^2 p} \tag{10.9}$$

with $c_1 = 6e^{2\delta}$. The proof of this result can be found in appendix 7. By comparing the VC bounds (10.9) and the Hoeffding inequality (10.4) we note that the proportionality factor $\Delta(2p)$ plays the role of the effective number of elements in the class.

In the case of a class of functions with finite VC dimension, the prefactor $\Delta(p)$ only grows like a power of p for $p > d_{\text{VC}}$, and we again conclude that the differences between the observed frequencies v_f^p and the probabilities ε_f will shrink uniformly as $p \to \infty$. This is nicely illustrated by applying the inequality (10.8) for the growth function and introducing the variable $\alpha = p/d_{\text{VC}}$ (for $\alpha > 1$):

$$\text{Prob}\left(\max_{f \in \mathcal{F}} |v_f^p - \varepsilon_f| > \delta\right) \le c_1 \exp\left(-d_{\text{VC}}(\alpha\delta^2 - \ln(2\alpha) - 1)\right). \tag{10.10}$$

In many applications, and particularly those considered in the statistical mechanics literature, the regime of interest is the analogue of a thermodynamic limit in which $d_{\text{VC}} \to \infty$. In that case the right hand side of (10.10) has a threshold behaviour that depends on the accuracy δ. There is an accuracy threshold

$$\delta_{\text{th}}(\alpha) = \sqrt{(\ln(2\alpha) + 1)/\alpha} \tag{10.11}$$

above which the right hand side of (10.10) vanishes in the thermodynamic limit. Therefore, with probability 1 all the error probabilities ε_f lie in an interval of radius $\delta_{\text{th}}(\alpha)$ centred at the corresponding frequency v_f^p over a test sample of size $p = \alpha d_{\text{VC}}$. The above bound can be made sharper by some combinatorial tricks [160] leading to a threshold $\delta_{\text{th}}(\alpha) = \sqrt{\ln \alpha/(2\alpha)}$.

There is an interesting variant of the Vapnik–Chervonenkis theorem for the case of a learnable rule. The Hoeffding inequality gives a bound which is independent of the observed frequency of error ε_f. However, in the context of generalization, one is particularly interested in the convergence properties for the case in which the observed frequencies are close to zero. In particular, for learnable problems, one may focus on student functions from the version space, i.e. on those making no mistake at all on the test set. As we will see, one can obtain much sharper bounds for this situation.

Let us start by noting that the Hoeffding inequality may be replaced by a sharper bound. The probability that the observed frequency v_f for a given function f is found to be equal to 0 while the true error ε is larger than δ, can be bounded as follows:

$$\text{Prob}\left(v_f^p = 0 \text{ and } \varepsilon_f > \delta\right) = \int_\delta^1 d\varepsilon_f \, P(\varepsilon_f)\,(1 - \varepsilon_f)^p \le (1 - \delta)^p \le e^{-\delta p},$$

(10.12)

where $P(\varepsilon_f)$ is the probability that the true error is equal to ε_f. We see that ε_f now decreases roughly as $1/p$ to be compared with the $1/\sqrt{p}$ behaviour observed in the Hoeffding inequality (10.2).

Consider now the version space $\mathcal{F}_p^* = \{f \,|\, f \in \mathcal{F} \text{ and } v_f^p = 0\}$ formed by all functions that score perfectly on the p training examples. We will assume that this class is not empty, i.e. we are considering the case of a learnable rule. The following improved VC bound can be derived by essentially the same argument as that used in the original VC proof

$$\text{Prob}\left(\max_{f \in \mathcal{F}_p^*} \varepsilon_f > \delta\right) \le 4\,\Delta(2p)\,2^{-\delta p}.$$

(10.13)

Note the important improvement over the VC theorem (10.9), with a factor δ rather than δ^2 in the exponent of the right hand side of the inequality. Considering again the thermodynamic limit $p \to \infty$ and $d_{\text{VC}} \to \infty$ with a fixed value of the ratio $\alpha = p/d_{\text{VC}}$ we conclude that (for $\alpha > 1$) the accuracy threshold is given by

$$\delta_{\text{th}}(\alpha) = \frac{1 + \ln(2\alpha)}{\alpha \ln 2}.$$

(10.14)

By a more refined argument and replacing the upper bound by the exact asymptotic expression for the combinatorial sum appearing in (10.7), the accuracy threshold may be further improved to [161]

$$\delta_{\text{th}}(\alpha) = \frac{2\alpha \ln(2\alpha) - (2\alpha - 1)\ln(2\alpha - 1)}{\alpha \ln 2} =: \varepsilon^{\text{VC}}(\alpha).$$

(10.15)

We conclude that all the error probabilities ε_f of the compatible students are smaller than $\varepsilon^{\text{VC}}(\alpha)$ with probability 1 in the thermodynamic limit.

Since the VC dimension characterizes the classification diversity of a hypothesis class $\mathcal{F}$, we expect that it must also be related to the storage capacity of the classifiers under consideration. In fact, it is not difficult to prove from the Sauer lemma (10.8) that the storage capacity $\alpha_c = p_c/d_{VC}$, where p_c is the maximum number of random examples that can be correctly stored, must be smaller than 2 (cf. problem 10.5). The appearance of the VC dimension in the problems of both storage and generalization points to an interesting relation between them. If a class of classifiers is confronted with an example set of size much smaller than its VC dimension it can reproduce the set without exploiting possible correlations coded in the classifications. In this region the system works as a pure memory and the generalization ability is rather poor. If, on the other hand, the size of the training set is much larger than the VC dimension the system is well above its storage capacity and has in general no chance to implement all the classifications. The only way to nevertheless reproduce the whole training set is to exploit all the possible correlations coming from the fact that the training set classifications were produced by a teacher function. In this way an alignment between teacher and student builds up which results in an appreciable generalization ability. In this sense *generalization sets in where memorization ends*. A system that can implement all possible classifications is a perfect storage device and (for this very reason!) fails completely to generalize. On the other hand a system with very small VC dimension can only store very few items but generalizes rather quickly (of course only to one of the few classifications it is able to realize). This highlights the trade-off always present in the modelling of data: a complicated model will be able to reproduce all the features but needs large data sets for sufficient generalization. A simple model will quickly generalize but may be unable to reproduce the data, so that the problem becomes unrealizable. The best model is hence the simplest one that can reproduce all the data, a principle sometimes referred to as *Occam's razor*.

10.4 Comparison with statistical mechanics

The VC bounds derived above are very general and consequently it is not known how tight they are in special situations. It is hence tempting to test them against explicit results obtained by statistical mechanics for the specific scenario of a student perceptron learning from a teacher perceptron. As we have argued before, statistical mechanics is designed to study typical properties rather than worst case situations. However, as we will see, it is also possible to analyse *partial* worst case scenarios and to extract in this way information on some "typical worst case".

As an example we will analyse the generalization error of the *worst* student from the version space. This corresponds to a partial worst case analysis since we do not include the worst possible teacher and the worst possible distribution of the examples. Instead we will use our standard distribution (1.5) for the examples and

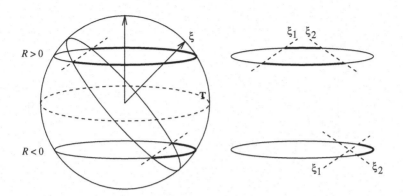

Fig. 10.1. Left: Three-dimensional sketch of the student space. Two rings corresponding to fixed overlaps $R > 0$ and $R < 0$ with the teacher **T** are shown. If a pattern ξ is added to the training set, the plane perpendicular to it cuts away that part of the rings not compatible with the teacher classification. Right: Two patterns leave always a connected part of the ring if $R < 0$. For $R > 0$, however, it is possible that the part of the ring belonging to the version space is disconnected. This gives rise to replica symmetry breaking for $R > 0$.

average over the teacher distribution as before, in this way characterizing what may be called the "typical worst student".

The calculation is rather similar to the one performed in section 2.3 to determine the generalization behaviour of the typical compatible student. There we found that the version space can be decomposed into slices of constant overlap R with the teacher, that students with $R = q$ exponentially dominate in number, and therefore display the typical generalization ability. The worst student, on the other hand, is determined by the *smallest* value $R_{\min}$ of R for which the corresponding slice of the version space is still not empty (cf. fig. 10.1). This slice can be identified from the fact that the corresponding value of the self-overlap q should go to 1. Considering the limit $q \to 1$ in the saddle point equation (A2.34) for q we find to leading order

$$1 - R_{\min}^2 = 2\alpha \int_0^\infty Dt\, H\left(\frac{R_{\min}t}{\sqrt{1 - R_{\min}^2}}\right)t^2, \tag{10.16}$$

and performing the integration we finally obtain the following equation determining $R_{\min}$:

$$1 - R_{\min}^2 = \frac{\alpha}{\pi}\left(\arccos R_{\min} - R_{\min}\sqrt{1 - R_{\min}^2}\right). \tag{10.17}$$

The numerical solution of this equation is shown in fig. 10.2. It reflects the expected behaviour $R_{\min}(\alpha = 0) = -1$ and $R_{\min} \to 1$ for $\alpha \to \infty$. Moreover the result $R_{\min}(\alpha = 2) = 0$ illustrates the fact that beyond the storage limit, which is $\alpha_c = 2$ in this case, the perceptron really needs the rule behind the examples in

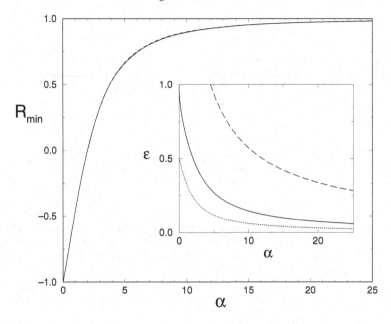

Fig. 10.2. Overlap R_{min} of the worst student in the version space as a function of the training set size α in replica symmetry (full line) and one-step replica symmetry breaking (dotted line). The corrections are only minimal. The inset shows the generalization error of the worst student in the version space (full) together with that of the typical student (dotted) and the upper bound $\varepsilon^{\mathrm{VC}}$ (dashed) resulting from the VC theorem.

order to stay in the version space. Whereas for $\alpha = \alpha_c$ the worst student can still reproduce the examples by treating them as random classifications ($R = 0$), for larger values of α a correlation with the teacher ($R > 0$) is indispensable to score perfectly on all the examples.

In the inset of fig. 10.2, we also show the resulting dependence of the generalization error of the worst student $\varepsilon^{\mathrm{ws}}(\alpha) = \arccos(R_{\mathrm{min}}(\alpha))/\pi$, together with the result $\varepsilon(\alpha)$ for the typical student as resulting from (2.42) and the threshold $\varepsilon^{\mathrm{VC}}(\alpha)$ predicted by the VC bound, cf. (10.15). For all α we have $\varepsilon \leq \varepsilon^{\mathrm{ws}} \leq \varepsilon^{\mathrm{VC}}$ as it should be. For large α one finds from (10.17) that $\varepsilon^{\mathrm{ws}} \sim 3/(2\alpha)$, to be compared with $\varepsilon^{\mathrm{VC}} \sim \ln\alpha/\alpha$ and $\varepsilon \sim 0.625/\alpha$.

We conclude that the VC bound for perceptrons trained by a teacher perceptron overestimates the worst case performance by a factor $\ln\alpha$ for large α. In fact the "typical worst case performance" of a student in the version space has the same asymptotic $1/\alpha$ decay of the generalization error as the typical student, albeit with a somewhat larger prefactor. One might hence speculate that in learnable situations the worst case bound of the VC theorem is over-pessimistic. However, this is not the case, as can be illustrated by the simple learning scenario presented in problem

10.10: the VC bound is found to be saturated when the worst possible teacher is considered.

The above results rely on the assumption of replica symmetry. On the other hand, a simple geometric argument shows that the part of the rim $R = \mathbf{JT}/N$ belonging to the version space is always connected for $R < 0$ only. For $R > 0$ it may be cut in separate pieces leading to a disconnected set (cf. fig. 10.1). This insight suggests that replica symmetry may be broken when $R_{\min} \geq 0$, i.e. for $\alpha \geq 2$. Testing the stability of the replica symmetric solution to transversal fluctuations in replica space along the lines of appendix 4 one indeed finds an instability for $\alpha \geq \alpha_{AT}$ with α_{AT} given by $\varepsilon^{ws}(\alpha_{AT}) = 1/\alpha_{AT}$, i.e. $\alpha_{AT} = 2$, in agreement with the geometric argument. A one-step replica symmetry-breaking calculation for $\alpha > \alpha_{AT}$ reveals that the corrections to ε^{ws} are very small for all α. In particular the asymptotic behaviour $\varepsilon^{ws} \sim 3/(2\alpha)$ for large α remains unchanged [162].

The above analysis of a partial worst case scenario narrows the gap between the concepts of statistical mechanics and mathematical learning theory. Interestingly, it is also possible to move in the other direction and to apply methods from mathematical statistics to questions typical of statistical mechanics. As example we briefly discuss an upper bound for the generalization error of the *typical* student derived from the VC theory [163].

Consider again the division of the version space corresponding to p examples into two parts of relative size P and $1 - P$ by example $\boldsymbol{\xi}^{(p+1)}$ as shown in fig. 3.1. Similarly to (3.32) we may note that the generalization error of the typical compatible student is always smaller than half the average information gain (cf. problem 2.9):

$$\varepsilon_{\text{Gibbs}}(\alpha) = 2P(1 - P) \leq \frac{1}{2}(-P \log_2 P - (1 - P)\log_2(1 - P)) = \frac{1}{2}\Delta I(\alpha).$$

$$(10.18)$$

Summing up all these inequalities with $0 < p < \alpha d_{VC}$ we find that the *cumulative* Gibbs error

$$\frac{1}{d_{VC}} \sum_{p=1}^{\alpha d_{VC}} \varepsilon_{\text{Gibbs}} \sim \int_0^\alpha d\alpha' \varepsilon(\alpha') \qquad (10.19)$$

is bounded by the *total* information gain, which in turn is bounded by $\log_2 \Delta(\alpha d_{VC})$ corresponding to the case that all the $\Delta(\alpha d_{VC})$ possible classifications are equally probable. On the other hand from (10.8) it follows that for $\alpha > 1$ the logarithm of the growth function behaves like $\log_2 \Delta(\alpha d_{VC}) \sim (1 + \ln \alpha)$, which together with (10.19) suggests that $\varepsilon \lesssim 1/\alpha$ for large α. Using more refined techniques [163] one can indeed show rigorously that

$$\varepsilon_{\text{Gibbs}}(\alpha) \leq \frac{2}{\alpha} \tag{10.20}$$

asymptotically for large α. Note that this bound is rather tight in the case of the perceptron, where we have $\varepsilon \sim 0.625/\alpha$. Considering the cumulative error it is hence possible to bound the typical behaviour using results from the worst case analysis.

10.5 The Cramér–Rao inequality

The Vapnik–Chervonenkis theorem and its variations bound the actual performance of the system by that of the worst case. The Cramér–Rao bound gives a complementary picture by comparing the actual performance with the best possible case. To introduce this bound, we first return to the concept of the Fisher information already discussed in section 9.7. Consider a probability distribution $P_\lambda(x)$ which depends on an unknown parameter λ. We would like to quantify how much information is provided about the value of λ, when a sampling x from $P_\lambda(x)$ is made available. As we will argue below, the Fisher information F_λ,

$$F_\lambda = \left\langle \left(\frac{\partial \ln P_\lambda}{\partial \lambda} \right)^2 \right\rangle = \int dx \left(\frac{\partial \ln P_\lambda(x)}{\partial \lambda} \right)^2 P_\lambda(x), \tag{10.21}$$

is an adequate measure. Firstly, it is obviously a positive quantity, $F_\lambda \geq 0$. Secondly, it agrees with the intuitive notion of additivity of information for independent samplings. Indeed let x_1 and x_2 be independent samplings from the probability distributions $P_\lambda^1(x_1)$ and $P_\lambda^2(x_2)$. We denote the corresponding Fisher information by F_λ^1 and F_λ^2 respectively. We can however also consider the vector random variable (x_1, x_2) as a sampling from $P_\lambda(x_1, x_2) = P_\lambda^1(x_1)P_\lambda^2(x_2)$. Its Fisher information is found to be $F_\lambda = F_\lambda^1 + F_\lambda^2$. Note that this additivity can also be applied for p independent samplings $(x_1, x_2, \ldots, x_p)$ from the same distribution $P_\lambda(x)$, the total Fisher information being equal to pF_λ with F_λ the information per sampling.

So far we have not explained why the Fisher information is a good measure of the information provided by a sampling about the value of λ. The argument for this is provided by the Cramér–Rao inequality. Indeed, this inequality gives a bound, expressed in terms of the Fisher information, on how well the parameter λ can be estimated from an observed sample x. Let $y(x)$ be an *unbiased estimator* of λ, meaning that it is a random quantity, depending on x (but not on the unknown λ), with $\langle y(x) \rangle = \lambda$. Defining $\delta y = y - \langle y \rangle$, the Cramér–Rao bound stipulates that

$$\langle \delta y^2 \rangle \geq F_\lambda^{-1}. \tag{10.22}$$

In words: the best unbiased estimate has a mean square error which is at least equal to the reciprocal of the Fisher information. This is in agreement with the intuitive observation that a sampling which conveys a lot of information about the parameter λ allows (in principle) the construction of an estimator with a very small mean square error.

The Cramér–Rao bound is an immediate consequence of the Schwarz inequality since

$$\langle \delta y^2 \rangle \left\langle \left(\frac{\partial \ln P_\lambda}{\partial \lambda} \right)^2 \right\rangle \geq \left\langle \delta y \frac{\partial \ln P_\lambda}{\partial \lambda} \right\rangle^2 = \left(\frac{\partial}{\partial \lambda} \langle y(x) \rangle \right)^2 = 1 \tag{10.23}$$

where the definition of y has been used. Furthermore, it can easily be seen that the bound (10.22) is tight, cf. problem 10.11. In other words, it cannot be improved without further information on P_λ. This however does not, of course, imply that the upper bound is realized in every specific case.

In the context of neural networks, x and λ are typically high dimensional vectors with x corresponding to the examples ξ on the N-sphere for the unsupervised problem, or to the pair (ξ, σ_T) for the supervised problem, and λ playing the role of the symmetry-breaking vector $\mathbf{B}$ or teacher vector $\mathbf{T}$ respectively.

To illustrate the application of the Cramér–Rao bound to a learning problem studied in statistical mechanics, we consider the unsupervised problem of chapter 8. Examples ξ are sampled from a distribution with a single unknown symmetry-breaking direction $\mathbf{B}$. Their distribution may be written in the form $P_\mathbf{B}(\xi) \sim \delta(\xi^2 - N)\exp(-V^*(h))$, with the alignment $h = \mathbf{B}\xi/\sqrt{N}$, cf. (8.3). We start by noting that the $\mathbf{J}$-vectors which were constructed in chapter 8 using various learning rules produce in fact unbiased estimators of $\mathbf{B}$. Indeed they have, in the thermodynamic limit, a self-averaging overlap R with $\mathbf{B}$, while as a result of the rotational symmetry of the pattern distribution around $\mathbf{B}$, their average orientation coincides with that of $\mathbf{B}$. Hence the average of $\mathbf{J}/R$ is exactly equal to $\mathbf{B}$, and $\mathbf{J}/R$ is thus an unbiased estimator of $\mathbf{B}$.

To apply the Cramér–Rao bound to this situation, we need the generalization of (10.22) to the multi-dimensional case, which we quote here without further proof [164]:

$$\left\langle \left(\frac{\mathbf{J}}{R} - \mathbf{B} \right) \left(\frac{\mathbf{J}}{R} - \mathbf{B} \right) \right\rangle \geq \left\langle p \frac{\partial \ln P_\mathbf{B}}{\partial \mathbf{B}} \frac{\partial \ln P_\mathbf{B}}{\partial \mathbf{B}} \right\rangle^{-1}. \tag{10.24}$$

The Cramér–Rao bound is now a matrix inequality: the difference between the matrices from the l.h.s. and r.h.s. respectively should be a positive matrix. The appearance of a factor $1/p$ in the r.h.s. of (10.24) comes from the fact that the unbiased estimator $\mathbf{J}$ was constructed on the basis of $p = \alpha N$ independent samplings of the distribution $P_\mathbf{B}$, so that the corresponding Fisher information is, by additivity, equal to p times that of a single sampling.

The inequality (10.24) is greatly simplified if we take into account the rotational symmetry around $\mathbf{B}$, which implies that the above matrices are diagonal. Indeed one has

$$\frac{\partial \ln P_\mathbf{B}}{\partial B_i} = \frac{\partial \ln P_\mathbf{B}}{\partial h} \frac{\partial h}{\partial B_i} = -\frac{dV^*(h)}{dh} \frac{\xi_i}{\sqrt{N}}. \tag{10.25}$$

Taking into account that $\langle \xi_i \xi_j \rangle = \delta_{ij}$ and $\langle J_i^2 \rangle = 1 - R^2$ along any axis orthogonal to $\mathbf{B}$, we conclude that the inequality (10.24) along such an axis reduces to

$$\frac{1 - R^2}{R^2} \geq \frac{1}{\alpha} \left\langle \left(\frac{dV^*(h)}{dh} \right)^2 \right\rangle^{-1}. \tag{10.26}$$

One can verify by comparison of (10.26) with (8.33) that the optimal performance realized by the Bayes overlap satisfies the Cramér–Rao bound, as it should. Furthermore, in the limit $R \to 1$, one obtains from (10.26) that

$$R \leq 1 - \frac{1}{2\alpha} \left\langle \left(\frac{dV^*(h)}{dh} \right)^2 \right\rangle^{-1}. \tag{10.27}$$

This upper bound coincides exactly with the asymptotic behaviour of the Bayes overlap in the limit $\alpha \to \infty$, see (8.37).

The fact that the Bayes overlap in the unsupervised problem saturates the Cramér–Rao bound for $\alpha \to \infty$ is reassuring. In particular, the ubiquitous $1/p$ or $1/\alpha$ behaviour follows from the additivity of the Fisher information for independent samplings. However, one has to realize that the Cramér–Rao inequality provides no information for non-smooth distributions (because the Fisher information diverges) and cannot be applied to cases in which the parameter λ takes discrete values (because one cannot calculate the derivative), whereas statistical mechanics calculations can still be performed in these cases. In particular, the $1/\alpha$ approach of R to 1 derived above, appearing for *smooth unsupervised* problems, has to be contrasted with the typical $1/\alpha^2$ behaviour, corresponding to $\varepsilon \sim 1/\alpha$, for e.g. the supervised problems characterized by a sharp decision boundary. On the other hand, the Cramér–Rao bound has a range of application which is wider in several respects than that of statistical mechanics. In particular, one need not consider the thermodynamic limit and the distribution of examples is completely general. Furthermore, it is possible to show that the overlap for on-line learning following the natural gradient, cf. section 9.7, also saturates the Cramér–Rao bound asymptotically for large example sets [137]. Hence on-line learning is, for smooth distributions, asymptotically as efficient as the optimal off-line procedure, a fact that we proved explicitly for the unsupervised problem in chapter 9.

10.6 Discussion

Statistics and statistical mechanics offer different and in many ways complementary approaches to the study of learning. The specific techniques used by either field determine to a large extent the type of results that can be obtained. While generality is the main strength of statistics, it is also its weakness since it does not allow one to discriminate between various options, such as learning algorithms, architectures, and other variations in the learning procedure. Because statistics proceeds mostly on the basis of inequalities, the obvious price to pay for this generality is that the results correspond to extreme cases and it remains unclear how tight the bounds are in a typical realization of the problem. Examples include the worst case for the Vapnik–Chervonenkis theorem and the best case for the Cramér–Rao bound.

On the other hand, statistical mechanics focuses on the calculation of self-averaging quantities, and hence on results which are typical. Nevertheless, one can also use these techniques to study, to a certain extent at least, worst and best cases; cf. the calculation for the worst student in the version space in this chapter or the analysis for the Bayes optimal student in section 3.6. The explicit results obtained by statistical mechanics confirm that in many situations there may indeed be substantial deviations from the statistics bounds and large differences between various learning strategies. For example, in the two-perceptron scenario we found for both the typical and the worst student from the version space a $1/\alpha$ decay of the generalization error, to be compared with a $\ln \alpha/\alpha$ prediction of the VC theorem and a $1/\sqrt{\alpha}$ result for Hebb learning. The discrepancies can be even more pronounced in the case of discontinuous learning, see for example [165].

Note also that a large class of results from statistics are based on the limit of infinite sampling, $p \to \infty$ but N finite, involving for example the central limit theorem, while in statistical mechanics we can study the effect of a finite fraction $\alpha = p/N$ (but, admittedly, only for $N \to \infty$).

Also, since many bounds derived in statistics either become trivial or do not apply to non-smooth probability distributions or variables which take discrete values, the results based on statistics do not provide information in these cases, whereas the statistical mechanics calculations can still be performed. Discontinuities in the learning process typical of such situations show up in the statistical mechanics treatment as phase transitions which, although strictly speaking only occurring in the thermodynamic limit, already characterize the performance of systems with moderately many degrees of freedom. We finally mention that while the linear discriminant function, implemented by the perceptron, is very specific, the corresponding properties such as capacity, generalization error, etc. appear to be rather typical and reproduce many of the features of more complicated architectures. A detailed study of this model and its variations therefore provides a rich and instructive addition to the results obtained from statistics.

Finally, we briefly review some of the literature. The connection between the VC approach and learning was discussed in [13, 166], see also [167], while the VC dimension for multilayer networks was estimated in [158]. The first derivation of the VC theorem appeared in the PhD thesis of Vapnik around 1965, see also [168]. Here, we have closely followed the presentation and derivation of an improved VC theorem [160], see also [163]. The worst student analysis for the teacher–student perceptron scenario is discussed in [162], while an alternative worst case scenario was introduced in [169]. The application of the Cramér–Rao inequality to neural networks was used to prove asymptotic optimality of on-line learning in [137], see also section 9.7. A general introduction to the problems discussed in this chapter is to be found in [170].

10.7 Problems

10.1 Verify that the number of dichotomies (6.18) derived by Cover satisfies but does not saturate the Sauer bound. Can you explain why the bound is not saturated?

10.2 Show that the inequality (10.7) becomes tight in the thermodynamic limit.

10.3 Prove the VC bound for the learnable case (10.13) by using the methods of appendix 7 [160].

10.4 Consider the Sauer lemma in the thermodynamic limit by assuming $p = \alpha N$ and $d_{VC} = \alpha_{VC} N$ when $N \to \infty$. Using Stirling's formula, approximating the sum by an integral, and using a saddle point argument for the asymptotic evaluation of the integral show that

$$\frac{1}{N} \log \Delta(p) \begin{cases} = \alpha \ln 2 & \text{for} \quad \alpha \leq 2\alpha_{VC} \\ \leq \alpha \ln \alpha + \alpha_{VC} \ln \alpha_{VC} \\ \quad - (\alpha - \alpha_{VC}) \ln(\alpha - \alpha_{VC}) & \text{otherwise.} \end{cases}$$

$$(10.28)$$

10.5 Show by using Sauer's lemma that the storage capacity of a classifier system, $\alpha_c = p_c/d_{VC}$, is always smaller than 2, where p_c is the maximum number of random examples which may be stored correctly. Note that for the case of the perceptron with continuous components, $d_{VC} = N$ and the upper bound is saturated. Consider in addition a perceptron with couplings that are either 0 or 1. Show that the VC dimension is again equal to N, and compare the result with the storage capacity determined in problem 6.12.

10.6 Consider the class of systems classifying natural numbers n according to the rule $\sigma(n) = \text{sgn}(\sin(kn))$ with a real parameter k. Show that although there is only one parameter the VC dimension is nevertheless infinite [171].
(Hint: Assume you are given the classification of all numbers $n < N$ with arbitrarily large N and convince yourself that you still cannot predict the classification of N.)

10.7 Show that it is impossible to find a real number k such that the mapping $\sigma(n) = \text{sgn}(\sin(kn))$ realizes the classifications $\sigma(1) = 1, \sigma(2) = 1, \sigma(3) = -1, \sigma(4) = 1$. How do you reconcile this result with the solution of the previous problem?

10.8 Consider again the high–low game already discussed in problem 1.4.

(a) Evaluate the worst case probability appearing in the VC theorem for a learnable task (10.13) for this case and verify that it satisfies the VC bound.

(b) Consider now the problem with the special teacher who classifies all examples as 1. A student with threshold x has, upon presentation of an example set $\{y_i\}$, the following test and generalization error:

$$v_x^p = \frac{1}{p} \sum_{i=1}^{p} \theta(x - y_i), \qquad (10.29)$$

$$\varepsilon_x = x.$$

In order to evaluate the worst case deviation, we have to estimate

$$\text{Prob}\left(\sup_{x \in [0,1]} |v_x^p - \varepsilon_x| > \delta \right), \qquad (10.30)$$

where the probability is with respect to the random variables y_i. We now make the gratifying observation that this problem has been addressed and solved in an entirely different context, namely that of empirical distribution functions, and goes under the name of the Dvoretzky–Kiefer–Wolfowitz theorem. Consult [154] to understand this link and compare the result with the VC theorem.

10.9 Consider the generalization error for the worst student of the version space. Show that the annealed approximation gives sensible results for the perceptron with binary couplings, but completely fails when the couplings are continuous.

10.10 Consider the problem of learning indicator functions on the interval $(0, 1)$. A teacher is defined by an interval (t_1, t_2) and the teacher output on an input

$y \in (0, 1)$ is 1 if $t_1 < y < t_2$ and 0 otherwise. Assume that both the inputs y and the teacher thresholds t_1, t_2 are drawn independently at random from the unit interval with constant probability density.

(a) Show that when choosing p points y_i then for large p the *average* distance between neighbouring points is $1/p$ whereas the *largest* distance between neighbouring points scales as $(\ln p)/p$.

(b) Using these results show that for a typical teacher the generalization error of the worst possible student decays asymptotically as $1/p$.
(Hint: Use your experience from solving problem 10.8.)

(c) In the present problem the hardest teacher is the "empty" one which gives the output 0 for all inputs. Show that in this case the generalization error of the worst student decreases only as $\ln p/p$ for large p.

Note that this result corroborates the necessity of the logarithmic term in the VC bound for a complete worst case scenario.

10.11 Calculate the Fisher information for a Gaussian distribution with known dispersion σ^2 but unknown average λ,

$$P_\lambda(x) = \frac{e^{-(x-\lambda)^2/2\sigma^2}}{\sqrt{2\pi}\sigma}, \tag{10.31}$$

and argue that it is indeed a measure of the information that a sampling x from $P_\lambda(x)$ conveys about the value of λ. Show that, in this example, the Cramér–Rao bound is saturated.
(Hint: Take $y(x) = x$ as an unbiased estimator for λ.)

11

A Bird's Eye View: Multifractals

For a fixed set of input examples, one can decompose the N-sphere into cells each consisting of all the perceptron coupling vectors $\mathbf{J}$ giving rise to the same classification of those examples. Several aspects of perceptron learning discussed in the preceding chapters are related to the geometric properties of this decomposition, which turns out to have random multifractal properties. Our outline of the mathematical techniques related to the multifractal method will of course be short and ad rem; see [172, 173] for a more detailed introduction. But this alternative description provides a deeper and unified view of the different learning properties of the perceptron. It highlights some of the more subtle aspects of the thermodynamic limit and its role in the statistical mechanics analysis of perceptron learning. In this way we finish our discussion of the perceptron with an encompassing multifractal description, preparing the way for the application of this approach to the analysis of multilayer networks.

11.1 The shattered coupling space

Consider a set of $p = \alpha N$ examples $\boldsymbol{\xi}^{\mu}$ generated independently at random from the uniform distribution on the N-sphere. Each hyperplane perpendicular to one of these inputs cuts the coupling space of a spherical perceptron, which is the very same N-sphere, into two half-spheres according to the two possible classifications of the example. The p examples hence generate a *random partition* of the N-sphere into a set of at most 2^p cells

$$C(\boldsymbol{\sigma}) = \{\mathbf{J} \mid \sigma^{\mu} = \text{sgn}(\mathbf{J}\boldsymbol{\xi}^{\mu})\} \tag{11.1}$$

labelled by the different possible output sequences $\boldsymbol{\sigma} = \{\sigma^{\mu}\}$. Coupling vectors $\mathbf{J}$ from the same cell realize the same classification of the examples. Figure 11.1 shows a simple example for small values of both N and p.

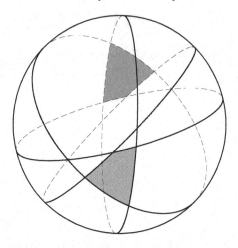

Fig. 11.1. Random partition of the coupling space of a spherical perceptron with $N = 3$ inputs by a set of $p = 4$ examples. Note that only $14 < 2^4$ cells were generated. Shaded is a pair of mirror cells which correspond to the transformation $(\mathbf{J}, \boldsymbol{\sigma}) \mapsto (-\mathbf{J}, -\boldsymbol{\sigma})$.

Due to the random orientations of the hyperplanes the size and shape of the cells vary greatly. In particular, many classifications may turn out to be impossible so that their corresponding cell has in fact zero size. On the other hand it is clear that to every cell associated with an output sequence $\boldsymbol{\sigma}$ there is a "mirror cell" with outputs $-\boldsymbol{\sigma}$ of exactly the same shape and size which may be generated by inversion of all coupling vectors forming the original cell at the centre of the N-sphere.

The volume of the cell corresponding to the output sequence $\boldsymbol{\sigma}$ is given by

$$\Omega(\boldsymbol{\sigma}) = \int d\mu(\mathbf{J}) \prod_{\mu=1}^{p} \theta\left(\frac{\mathbf{J}\boldsymbol{\xi}^{\mu}\sigma^{\mu}}{\sqrt{N}}\right). \tag{11.2}$$

The integration measure ensures the normalization

$$\operatorname{Tr}_{\boldsymbol{\sigma}} \Omega(\boldsymbol{\sigma}) = 1, \tag{11.3}$$

implying that $\Omega(\boldsymbol{\sigma})$ may be interpreted as the probability that the output sequence $\boldsymbol{\sigma}$ is realized by a coupling vector $\mathbf{J}$ drawn at random from the uniform distribution on the N-sphere.

In order to characterize the sizes of the cells in the thermodynamic limit, we recall that non-trivial perceptron learning requires the number of examples to scale as $p = \alpha N$, for $N \to \infty$. We thus anticipate that the typical cell size is exponentially small in N. Therefore the cell *size* is best characterized by the quantity

$$k(\boldsymbol{\sigma}) = -\frac{1}{N} \ln \Omega(\boldsymbol{\sigma}), \tag{11.4}$$

which tells us with which exponent a given cell size goes to zero for $N \to \infty$. The distribution of cell sizes may be specified by the *number* of cells of given size

$$\mathcal{N}(k) = \mathop{\mathrm{Tr}}_{\boldsymbol{\sigma}} \delta(k - k(\boldsymbol{\sigma})), \tag{11.5}$$

which, for typical values of k, will be exponential in N. It is thus appropriate to describe the cell size distribution by

$$c(k) = \frac{1}{N} \ln \mathcal{N}(k) \tag{11.6}$$

giving the rate at which the number of cells of given size k increases exponentially with N.

In the theory of multifractals the function $c(k)$ is called the *multifractal spectrum*.[1] Roughly speaking all subsets of a given size k form a fractal with fractal dimension $c(k)$. If $c(k)$ is a constant, i.e. independent of k, the object under consideration is a simple fractal which can be described by just a single fractal dimension. The defining property of multifractals is that subsets corresponding to different parameters k have *different* fractal dimensions. Therefore a whole nontrivial function $c(k)$ is necessary to completely characterize the scaling properties of a multifractal.

Both $k(\boldsymbol{\sigma})$ and $c(k)$ still depend on the random example sequence $\{\boldsymbol{\xi}^\mu\}$. However, for $N \to \infty$ we expect both quantities to be self-averaging. This assumption may be checked *a posteriori* from the results obtained and is also corroborated by numerical simulations [174]. It is thus sufficient to calculate the averages of $k(\boldsymbol{\sigma})$ and $c(k)$ respectively over the distribution of inputs to obtain, with probability 1, the correct result for any particular input set $\{\boldsymbol{\xi}^\mu\}$.

11.2 The multifractal spectrum of the perceptron

The averaged multifractal spectrum of the perceptron may be calculated explicitly by using a variant of the so-called thermodynamic formalism for multifractals [175, 176]. To this end it is useful to interpret $c(k)$ as the microcanonical entropy of a spin system $\boldsymbol{\sigma}$ with energy $k(\boldsymbol{\sigma})$. As such it may be obtained from the corresponding ensemble averaged free energy

$$f(\beta) = -\frac{1}{N\beta} \left\langle\!\!\left\langle \ln \mathop{\mathrm{Tr}}_{\boldsymbol{\sigma}} e^{-\beta k(\boldsymbol{\sigma})} \right\rangle\!\!\right\rangle_{\boldsymbol{\xi}^\mu} \tag{11.7}$$

[1] In the multifractal literature it is conventionally denoted by $f(\alpha)$.

via a Legendre transform. Indeed, using (11.6) we easily find

$$\operatorname*{Tr}_{\sigma} e^{-\beta k(\sigma)} = \int dk \, \mathcal{N}(k) \, e^{-\beta N k} = \int dk \, \exp(N[c(k) - \beta k]), \qquad (11.8)$$

implying for $N \to \infty$

$$-\beta f(\beta) = \max_k [c(k) - \beta k], \qquad (11.9)$$

or equivalently

$$c(k) = \min_\beta [\beta k - \beta f(\beta)]. \qquad (11.10)$$

On the other hand, recalling the definition (11.4) of $k(\sigma)$ we may rewrite $f(\beta)$ in the form

$$f(\beta) = -\frac{1}{N\beta} \left\langle\!\!\left\langle \ln \operatorname*{Tr}_{\sigma} \Omega^\beta(\sigma) \right\rangle\!\!\right\rangle_{\xi^\mu} \qquad (11.11)$$

relating the free energy to the *moments*[2] of the distribution of cell sizes $\Omega(\sigma)$.

The quenched average in (11.11) can now be accomplished by an interesting variant of the replica trick [177] which uses *two* sets of replicas, one denoted by $a = 1, \dots, n$ to convert the logarithm in the usual way and a second one $\gamma = 1, \dots, \beta$ to represent the β-th power of the cell volume. As in the conventional replica trick we first calculate $f(\beta)$ for integer values of β and assume that a meaningful continuation to real values may be found at the end. In contrast to the usual replica trick, however, β is a free parameter not necessarily tending to zero.

We therefore start with

$$\left\langle\!\!\left\langle (\operatorname*{Tr}_{\sigma} \Omega^\beta(\sigma))^n \right\rangle\!\!\right\rangle_{\xi^\mu} = \left\langle\!\!\left\langle \operatorname*{Tr}_{\sigma^a} \int \prod_{a=1}^n \prod_{\gamma=1}^\beta d\mu(\mathbf{J}^{a\gamma}) \prod_{a,\gamma,\mu} \theta\left(\frac{\mathbf{J}^{a\gamma}\xi^\mu \sigma^{\mu a}}{\sqrt{N}}\right) \right\rangle\!\!\right\rangle_{\xi^\mu}. \qquad (11.12)$$

Note that the output sequence σ only carries one replica index. Coupling vectors with the same index a therefore correspond to the same output sequence σ^a and consequently belong to the *same* cell. Similarly those with different first indices belong to *different* cells.

With the help of the techniques of appendix 2 the average over the inputs ξ^μ can now be performed and after introducing the order parameters

$$q_{\gamma\delta}^{ab} = \frac{1}{N} \sum_i J_i^{a\gamma} J_i^{b\delta} \qquad (11.13)$$

---

[2] The analysis of the moments of the measure under consideration is central to the theory of multifractals, where $f(\beta)$ is called the *mass exponent* and is usually denoted by $\tau(q)$.

the various integrals may be disentangled and the resulting expression may be written as a saddle point integral over the order parameters in the usual way.

Let us start by investigating the results obtained under the assumption of replica symmetry at the saddle point. It is important to realize that due to the second replica index we must already introduce two different overlaps at the replica symmetric level. More precisely, the appropriate replica symmetric ansatz for the order parameters is

$$q_{\gamma\delta}^{ab} = \begin{cases} 1 & \text{if} \quad a = b, \gamma = \delta \\ q_1 & \text{if} \quad a = b, \gamma \neq \delta \\ q_0 & \text{if} \quad a \neq b, \end{cases} \tag{11.14}$$

with q_1 denoting the typical overlap between two couplings from the same cell (same first index) and q_0 characterizing the typical overlap between couplings from different cells (different first indices). Note that both q_1 and q_0 are functions of β which in turn is related to k via $k = \partial(\beta f(\beta))/\partial\beta$ (cf. (11.10)). Hence q_0 is the typical overlap between different cells *of the same size*.

Using the ansatz (11.14) the resulting expressions can be simplified in a way rather similar to a conventional replica calculation within one-step replica symmetry breaking (cf. appendix 5), finally giving rise to

$$-\beta f(\beta) = \underset{q_0, q_1}{\text{extr}} \left[\frac{\beta - 1}{2} \ln(1 - q_1) + \frac{1}{2} \ln(1 - q_1 + \beta(q_1 - q_0)) \right.$$
$$+ \frac{\beta q_0}{2(1 - q_1 + \beta(q_1 - q_0))}$$
$$\left. + \alpha \int Dt_0 \ln \left[2 \int Dt_1 \, H^\beta \left(\frac{\sqrt{q_0} \, t_0 + \sqrt{q_1 - q_0} \, t_1}{\sqrt{1 - q_1}} \right) \right] \right]. \tag{11.15}$$

Inspection of the saddle point equations corresponding to this expression reveals that $q_0 = 0$ is always a solution. This should not come as a surprise. After all q_0 is the typical overlap between two coupling vectors from different cells and since the cells cover the whole N-sphere $q_0 = 0$ is very plausible. It is in accordance also with the existence of mirror cells shown in fig. 11.1 since for each vector **J** of a given cell the vector $-$**J** belongs to a cell of exactly the same size. Anticipating the implications of this symmetry the whole calculation could have been done without introducing the replica index a at all, i.e. an *annealed* average of $\Omega^\beta(\sigma)$ could have been calculated (see problem 11.2). Note, however, that $q_0 = 0$ may not be the only solution of the saddle point equation and more work is needed to determine the correct extremum in (11.15) if several solutions exist (see below).

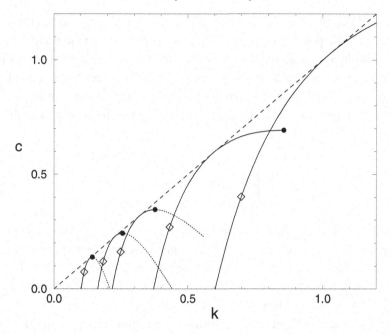

Fig. 11.2. Multifractal spectrum $c(k)$ characterizing the cell size distribution of the spherical perceptron for $\alpha = 0.2, 0.35, 0.5, 1.0$ and 2.0 (from left to right) as obtained within the replica symmetric ansatz. The dots denote the maxima of the respective curves; to the left of the diamonds the results are unstable to replica symmetry breaking. The dotted parts correspond to regions with singular free energy (11.11), see text.

Using $q_0 = 0$ the expression (11.15) for the free energy can be further simplified to yield

$$
-\beta f(\beta) = \operatorname*{extr}_{q_1} \left[\frac{\beta - 1}{2} \ln(1 - q_1) + \frac{1}{2} \ln(1 + (\beta - 1)q_1) \right.
$$
$$
\left. + \alpha \ln 2 \int Dt \, H^\beta\!\left(\frac{\sqrt{q_1}\, t}{\sqrt{1 - q_1}} \right) \right]. \quad (11.16)
$$

The final extremization in q_1 has to be done numerically. With the help of (11.10) the multifractal spectrum $c(k)$ may then be determined for different values of α. Figure 11.2 displays some results obtained in this way.

As expected we find a smaller number of large cells at small values of α and an increasing number of smaller cells (corresponding to larger values of k) for larger values of α. The maxima of the multifractal spectra, marked by the dots in the figure, specify the size $k_0 = \operatorname{argmax} c(k)$ and number $c(k_0) = \max c(k)$ of the *most frequent* cells, which exponentially dominate the total *number* of cells. On the other hand, although the most numerous these cells cover only a negligible part of the surface of the N-sphere. In fact grouping together cells of the same size in (11.3) we find

$$1 = \underset{\sigma}{\mathrm{Tr}}\,\Omega(\sigma) = \int dk\,\mathcal{N}(k)\,e^{-Nk} = \int dk \exp(N[c(k) - k]) \tag{11.17}$$

implying that for $N \to \infty$ the *volume* of the coupling space is dominated by cells of size k_1 defined by

$$\frac{dc}{dk}(k_1) = 1. \tag{11.18}$$

Cells of larger size are too rare, those more frequent are too small to matter. We hence find that the total number of cells and the total volume they cover are dominated by cells of different sizes k_0 and k_1 respectively.[3] Note also that (11.17) implies that the line $c(k) = k$ is tangent to the multifractal spectrum $c(k)$ at $k = k_1$ for all values of α (cf. fig. 11.2).

Let us now see how these geometric features are related to the learning properties of the perceptron. A randomly chosen cell has size k_0 with probability 1 as $N \to \infty$, because all other sizes are exponentially rare. But picking a cell at random is the same as requiring a randomly selected output sequence σ for the given inputs ξ^μ, which is equivalent to the storage problem discussed in chapter 6. We therefore find that e^{-Nk_0} is nothing but the typical value of the Gardner volume $\Omega(\xi^\mu, \sigma^\mu)$ as defined in (6.5) for $\kappa = 0$. In fact from (11.9) it follows that $k \to k_0$ implies $\beta \to 0$ and it is not difficult to show that (6.13) is equivalent to (11.16) in this limit (see problem 11.3). Correspondingly we find $k_0 \to \infty$ when α approaches the storage capacity $\alpha_c(\kappa = 0) = 2$ showing that the typical cell size tends to zero and with probability 1 no coupling vector can be found which implements a random output sequence σ. For $\alpha > \alpha_c$ the cell size distribution $c(k)$ is monotonically increasing and the typical cell is empty in the sense that the corresponding k-value is $+\infty$. The storage properties of the spherical perceptron as determined within the Gardner approach in section 6.1 are hence encoded in the maxima of the multifractal spectrum.

But this spectrum tells us more: in addition to the size k_0 we also know the *number* $c(k_0)$ of typical cells. This number is the central quantity in Cover's approach to the storage problem discussed in section 6.2. In fact for $\alpha < 2$ we find from $k_0 < \infty$ and (11.10) $c(k_0) = -\lim_{\beta \to 0}(\beta f(\beta))$, which by using (11.16) yields $c(k_0) = \alpha \ln 2$. Hence for $\alpha < 2$ with probability 1 all of the $2^{\alpha N}$ cells are realized, in complete agreement with the findings of section 6.2. For $\alpha > 2$ we have $k_0 \to \infty$ resulting in $c(k_0) < \alpha \ln 2$ and only an exponentially small fraction of all possible classifications may be realized (cf. problems 11.5 and 6.4). A random

---

[3] This is again more or less the defining property of multifractals: different moments of the distribution are dominated by different fractal subsets.

colouring is therefore not linearly separable with probability 1. We thus see that the multifractal method nicely reconciles the previously complementary approaches to the storage problem of the perceptron due to Cover and Gardner respectively: the horizontal axis in fig. 11.2 corresponds to the Gardner approach of *measuring* cell sizes whereas the vertical axis represents Cover's method of *counting* the number of cells.

On the other hand, instead of choosing at random a classification of the examples and discussing the corresponding cell properties, we may draw a *vector* **T** at random from the uniform distribution on the N-sphere and ask for the size of the cell to which it belongs. For finite N, this size is of course a random quantity. But we recall that in the thermodynamic limit the cells of size k_1 completely fill the surface of the N-sphere apart from an exponentially small part. Hence the randomly chosen vector **T** will lie in a cell of size k_1 with probability 1. But the very same cell will comprise by definition all coupling vectors **J** which classify the inputs exactly like **T**. Its size is therefore nothing but the volume of the version space at given value of α as calculated in section 2.3. The behaviour of the generalization error ε as a function of the training set size α is hence also coded in the multifractal spectrum, namely by the point of contact between $c(k)$ and the line $c = k$. Again it is not difficult to derive (2.41) from the general expression (11.16) for the multifractal spectrum using the limit $\beta \to 1$ (cf. problem 11.3). In fact anticipating $q_0 = 0$, the calculation of the multifractal spectrum which gave rise to (11.16) is in this limit identical to the $n \to 1$ replica trick used in section 2.3.

It is possible to give an interpretation also to the points between k_1 and k_0 on the multifractal spectrum: they correspond to learning problems with noisy teachers and interpolate between the noise free generalization task described by k_1 and the storage problem related to k_0, see [178] for details.

The results obtained still depend on the assumptions of replica symmetry and $q_0 = 0$. A careful stability analysis [179] reveals that both assumptions break down at

$$\beta_\pm = 1 \pm \frac{\sqrt{\alpha}}{q_1(\alpha)} \tag{11.19}$$

so that the calculated multifractal spectra are not reliable for $\beta > \beta_+ > 0$ and $\beta < \beta_- < 0$. Moreover, for all $\beta < 0$ there is a discontinuous transition with q_1 jumping from its saddle point value to $1/(1 - \beta)$ and thus giving rise to a singular free energy. It is tempting to relate these divergences to the existence of *empty* cells $\Omega(\sigma) = 0$ blowing up the sum (11.11) for negative β. This interpretation could open the way to relate the multifractal spectrum also to the VC dimension of

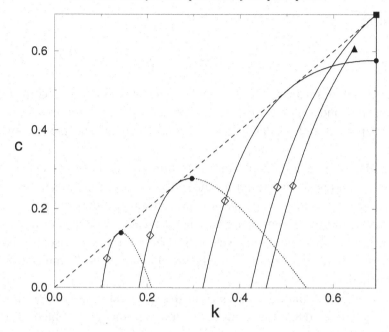

Fig. 11.3. Multifractal spectrum $c(k)$ characterizing the cell size distribution of the Ising perceptron for $\alpha = 0.2, 0.4, 0.833, 1.245$ and 1.4 (from left to right) as obtained within the replica symmetric ansatz. The dots denote the maxima of the respective curves; to the left of the diamonds the results are unstable to replica symmetry breaking. The dotted parts correspond to regions with singular free energy (11.11), see text. For $\alpha = 1.4$ the continuous part of the spectrum ends at the triangle and the spectrum is completed by the isolated point $(\ln 2, \ln 2)$ indicated by the square.

the perceptron; however, so far mathematical problems have thwarted attempts to make this connection explicit.

In order to indicate the limited reliability of the RS results for the multifractal spectrum, the parts of $c(k)$ with negative slope (corresponding to $\beta < 0$) are dotted in fig. 11.2 whereas the values of β_+ are delimited by the diamond. It should be noted that one can show from (11.19) that the replica symmetric results using $q_0 = 0$ are correct in the whole interval $[k_1, k_0]$ for all values of α. Hence these parts of the multifractal spectra are correctly determined by (11.16).

By an analogous calculation one can determine the multifractal spectrum of the Ising perceptron; see fig. 11.3 for a representative selection of results. We briefly discuss some points which highlight the peculiarities of neural networks with discrete couplings; for a detailed analysis see [179]. For the Ising perceptron the coupling space consists of the corners of the N-dimensional hypercube and accordingly cells are collections of discrete points. The "volume" of a cell is just the number of points times 2^{-N}, i.e. in (11.2) we have to make the replacement

$$\int d\mu(\mathbf{J}) \mapsto \frac{1}{2^N} \operatorname*{Tr}_{\mathbf{J}}.$$ (11.20)

There is hence a smallest non-zero cell volume $\Omega_{\min} = 2^{-N}$ corresponding to an upper bound $k_{\max} = \ln 2$ for k. Results for $c(k)$ for larger values of k would represent cells containing a fraction of a point and are not shown in fig. 11.3.

For small values of α the multifractal spectrum of the Ising perceptron is very similar to the corresponding result for the spherical case. This was to be expected because the cells are still rather large, comprising a huge number of points, and the discrete nature of the coupling space does not yet matter. The special values k_0 and k_1 have of course the same meaning as in the spherical case and also the instability for the parts with negative slope β and the transition to replica symmetry breaking at β_+ are similar.

With increasing α the differences from the spherical case become more pronounced. For $\alpha \cong 0.833$ one finds $k_0 = \ln 2$ (see fig. 11.3) which means that the typical cells only contain a single point of the hypercube. For larger values of α the typical cells are empty and with probability 1 no Ising coupling vector can be found which implements a random input–output mapping. The requirement $k_0 = \ln 2$ therefore defines the storage capacity α_c and the numerical value is of course the same as found in section 6.3.

Increasing α further we reach the point where even the cells dominating the volume are so small that they only contain a single coupling vector. At the corresponding value $\alpha \cong 1.245$ a randomly chosen vector $\mathbf{T}$ belongs almost certainly to a cell with no other element in it. This marks the discontinuous transition to perfect generalization found in section 7.2. As in the storage problem, the discrete structure of the coupling space prevents a continuous decrease of the size of the version space and a discontinuous transition takes place. The prescription to determine the two transitions from $k_0 = \ln 2$ and $k_1 = \ln 2$ respectively is of course identical to the zero-entropy criterion used in sections 6.3 and 7.2 (cf. problem 11.4).

For even larger values of α a discontinuous transition to $q_1 = 1$ in the calculation of the free energy gives rise to a *gap* in the multifractal spectrum. The continuous part ends at some value $k_{\max} < \ln 2$ and the spectrum is completed by the isolated point $(\ln 2, \ln 2)$ as shown in fig. 11.3 for the special case $\alpha = 1.4$. This point corresponds to a large number (namely 2^N) of cells comprising just a single coupling vector which dominate both the number of cells and the volume of the coupling space. There are a few other cells which are much larger and a whole interval of cell sizes which are not realized at all.

Let us finally note that in the case of the Ising perceptron it is possible to determine the function $c(k)$ numerically by exact enumeration techniques giving a valuable check of the analytical results [174].

11.3 The multifractal organization of internal representations

A slight modification of the techniques introduced in the previous section also provides an improved understanding of the storage and generalization properties of neural networks with internal degrees of freedom, such as multilayer networks. The method is most concisely demonstrated for the reversed wedge perceptron introduced in section 7.3 as a toy model for multilayer networks.

We first return to the storage problem for the reversed wedge perceptron studied in problem 7.6. Using the input–output relation (7.11) and assuming without loss of generality $\sigma^\mu = 1$ for all μ, the Gardner volume for an input sequence $\{\boldsymbol{\xi}^\mu\}$ is given by

$$\Omega(\boldsymbol{\xi}^\mu) = \int d\mu(\mathbf{J}) \prod_\mu \theta_\gamma \left(\frac{\mathbf{J}\boldsymbol{\xi}^\mu}{\sqrt{N}} \right), \qquad (11.21)$$

where $\theta_\gamma(x) = \theta((x - \gamma)x(x + \gamma))$ is the appropriate indicator function. For the quenched entropy we find within the replica symmetric ansatz

$$s = \frac{1}{N} \langle\!\langle \ln \Omega(\boldsymbol{\xi}^\mu) \rangle\!\rangle_{\boldsymbol{\xi}^\mu} = \underset{q}{\text{extr}} \left[\frac{1}{2} \ln(1 - q) + \frac{q}{2(1 - q)} + \alpha \int Dt \ln H_\gamma(t) \right] \qquad (11.22)$$

where

$$H_\gamma(t) = H\left(\frac{\sqrt{q}\, t + \gamma}{\sqrt{1 - q}} \right) - H\left(\frac{\sqrt{q}\, t}{\sqrt{1 - q}} \right) + H\left(\frac{\sqrt{q}\, t - \gamma}{\sqrt{1 - q}} \right). \qquad (11.23)$$

Taking the limit $q \to 1$ yields for the storage capacity

$$\alpha_c^{-1} = \int_0^{\gamma/2} Dt\, t^2 + \int_{\gamma/2}^\infty Dt\, (t - \gamma)^2. \qquad (11.24)$$

This expression vastly overestimates the storage capacity. In fact, it is known that replica symmetry is broken at $\alpha = \alpha_c$ for all $\gamma > 0$ and a calculation using one-step RSB yields significantly reduced values for α_c [106]. The intuitive reason for the occurrence of replica symmetry breaking is a highly disconnected solution space which results from the existence of exponentially many choices in the internal representations that specify whether a positive output of the examples is realized by local fields larger than γ or belonging to the interval $(-\gamma, 0)$. As a result replica symmetry breaks down and a reliable calculation of the storage capacity necessitates RSB.

While it is obvious (cf. fig. 7.2) that the Gardner volume is disconnected for *all* values of α, the instability to RSB occurs only for $\alpha > \alpha_{RSB}(\gamma) > 0$, indicating that the relation between the structure of the solution space and the stability of replica symmetry is more subtle. The organization of internal representations turns out to be the key to an improved understanding of this relation. Indeed the total Gardner volume (11.21) may be decomposed into cells corresponding to a specific choice of the internal representations by writing

$$\Omega(\xi^\mu) = \underset{\tau}{\mathrm{Tr}}\, \Omega(\tau;\xi^\mu) \tag{11.25}$$

with

$$\Omega(\tau;\xi^\mu) = \int d\mu(\mathbf{J}) \prod_\mu \theta_\gamma\left(\frac{\mathbf{J}\xi^\mu}{\sqrt{N}}\right) \theta\left(\frac{\mathbf{J}\xi^\mu}{\sqrt{N}}\tau^\mu\right). \tag{11.26}$$

The first term in the product over μ selects all couplings $\mathbf{J}$ realizing the correct output whereas the second θ-function additionally subdivides the total solution volume into subsets corresponding to specific internal representation vectors $\tau = \{\tau^\mu\}$. Here $\tau^\mu = +1$ stands for $\mathbf{J}\xi^\mu/\sqrt{N} > \gamma$ and $\tau^\mu = -1$ indicates $-\gamma < \mathbf{J}\xi^\mu/\sqrt{N} < 0$.

We now introduce the logarithmic volume scale $k(\tau;\xi^\mu) = -\ln \Omega(\tau;\xi^\mu)/N$ and calculate the number $\mathcal{N}(k) = \exp(N\,c(k))$ of cells of a given volume in a similar way as in the previous section. Assuming replica symmetry, again two order parameters have to be introduced: q_1 giving the typical overlap between two coupling vectors realizing the same internal representation of all inputs and q_0 denoting the typical overlap between two coupling vectors belonging to cells of equal size but corresponding to different internal representation vectors σ. The expression for the free energy is (cf. (11.15))

$$-\beta f(\beta) = \underset{q_0,q_1}{\mathrm{extr}}\left[\frac{\beta-1}{2} \ln(1-q_1) + \frac{1}{2}\ln(1-q_1 + \beta(q_1-q_0)) \right.$$
$$+ \frac{\beta q_0}{2(1-q_1+\beta(q_1-q_0))} \tag{11.27}$$
$$\left. + \alpha \int Dt_0 \ln \int Dt_1 \left(H_+^\beta + (H_- - H_0)^\beta\right)\right],$$

where

$$H_\pm = H\left(\frac{\pm\gamma + \sqrt{q_0}t_0 + \sqrt{q_1-q_0}t_1}{\sqrt{1-q_1}}\right), \qquad H_0 = H\left(\frac{\sqrt{q_0}t_0 + \sqrt{q_1-q_0}t_1}{\sqrt{1-q_1}}\right).$$

Clearly we cannot generally expect $q_0 = 0$ any more, in fact q_0 should be similar to the value of q in the standard Gardner approach that gives the overlap of two

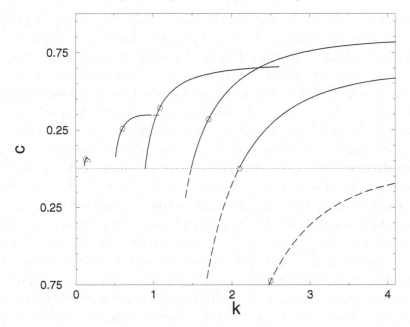

Fig. 11.4. The multifractal spectrum characterizing the decomposition of the Gardner volume of the reversed wedge perceptron into cells corresponding to different internal representations for $\gamma = 1$ and $\alpha = 0.1, 0.5, 1.0, 2.0$, together with $\alpha = \alpha_{\text{disc}} \sim 3.0$ and $\alpha = \alpha_c \sim 4.6$ (from left to right). Parts with negative slope are indicated by dotted lines; dashed lines correspond to negative values of c. The circles denote the sizes k_1 of cells dominating the total Gardner volume.

couplings from the solution space irrespective of the internal representation they implement.

Figure 11.4 shows some typical results for the multifractal spectrum obtained from a numerical analysis of (11.27). Qualitatively the behaviour is similar to the simple perceptron. Again the maxima of the curves give the size and number of the most frequent cells whereas the volume of the solution space is dominated by cells of size k_1 defined by (11.18).

For small values of α the typical cell is non-empty, i.e. $k_0 < \infty$, and all possible internal representations may be realized, i.e. $c(k_0) = \alpha \ln 2$. With increasing storage ratio the cells become smaller and more numerous until at a certain value of α it is impossible to realize all the $2^{\alpha N}$ different internal representations and accordingly $k_0 \to \infty$ and $c(k_0) < \alpha \ln 2$. Note that the storage problem can be solved as long as there is at least a *single* internal representation τ left. Therefore we expect that the storage capacity α_c corresponds to the point where $c(k_0) = \lim_{k \to \infty} c(k) = 0$. Before this happens, however, there is another value $\alpha_{\text{disc}} < \alpha_c$ for which $c(k_1)$ becomes negative. At this point the number of cells dominating the solution space *volume* becomes sub-exponential in N. It turns out that $\alpha_{\text{disc}} \cong \alpha_{\text{RSB}}$ for most values of γ. For $\alpha < \alpha_{\text{disc}}$ the Gardner volume is dominated by an exponentially large number of cells. Two vectors $\mathbf{J}^a$ and $\mathbf{J}^b$ picked at random from the solution space will therefore with overwhelming probability belong to *different* internal representations and the mutual overlap will always be given by q_0. Hence, although the Gardner volume consists of a huge number of disconnected domains, only *one* overlap scale is observable and a replica symmetric description is appropriate. For $\alpha > \alpha_{\text{disc}}$ on the other hand only a few cells of size k_1 remain, which however still dominate the solution volume. There is then a non-zero probability drawing two coupling vectors from the *same* cell and the second overlap q_1 becomes relevant. In the standard Gardner calculation focusing on the total solution space this shows up as an instability of the RS saddle point. The multifractal method therefore clarifies that the transition to RSB is related to $c(k_1) = 0$ whereas the storage capacity is given by $c(k_0) = 0$. If the determination of $c(k_0)$ can be done within replica symmetry the multifractal technique is clearly advantageous when compared with the one-step RSB calculation of the total Gardner volume. Both calculations are of comparable mathematical complexity but the former is believed to be exact whereas the latter is just the first step of an approximate scheme.

The values for α_c and the point where $c(k_0) = 0$ as well as α_{disc} and α_{RSB} respectively do not coincide exactly, which can be traced back to differences between (11.27) and the expression for the quenched entropy of the Gardner volume in one-step RSB. The reason for this discrepancy is that the notions of cells of different internal representations and of ergodic components are not equivalent [177]. However, these quantitative differences are small and do not invalidate the qualitative insights offered by the multifractal method.

The above analysis of the storage properties can be extended to the generalization problem for the reversed wedge perceptron. In addition to the number and size of the cells the multifractal spectrum then describes the relative *orientation* of cells with respect to the teacher coupling $\mathbf{T}$. The calculation allows one to determine the respective importance of shrinkage and disappearance of cells for the decrease of the generalization error with increasing training set size and gives a detailed understanding of the discontinuous transition from the poorly to the well generalizing phase discussed in section 7.3. In the former the multifractal spectrum is very similar to the results for the pure storage problem shown in fig. 11.4, underlining how poorly the rule behind the examples is detected. Moreover one always finds $c(k_1) > 0$ in the dominating phase, which explains why replica symmetry always holds in the generalization problem even though the version space disconnected.

11.4 Discussion

Many interesting insights into the learning properties of simple neural network models can be gained by analysing the tessellation of the coupling space induced by random inputs. The geometrical scaling properties of the evolving random cell structure are quantitatively characterized by a multifractal spectrum which can be calculated explicitly within the framework of statistical mechanics. For the simple perceptron this method unifies the complementary approaches of Cover and Gardner to the storage problem and also incorporates a description of the generalization properties. When used for the analysis of networks with internal degrees of freedom it makes possible a detailed characterization of the organization of internal representations, which is hidden in the standard Gardner calculation of the total volume of the version space. As a result the subtle relation between the instability of replica symmetry and the connectedness of the solution space can be further clarified and replica symmetric expressions may be used to investigate systems which within the standard framework would require replica symmetry breaking.

Let us close with a short guide to the literature. The relevance of the distribution of cell sizes for the learning properties of the perceptron was first mentioned in [78]. The first explicit calculation of a multifractal spectrum was performed for the storage problem of a reversed wedge perceptron in [177]. A detailed analysis of the spherical and the Ising perceptron was given in [179]; a variation including finite training errors can be found in [180]. Multifractal properties of the coupling distribution prior to learning in the Ising perceptron are discussed in [181]. The generalization problem for the reversed wedge perceptron is analysed in [182], and the Ising reversed wedge perceptron is treated in [183]. The application of the method to simple multilayer networks is presented in [184, 185, 186]. An interesting related method using a different indicator function for the existence of a cell is discussed in [187].

11.5 Problems

11.1 Show that no orientation of hyperplanes can be found which generates more than 14 cells in fig. 11.1.

11.2 Re-derive the result (11.16) for the multifractal spectrum of the spherical perceptron by using the annealed average of $\Omega^\beta(\sigma)$ instead of the quenched one employed in (11.11). Why does this calculation correspond to $q_0 = 0$?

11.3 Show that (11.9) implies that $k = k_0$ corresponds to $\beta = 0$ and $k = k_1$ to $\beta = 1$. Using these correspondences derive the expression (6.13) for the quenched entropy of the Gardner volume and (2.41) for the quenched entropy of the version space from the appropriate limits of the multifractal spectrum (11.16).

11.4 Performing the replacement (11.20) in (11.2) show that the requirements $k_0 = \ln 2$ and $k_1 = \ln 2$ for the determination of the storage capacity and the transition to perfect generalization respectively in the Ising perceptron are identical to the respective zero-entropy criteria as used in sections 6.3 and 7.2.

11.5 Show from (11.16) that the total number of cells is for $\alpha \geq 2$ described by

$$\lim_{k\to\infty} c(k) = \alpha \ln \alpha - (\alpha - 1) \ln(\alpha - 1). \tag{11.28}$$

Compare this expression with the asymptotic form of the Cover result (6.18) obtained in problem 6.4.

(Hint: For $\alpha > 2$ the limit $\beta \to 0$ implies $q_1 \to 1$ with $\beta/(1 - q_1)$ remaining of order 1 in agreement with the fact that the most numerous cells are vanishingly small, $k_0 \to \infty$. Using this scaling one finds $\lim_{\beta\to 0} \beta k(\beta) = 0$.)

11.6 In problem 3.8, we found that for all α the version space is cut into two parts with probability 1 by a random new example. On the other hand, from the Cover result (6.18) it follows that the total number of classifications, hence the total number of cells, no longer increases exponentially with p for $p > 2N$. How can these two results be reconciled?

11.7 In problem 10.10 the worst possible teacher for the learning of indicator functions on the unit interval was considered. It is tempting to use the results of the multifractal analysis to pose a similar question for perceptron learning. Performing the limit $\beta \to \infty$ in (11.15) one can extract information about the *largest* cell, which corresponds to the "hardest teacher". To perform this limit one has to note that q_0 and q_1 converge to a single q-value, since only a single cell survives. Introducing $x = \beta(q_1 - q_0)$, show that

$$f(\beta \to \infty) = - \operatorname*{extr}_{q,x} \left[\frac{q}{2(1 - q + x)} + \frac{1}{2} \ln(1 - q) \right.$$
$$\left. + \alpha \int Dt \operatorname*{extr}_z \left(-\frac{1 - q}{2x} z^2 + \ln H\left(\frac{\sqrt{q}t}{\sqrt{1 - q}} + z \right) \right) \right]. \tag{11.29}$$

Extract from this expression the asymptotic behaviour of the generalization error for large values of α by self-consistently assuming $x \to 3/2$ and $1 - q \sim 1/(\alpha^{2/3} \ln \alpha)$ in this limit. Compare the result with the VC theorem and discuss its applicability as well as the reliability of (11.29) (see [169] for more details).

12

Multilayer Networks

In the preceding chapters we have described various properties of learning in the perceptron, exploiting the fact that its simple architecture allows a rather detailed mathematical analysis. However, the perceptron suffers from a major deficiency that led to its demise in the late 1960s: being able only to implement linearly separable Boolean functions its computational capacities are rather limited. An obvious generalization is feed-forward multilayer networks with one or more intermediate layers of formal neurons neurons between input and output (cf. fig. 1.1c). On the one hand these may be viewed as being composed of individual perceptrons, so that their theoretical analysis may build on what has been accomplished for the perceptron. On the other hand the addition of internal degrees of freedom makes them computationally much more powerful. In fact multilayer neural networks are able to realize *all* possible Boolean functions between input and output, which makes them an attractive choice for practical applications. There is also a neurophysiological motivation for the study of multilayer networks since most neurons in biological neural nets are *inter*neurons neither directly connected to sensory inputs nor to motor outputs.

The higher complexity of multilayer networks as compared to the simple perceptron makes the statistical mechanics analysis of their learning abilities more complicated and in general precludes the general and detailed characterization which was possible for the perceptron. Nevertheless, for tailored architectures and suitable learning scenarios very instructive results may be obtained, some of which will be discussed in the present chapter.

Given the greater complexity of the standard learning setup for multilayer networks, the simplifications gained by restricting ourselves to the on-line learning prescription are even more decisive than for the perceptron. We will therefore devote a whole chapter to reviewing some techniques and results obtained for on-line learning in multilayer networks and defer this topic to chapter 13.

12.1 Basic architectures

A feed-forward multilayer neural network is defined by a number of layers of formal neurons with directed synaptic couplings connecting successive layers only, cf. section 1.1. Whereas the lay-out of the perceptron is more or less fixed, there is substantial variability in architecture in the class of multilayer networks, which may differ in the number and size of the hidden layers. For a meaningful theoretical analysis it is first necessary to select some simple cases which still show most of the relevant properties. As a first step we restrict ourselves again to networks with a single output unit. Since there are no couplings between the elements of a given layer, networks with several outputs are only slightly more complicated than an ensemble of single output nets.

Moreover one can show that a feed-forward neural network with a *single* hidden layer made of sufficiently many units is already able to implement *any* Boolean function between input layer and output [188]. This remarkable fact allows us to restrict our attention further to networks with just one hidden layer. Incidentally we note that the corresponding result for networks with continuous neurons [189] states that a multilayer net with a single hidden layer can approximate any function of the input variables to any desired degree of accuracy by including a sufficient number of units in the hidden layer[1] (see also problem 12.3).

A multilayer network with one hidden layer containing K elements is hence specified by K coupling vectors $\mathbf{J}_1, \ldots, \mathbf{J}_K$ connecting the N inputs S_i with the hidden units $\tau_1, \ldots, \tau_K$ (cf. fig. 12.1). The activity of the hidden units for a given input $\mathbf{S}$ is given by

$$\tau_k = \mathrm{sgn}\left(\frac{\mathbf{J}_k \mathbf{S}}{\sqrt{N}}\right) \qquad k = 1, \ldots, K. \tag{12.1}$$

The vector $\boldsymbol{\tau} = (\tau_1, \ldots, \tau_K)$ is referred to as the *internal representation* of the input $\mathbf{S}$. The activity state of the hidden units determines the output σ via couplings $W_1, \ldots, W_K$ according to

$$\sigma = \mathrm{sgn}\left(\frac{1}{\sqrt{K}} \sum_{k=1}^{K} W_k \tau_k\right) = \mathrm{sgn}\left(\frac{\mathbf{W}\boldsymbol{\tau}}{\sqrt{K}}\right). \tag{12.2}$$

Even networks with a single hidden layer are still quite complicated and no general analysis within the framework of statistical mechanics has been possible so far. As a further simplification we therefore assume that the number K of hidden units is much less than the number N of input units. In the thermodynamic limit $N \to \infty$ which we will eventually always consider this means that either K

---

[1] This result is closely related to a remarkable theorem by Kolmogorov [190] motivated by the 13th problem of Hilbert. Loosely speaking this theorem states that any non-linear function of many variables may be written as linear combination of functions of a single variable.

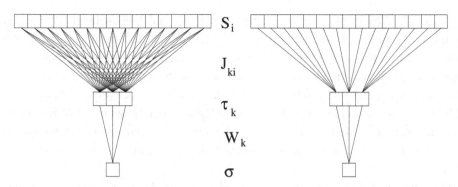

Fig. 12.1. Fully connected (left) and tree (right) architecture of a multilayer network with one hidden layer.

remains of order 1 or $K \lesssim \ln N$. Moreover, in general we will assume that the number of hidden units does not change during the learning process although this excludes some of the interesting heuristic learning rules in which hidden units are added until a desired task can be performed (cf. problem 12.7).

For $K \ll N$ it is quite conceivable that the learning abilities of a multilayer network are not substantially influenced if the few couplings from the hidden to the output layer are not modified at all [191]. Somewhat more generally, we may assume that the mapping from the internal representation $\boldsymbol{\tau}$ to the output σ is coded in a *prewired* Boolean function $F(\boldsymbol{\tau})$ and the whole learning process concerns only the adaptation of the couplings $\mathbf{J}_1, \ldots, \mathbf{J}_K$ between inputs and hidden units. Popular choices for F include

$$F(\tau_1, \ldots, \tau_K) = \prod_{k=1}^{K} \tau_k \qquad (12.3)$$

and

$$F(\tau_1, \ldots, \tau_K) = \text{sgn}\left(\frac{1}{\sqrt{K}} \sum_{k=1}^{K} \tau_k\right), \qquad (12.4)$$

giving rise to what are called the *parity* and the *committee* machine respectively [192]. Note that in order to implement the parity function (12.3) with the help of McCulloch–Pitts neurons one needs an additional layer of hidden units. On the other hand the committee machine is easily realized by simply choosing $W_k = 1$ for all k. Note also that for the case of Ising couplings $W_k = \pm 1$ the committee machine is already the most general two-layer network since the input–output mapping is invariant under the transformation $J_{ki} \mapsto -J_{ki}, W_k \mapsto -W_k$.

We therefore finally end up with the two prototypes of multilayer networks shown in fig. 12.1. The important remaining difference between these two architectures lies in the connection between input and hidden layers. Whereas in the *tree-structured* architecture each hidden unit is fed from *different* input units, in the *fully connected* architecture all hidden units are connected to *all* inputs. The situations are therefore sometimes also referred to as *non-overlapping* and *overlapping* receptive fields of the hidden units respectively. Note that the fully connected case has a factor K more adaptable couplings between input and hidden layer. For the tree-structured architecture it is convenient to change the normalization of the fields at the hidden units and replace $\sqrt{N}$ by $\sqrt{N/K}$ in (12.1).

One may well wonder how many of the spectacular computational abilities of multilayer networks alluded to in the introduction to the present chapter survive the severe simplifications made above. In fact a committee machine with $K = 3$ may seem rather "perceptron-like" so that our hopes of substantially improving on the performance of the perceptron might be in vain. As we will see there are indeed situations in which the simple multilayer architectures described above show learning properties rather similar to the perceptron. Still there are also important improvements over the capabilities of the perceptron. Note also that in the light of the findings of chapter 10 modest results for the storage capacity of these special multilayer architectures imply attractive generalization abilities.

As basic learning tasks we will again consider the storage problem, i.e. the ability of the network to implement input–output mappings generated independently at random, and the generalization problem in which a target mapping has to be inferred from labelled examples. In the latter case it is as before convenient to think of the rule to be learned as being represented by a teacher network. Although teacher and student must of course have the same input dimension they may well differ in their hidden architecture. The general case of M hidden units of the teacher and K hidden units of the student includes the *unrealizable* case ($K < M$), the *realizable* one ($K = M$), and the so-called *over-realizable* situation ($K > M$) in which the complexity of the student is larger than that of the teacher. All three cases show interesting generalization behaviour.

As in the case of the perceptron, the statistical mechanics techniques are linked with the thermodynamic limit $N \to \infty$ and non-trivial results are obtained only if the number p of examples scales with the size of the system. Contrary to the perceptron, for which the dimension of the input space, the number of adjustable parameters and the VC dimension all coincide, for multilayer networks different scaling regimes may be of interest. For the tree architecture the obvious choice is again $p = \alpha N$. For fully connected networks both the scalings $p = \alpha N$ and $p = \alpha N K$ make sense and correspond to different regimes in the generalization process.

From our experience with the perceptron we expect that the statistical mechanics analysis of the different learning scenarios will give rise to equations for suitable order parameters specifying the overlap between teacher and student coupling vectors. The expressions for the generalization error as a function of these order parameters can in principle be derived in an analogous way as (2.3) was derived for the perceptron, although the results may easily get rather cumbersome. For the tree architecture there is a unique mapping between the sub-perceptrons between input and hidden layer of teacher and student and moreover all sub-perceptrons have the same statistical properties. This makes it possible to take advantage of the results obtained for the perceptron.

Consider first the realizable situation of a tree parity machine learning from a teacher of the same architecture. According to (12.3) the two respective outputs will be different if there is an *odd* number of disagreements in the hidden layer. We denote by ε_k the probability that the student hidden unit k disagrees with the corresponding hidden unit of the teacher and by Prob(odd/even) the probabilities of an odd or even number of disagreements respectively. From the permutation symmetry of the parity function (12.3) and the self-averaging property of the generalization error of the individual perceptrons we infer $\varepsilon_k = \varepsilon_\tau$ for all k and find [193]

$$
\begin{aligned}
(1 - 2\varepsilon_\tau)^K &= ((1 - \varepsilon_\tau) - \varepsilon_\tau)^K \\
&= \mathrm{Prob(even)} - \mathrm{Prob(odd)} \\
&= (1 - \varepsilon^{\mathrm{PAR}}) - \varepsilon^{\mathrm{PAR}} \\
&= 1 - 2\varepsilon^{\mathrm{PAR}}
\end{aligned}
$$

resulting in

$$
\varepsilon^{\mathrm{PAR}} = \frac{1}{2}\left(1 - (1 - 2\varepsilon_\tau)^K\right). \tag{12.5}
$$

For the committee tree the calculation is more involved since the different internal representations of the teacher are not equivalent to each other. For $K = 3$, e.g., outputs with teacher internal representation $(+, +, +)$ are only misclassified by the student if two of his hidden units fail to reproduce the respective teacher values. If on the other hand the internal representation of the teacher is $(+, +, -)$ the student fails if he makes one error at the $+$-sites and no error at the $-$-site or if he gets both $+$-sites wrong. Together this gives rise to

$$
\varepsilon^{\mathrm{COM}}_{K=3} = \varepsilon_\tau^3 - \frac{3}{2}\varepsilon_\tau^2 + \frac{3}{2}\varepsilon_\tau. \tag{12.6}
$$

Working through the combinatorial complications for larger values of K one finds,

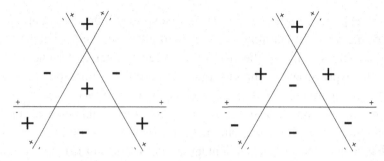

Fig. 12.2. Partition of the input space according to the output of a parity machine (left) and committee machine (right) with $K = 3$ hidden units and non-zero threshold each.

assuming again $\varepsilon_k = \varepsilon_\tau$ for all k [194],

$$\varepsilon_K^{COM} = \frac{1}{2} - \frac{1}{2\pi^2} \sum_{k=0,\,\text{even}}^{K-1} \binom{K}{k} \left[\frac{\Gamma(\frac{K-k}{2})\,\Gamma(\frac{k+1}{2})}{\Gamma(\frac{K+1}{2})} \right]^2 (1 - 2\varepsilon_\tau)^{K-k}. \qquad (12.7)$$

For large values of K (but still $K \ll N$) one may simplify this expression by noting that the main contributions in the k-sum come from large k. Using Stirling's formula for the asymptotic behaviour of the Γ-function one finds

$$\varepsilon_{K \to \infty}^{COM} = \frac{1}{\pi} \arccos(1 - 2\varepsilon_\tau). \qquad (12.8)$$

This simple result can be derived directly by assuming that for large K the hidden units are only very weakly correlated and proceeding in complete analogy with the derivation of (2.3) (cf. problem 12.4).

12.2 Bounds

Due to the more complex architecture the learning and generalization properties of multilayer networks are more difficult to analyse than those of the perceptron. Consequently exact results are rarely possible and in general require considerable mathematical effort. Under these circumstances approximations which may be derived by relatively simple means are of particular interest.

Let us first try to generalize the Cover approach to the storage problem to multilayer networks. Instead of a single separating hyperplane characteristic of the perceptron we have now K such planes corresponding to the K sub-perceptrons of the multilayer network. These hyperplanes form a *partition* of the input space into regions with different overall classification. Figure 12.2 gives an impression of these partitions for the $K = 3$ parity and committee machine.

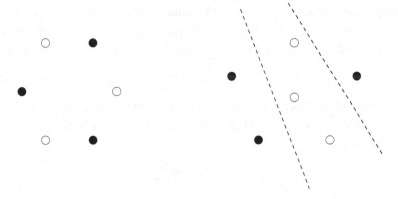

Fig. 12.3. Two sets of $p = 6$ inputs in $N = 2$ dimensions. White (black) circles denote a positive (negative) output. Whereas it is impossible to implement the labelling shown on the left with a $K = 2$ parity machine all labellings can be realized with such a machine for the relative orientation of inputs given on the right.

Similarly to the analysis described in section 6.2 we could now try to count the number of different classifications of p inputs which may be induced by different orientations of the hyperplanes. To this end we would have to determine the change in the number of possible partitions when adding a new input. The main obstacle rendering this approach impossible is that the number of different partitions not only depends on the number of the inputs but also on their *relative location* with respect to each other. This is demonstrated in fig. 12.3 for a simple example. Unlike the case of the perceptron we hence do not get the same number of partitions for all sets of p inputs in general position. This precludes the derivation of a simple recursion relation similar to (6.17).

Although a complete analysis along the lines of the Cover approach is hence impossible we may derive a useful *bound* for the storage capacity of multilayer nets. Consider for definiteness a network with K hidden units and tree structure. For $p = \alpha N$ inputs in general position we know from (6.18) that each sub-perceptron may maximally realize $C(p, N/K)$ different classifications and there are hence at most $[C(p, N/K)]^K$ different internal representations possible. The number of different output strings must clearly be less than the number of internal representations since several internal representations are mapped to the same output. Using the inequality (10.7) we hence find that the ratio between the number of different output sequences and the number of different input sets is bounded from above by

$$\frac{[C(p, N/K)]^K}{2^p} \lesssim \exp(N[1 + \ln \alpha + \ln K - \alpha \ln 2]). \tag{12.9}$$

The storage capacity α_c is defined as the value of α at which this ratio becomes less than $1/2$. For large N this happens abruptly when the exponent changes sign. We therefore find $\alpha_c < \alpha^{\mathrm{MD}}$ with α^{MD} defined as the solution of the equation

$$0 = 1 + \ln \alpha^{\mathrm{MD}} + \ln K - \alpha^{\mathrm{MD}} \ln 2. \tag{12.10}$$

This is the so-called *Mitchison–Durbin* bound for the storage capacity of a tree-structured multilayer network with K hidden units [195]. For large values of K we find asymptotically

$$\alpha_c \lesssim \alpha^{\mathrm{MD}} \sim \frac{\ln K}{\ln 2}. \tag{12.11}$$

A similar calculation for the fully connected architecture yields asymptotically

$$\alpha_c \lesssim \alpha^{\mathrm{MD}} \sim K \frac{\ln K}{\ln 2}. \tag{12.12}$$

These bounds give a valuable orientation for more precise calculations using the replica method (cf. problem 12.6).

Turning to the generalization problem, approximate results for the dependence of the generalization error on the training set size may be obtained from the annealed approximation as used for the perceptron in section 2.1. This is particularly simple for tree architectures since the relations (12.5) and (12.7) between the generalization error and the overlaps of sub-perceptrons in the tree allow one to easily derive the entropic and energetic parts.

For the parity tree, e.g., we find (cf. (2.6))

$$\begin{aligned} s^{\mathrm{ann}}(\varepsilon) &= \frac{1}{2} \ln(1 - R^2(\varepsilon)) + \alpha \ln(1 - \varepsilon) \\ &= \frac{1}{2} \ln\left(1 - \sin^2\left(\frac{\pi}{2}(1 - 2\varepsilon)^{1/K}\right)\right) + \alpha \ln(1 - \varepsilon) \end{aligned} \tag{12.13}$$

and a simple numerical extremization yields an approximation for the generalization error $\varepsilon(\alpha)$ as a function of the training set size as shown in fig. 12.4. For all values of $K > 2$ there is a discontinuous transition from the pure guessing state characterized by $\varepsilon = 0.5$, which takes place when the maximum of $s^{\mathrm{ann}}(\varepsilon)$ in the open interval $(0, 0.5)$ coincides with $s^{\mathrm{ann}}(0.5)$. Within the annealed approximation we hence find retarded learning as discussed already in sections 7.3 and 8.3 for all values of $K > 1$. As we will see below (cf. section 12.4), the exact results are qualitatively similar to these simple approximations.

Results for the committee tree, which may be obtained similarly using (12.8) for $K \to \infty$ or inverting (12.7) numerically for finite K, are included in fig. 12.7.

Interestingly, the annealed approximation for the entropy of the generalization problem may also be used to derive a *lower bound* to the *storage capacity* α_c [196].

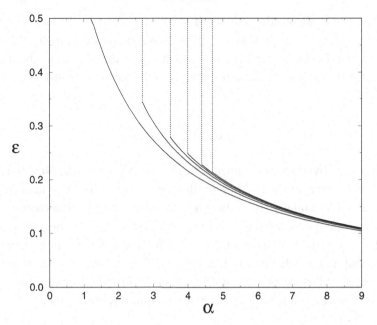

Fig. 12.4. Results for the generalization error as a function of the training set size for a parity machine of tree architecture with $K = 2, 3, 4, 5, 6$ and 7 hidden units (from left to right) as obtained within the annealed approximation (12.13).

This is again particularly effective for the parity tree. Let us first note that the points $\alpha_d^{\text{ann}}(K)$ of the discontinuous drop of ε from the initial value 0.5 as obtained within the annealed approximation are lower bounds for the true transition points $\alpha_d(K)$, see also fig. 12.6. The reason is as follows. The transitions occur when $s(0.5, \alpha)$ is equal to the maximum of $s(\varepsilon, \alpha)$ in the interval $0 < \varepsilon < 0.5$. For $\varepsilon = 0.5$ annealed and quenched entropy coincide since $R = 0$, whereas for $\varepsilon < 0.5$ the annealed entropy is an upper bound to the true entropy. The transition within the exact theory can therefore never precede the one within the annealed approximation. Moreover, $\varepsilon = 0.5$ for $\alpha < \alpha_d$ means that the student can reproduce all mappings without alignment with the teacher, i.e. considering the outputs as uncorrelated with the inputs. The task is then identical to the storage problem and we must therefore have $\alpha_d \leq \alpha_c$.

Anticipating that the transition occurs for large values of K at larger and larger values of α and jumps to smaller and smaller values of ε (cf. fig. 12.4), we may derive the large-K behaviour of α_d^{ann} from the asymptotic form of $s^{\text{ann}}(\varepsilon)$ for small ε. From (12.13) it is easy to show that in this limit

$$s^{\text{ann}}(\varepsilon) \sim \ln 2 + \ln \varepsilon - \ln K - \alpha\varepsilon. \tag{12.14}$$

Extremizing in ε and putting the result equal to $s^{\text{ann}}(\varepsilon = 0.5) = \alpha \ln 2$ we find to leading order $\alpha_d \sim \ln K / \ln 2$. This *lower* bound asymptotically matches the Mitchison–Durbin bound (12.11) which constitutes an *upper* bound! The asymptotic behaviour of the storage capacity of the parity tree must hence be given by

$$\alpha_c \sim \frac{\ln K}{\ln 2}, \qquad (12.15)$$

which is a non-trivial result obtained solely from simple bounds. Note that in view of problem 10.5 this result also implies that for the parity tree with large K the VC dimension is substantially larger than the number N of free parameters.

Of course the general bounds derived in chapter 10 also apply to multilayer networks. In particular the bound (10.20) for the generalization error gives a valuable hint on the behaviour to be expected. Finally, high-temperature learning as introduced at the end of section 4.2 may also be used effectively for obtaining approximate results on learning scenarios with multilayer networks.

12.3 The storage problem

The problem of implementing *random* input–output mappings forms a suitable starting point for the investigation of the learning abilities of multilayer networks. In the present section we will hence briefly discuss some of the peculiarities of the storage problem related to the existence of hidden units.

Let us first consider a network with tree architecture and fixed hidden-to-output mapping $\sigma = F(\tau_1, \ldots, \tau_K)$. The joint volume of couplings $\mathbf{J}_k$ realizing p input–output pairs $\{\boldsymbol{\xi}^\mu, \sigma^\mu\}$ is given by

$$\Omega(\boldsymbol{\xi}^\mu, \sigma^\mu) = \int \prod_{k=1}^{K} d\mu(\mathbf{J}_k) \prod_{\mu} \theta\left(\sigma^\mu F\left(\frac{\mathbf{J}_1 \boldsymbol{\xi}_1^\mu}{\sqrt{N/K}}, \ldots, \frac{\mathbf{J}_K \boldsymbol{\xi}_K^\mu}{\sqrt{N/K}}\right)\right), \qquad (12.16)$$

where

$$d\mu(\mathbf{J}_k) = \prod_{i=1}^{N/K} \frac{d J_{ki}}{\sqrt{2\pi e}} \qquad (12.17)$$

and $\boldsymbol{\xi}_k^\mu$ denotes the proper part of the input feeding the k-th hidden unit (cf. fig. 12.1).

The calculation of the average of $\ln \Omega(\boldsymbol{\xi}^\mu, \sigma^\mu)$ over the standard unbiased distributions of $\boldsymbol{\xi}^\mu$ and σ^μ follows the usual procedure outlined in appendix 2. The energetic part $G_E(q^{ab})$ may be written most concisely by splitting the integration variables λ_k^a into their sign, τ_k^a, and their absolute value according to

$$\int \prod_{k,a} d\lambda_k^a \, f(\lambda_k^a) = \underset{\{\tau_k^a\}}{\text{Tr}} \int_0^\infty \prod_{k,a} d\lambda_k^a \, f(\lambda_k^a \tau_k^a). \tag{12.18}$$

Using the replica and site symmetric ansatz

$$q_k^{ab} = \frac{K}{N} \sum_{i=1}^{N/K} J_{ki}^a J_{ki}^b = q \qquad \text{for} \quad a \neq b \tag{12.19}$$

for the order parameter matrix we find for the quenched entropy

$$s(\alpha) = \underset{q}{\text{extr}} \left[\frac{1}{2} \ln(1-q) + \frac{q}{2(1-q)} \right.$$
$$\left. + \alpha \int \prod_k Dt_k \ln \left(\underset{\{\tau_k\}}{\text{Tr}} \, \theta(F(\tau_1, \dots, \tau_K)) \prod_k H\left(\frac{\sqrt{q} t_k \tau_k}{\sqrt{1-q}} \right) \right) \right]. \tag{12.20}$$

This result has a simple interpretation. Comparing (12.20) with the entropy of the perceptron (6.13) we realize that the expression under the logarithm is nothing but the sum over all possible internal representations yielding the correct output weighted by the product of Gardner volumes of the individual sub-perceptrons for the corresponding internal representation.

As discussed in section 6.1 the storage capacity can be determined from the limit $q \to 1$ in the expression for the entropy. Taking this limit in (12.20) we obtain

$$\frac{1}{\alpha_c} = K \int_0^\infty Dt \, t^2 \, g(t) \tag{12.21}$$

with the function $g(t)$ depending on the special Boolean function $F(\tau_1, \dots, \tau_K)$ under consideration. Using (12.3) and (12.4) we find

$$g^{\text{PAR}}(t) = [2H(t)]^{(K-1)} \tag{12.22}$$

for the parity tree (cf. problem 12.6) and

$$g^{\text{COM}}(t) = \sum_{k=0}^{(K-1)/2} \binom{K-1}{k} [H(t)]^{K-1-k} [1 - H(t)]^k \tag{12.23}$$

for the committee tree.

The values for the storage capacity α_c obtained from these expressions are rather large. For the parity tree one finds e.g. $\alpha_c = 5.5, 10.4, 16.6$ and 24.1 for $K = 2, 3, 4$ and 5 whereas for the committee tree one gets $\alpha_c = 4.02, 5.78$ and 7.31 for $K = 3, 5$ and 7. This is reminiscent of the situation for the reversed wedge perceptron discussed in problem 7.6. Moreover using (12.22) and (12.23) one finds for a large number of hidden units K that $\alpha_c \sim K^2$ for the parity tree and $\alpha_c \sim \sqrt{K}$

for the committee tree. Both asymptotic behaviours violate the Mitchison–Durbin bound (12.11) and expression (12.21) for the storage capacity can therefore not be correct.

A stability analysis of the replica symmetric saddle point used in the derivation of (12.20) along the lines of appendix 4 reveals that replica symmetry is indeed broken for $\alpha > \alpha_{AT}$ with $\alpha_{AT} < \alpha_c$ and therefore a reliable determination of the storage capacity of multilayer networks in general requires replica symmetry breaking. As in the case of the reversed wedge perceptron the intuitive reason for the occurrence of replica symmetry breaking lies in the possibility of different internal representations and the ensuing disconnectedness of the solution space.

Calculations of the storage capacity using one-step replica symmetry breaking as described in appendix 5 have been performed for both the parity [197] and the committee tree [198, 199]. In all cases reduced values for the storage capacity are found, often in good agreement with numerical findings. For the parity tree one may show that within one-step replica symmetry breaking the storage capacity obeys the exact asymptotics (12.15), which may serve as an indication that this level of replica symmetry breaking might already yield the exact result as in the somewhat related random energy model [79, 76].

For the committee tree the calculations are rather involved and so far nobody has succeeded in deriving the asymptotic result for α_c for $K \to \infty$ within the above framework. Progress is possible however by using a variant of the multifractal techniques introduced in chapter 11 [184]. Again similarly to the analysis of the reversed wedge perceptron (cf. section 11.3) we decompose the total Gardner volume (12.16) into cells corresponding to different internal representations according to

$$\Omega(\boldsymbol{\xi}^\mu, \sigma^\mu) = \sum_{\boldsymbol{\tau}} \Omega(\boldsymbol{\tau}; \boldsymbol{\xi}^\mu, \sigma^\mu) \tag{12.24}$$

with

$$\Omega(\boldsymbol{\tau}; \boldsymbol{\xi}^\mu, \sigma^\mu) =$$

$$\int \prod_{k=1}^{K} d\mu(\mathbf{J}_k) \prod_{\mu} \theta\left(\sigma^\mu F\left(\frac{\mathbf{J}_1 \boldsymbol{\xi}_1^\mu}{\sqrt{N/K}}, \dots, \frac{\mathbf{J}_K \boldsymbol{\xi}_K^\mu}{\sqrt{N/K}}\right)\right) \prod_k \theta\left(\tau_k \frac{\mathbf{J}_k \boldsymbol{\xi}_k^\mu}{\sqrt{N/K}}\right). \tag{12.25}$$

Defining again $k(\boldsymbol{\tau}; \boldsymbol{\xi}^\mu, \sigma^\mu) = -(\ln \Omega(\boldsymbol{\tau}; \boldsymbol{\xi}^\mu, \sigma^\mu))/N$ the distribution $c(k)$ of the sizes of these cells may be calculated from the corresponding free energy

$$-\beta f(\beta) = \frac{1}{N}\left\langle\!\left\langle \ln \operatorname{Tr}_{\boldsymbol{\tau}} \Omega^\beta(\boldsymbol{\tau}; \boldsymbol{\xi}^\mu, \sigma^\mu) \right\rangle\!\right\rangle \tag{12.26}$$

via a Legendre transformation. As in chapter 11 the total number of internal representations is related to the maximum $c(k_0)$ of the multifractal spectrum $c(k)$ whereas $c(k_1)$ with k_1 defined by (11.18) characterizes the number of cells dominating the total Gardner volume $\Omega(\xi^\mu, \sigma^\mu)$. A replica symmetric calculation similar to the one which yielded (11.27) gives [184]

$$
-\beta f(\beta) = \underset{q_0, q_1}{\text{extr}} \left[\frac{\beta - 1}{2} \ln(1 - q_1) + \frac{1}{2} \ln(1 - q_1 + \beta(q_1 - q_0)) \right.
$$
$$
+ \frac{\beta q_0}{2(1 - q_1 + \beta(q_1 - q_0))}
$$
$$
+ \alpha \int \prod_k Dt_k \ln \underset{\tau}{\text{Tr}} \, \theta \left(\frac{1}{\sqrt{K}} \sum_k \tau_k \right)
$$
$$
\left. \times \int \prod_k Ds_k \, H^\beta \left(\frac{\sqrt{q_1 - q_0} s_k + \sqrt{q_0} \tau_k t_k}{\sqrt{1 - q_1}} \right) \right].
\tag{12.27}
$$

The storage capacity is identified with the value of α for which $c(k_0)$ becomes negative since then the typical number of available internal representations becomes exponentially small. From (12.27) one finds in this way for large K to dominant order

$$
\alpha_c \sim \frac{16}{\pi} \sqrt{\ln K}.
\tag{12.28}
$$

A stability analysis shows that the replica symmetric saddle point used in this calculation is marginally stable for $K \to \infty$, so that (12.28) is believed to be the correct asymptotic behaviour of the storage capacity of the committee tree. Note that the Mitchison–Durbin bound is obeyed.

The main reason for the enhanced storage abilities of multilayer networks as compared with the perceptron is the additional degrees of freedom in the hidden layer. The detailed organization of internal representations expressing the division of labour between the different hidden units may be characterized by the correlations

$$
c_{i_1, \dots, i_n} = \frac{1}{\alpha N} \sum_\mu \tau_{i_1}^\mu \tau_{i_2}^\mu \cdots \tau_{i_n}^\mu.
\tag{12.29}
$$

It turns out that for α tending to the storage capacity α_c these correlations approach specific values characteristic of the Boolean function $F(\tau_1, \dots, \tau_K)$ between hidden units and outputs. They can be calculated explicitly by using an extension of the methods introduced in section 6.4 [200, 201]. For a permutation-symmetric Boolean function $F(\tau_1, \dots, \tau_K)$ the correlation coefficients only depend on the number of hidden units included, i.e. $c_{i_1, \dots, i_n} = c_n$.

Complementary to calculating the c_n for different Boolean functions one may *replace* $F(\tau_1, \dots, \tau_K)$ by the specific values of the correlation coefficients c_n, thereby approximating the multilayer network by an ensemble of *correlated perceptrons* [202]. This allows one to consider smooth transitions between multilayer networks with different hidden-to-output mappings $F(\tau_1, \ldots, \tau_K)$.

Considering finally fully connected networks we only report a few results. The main new feature is the permutation symmetry between hidden units, related to the fact that all hidden units are fed from the same inputs (cf. fig. 12.1). In the statistical mechanics calculation this gives rise to the additional order parameters

$$C_{kl}^a = \frac{1}{N} \sum_i J_{ki}^a J_{li}^a \quad \text{and} \quad D_{kl}^{ab} = \frac{1}{N} \sum_i J_{ki}^a J_{li}^b \quad (12.30)$$

expressing the correlation between hidden units induced by the couplings to the same input. For small values of α the network is in the *permutation symmetric* phase in which solutions related to each other by a permutation of the hidden units belong to the same solution volume. Increasing α generally leads to a state with *broken permutation symmetry* where solutions with different permutations of hidden units are no longer connected with each other. Assuming replica and site symmetry one can show for the committee machine that $D \to C$ (as $q \to 1$) for $\alpha \to \alpha_c$ and that $C = -1/(K-1)$ at the storage capacity. This weak anti-correlation between the hidden units is consistent with the fact that at the storage capacity most inputs have an internal representation with $(K+1)/2$ of the τ_k equal to the desired output and $(K-1)/2$ of them opposite to the output. For large K these correlations disappear, suggesting that in this limit the storage capacity is just equal to the result for the tree architecture multiplied by K. A more precise investigation using multifractal techniques however yields [203]

$$\alpha_c \sim \frac{16}{\pi - 2} K \sqrt{\ln K}. \quad (12.31)$$

Comparing this result with (12.28) one realizes that the small correlation continues to play a role and modifies the prefactor of the asymptotic behaviour. For the fully connected parity machine one finds $\alpha_c \sim K \ln K / \ln 2$ [204], which again saturates the Mitchison–Durbin bound (12.12).

12.4 Generalization with a parity tree

As an instructive example for the problem of learning a rule from examples with a multilayer network we consider the realizable problem in which a parity tree with K hidden units learns a target classification provided by another parity tree with exactly the same architecture. Denoting as usual the couplings of the teacher network by $\mathbf{T}_k$ the version space volume is given by

$$\Omega(\xi^\mu, \mathbf{T}_k) = \int d\mu(\mathbf{J}) \prod_\mu \theta \left(\prod_k \frac{\mathbf{T}_k \xi_k^\mu}{\sqrt{N/K}} \prod_k \frac{\mathbf{J}_k \xi_k^\mu}{\sqrt{N/K}} \right). \tag{12.32}$$

The by now standard calculation of the quenched entropy is most conveniently done by employing the teacher–student symmetry and using the $n \to 1$ version of the replica trick (cf. section 2.3). Within replica symmetry, which is known to hold for this case, one finds

$$s(\alpha) = \operatorname*{extr}_R \left[\frac{1}{2} \ln(1 - R) + \frac{R}{2} \right.$$

$$+ 2\alpha \int \prod_k Dt_k \left(\operatorname*{Tr}_{\{\tau_k\}} \theta \left(\prod_k \tau_k \right) \prod_k H \left(\frac{\sqrt{R} t_k \tau_k}{\sqrt{1 - R}} \right) \right)$$

$$\times \left. \ln \left(\operatorname*{Tr}_{\{\tau_k\}} \theta \left(\prod_k \tau_k \right) \prod_k H \left(\frac{\sqrt{R} t_k \tau_k}{\sqrt{1 - R}} \right) \right) \right], \tag{12.33}$$

clearly resembling (12.20). Now by a similar argument to that used in the derivation of (12.5) one can show that

$$\operatorname*{Tr}_{\{\tau_k\}} \theta \left(\prod_k \tau_k \right) \prod_k H \left(\frac{\sqrt{R} t_k \tau_k}{\sqrt{1 - R}} \right) = \frac{1}{2} \left(1 + \prod_k \left(2H \left(\frac{\sqrt{R} t_k \tau_k}{\sqrt{1 - R}} \right) - 1 \right) \right). \tag{12.34}$$

Using the fact that $2H(x) - 1$ is an odd function of x and expanding the logarithm the result for the quenched entropy can be written as [193]

$$s(\alpha) = \operatorname*{extr}_R \left[\frac{1}{2} \ln(1 - R) + \frac{R}{2} - \alpha \ln 2 \right.$$

$$+ \alpha \sum_{m=2,4,\ldots}^\infty \frac{1}{m(m-1)} \left[\int Dt \left(2H \left(\frac{\sqrt{R} t_k \tau_k}{\sqrt{1 - R}} \right) - 1 \right)^m \right]^K \right]. \tag{12.35}$$

This form is particularly useful for the numerical determination of the extremum since it involves only a single integration. The results for $\varepsilon(\alpha)$ obtained by numerically solving the saddle point equation corresponding to (12.35) and using (12.5) are shown in fig. 12.5 for different values of K. They are qualitatively rather similar to those obtained within the annealed approximation and shown in fig. 12.4.

Two points deserve special attention. Firstly, as in the annealed approximation, we find retarded learning for all values of $K > 1$, i.e. for small α the generalization error remains equal to 0.5. This is related to the inversion symmetry of the parity function (12.3), see problem 12.11. With increasing training set size there is a

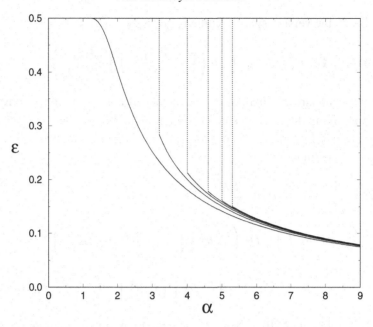

Fig. 12.5. Generalization error as a function of the training set size for a parity machine of tree architecture with $K = 2, 3, 4, 5, 6$ and 7 hidden units (from left to right) as obtained from the numerical extremization of (12.35).

transition to non-trivial generalization with $\varepsilon < 0.5$ which sets in continuously (at $\alpha = \pi^2/8$) for $K = 2$ but occurs *discontinuously* at a certain value $\alpha_d(K)$ for all $K > 2$. Secondly, for large α the curves for different values of K become very similar. In fact considering the limits $\alpha \to \infty$ and $R \to 1$ in (12.35) one may show that the asymptotic decay of the generalization error is *independently* of K given by

$$\varepsilon \sim \frac{1}{\sqrt{\pi} \, | \int dt \, H(t) \ln H(t)|} \frac{1}{\alpha} \cong \frac{0.625}{\alpha}, \tag{12.36}$$

which coincides with the asymptotic result for the perceptron as determined in problem 2.10 (see also problem 12.10). The asymptotic decay of the generalization error is hence solely determined by the dimension of the input space N. Investigating on the other hand the dependence on K of the value α_d at which the generalization error drops discontinuously from $\varepsilon = 0.5$ one finds that it scales asymptotically as $\alpha_d \sim \ln K / \ln 2$, i.e. exactly like the storage capacity and the VC dimension. This is shown in fig. 12.6. Hence although the asymptotic decay of the generalization error is insensitive to the particular value of the VC dimension, the threshold at which non-trivial generalization sets in is closely related to the

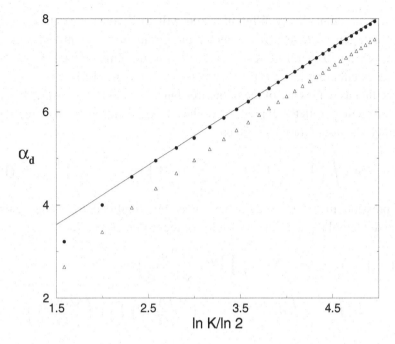

Fig. 12.6. Value α_d of the training set size at which the discontinuous transition to non-trivial generalization takes place in a parity tree as a function of the number K of hidden units as resulting from the quenched theory (12.35) (circles) and the annealed approximation (12.13) (triangles). The line describes the asymptotic behaviour (12.15) of the storage capacity.

storage abilities of the network and "generalization starts where learning ends" in accordance with the general discussion of section 10.3.

12.5 Generalization with a committee tree

Due to the high symmetry of the parity machine a comparatively simple analysis of its storage and generalization abilities was possible. On the other hand the parity function from the hidden layer to the output cannot be implemented in a simple way using McCulloch–Pitts neurons. In this respect the committee machine is a much more natural representative of a multilayer network. Unfortunately its detailed investigation is more involved.

In the present section we will study the realizable generalization scenario in which a committee tree with K hidden units learns a target classification provided by a teacher network of exactly the same architecture. Considering the limit $K \rightarrow \infty$ we will find that the general behaviour is rather similar to the perceptron case, which corresponds to $K = 1$. It is therefore believed that also for intermediate values of K no dramatically different results will arise. Since the detailed analysis of the case of general K involves rather tedious calculations and intricate numerical procedures we will therefore restrict ourselves to the limiting case $K \to \infty$, in which the calculations benefit from asymptotic results like (12.8).

Proceeding as in the case of the parity tree but replacing (12.3) by (12.4) we find for the energetic part in the expression of the quenched entropy using a replica and site symmetric ansatz for the overlaps

$$G_E = \ln 2 \int \prod_k Dt_k \left[\underset{\{\tau_k\}}{\text{Tr}}\, \theta\left(\frac{1}{\sqrt{K}} \sum_k \tau_k\right) \prod_k H\left(\frac{\sqrt{R}\, t_k \tau_k}{\sqrt{1-R}}\right) \right]^n. \qquad (12.37)$$

The expression in the square brackets may be simplified by using again the celebrated integral representation (A1.19) of the θ-function to find

$$[\cdots] = \underset{\{\tau_k\}}{\text{Tr}}\, \theta\left(\frac{1}{\sqrt{K}} \sum_k \tau_k\right) \prod_k H\left(\frac{\sqrt{R}\, t_k \tau_k}{\sqrt{1-R}}\right)$$

$$= \int_0^\infty \frac{d\Lambda}{2\pi} \int d\hat{\Lambda}\, e^{i\Lambda\hat{\Lambda}} \underset{\{\tau_k\}}{\text{Tr}} \exp\left(-\frac{i\hat{\Lambda}}{\sqrt{K}} \tau_k\right) \prod_k H\left(\frac{\sqrt{R}\, t_k \tau_k}{\sqrt{1-R}}\right)$$

$$= \int_0^\infty \frac{d\Lambda}{2\pi} \int d\hat{\Lambda}\, e^{i\Lambda\hat{\Lambda}} \prod_k \left(\underset{\tau}{\text{Tr}} \exp\left(-\frac{i\hat{\Lambda}}{\sqrt{K}} \tau\right) H\left(\frac{\sqrt{R}\, t_k \tau}{\sqrt{1-R}}\right) \right).$$

Expanding to second order in $1/\sqrt{K}$, performing the trace over the internal representations, using the abbreviation

$$H_k = H\left(\frac{\sqrt{R}\, t_k}{\sqrt{1-R}}\right),$$

and re-exponentiating we find to order $1/K$

$$[\cdots] = \int_0^\infty \frac{d\Lambda}{2\pi} \int d\hat{\Lambda} \exp\left(i\Lambda\hat{\Lambda} + i\hat{\Lambda}\frac{1}{\sqrt{K}} \sum_k (1 - 2H_k) \right.$$

$$\left. - \frac{\hat{\Lambda}^2}{2}\left(1 - \frac{1}{K} \sum_k (1 - 2H_k)^2\right) \right).$$

Hence the integrand in (12.37) does not depend on all the individual integration variables t_k but only on the combination $\sum_k (1 - 2H_k)$. By the central limit theorem

$$\frac{1}{\sqrt{K}} \sum_k (1 - 2H_k)$$

is a Gaussian random variable with zero mean and variance

$$\int Dt \left(1 - 2H\left(\frac{\sqrt{R}\, t_k}{\sqrt{1-R}}\right)\right)^2 = \frac{2}{\pi} \arcsin R =: R_{\text{eff}}. \qquad (12.38)$$

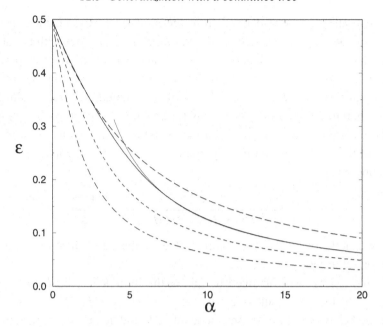

Fig. 12.7. Generalization error as a function of the training set size for a committee machine of tree architecture in the limit of infinitely many hidden units, $K \to \infty$ (full line). Also shown are the results of the annealed approximation for $K \to \infty$ (long-dashed) and $K = 3$ (dashed) and for the perceptron (dashed–dotted) corresponding to $K = 1$. The thin line is the asymptotic result (12.41).

We may therefore use the replacement

$$\int \prod_k Dt_k \, f\left(\frac{1}{\sqrt{K}} \sum_k (1 - 2H_k), \frac{1}{K} \sum_k (1 - 2H_k)^2\right) = \int Dt \, f(\sqrt{R_{\text{eff}}}\, t, R_{\text{eff}})$$

and obtain

$$G_E = \ln 2 \int Dt \left[\int_0^\infty \frac{d\Lambda}{2\pi} \int d\hat{\Lambda} \exp\left(i\hat{\Lambda}(\Lambda + \sqrt{R_{\text{eff}}}\, t) - \frac{1 - R_{\text{eff}}}{2}\hat{\Lambda}^2\right)\right]^n$$

$$= \ln 2 \int Dt \, H^n\left(\frac{\sqrt{R_{\text{eff}}}\, t}{\sqrt{1 - R_{\text{eff}}}}\right). \tag{12.39}$$

This expression is exactly equivalent to the corresponding quantity for the simple perceptron after the replacement $R \mapsto R_{\text{eff}}$. We therefore finally find for the quenched entropy

$$s(\alpha) = \operatorname*{extr}_R \left[\frac{1}{2}\ln(1 - R) + \frac{R}{2} + 2\alpha \int Dt \, H\left(\frac{\sqrt{R_{\text{eff}}}\, t}{\sqrt{1 - R_{\text{eff}}}}\right) \ln H\left(\frac{\sqrt{R_{\text{eff}}}\, t}{\sqrt{1 - R_{\text{eff}}}}\right)\right]. \tag{12.40}$$

The generalization error derived from the numerical extremization in (12.40) and $\varepsilon = \arccos(R_{\text{eff}})/\pi$ (cf. 12.8) is shown in fig. 12.7 together with the annealed approximation for $K = 3$ and $K \to \infty$ and the result for the perceptron corresponding to $K = 1$. It is clearly seen that the generalization behaviours of the committee tree for $K = 1$ and $K \to \infty$ are qualitatively rather similar and one may therefore expect that the results for general K do not differ significantly from these extreme cases. In particular there are no discontinuous transitions as in the case of the parity tree and the asymptotic decay of ε is algebraic. In fact from (12.40) one finds

$$\varepsilon \sim 2\frac{\sqrt{2}}{\alpha \int Dt \, \exp(-t^2/2) \, (H(t))^{-1}} \sim \frac{1.25}{\alpha} \qquad (12.41)$$

which is exactly twice the asymptotic value of the generalization error of the perceptron (cf. (2.50)).

Note that (12.41) was obtained by taking the limit $K \to \infty$ *before* the limit $\alpha \to \infty$. In fact the result is correct only for $\alpha \lesssim \sqrt{K}$. For $\alpha > \sqrt{K}$ the asymptotic behaviour of $\varepsilon(\alpha)$ is independent of K and therefore identical to that of the perceptron as given in (2.50), a remarkable result the origin of which is clarified in problem 12.10.

The initial decay of the generalization error with the size of the training set is slower for a large committee tree than for the perceptron. This is in accordance with the fact that in the former case the storage capacity and therefore also the VC dimension are significantly larger. However, unlike in the case of the parity tree no retarded learning occurs and it seems impossible here to extract the result (12.28) from the learning curves $\varepsilon(\alpha, K)$. As with the perceptron the simple rule that "generalization starts where memorization ends" therefore does not show up in a straightforward manner in the learning behaviour of a committee machine. This is related to the fact that there is a positive correlation between the output and the hidden units (cf. problem 12.11).

12.6 The fully connected committee machine

As an example of learning in a fully connected multilayer network we will in this section consider the realizable scenario of a fully connected committee machine with $K \to \infty$ hidden units learning a classification provided by a teacher network of the same architecture. We will only briefly discuss the additional features which appear in this situation since the detailed calculations become rather lengthy. A thorough and very readable analysis of this important case is given in [205].

The main qualitatively new aspect in learning with a fully connected architecture is the permutation symmetry between hidden units and its possible spontaneous breakdown due to correlations between particular hidden units of teacher and student. This possible *specialization of hidden units* causes the main differences between the generalization behaviour of the tree architecture and that of the fully connected committee machine.

As in the storage problem this possibility shows up in the calculations by the emergence of additional order parameters of the form (12.30). For the generalization problem the most important family is given by

$$R_{kl}^a = \frac{1}{N} \mathbf{T}_k \mathbf{J}_l^a, \tag{12.42}$$

describing the overlap between different sub-perceptrons of teacher and student. A suitable ansatz for these order parameters which allows further analytical progress combines replica symmetry, which can again be shown to hold, with the assumption of *partial committee symmetry* and is of the form

$$R_{kl}^a = R + \Delta R \, \delta(k, l), \tag{12.43}$$

with the Kronecker symbol $\delta(k, l)$ defined in (A1.13).

This ansatz generalizes the assumption of site symmetry used in the analysis of the storage capacity to the generalization problem. For $\Delta R = 0$ it describes a *permutation symmetric state* in which each hidden unit of the student has the same alignment with all hidden units of the teacher. If on the other hand $\Delta R > 0$ every hidden unit of the student is correlated with one hidden unit of the teacher and the mentioned specialization of hidden units sets in. Note that more general situations are conceivable, e.g. two student hidden units trying to imitate the same hidden unit of the teacher; however, the above ansatz is the simplest one capable of showing specialization at all and has been shown to yield results in accordance with numerical simulations.

Treating the remaining order parameters describing the self-overlap of the student in an analogous way, the analysis may be completed similarly as for the committee tree. One finally ends up with saddle point equations for five order parameters which are to be solved numerically.

Defining α as $\alpha = p/(NK)$, i.e. as the ratio between the number of examples and the number of adaptable couplings in the network, the following results are found [205]. For small training set sizes, $\alpha = O(1/K)$, the permutation symmetric state characterized by $\Delta R = 0$ is stable and no specialization of hidden units occurs. The generalization error decreases in this regime from its initial value 0.5 to an *intermediate plateau* at

$$\varepsilon_{\text{pl}} = \frac{1}{\pi} \arccos \frac{2}{\pi} \cong 0.28. \tag{12.44}$$

The approach to ε_{pl} is algebraic, $(\varepsilon - \varepsilon_{\text{pl}}) \sim \text{const}/\alpha$. Despite the initial decrease of the generalization error perfect learning is hence impossible in this phase. This failure is related to the symmetry between the hidden units of the student and signals an inefficient degree of division of labour among them. The limited number of examples in the training set, which is of the order of the input dimension N, is just sufficient to adapt the couplings of the *individual* sub-perceptrons to the task but does not yet allow their interaction to be optimized.

The permutation symmetric state remains a solution of the saddle point equations when α is increased to order 1 such that the number of examples becomes comparable to the number of adaptive couplings in the network. However, at $\alpha = \alpha_d \cong 7.65$ a *discontinuous* transition to a *specialized* state with $\Delta R > 0$ occurs, followed by an algebraic decay of the generalization error to zero. The detailed asymptotic behaviour is given by (12.41) as found for the committee tree if different sub-perceptrons of the teacher are orthogonal to each other.

The generalization behaviour in a fully connected multilayer network therefore consists of three phases. Initially the different sub-perceptrons adjust to the task individually. Fed by the same inputs they realize on average identical configurations. The generalization error decreases continuously during this phase and reaches a plateau value. Next a discontinuous drop in the generalization error occurs, related to the transition from the permutation symmetric state to one with hidden units specializing in the performance of one particular hidden unit of the teacher. Being related to the spontaneous breakdown of the permutation symmetry between the hidden units of the student, this transition corresponds to the adaptation of *discrete* degrees of freedom in the learning process, and its discontinuous character is in accordance with our experience gained in chapter 7. Finally the fine-tuning of the student couplings to the values of the teacher results in a second phase of continuous decrease of the generalization error reaching asymptotically $\varepsilon = 0$ as characteristic of a realizable problem.

12.7 Summary

Multilayer neural networks are powerful information processing devices. Even a single intermediate layer of sufficiently many hidden units allows the implementation of an arbitrary Boolean function between input and output. A detailed analysis within the framework of statistical mechanics is, however, possible only for very restricted architectures. Therefore approximate methods permitting a rough characterization of the abilities of a multilayer network with reasonable mathematical effort are of particular importance.

Multilayer networks with a number K of hidden units much smaller than the input dimension N are accessible to a detailed statistical mechanics analysis because the incoming fields at the hidden units are Gaussian random variables. In particular if one assumes a tree architecture with hidden units fed by disjoint subsets of the input and a fixed Boolean function F between the internal representation in the hidden layer and the output the calculations may efficiently build on the results obtained for the perceptron. In the present chapter we have mainly dealt with the parity and committee machine but several of the results may be generalized to a general *permutation symmetric* Boolean function as shown in problems 12.9–12.11. Although these special architectures are rather "perceptron-like" they show interesting new features both in their storage and generalization behaviour.

In the storage problem the main complication lies in the likely occurrence of replica symmetry breaking related to a disconnected solution space due to the possibility of different internal representations giving rise to the same output. This is very similar to what has already been discussed for the reversed wedge perceptron in chapter 7. For large number of hidden units K (but still $K \ll N$) the storage capacity may diverge with K, implying that also the VC dimension becomes significantly larger than the dimension N of the input space.

The initial phase of the generalization behaviour depends decisively on the correlations between the hidden units and the output (cf. problem 12.11). If the Boolean function F is such that in order to realize a positive output the majority of the hidden units must show a particular sign (as in the case of the committee machine) the generalization error decreases from its initial value 0.5 immediately if $\alpha > 0$. This is reasonable since the information about the teacher classification at the output is to a certain extent directly transferred to the hidden units. If on the other hand the Boolean function does not give rise to correlations between the values of the hidden units and the output (as in the case of the parity machine) the generalization error remains at 0.5 for some interval of α and the system exhibits retarded learning.

For large training set size α the same algebraic decay of the generalization error is found as for the perceptron. When considering the case of large number of hidden units one has to keep in mind that the limits $K \to \infty$ and $\alpha \to \infty$ do not commute.

New features of the learning behaviour show up for fully connected architectures. Since all hidden units are now connected to exactly the same inputs there is full permutation symmetry in the hidden layer. Learning proceeds now in two distinct phases. If the number of examples is just of the order of the input dimension all sub-perceptrons adapt individually and the system settles into a permutation symmetric state in which the overlap between all pairs of hidden units of teacher and student is the same. The generalization error approaches an intermediate plateau value $\varepsilon_{pl} > 0$ in this phase. Further progress is possible only with a more efficient division of labour between the hidden units. This requires a number of examples of the order KN, which is the number of adaptable parameters in the system. It gives rise to a breaking of the permutation symmetry resulting in a specialization of the hidden units of the student to those of the teacher. After a discontinuous drop of the generalization error at this symmetry-breaking transition the final decay of ε towards zero is again algebraic.

With the internal representations acting as discrete degrees of freedom explicit learning algorithms for multilayer networks have to cope with the same difficulties already discussed in section 7.4 for the Ising perceptron. In fact no fast, reliable, and universal learning algorithm for multilayer networks with non-differentiable transfer function is known.   Different heuristics (see e.g. [195, 191]) work reasonably well for some setups and fail in others. This problem is much less severe within the framework of on-line learning to be discussed in the next chapter.

We finally again collect some of the basic references. The first complete analysis of the storage problem for a multilayer network from the point of view of statistical mechanics was given in [197] and dealt with the parity tree. The storage properties of the committee machine were discussed in [198, 199], and the asymptotic result for the storage capacity in the limit of large K was first obtained in [184] using the multifractal analysis of the space of internal representations. The generalization behaviour of a parity tree with $K = 2$ hidden units was discussed in [206], and the complete analysis for general K was given in [193]. The generalization properties of the committee tree with $K \to \infty$ were first given in [207], and the case of the fully connected committee machine was thoroughly analysed in [205]. The existence of an intermediate plateau for the fully connected architecture was also discussed in [208, 209] on the basis of the annealed approximation. The generalization properties of multilayer networks with tree architecture and a general permutation invariant Boolean function between hidden units and output were elucidated in [210]. A simple over-realizable scenario was discussed in [211]. Some aspects of optimal learning in multilayer networks were considered in [212].

12.8 Problems

12.1 Show by using the results of chapter 10 that a perceptron can at most implement of order e^{N^2} different Boolean functions between input and output.

12.2 Consider as input examples all vectors $\boldsymbol{\xi}$ with binary components $\xi_i = \pm 1$, $i = 1, \ldots, N$. Show that any classification of those examples, i.e. any Boolean function of N variables, may be implemented by a multilayer network by introducing "grandmother cells", i.e. nodes in the hidden layer which become activated for one and only one input example [213].

12.3 Consider a feed-forward network with a single input ξ and a linear output node. Show by geometric considerations that the network can approximate to any desired accuracy any function $\sigma_T(\xi)$, provided enough nodes are available in the hidden layer.

(Hint: Consider two hidden nodes and show that $g(J_1x - \theta_1) - g(J_2x - \theta_2)$ contributes a localized pulse to the output. By superposition of such pulses, any function may be reconstructed.)

12.4 Consider the teacher–student scenario with two committee machines of identical architecture. For a very large number K of hidden units (but still $K \ll N$) one expects the different hidden units of the same machine to be only very weakly correlated with each other. Since each pair of teacher–student hidden units agrees with probability $(1 - \varepsilon_\tau)$ and disagrees with probability ε_τ, the local fields at teacher and student output become Gaussian distributed variables with zero mean, unit variance, and correlation $(1 - 2\varepsilon_\tau)$. Denoting by R the overlap between corresponding teacher and student sub-perceptrons between input and hidden layer show that

$$\varepsilon_{K \to \infty}^{\text{COM}} = \frac{1}{\pi} \arccos\left(\frac{2}{\pi} \arcsin(R)\right), \tag{12.45}$$

verifying (12.8).

12.5 Show by using the annealed approximation that the storage capacity α_c of an Ising parity tree, i.e. with couplings $J_i = \pm 1$, must be less than or equal to 1. Show then that this bound is indeed saturated for all $K > 1$.

12.6 Verify the replica symmetric expressions (12.21) and (12.22) for the storage capacity α_c of the parity tree and show that asymptotically $\alpha_c^{\text{RS}} \sim K^2$, violating the Mitchison–Durbin bound (12.11).

12.7 Consider the storage problem for a fully connected parity machine and employ the following learning algorithm which *adds hidden units* in the process of learning [214]. The algorithm starts with a perceptron with *adaptable threshold*. When it becomes impossible to realize all the desired input–output mappings by adapting the couplings and the threshold of this perceptron, a second perceptron of the same type and fed by the same inputs is added and the overall output is taken to be the product of the two-perceptron outputs. The second perceptron corrects the errors of the first by giving an output $+1$ for all inputs classified correctly by the first perceptron and -1 if its classification was wrong. The output of the second perceptron is therefore *biased*. When the storage capacity of this $K = 2$ parity machine is reached a third hidden unit is added and so on. Show by using the results of problem 6.9 that the storage capacity reached by this special learning algorithm behaves asymptotically as $\alpha_c \sim K \ln K$, saturating the Mitchison–Durbin bound (12.12).

12.8 Show by combining (12.39) with the entropic part for Ising couplings (cf. (7.8)) that a committee tree with couplings $J_i = \pm 1$ and $K \to \infty$ learning from a teacher of the same architecture shows a discontinuous transition to perfect generalization at $\alpha_d \cong 1.07$. Compare this with the corresponding result for the Ising perceptron discussed in section 7.2.

12.9 Consider the realizable teacher–student scenario of two two-layered neural networks of tree architecture with a *general permutation invariant* Boolean function $F(\tau_1, \ldots, \tau_K)$ between hidden units and output [210]. Defining

$$\operatorname*{Tr}_{\{\tau_k | \sigma\}} \cdots \tag{12.46}$$

as the restricted trace over all those internal representations $\{\tau_k\}$ which give rise to the output σ show that the generalization error and the quenched entropy are given by

$$\varepsilon = \frac{1}{2K} \operatorname*{Tr}_{\sigma} \operatorname*{Tr}_{\{\tau_k^T | \sigma\}} \operatorname*{Tr}_{\{\tau_k^J | -\sigma\}} \prod_k \left(1 - \frac{1}{\pi}\arccos(\tau_k^J \tau_k^T R)\right), \tag{12.47}$$

and

$$s = \operatorname*{extr}_R \left[\frac{1}{2}\ln(1-R) + \frac{R}{2} + \alpha \int \prod_k Dt_k \operatorname*{Tr}_{\sigma} \right.$$
$$\left. \times \left(\operatorname*{Tr}_{\{\tau_k | \sigma\}} \prod_k H\left(\sqrt{\frac{R}{1-R}}\tau_k t_k\right)\right) \ln \left(\operatorname*{Tr}_{\{\tau_k | \sigma\}} \prod_k H\left(\sqrt{\frac{R}{1-R}}\tau_k t_k\right)\right) \right] \tag{12.48}$$

respectively, with R denoting the overlap between corresponding sub-perceptrons of teacher and student.

12.10 Considering the large-α behaviour for the setup of the previous problem show that for $R \to 1$ one finds from (12.47) and (12.48)

$$\varepsilon \sim \frac{N_{\mathrm{db}}}{2^K} \frac{1}{\pi}\sqrt{2(1-R)}, \tag{12.49}$$

and

$$s \sim \operatorname*{extr}_R \left[\frac{1}{2}\ln(1-R) + \frac{R}{2} + \alpha \frac{N_{\mathrm{db}}}{2^K}\sqrt{1-R}\sqrt{\frac{2}{\pi}}\int dt\, H(t)\ln H(t) \right] \tag{12.50}$$

where N_{db} denotes the number of internal representations at the *decision boundary* of F, i.e. of those configurations $\{\tau_k\}$ for which flipping a single τ_k may result in a different output. Performing the extremization in R show that the asymptotic decay of the generalization error with α is *independently of* $F(\tau_1, \ldots, \tau_K)$ given by

$$\varepsilon \sim \frac{1}{\sqrt{\pi} \ |\int dt \ H(t) \ln H(t)|} \frac{1}{\alpha} \tag{12.51}$$

coinciding with the result (2.50) for the perceptron.

12.11 Consider now the generalization behaviour of the setup of problem 12.9 with general permutation invariant Boolean decoder functions for small α. Show that in this limit one finds from (12.47) and (12.48)

$$\varepsilon \sim 2c_0(1 - c_0) - \frac{4K}{\pi} c_1^2 R + \cdots \tag{12.52}$$

and

$$s \sim \underset{R}{\mathrm{extr}} \left[-\frac{R^2}{4} + \alpha c_0 \ln c_0 + \alpha c_1 \ln c_1 + \frac{\alpha K}{\pi} \frac{c_1^2}{c_0(1 - c_0)} R + \cdots \right] \tag{12.53}$$

respectively, where

$$c_0 = \frac{1}{2^K} \underset{\{\tau_k|+\}}{\mathrm{Tr}} = 1 - \frac{1}{2^K} \underset{\{\tau_k|-\}}{\mathrm{Tr}} \tag{12.54}$$

and

$$c_1 = \frac{1}{2^K} \underset{\{\tau_k|+\}}{\mathrm{Tr}} \tau_l = -\frac{1}{2^K} \underset{\{\tau_k|-\}}{\mathrm{Tr}} \tau_l \tag{12.55}$$

are generalizations of the correlation coefficients defined in (12.29) for the storage problem. Performing the extremization in R show that for $c_1 \neq 0$ the generalization error decreases immediately for $\alpha > 0$ whereas for $c_1 = 0$ one finds retarded learning.

12.12 Consider a perceptron learning from a fully connected committee machine with infinitely many hidden units ($K \to \infty$) and orthogonal sub-perceptrons, $\mathbf{T}_k \mathbf{T}_l = N \delta_{kl}$. Assuming that for $\alpha \to \infty$ the student vector will approach the centre of mass of the teacher vectors $\mathbf{T}_k$ show that the generalization error will converge to

$$\varepsilon_r = \frac{1}{\pi} \arccos \sqrt{\frac{2}{\pi}}. \tag{12.56}$$

(Hint: Use the fact that

$$\frac{\mathbf{J}\boldsymbol{\xi}}{\sqrt{N}} \quad \text{and} \quad \frac{1}{\sqrt{K}} \sum_k \text{sgn}\left(\frac{\mathbf{T}_k\boldsymbol{\xi}}{\sqrt{N}}\right) \qquad (12.57)$$

are correlated Gaussian variables.)

13

On-line Learning in Multilayer Networks

The widespread use in applications of on-line learning in multilayer networks makes their theoretical study a subject of prime importance. Even though there are many *ad hoc* recipes on how to proceed with the details of the architecture and the training rules, a deeper understanding has been lacking. We will start with a study of the simplified multilayer architectures introduced in the previous chapter, namely the parity tree and committee machines. We will find that they share several features with the perceptron, but at the same time differences arise which are typical of the multilayer structure. The theory for more general multilayer machines with a sign transfer function becomes quite involved. It thus comes as a pleasant surprise that one can derive explicit evolution equations for fully connected multilayer networks with a smooth activation function. This allows one to study and obtain more insight into several important issues mentioned earlier, such as the origin of plateaus.

13.1 The committee tree

We start the detailed discussion of on-line learning in multilayer networks with one of the simpler situations, namely a student committee machine of tree architecture with K hidden units characterized by the set of synaptic vectors $\mathbf{J}_k$, learning from a teacher machine with the same architecture with synaptic vectors $\mathbf{T}_k, k = 1, \ldots, K$. Since the calculations are very similar to those for the perceptron corresponding to $K = 1$, we can dispense with the details and refer to section 9.1 for guidance. The examples $\boldsymbol{\xi}^\mu$ consist of random and independent sub-pieces $\boldsymbol{\xi}_k^\mu$ which are presented subsequently to the hidden unit with synaptic vector $\mathbf{J}_k^\mu$, constructed from the examples preceding μ. Recalling that both $\boldsymbol{\xi}_k^\mu$ and $\mathbf{J}_k^\mu$ are

237

vectors of dimension N/K the on-line learning rule has the form

$$\mathbf{J}_k^{\mu+1} = \mathbf{J}_k^{\mu} + \frac{1}{\sqrt{N/K}} F_k^{\mu} \boldsymbol{\xi}_k^{\mu}. \tag{13.1}$$

The learning amplitude F_k^{μ} may in principle depend on all the information available, including for example the state of the other student units $k' \neq k$.

Similarly to the treatment of on-line learning for the perceptron we introduce the order parameters

$$\rho_k^{\mu} = \frac{\mathbf{J}_k^{\mu} \mathbf{T}_k}{N/K} \quad \text{and} \quad Q_k^{\mu} = \frac{(\mathbf{J}_k^{\mu})^2}{N/K}. \tag{13.2}$$

In the thermodynamic limit these quantities become self-averaging functions of $\alpha = p/N$ and obey the evolution equations

$$\frac{d\rho_k}{d\alpha} = K \langle F_k u_k \rangle, \tag{13.3}$$

$$\frac{dQ_k}{d\alpha} = K \langle F_k (F_k + 2t_k) \rangle. \tag{13.4}$$

These equations are identical in form to the perceptron equations (9.9) and (9.11) with the training size α replaced by $K\alpha = p/(N/K)$. The average is with respect to the randomly chosen examples $\boldsymbol{\xi}_k$,

$$u_k = \frac{\mathbf{T}_k \boldsymbol{\xi}_k}{\sqrt{N/K}} \tag{13.5}$$

is the local field of the teacher, and the local field

$$t_k = \frac{\mathbf{J}_k \boldsymbol{\xi}_k}{\sqrt{N/K}} \tag{13.6}$$

is that of a *new* example $\boldsymbol{\xi}_k$ with the vector $\mathbf{J}_k$ constructed on the basis of preceding examples. The evolution equations (13.3)–(13.4) must be supplemented with the specific form of the learning amplitude F_k. The average over the examples can then be easily performed by noting that u_k and $t_k/\sqrt{Q_k}$ form pairs of correlated Gaussian random variables with

$$\langle u_k \rangle = \left\langle \frac{t_k}{\sqrt{Q_k}} \right\rangle = 0,$$

$$\langle u_k u_l \rangle = \left\langle \frac{t_k}{\sqrt{Q_k}} \frac{t_l}{\sqrt{Q_l}} \right\rangle = \delta(k, l),$$

$$\left\langle u_k \frac{t_l}{\sqrt{Q_l}} \right\rangle = \frac{\rho_k}{\sqrt{Q_k}} \delta(k, l) = R_k \delta(k, l), \tag{13.7}$$

with $\delta(k, l)$ defined in (A1.13). From the properly normalized overlaps $R_k =$

$\rho_k / \sqrt{Q_k}$, the generalization error of the corresponding hidden units follows as $\varepsilon_k = (\arccos R_k)/\pi$, and the generalization error of the committee machine can be obtained from (12.7) for the particular case $\varepsilon_k = \varepsilon_\tau$ for all values of k.

As a first application of the above formulas, we turn to the simple case of Hebb learning, corresponding to the choice

$$F_k = \eta \, \sigma_T = \eta \, \mathrm{sgn} \left(\sum_{k'=1}^{K} \mathrm{sgn} \, u_{k'} \right). \tag{13.8}$$

The multi-Gaussian integrals in (13.3)–(13.4) are easily evaluated if one realizes that the only non-zero contributions come from the cases where the hidden units $k' \neq k$ are in a tie, i.e. $\sum_{k' \neq k} \mathrm{sgn} \, u_{k'} = 0$. One thus finds

$$\left\langle u_k \, \mathrm{sgn} \left(\sum_{k'=1}^{K} \mathrm{sgn} \, u_{k'} \right) \right\rangle = \frac{1}{2^{K-1}} \binom{K-1}{\frac{K-1}{2}} \sqrt{\frac{2}{\pi}},$$

$$\left\langle t_k \, \mathrm{sgn} \left(\sum_{k'=1}^{K} \mathrm{sgn} \, u_{k'} \right) \right\rangle = \frac{1}{2^{K-1}} \binom{K-1}{\frac{K-1}{2}} \rho_k \sqrt{\frac{2}{\pi}}. \tag{13.9}$$

After integration of the equations for ρ_k and Q_k, with initial conditions $\rho_k(0) = Q_k(0) = 0$, one concludes

$$R_k(\alpha) = \left(1 + \frac{2^{2K-3} \, \pi}{K \, \alpha \left(\frac{K-1}{\frac{K-1}{2}} \right)^2} \right)^{-1/2}. \tag{13.10}$$

In particular, for $K = 3$, we find

$$R_k(\alpha) = \left(1 + \frac{2\pi}{3\alpha} \right)^{-1/2}. \tag{13.11}$$

The generalization error ε follows from (12.7). For $\alpha \to 0$ (and all initial overlaps equal to zero) one finds that $\varepsilon(\alpha) \approx 1/2 - \sqrt{17\alpha/32\pi^3}$, while the asymptotic decay is given by $\varepsilon(\alpha) \sim \sqrt{3/(2\pi\alpha)}$. A similar asymptotic behaviour is found for other finite values of K. Turning to the limit $K \to \infty$ the following explicit result may be obtained, cf. problem 13.2:

$$\varepsilon(\alpha) = \frac{1}{\pi} \arccos \left[\frac{2}{\pi} \arcsin \left(1 + \frac{\pi^2}{4\alpha} \right)^{-1/2} \right], \tag{13.12}$$

implying $\varepsilon(\alpha) \approx 1/2 - 4\sqrt{\alpha}/\pi^3$ for $\alpha \to 0$ and $\varepsilon(\alpha) \sim \sqrt{2}/(\pi\alpha^{1/4})$ for $\alpha \to \infty$. Note that as in off-line learning, the limits $\alpha \to \infty$ and $K \to \infty$ do not commute. To get an idea of the deterioration of the generalization ability with K of Hebb

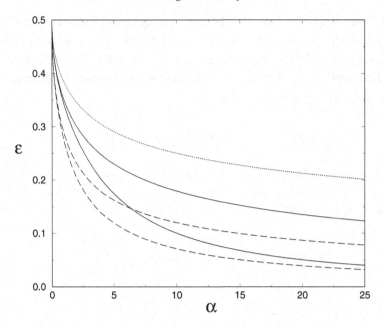

Fig. 13.1. Generalization error of a student tree committee machine with $K = 3$ learning from a teacher with the same architecture by the optimal learning rule (lower full line), cf. (13.16), and the Hebbian rule (upper full line), cf. (13.11). For comparison, we have included the corresponding results for the usual $K = 1$ perceptron (dashed lines) and the Hebbian $K = \infty$ result (dotted line), cf. (13.12).

learning in a committee tree, we have shown the generalization error in fig. 13.1 for the cases $K = 1$, $K = 3$ and $K = \infty$.

To put the Hebb result into perspective, we now turn to the optimal scenario. Again the calculations are very similar to those for $K = 1$, but the algebra is more tedious. We just reproduce the major steps in the calculation. Since ε is a monotonic function of the overlaps $R_k = \rho_k/\sqrt{Q_k}$, we seek to maximize $dR_k/d\alpha$. From (13.3)–(13.4) it follows that the optimal learning amplitude is given by

$$F_{k,\text{opt}} = -t_k + \frac{Q_k}{\rho_k} \langle u_k \rangle|_{(t_1,\dots,t_K),\sigma_T}, \qquad (13.13)$$

to be compared with (9.28). The average is over the unknown degrees of freedom, namely over the states u_k of the teacher units, given the known teacher classification and the hidden states of the student. By evaluating the Gaussian integrals for the simplest non-trivial case $K = 3$, one finds

$$F_{k,\text{opt}} = \frac{\sigma_T}{\sqrt{2\pi}} \frac{\sqrt{Q_k(1 - R_k^2)}}{R_k} \exp\left(-\frac{R_k^2}{2(1 - R_k^2)} \frac{t_k^2}{Q_k}\right) v_k(x_1, x_2, x_3), \quad (13.14)$$

where the variables x_k, $k = 1, 2, 3$, are defined as

$$x_k = \frac{R_k}{\sqrt{1 - R_k^2}} \frac{\sigma_T \, t_k}{\sqrt{Q_k}}. \tag{13.15}$$

Moreover

$$v_1(x_1, x_2, x_3) =$$
$$\frac{H(-x_2) \, H(x_3) + H(x_2) \, H(-x_3)}{H(-x_2) \, H(-x_3) + H(-x_1) \, [H(-x_2) \, H(x_3) + H(x_2) \, H(-x_3)]},$$

with similar results for $k = 2, 3$ following by permutation of the indices. This result bears some resemblance to the $K = 1$ result (9.33), with the important difference that the optimal amplitude $F_{k,\text{opt}}$ now depends on the cross-information from other hidden student units $k' \neq k$. In fact, one can also formulate an optimized algorithm in which only local information is used, i.e. $F_{k,\text{opt}}$ must not depend on $t_{k'}$, $k' \neq k$. It turns out that this problem is equivalent to that of a usual perceptron with output noise, cf. problem 13.4.

Proceeding with (13.14) one finds by substitution of $F_{k,\text{opt}}$ into (13.3)–(13.4) that the equation for R_k decouples from that for the length Q_k, and obtains

$$\frac{dR_k}{d\alpha} = \frac{3}{4\pi} \frac{1 - R_k^2}{R_k} \int \prod_{k'=1}^{3} Dy_{k'} \, e^{-y_k^2} \, w_k(y_1, y_2, y_3) \tag{13.16}$$

where

$$w_1(y_1, y_2, y_3) =$$
$$\prod_{k'=1}^{3} \left(\frac{\sqrt{1 - R_{k'}^2}}{R_{k'}} e^{y_{k'}^2 - y_{k'}^2/2R_{k'}^2} \right) \frac{[H(-y_2) \, H(y_3) + H(y_2) \, H(-y_3)]^2}{r_1(y_1, y_2, y_3) \, [1 - r_1(y_1, y_2, y_3)]} \tag{13.17}$$

and

$$r_1(y_1, y_2, y_3) = H(y_2) \, H(y_3) + H(y_1) \, [H(-y_2) \, H(y_3) + H(y_2) \, H(-y_3)]. \tag{13.18}$$

The results for $k = 2, 3$ again follow by permutation of the indices. As for the perceptron, the equation for the length of the synaptic vector is simply related to that of the overlap by

$$\frac{1}{\sqrt{Q_k}} \frac{d\sqrt{Q_k}}{d\alpha} = \frac{1}{R_k} \frac{dR_k}{d\alpha} \tag{13.19}$$

so that the observed length may be used to directly measure the overlap (cf. problem 9.8).

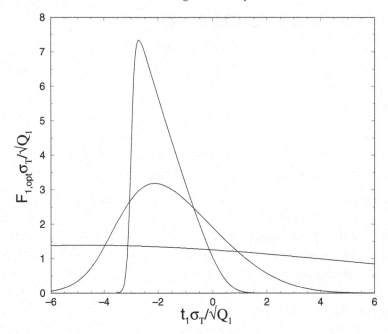

Fig. 13.2. Scaled optimal learning amplitude $F_{1,\text{opt}}\sigma_T/\sqrt{Q_1}$ as a function of $t_1\sigma_T/\sqrt{Q_1}$, with $t_2\sigma_T/\sqrt{Q_2} = -3$ and $t_3\sigma_T/\sqrt{Q_3} = 3$, with the values of the overlaps $R_1 = R_2 = R_3$ equal to 0.1, 0.5, 0.9 respectively (from top to bottom).

The resulting generalization error ε is found by combining the solution of (13.16) with (12.7). The result is shown in fig. 13.1, together with the results for Hebb learning. For $\alpha \to 0$ optimal learning and Hebb learning coincide, as expected. For the asymptotic approach of ε to zero however, one finds for optimal learning in both the $K = 1$ and $K = 3$ case the ubiquitous $1/\alpha$ decay. More surprisingly the proportionality factors are *exactly* the same! Hence asymptotic learning is no more difficult for the tree architecture than it is for the simple perceptron. This result turns out to be quite general, valid for all K, persisting even in the presence of output noise [215], and is also true for a parity tree machine, as we will see below.

The above calculations and results for optimal learning appear to be rather similar to those for the perceptron. However, a distinctive feature of multilayer networks is observed when we focus on the form of the learning amplitude, as shown in fig. 13.2. Considering the simplest case of all R_k equal, one observes that the scaled amplitude $F_{1,\text{opt}}\sigma_T/\sqrt{Q_1}$ as a function of $t_1\sigma_T/\sqrt{Q_1}$ has, for large negative values of $t_1\sigma_T/\sqrt{Q_1}$, a behaviour strikingly different from that of the perceptron. This situation corresponds to examples in which the hidden student unit under consideration gives, with "great conviction", a classification which disagrees with the teacher output. In the simple perceptron, such an occurrence gives rise to a large correction of the student, whereas here the correction is in fact very small. In anthropomorphic terms, the hidden unit of the student shifts the responsibility for a correct classification on to the two *other* members of the committee, and decides not to worry about his own classification. Hence no correction of its synaptic vector is performed. As expected this automatic division of labour will become more pronounced as the student gains more experience, i.e. as R_k gets closer to 1.

13.2 The parity tree

The scenario of a student parity machine learning from a teacher parity machine may be discussed in the same way as for the committee machine. Exactly the same equations (13.1)–(13.7) apply. The main difference resides in the choice of the learning algorithm, which should be adapted to the fact that the output is now the product of the outputs of the hidden units. For example, the Hebb rule fails completely as a learning algorithm for parity machines, cf. problem 13.5. Hence we consider another algorithm, inspired by the perceptron learning rule, namely the so-called least action algorithm [195]. In this rule, the **J**-vector of the unit with the smallest absolute value of the local field is corrected following the perceptron rule when the parity machine makes an error. Least action refers to the fact that one assigns the "labour" of the correction to the unit with the smallest degree of conviction about its classification. For simplicity we limit our discussion to the case $K = 2$. This leads to the following choice of the learning amplitude, cf. (9.19) where $\mathrm{sgn}(u)$ has been replaced by $-\mathrm{sgn}(t)$ since the output of the teacher hidden unit is not available:

$$F_k = -\theta(-u_1 u_2 t_1 t_2)\,\theta(|t_j| - |t_k|)\,\mathrm{sgn}(t_k),\tag{13.20}$$

with $j \neq k$. The resulting evolution equations for the overlap parameters follow by inserting this expression into (13.3) and (13.4). Since the integrals cannot be evaluated explicitly, we focus on the limiting regimes, and again for simplicity limit our discussion to the symmetric case $Q = Q_1 = Q_2$ and $\rho = \rho_1 = \rho_2$. We first investigate the poor performance regime of both Q and $R = \rho/\sqrt{Q}$ being small. One finds

$$\frac{dR}{d\alpha} \approx -\left(\frac{1}{4} - \frac{2}{\pi^{3/2}}\sqrt{Q}\right)\frac{R}{Q},\tag{13.21}$$

$$\frac{dQ}{d\alpha} \approx \frac{1}{2} - 2\frac{\sqrt{2}-1}{\sqrt{\pi}}\sqrt{Q}.\tag{13.22}$$

The following conclusions may be drawn from these equations. First if $R = 0$ at $\alpha = 0$ we find $R = 0$ for all α, i.e. learning from scratch is impossible. Generalization requires a minimum of pre-knowledge corresponding to an initial R larger than zero. As discussed before, this result is strictly valid in the thermodynamic limit of the system only. Fluctuations due to finite size allow escape from the $R = 0$ fixed point, but this takes a long time and produces an initial plateau in the learning curve $\varepsilon(\alpha)$. A more surprising finding is that a student can only start to generalize after the length of his vector has reached a critical value $Q_c = \pi^3/64$. For smaller lengths, one has $dR/d\alpha < 0$, leading to a decay of the overlap. To avoid this problem the algorithm should be supplemented with an annealing schedule for the *initial* phase of learning, starting with a learning amplitude which is sufficiently small, cf. problem 13.6.

Turning to the high performance regime $R \approx 1$, one finds

$$\frac{dR}{d\alpha} \approx -\frac{1}{Q}\left(\frac{\sqrt{2}}{\pi}\sqrt{1-R} - \frac{4}{\sqrt{2\pi}}(1-R)\sqrt{Q}\right) \tag{13.23}$$

$$\frac{dQ}{d\alpha} \approx \frac{2\sqrt{2}}{\pi}\sqrt{1-R} - \frac{4}{\sqrt{2\pi}}(1-R)\sqrt{Q} \tag{13.24}$$

implying the asymptotic behaviour $R \sim 0.24\,\alpha^{-2/3}$ and for the generalization error $\varepsilon \sim 0.44\,\alpha^{-1/3}$. This result is similar to that for the perceptron, cf. (9.22).

We now turn to a discussion of the optimal learning strategy. Since the calculations are again similar to those reviewed earlier for the perceptron and the committee machine, we only give the results and refer to [216] for more details. As we will see several of the distinctive features of the least action algorithm are not found in the optimal strategy.

As in the off-line case, the parity machine is found to be technically simpler than the committee machine, and the calculations may be performed for all K with the following final result:

$$\frac{dR_k}{d\alpha} = \frac{K}{2\pi}\frac{1-R_k^2}{R_k}\int\prod_{i=1}^{K}Du_i\exp\left(-\frac{u_k^2R_k^2}{1-R_k^2}\right) \tag{13.25}$$

$$\times \frac{\prod_{l\neq k}\left[H\left(-\frac{u_lR_l}{\sqrt{1-R_l^2}}\right) - H\left(\frac{u_lR_l}{\sqrt{1-R_l^2}}\right)\right]^2}{\sum_{\{b_i=\pm1\}}\delta\left(\prod_i b_i, 1\right)\prod_{j=1}^{K}H\left(-b_j\frac{u_jR_j}{\sqrt{1-R_j^2}}\right)}.$$

In the low performance regime one finds the simple result

$$\frac{dR_k}{d\alpha} \approx \frac{K}{2} \left(\frac{2}{\pi}\right)^K \frac{\prod\limits_{l \neq k} R_l^2}{R_k}. \tag{13.26}$$

One thus observes that $R_k = 0$ for any two or more branches is a fixed point of the dynamics, reflecting an inherent limitation of on-line learning. It is related to the retarded learning appearing in the off-line scenario. As mentioned before, it is the result of a symmetry in the architecture of this network, namely the fact that the output is unchanged if one inverts the signs of an even number of synaptic vectors. Note that such a plateau is not present in the committee machine because there is no inversion symmetry in this architecture. Considering the departure from the fixed point for initial conditions $R_k = R$ small but larger than zero, we note that it is exponential for $K = 2$, while it is a much slower power law for $K > 2$. This distinction is reminiscent of the qualitative differences which are also observed in the off-line case, cf. section 12.4. While the initial $R = 0$ plateau, also observed in the least action algorithm, cannot be avoided, we do find, in contrast to the latter non-optimized algorithm, that there is no minimum length Q_c required for learning. This is not really surprising since the optimal algorithm incorporates an optimal annealing of the learning rate.

Turning to the $\alpha \to \infty$ and $R_k \to R \to 1$ regime, the following evolution equation is obtained:

$$\frac{dR}{d\alpha} \sim \frac{K}{2\pi} [2(1 - R)]^{3/2} \int Dx \, \frac{e^{-x^2/2}}{H(x)}. \tag{13.27}$$

One notes that all the perceptron branches learn at the same rate. After rescaling $\alpha_K = K\alpha$, representing the number of examples divided by the number of couplings in a single branch, this rate is independent of K. From $\varepsilon_k = \arccos R_k/\pi$ and formula (12.5) for the generalization error of the parity machine itself, one derives the asymptotic result

$$\varepsilon \sim \sum_k \varepsilon_k \sim \frac{2}{\alpha} \left(\int Dx \, \frac{e^{-x^2/2}}{H(x)} \right)^{-1}. \tag{13.28}$$

Note that even though the generalization error of the machine is the sum of the individual errors in this limit, the whole machine in fact learns at the same rate as the hidden units if we measure the training set size appropriately by α instead of $K\alpha$. The $1/\alpha$ decay is the only law compatible with this peculiar property. Furthermore, the proportionality coefficient is independent of K and exactly the same as for the simple perceptron, as in (9.36)! Hence for both the committee and parity machine with tree structure, the optimal asymptotic approach is identical to that of the perceptron. This conclusion remains valid in the presence of output noise, cf. problem 13.7.

13.3 Soft committee machine

The analysis of fully connected machines with a sign transfer function appears to be extremely involved, and will not be further discussed here. Instead we turn to a committee machine with smooth transfer functions g for the hidden units. For simplicity we consider a linear output unit. The network is trained by gradient descent on the quadratic output error. As we have already noticed for the simple perceptron, cf. section 9.4, it turns out that for a judicious choice of the transfer function, all integrals may be explicitly performed, simplifying the analysis of the evolution equations for the order parameters enormously.

The student and teacher committee machine are characterized by the set of N-dimensional synaptic vectors $\{\mathbf{J}_k, k = 1, \ldots, K\}$ and $\{\mathbf{T}_m, m = 1, \ldots, M\}$, where K and M are the number of hidden units for student and teacher respectively. We will restrict the subsequent analysis to the case of a learnable scenario $K = M$ with an isotropic teacher with mutually orthogonal weight vectors lying on the N-sphere, $\mathbf{T}_m \mathbf{T}_n = N\delta(m, n)$. But we will also mention results for over-realizable $K > M$ and unrealizable $K < M$ scenarios as well as for the graded teacher with some dominant weight vectors larger than others. We train by on-line gradient descent on the quadratic output error

$$V(\mathbf{J}_1, \ldots, \mathbf{J}_k) = \frac{1}{2}\left[\sum_{k=1}^{K} g(t_k^{\mu}) - \sum_{m=1}^{M} g(u_m^{\mu})\right]^2, \qquad (13.29)$$

where

$$t_k^{\mu} = \frac{\mathbf{J}_k \boldsymbol{\xi}^{\mu}}{\sqrt{N}} \qquad (13.30)$$

and

$$u_m^{\mu} = \frac{\mathbf{T}_m \boldsymbol{\xi}^{\mu}}{\sqrt{N}}. \qquad (13.31)$$

The presentation of a new training example $\boldsymbol{\xi}^{\mu}$ thus results in an on-line update of the student vectors of the form

$$\mathbf{J}_k^{\mu+1} = \mathbf{J}_k^{\mu} + \frac{1}{\sqrt{N}} F_k^{\mu} \boldsymbol{\xi}^{\mu}, \qquad (13.32)$$

with

$$F_k^{\mu} = -\eta\left[\sum_{k'=1}^{K} g(t_{k'}^{\mu}) - \sum_{m'=1}^{M} g(u_{m'}^{\mu})\right] g'(t_k^{\mu}). \qquad (13.33)$$

The resulting evolution equations for the overlaps

$$R_{km} = \frac{\mathbf{J}_k \mathbf{T}_m}{\sqrt{N Q_{kk}}} \quad \text{and} \quad Q_{kl} = \frac{\mathbf{J}_k \mathbf{J}_l}{N} \tag{13.34}$$

may be calculated explicitly by invoking the Gaussian character of the variables t_k and u_m. The algebra is similar to the $K = 1$ case but is rather tedious. The specific use of the error function as transfer function $g(x) = 1 - 2H(x)$ allows all these averages to be calculated explicitly. We refer the reader to the literature [134, 217, 218] for the explicit result.

The resulting set of coupled first order equations may be integrated numerically, providing valuable insights into the learning process of the machine. A detailed *analytic* study is also possible if one focuses on specific situations of special interest. For example, the effect of the learning rate, the existence of plateaus induced by the permutation symmetry of the hidden units, the emergence of specialization of those units and the exponential asymptotic convergence to perfect generalization are key elements which may be documented in detail.

To illustrate how this is done, we will restrict ourselves to an analysis for small η of the following subspace, representing partial committee symmetry as introduced in section 12.6:

$$Q_{kl} = Q \, \delta(k, l) + C(1 - \delta(k, l))$$
$$R_{kl} = R \, \delta(k, l) + S(1 - \delta(k, l)). \tag{13.35}$$

Using the scaling $\alpha' = \alpha \eta$, the following evolution equations are found [218]:

$$\frac{dR}{d\alpha'} = \frac{2}{\pi} \frac{1}{(1 + Q)} \left[\frac{1 + Q - R^2}{\sqrt{2(1 + Q) - R^2}} - \frac{RS(K - 1)}{\sqrt{2(1 + Q) - S^2}} \right.$$
$$\left. - \frac{R}{\sqrt{1 + 2Q}} - \frac{(1 + Q)S(K - 1) - RC(K - 1)}{\sqrt{(1 + Q)^2 - C^2}} \right], \tag{13.36}$$

$$\frac{dS}{d\alpha'} = \frac{2}{\pi} \frac{1}{(1 + Q)} \left[\frac{1 + Q - S^2(K - 1)}{\sqrt{2(1 + Q) - S^2}} \right.$$
$$- \frac{RS}{\sqrt{2(1 + Q) - R^2}} - \frac{S}{\sqrt{1 + 2Q}}$$
$$\left. - \frac{(1 + Q)[R + S(K - 2)] - SC(K - 1)}{\sqrt{(1 + Q)^2 - C^2}} \right], \tag{13.37}$$

$$\frac{dQ}{d\alpha'} = \frac{4}{\pi} \frac{1}{(1+Q)} \left[\frac{R}{\sqrt{2(1+Q) - R^2}} + \frac{S(K-1)}{\sqrt{2(1+Q) - S^2}} \right.$$

$$\left. - \frac{Q}{\sqrt{1+2Q}} - \frac{C(K-1)}{\sqrt{(1+Q)^2 - C^2}} \right], \tag{13.38}$$

$$\frac{dC}{d\alpha'} = \frac{4}{\pi} \frac{1}{(1+Q)} \left[\frac{(1+Q)S - RC}{\sqrt{2(1+Q) - R^2}} \right.$$

$$+ \frac{(1+Q)[R + S(K-2)] - SC(K-1)}{\sqrt{2(1+Q) - S^2}}$$

$$\left. - \frac{C}{\sqrt{1+2Q}} - \frac{(1+Q)[Q + C(K-2)] - C^2(K-1)}{\sqrt{(1+Q)^2 - C^2}} \right]. \tag{13.39}$$

The generalization error, defined as the average quadratic output error on a random new example, is given by [218]

$$\varepsilon = \frac{K}{\pi} \left[\frac{\pi}{6} + \arcsin\left(\frac{Q}{1+Q}\right) + (K-1)\arcsin\left(\frac{C}{1+Q}\right) \right. \tag{13.40}$$

$$\left. -2\arcsin\left(\frac{R}{\sqrt{2(1+Q)}}\right) - 2(K-1)\arcsin\left(\frac{S}{\sqrt{2(1+Q)}}\right) \right].$$

As a first application of the above explicit set of evolution equations, we will study the properties of the symmetric phase, characterized by an absence of differentiation among student hidden units. In particular, there is no preferred overlap of the student units with one of the teacher vectors. Hence the symmetric subspace is defined by the conditions (13.35) with the additional constraint that $R = S$. Note that the "natural" initial conditions, appearing with probability 1 in the thermodynamic limit for a random initial choice of the student weight vectors of equal square length NQ, namely $R = S = C = 0$, belong to this symmetric subspace. Furthermore, one immediately verifies that the equations for R and S coincide when $R = S$, so that an initial condition of this type is propagated in time. The number of evolution equations is thus reduced to three.

The stationary solution may be found as follows. By substituting the solution for R from the condition $dQ/d\alpha' = 0$ into the condition $dC/d\alpha' = 0$, one verifies that $Q^2 = C^2$ at the steady state. Disregarding the unphysical solution $Q = -C$, one concludes that (13.36)–(13.39) with $R = S$ have the unique fixed point solution

$$Q_{pl} = C_{pl} = \frac{1}{2K-1}, \tag{13.41}$$

$$R_{pl} = S_{pl} = \frac{1}{\sqrt{K(2K-1)}}. \tag{13.42}$$

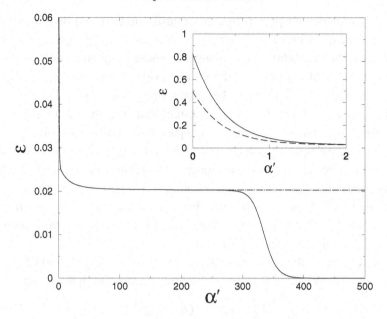

Fig. 13.3. The generalization error as a function of $\alpha' = \alpha\eta$, obtained by combining (13.36)–(13.39) with (13.40), for the initial conditions $(R, S, Q, C) = (0, 0, 0.5, 0)$ (dotted), $(0.1, 0.1, 0.5, 0)$ (dashed) and $(10^{-6}, 0, 0.5, 0)$ (full). The inset shows the behaviour for small α'. For small α' the dotted line is almost identical to the full one; for large α' it almost coincides with the dashed line.

The corresponding generalization error reads

$$\varepsilon_{\mathrm{pl}} = \frac{K}{\pi}\left[\frac{\pi}{6} - K\arcsin\left(\frac{1}{2K}\right)\right]. \tag{13.43}$$

A numerical analysis indicates that this fixed point is globally stable inside the symmetric subspace. There appear to be no run-away solutions or limit cycles.

A typical evolution of the generalization error is shown in fig. 13.3 by the dashed line: the generalization error converges monotonically to its final non-zero value (13.43). Unlike in perceptron problems with symmetry, see section 9.6, in which no learning at all takes place when one starts in a symmetric phase, we observe here an initial learning phase saturating on a non-trivial plateau, rather similar to off-line learning in a fully-connected architecture as discussed in section 12.6. But as in the perceptron case, the above fixed point turns out to be unstable outside the symmetric subspace. Hence asymmetric initializations will drive the parameters away from this subspace, and hidden unit specialization sets in.

Turning to the study of the incipient specialization, one has to distinguish between a dominant overlap R between a given student unit and a corresponding teacher unit and a secondary overlap $S \neq R$ with other teacher units. The escape from the symmetric subspace is then most easily investigated by a linear stability analysis for the quantities $r = R - R_{\text{pl}}, s = S - S_{\text{pl}}, q = Q - Q_{\text{pl}}, c = C - C_{\text{pl}}$. It turns out that the instability of the symmetric phase is signalled to lowest order by the differentiation of R from S. Only one eigenvalue is found to be strictly positive and the corresponding eigenvector has components $((K - 1), -1, 0, 0)$. From the implied relation $s = -r/(K - 1)$ at constant length of the vectors, we conclude that the departure from the symmetric subspace is by a mere rotation of the student vector towards the specific teacher vector which it is trying to implement. This simultaneous process – acquiring a stronger correlation with a specific teacher unit while decorrelating from the remaining units – is characteristic for an isotropic teacher, see fig. 13.3 for an illustration. For a graded teacher, specialization occurs by a cascade of escapes out of the symmetric subspace in an order following the decreasing overlaps with teacher units [218].

We finally turn to the asymptotic approach to the perfect solution $S = C = 0$ and $R = Q = 1$. We study the approach of this fixed point in the subspace

$$R_{kl} = R \, \delta(k, l) \qquad Q_{kl} = Q \, \delta(k, l). \tag{13.44}$$

In this regime the generalization error is given by

$$\varepsilon = \frac{K}{\pi} \left[\frac{\pi}{6} + \arcsin \left(\frac{Q}{1 + Q} \right) - 2 \arcsin \left(\frac{R}{\sqrt{2(1 + Q)}} \right) \right]. \tag{13.45}$$

By linearization with respect to $r = 1 - R$ and $q = 1 - Q$ with $C = S = 0$, one finds from (13.36)–(13.39)

$$\frac{d}{d\alpha} \binom{r}{q} = \frac{2}{\pi} \frac{\sqrt{3}}{9} \eta \begin{pmatrix} -4 & 3/2 \\ (4 - 2\eta\mu) & (-3 + \eta\mu) \end{pmatrix} \binom{r}{q} \tag{13.46}$$

with $\mu = \sqrt{3}(2/\pi)(K - 1 + 3/\sqrt{5})$. Note that we have also included here the non-linear terms in η, see [218] for details. The stability of the perfect solution requires that the eigenvalues of the matrix in (13.46) be negative. One immediately concludes that the exponential convergence to perfect generalization is only guaranteed for $0 < \eta < \eta_{\text{max}}$, with

$$\eta_{\text{max}} = \frac{\pi\sqrt{3}}{K - 1 + 3/\sqrt{5}}. \tag{13.47}$$

Since the eigenvalues are, for a small learning rate η, negative but equally small, the system will get trapped for a long time in the symmetric subspace. The plateau regime is significantly reduced upon increasing η. In fact, by inserting the results for r and q into the generalization error, one can identify the learning rate η_{opt} which leads to the fastest asymptotic decay. One finds $\eta_{\text{opt}} = 2\eta_{\text{max}}/3$. For $\eta > \eta_{\text{max}}$, the ability to reach an error-free solution is lost.

We have limited the above analysis to the subspace (13.35). The full picture turns out be much richer [219]. In particular, a numerical analysis of the full set of equations reveals that there exist many fixed points, marked by different values of the generalization error and different degrees of symmetry. For example for $K = M = 3$ and $\eta = 1$, thirteen fixed points were found. Furthermore with the learning rate η acting as a control parameter the fixed points can undergo bifurcations. Their properties affect the learning dynamics by producing cascades of plateaus in the generalization error and can even trap the student in a stable sub-optimal fixed point.

We close this section with a brief discussion of the unrealizable ($K < M$) and over-realizable ($K > M$) cases. In the over-realizable case, one finds that the learning process automatically prunes unnecessary hidden units. The lengths Q_{kk} of the corresponding units go to zero. The other units undergo a similar evolution as in the $K = M$ case, with an escape from the symmetric phase followed by specialization. The pruning of non-essential units is reminiscent of Occam's razor which we mentioned at the end of section 10.3. In the unrealizable case, the student units specialize in a cascade, after escape from the symmetric subspace, each to less and less dominant teacher nodes, while retaining some overlap with the discarded teacher units. The generalization error remains of course non-zero even in the asymptotic limit.

13.4 Back-propagation

We now go one step further and consider multilayer networks with possibly several hidden layers, in which all the synaptic vectors, including those feeding the output units, can be tuned. The back-propagation algorithm is by far the most popular procedure for doing so [220]. One may cite at least four major reasons for its success. First, as was mentioned before, such a network can approximate any function $f(\xi)$ of the input variables ξ to any desired degree of accuracy by including a sufficient number of units in the hidden layer. The second reason is that the back-propagation training rule, while being in fact nothing but a gradient descent algorithm, has the extremely nice feature of requiring only local information to perform the corrections, see below. The third reason is ease of application. The architecture and training algorithm are both very simple, and there is no need to incorporate any extra information besides the training set. The fourth reason is the uncanny success of such networks, in spite of their simplicity and generality, to reach a level of performance in widely different problems comparable to that of more problem-specific approaches.

It is possible to extend the calculations of the preceding section to the back-propagation network with output weights which are also adapted in the learning process, see for example [221]. Since the calculations and the main picture are similar to those for the simpler machines, we will not discuss these results. In view of the practical importance of back-propagation, we will however explain in more detail how it works. We consider a multilayer feed-forward network, such as introduced in chapter 1, see fig. 1.1.c, with units possessing a continuous rather than a binary activation function. In particular the output σ_k of a unit k, which receives its inputs from a set of other units l located in a preceding layer, is given by

$$\sigma_k = g\left(\sum_l J_{lk}\sigma_l\right), \tag{13.48}$$

where the activation or transfer function g is typically chosen to have a sigmoid form, going from -1 (bipolar form) or 0 (binary form) to $+1$. A popular choice is $g(x) = \tanh(\beta x)$, because it may be tuned between a linear perceptron ($\beta \to 0$) and a threshold sensitive perceptron ($\beta \to \infty$), while its derivative is conveniently expressed in terms of its own value by $g' = \beta(1 - g^2)$.

The purpose of the back-propagation algorithm is to minimize the total quadratic error E for a set of training examples ξ^μ, $\mu = 1, \ldots, p$, given by

$$E = \sum_\mu (\sigma_T^\mu - \sigma_0^\mu)^2, \tag{13.49}$$

where σ_0^μ is the value at the output node upon presentation of example ξ^μ and σ_T^μ is the required teacher output. For simplicity, we consider a system with a single output. Multiple outputs may be treated in exactly the same way.

Clearly the error E depends, through the resulting output value σ_0^μ, on the current choice of all the synaptic vectors $\mathbf{J} = \{J_{lk}\}$, i.e. $E = E(\mathbf{J})$. To decrease the error, we note that, using a Taylor expansion, a change δJ_{lk} of the synaptic strengths $\{J_{lk}\}$ results to lowest order in an error change of the form

$$\delta E = \sum_{[l,k]} \delta J_{lk} \frac{\partial E}{\partial J_{lk}}, \tag{13.50}$$

where the sums runs over all pairs $[l, k]$ of connected nodes. Gradient descent corresponds to the choice

$$\delta J_{lk} = -\eta \frac{\partial E}{\partial J_{lk}} \qquad \text{for all } [l, k], \tag{13.51}$$

which clearly guarantees a decrease of E. At first sight, it appears that the application of (13.51) requires a quite involved calculation to find all the relevant derivatives, except for the output nodes. But it turns out that this is not the case. We first note that the error E depends on the choice of J_{lk} only through the output

σ_k of the node which is fed by this weight. Hence

$$\frac{\partial E}{\partial J_{lk}} = \frac{\partial E}{\partial \sigma_k} \frac{\partial \sigma_k}{\partial J_{lk}}.$$ (13.52)

Furthermore, in view of (13.48), one has

$$\frac{\partial \sigma_k}{\partial J_{lk}} = \sigma_l \, g' = \beta \sigma_l (1 - \sigma_k^2),$$ (13.53)

where the prime stands for the derivative with respect to the argument. Hence (13.53) may be evaluated using local information only. The quantity

$$\frac{\partial E}{\partial \sigma_k} = \delta_k$$ (13.54)

is called the error contributed by node k. The essence of back-propagation is the observation that this factor can also be calculated locally. This is a crucial advantage for a hardware implementation, since no long-distance wiring is required. To show how such an error may be computed, suppose that the errors δ_k are known for the layer of nodes which is fed by a specific node l. Then δ_l is evaluated as

$$\delta_l = \frac{\partial E}{\partial \sigma_l} = \sum_k \frac{\partial E}{\partial \sigma_k} \frac{\partial \sigma_k}{\partial \sigma_l} = \sum_k \delta_k \, J_{lk} \, \beta \, (1 - \sigma_k^2)$$ (13.55)

where we have used the fact that E depends on σ_l only through the outputs σ_k of the nodes which are fed by l. We conclude from (13.55) that the error can be *back-propagated*: its value at a given node is the weighted sum of the errors of the nodes which it feeds.

13.5 Bayesian on-line learning

We close this chapter with an on-line procedure which is quite general and is not restricted to the thermodynamic limit. It is based on a Bayesian formulation of the learning process which we first briefly review, see also sections 3.6 and 8.3. One assumes that the probability distribution $P(\xi^\mu | \mathbf{T})$ generating the data set ξ^μ, $\mu = 1, \ldots, p$, is known, but that it depends on a set of unknown parameters $\mathbf{T}$. In neural network parlance, the data set can include besides the examples also their corresponding classifications while the parameters $\mathbf{T}$ are the set of teacher weights. Furthermore, the degree of prior belief or plausibility is expressed in terms of the prior distribution $P_0(\mathbf{J})$ which gives the probability that the choice $\mathbf{J}$ coincides with the teacher *a priori*. In other words the teacher is supposed to be sampled from this distribution. Using Bayes' theorem [116], one can now calculate the posterior distribution,

$$P(\mathbf{J}|\boldsymbol{\xi}^{\mu}) \sim P(\boldsymbol{\xi}^{\mu}|\mathbf{J}) \, P_0(\mathbf{J}), \qquad (13.56)$$

the *a posteriori* probability that $\mathbf{J}$ coincides with the teacher, which takes into account the observed examples. The proportionality constant is fixed by normalization.

Several specific choices can now be made. One may choose the *maximum a posteriori* prediction $\mathbf{J}_{\text{MAP}} = \text{argmax}_{\mathbf{J}} \, P(\mathbf{J}|\boldsymbol{\xi}^{\mu})$, which maximizes the posterior and is thus the most probable parameter value. The *maximum likelihood* prediction $\mathbf{J}_{\text{ML}} = \text{argmax}_{\mathbf{J}} \, P(\boldsymbol{\xi}^{\mu}|\mathbf{J})$ maximizes the likelihood of the examples. It coincides with the maximum a posteriori choice for a uniform prior. Finally one can make the centre of mass prediction $\mathbf{J} = \int d\mathbf{J}' \, \mathbf{J}' \, P(\mathbf{J}'|\boldsymbol{\xi}^{\mu})$, which is the posterior average. This choice is, as explained in section 3.6, Bayes optimal in the sense that the average overlap between the estimated and true vector will be maximal. We note in passing that uniform optimality, optimal in all realizations and for all criteria, cannot be achieved in general. For example the optimality on average usually differs from predictions which are optimal in the worst case, corresponding to the so called *minimax* choice; see [222] for more details.

The estimation of the posterior (13.56) involves *all* training examples $\boldsymbol{\xi}^{\mu}$, so it is intrinsically off-line. One may however formulate an on-line version by working with an adequate approximate form of the posterior, which is characterized by parameter values which are updated on-line. We will discuss two different choices of the posterior. First in the case of smooth distributions, it is known that the posterior converges, under quite general conditions and for the number p of independent examples tending to infinity, to a multi-dimensional Gaussian [222]. Hence to capture at least the correct asymptotic form, it is natural to assume the following Gaussian distribution for the posterior [147]:

$$P(\mathbf{J}|\boldsymbol{\xi}^{\mu}) \sim \exp\left(-\frac{1}{2}\sum_{i,j}^{N}(J_i - m_i) \, C_{i,j}^{-1} \, (J_j - m_j)\right) \qquad (13.57)$$

determined by the average $\mathbf{m} = \langle \mathbf{J} \rangle$ and the correlation matrix $\mathbf{C} = \langle (\mathbf{J} - \mathbf{m})(\mathbf{J} - \mathbf{m}) \rangle$, which are both functions of the number p of examples, $\mathbf{m} = \mathbf{m}(p)$ and $\mathbf{C} = \mathbf{C}(p)$. When a new example is presented, the new posterior is calculated by Bayes' theorem using the approximate posterior (13.57) instead of the exact one (13.56). This posterior is then used to find the updated values $\mathbf{m}(p + 1)$ and $\mathbf{C}(p + 1)$ of the parameters, which inserted into (13.57) yield the new approximation for the posterior after $(p + 1)$ examples. When applied to a smooth realizable rule, one can show that this procedure achieves asymptotically optimal error rates coinciding with our previous results obtained for optimized on-line learning, cf. section 9.6.

For non-smooth problems, the Gaussian approximation is expected to be rather poor. To illustrate how similar ideas may nevertheless be applied, we turn to on-line learning of a teacher with binary weights. In this case it is quite natural to work with a binary approximate posterior of the form [223]

$$P(\mathbf{J}|\xi^{\mu}) = \prod_i \left(\frac{1 + m_i(p)}{2} \delta(J_i - 1) + \frac{1 - m_i(p)}{2} \delta(J_i + 1) \right) \qquad (13.58)$$

characterized by the average bias $\mathbf{m} = \langle \mathbf{J} \rangle$. The rest of the procedure is then the same as for smooth networks. Upon presentation of a new example, a new posterior is calculated using (13.58) as the posterior after p examples, and the new value of the parameter $\mathbf{m}(p + 1)$ is calculated. In its application to a perceptron student learning from a perceptron teacher, both with binary weights, this algorithm works rather well [224], thereby overcoming the limitations pointed out at the end of section 9.8 for simple updating rules like (9.1).

13.6 Discussion

Arriving at the end of the multilayer chapters, one cannot fail to notice that these architectures are extremely rich and intricate, and the theoretical analysis so far only scratches the surface. But apart from its didactic and intellectual value, the existing theoretical machinery allows one to study specific questions or to test out new ideas in a systematic way rather than by trial and error. Furthermore, as we have seen in the transition from the perceptron to the multilayer networks, many features are quite robust and we expect that the properties observed in our toy multilayer networks will persist in more realistic scenarios.

Let us review briefly some of the new features which were documented in this chapter. The phenomenon that we referred to as division of labour is quite remarkable. When using optimal algorithms, the different units of the student are involved in a cooperative game to reproduce the answers of the teacher. Non-optimal algorithms on the other hand may seriously degrade the performance, by inducing the appearance of parasite phase transitions or, even worse, by failing to learn a learnable problem at all. As in perceptron learning, we have encountered the problem of plateaus, but appearing now as the result of a symmetry intrinsic to the architecture of the network, namely an inversion symmetry for the parity machine and a permutation symmetry for fully connected architectures. Furthermore the plateau is reached after a fast decrease of the generalization error and is characterized by non-trivial values of the order parameters.

As far as the literature is concerned, we have already mentioned the works on on-line learning in parity tree machines [225, 216] and committee tree machines [226, 227], the fully connected machines with smooth transfer function

[217, 218, 221] and the Bayesian on-line approach [147, 224]. See also [228] for the study of robustness diagrams when one estimates wrongly the output noise of the teacher, [219] for a further study of the influence of the learning rate and the initial conditions, [229] for optimized on-line learning over a fixed time-window and [230, 231] for an on-line Gibbs algorithm. More recently the case of restricted training has been investigated. The re-sampling of previously seen examples destroys the Gaussian nature of the distributions for u and t and the situation becomes much more complicated. For example, the latter distribution is then no longer described by a finite number of order parameters such as R and Q [232, 233].

13.7 Problems

13.1 Consider an α-dependent rate in the Hebb rule, cf. (13.8) with $\eta = \eta(\alpha)$. Show that the choice of the latter function which gives the lowest generalization error is in fact $\eta(\alpha)$ constant. In other words, the performance of the Hebb rule cannot be improved by introducing an annealing schedule.

13.2 Show by combining the result (13.10) with problem 12.4 that the generalization error for the committee machine with Hebb training is given by (13.12) when $K \to \infty$.

13.3 Consider learning by queries in the committee tree machine scenario, with questions orthogonal to the student vectors. Show that this strategy leads, for an optimal choice of the learning amplitude, to an asymptotic decay of the generalization error of the form

$$\varepsilon(\alpha) \sim \frac{2}{\pi^{3/2}} \exp\left(-\frac{\alpha}{\pi^2}\right). \tag{13.59}$$

13.4 Consider optimal learning in the committee tree machine scenario, but with the restriction that $F_{k,\mathrm{opt}}$ does not depend on the states of the other hidden units. Hence (13.13) is replaced by

$$F_{k,\mathrm{opt}} = -t_k + \frac{Q_k}{\rho_k} \langle u_k \rangle |_{t_k,\sigma_T}. \tag{13.60}$$

Show that the generalization error ε_k of a hidden unit of the student is exactly the same as that of a perceptron learning from a teacher with output noise level

$$a = \frac{1}{2^{K-1}} \binom{K-1}{\frac{K-1}{2}}, \tag{13.61}$$

to be used in (5.4). In other words, a hidden unit of the student perceives the teacher output classification as that of a teacher hidden unit corrupted by output noise due to the interference of the other teacher hidden units. Thanks to this equivalence the K-committee tree machine can in this case be solved explicitly for all K, see [227] for more details.

13.5 Consider the parity machine scenario with tree structure. Show from (13.1)–(13.7) that a student machine trained by the Hebb rule (13.8) with the sum replaced by a product fails to learn from a teacher parity machine.

13.6 Repeat the calculations leading to (13.21) and (13.22) with a learning amplitude proportional to the step size η. Show that the problem of a decreasing overlap for small lengths is cured by taking $\eta \sim \sqrt{Q}$ with a proportionality factor smaller than $8/\pi^{3/2}$.

13.7 Repeat the calculations for the $K = 2$ parity machine, trained by the least action algorithm of section 13.2, but now in the presence of output noise in the classification of the teacher. Show that there is a critical noise level, above which the generalization error no longer decays to zero for $\alpha \to \infty$ [225]. In other words, the problem becomes unlearnable when using this algorithm. Repeat the calculations with the optimal algorithm and show that the $1/\alpha$ asymptotic decay of the generalization error persists at all noise levels, with a proportionality factor identical to that of the perceptron (see [216] for details).

13.8 Train a feed-forward back-propagation network with two input nodes, two hidden nodes and one output node, to learn the XOR problem. Does the network always converge?

13.9 Consider the corrections of the standard back-propagation algorithm at some time t:

$$\delta J_{lk}(t) = -\eta S_{lk}(t), \tag{13.62}$$

where $S_{lk}(t)$ is the gradient at time t:

$$S_{lk}(t) = \frac{\partial E}{\partial J_{lk}}. \tag{13.63}$$

Suppose now that the dependence of E on J_{lk} has the form

$$E = a + bJ_{lk} + cJ_{lk}^2. \tag{13.64}$$

Prove that minimum error is realized by the so-called quick-prop choice [234]

$$\delta J_{lk}(t) = \delta J_{lk}(t - 1) \frac{S_{lk}(t)}{S_{lk}(t - 1) - S_{lk}(t)}. \tag{13.65}$$

Use this method to solve the XOR problem. Show that this *risk taking* algorithm often converges faster than standard back-propagation, but that it sometimes fails to converge at all.

13.10 According to a general theorem of Ruelle and Takens [235], the dynamics of a chaotic attractor with fractal dimension d can be reproduced exactly by a time discrete map $x(t+1) = F(x(t), \ldots, x(t-m))$ with m lying between d and $2d + 1$. Can you suggest on this basis a feed-forward back-propagation network which is a good candidate for learning a chaotic time series? For more details, see [236].

14

What Else?

In this book we have discussed how various aspects of learning in artificial neural networks may be quantified by using concepts and techniques developed in the statistical mechanics of disordered systems. These methods grew out of the desire to understand some strange low-temperature properties of disordered magnets; nevertheless their usefulness for and efficiency in the analysis of a completely different class of complex systems underlines the generality and strength of the principles of statistical mechanics.

In this final chapter we have collected some additional examples of non-physical complex systems for which an analysis using methods of statistical mechanics similar to those employed for the study of neural networks has given rise to new and interesting results. Compared with the previous chapters, the discussions in the present one will be somewhat more superficial – merely pointing to the qualitative analogies with the problems elucidated previously, rather than working out the consequences in full detail. Moreover, some of the problems we consider are strongly linked to information processing and artificial neural networks, whereas others are not. In all cases quenched random variables are used to represent complicated interactions which are not known in detail, and the typical behaviour in a properly defined thermodynamic limit is of particular interest.

14.1 Support vector machines

The main reason which prevents the perceptron from being a serious candidate for the solution of many real-world learning problems is that it can only implement linearly separable Boolean functions. In chapters 12 and 13 we have shown that this limitation can be overcome by introducing hidden layers of formal neurons. The input–output mapping in such multilayer networks may be considered as a two-step process. First the inputs are mapped to the internal representations. Due to the sigmoidal activation function of the hidden units this is a *non-linear transformation* from the input space to an abstract intermediate representation. Second the hidden-to-output mapping performs a linearly separable classification of the internal representations. The mapping from the input to the hidden layer therefore fulfils some preprocessing task in transforming a problem which is not linearly separable into one which is.

From the more general point of view of learning machines not necessarily related to artificial neural networks, this strategy may be generalized in the following way. The inputs **S**, which we continue to take to be N-dimensional real vectors, are mapped by a *general non-linear* transformation **Φ** to an intermediate *feature space*. The output is then determined by a *linearly separable* classification performed by a perceptron in this feature space.

Intuitively it seems rather clear that a sufficiently complex function **Φ** mapping the inputs to a sufficiently high-dimensional feature space should be able to unfold every classification in the input space to a linearly separable function in feature space. However, we are interested in systems which are able to *learn from examples* and at first sight the huge variability caused by the high (possibly infinite) dimension of the feature space seems to prohibit effective learning both in principle and in practice.

Two non-trivial observations have been made, however, which overcome these difficulties and which have turned the above program into one of the most promising approaches to practical problems in machine learning.

The first observation is that using the *maximally stable* perceptron as discussed in section 3.5 for performing the classification in the feature space results in a dramatically reduced VC dimension of the machine [155]. Let us again consider a training set $\{\boldsymbol{\xi}^\mu, \sigma_T^\mu\}$ of p inputs $\boldsymbol{\xi}^\mu$ together with the target outputs σ_T^μ. The coupling vector **J** of the maximally stable perceptron in feature space may then be written as (cf. (3.11))

$$\mathbf{J} \sim \sum_\mu x^\mu \sigma_T^\mu \mathbf{\Phi}(\boldsymbol{\xi}^\mu). \tag{14.1}$$

Only a subset of the embedding strengths x^μ is different from zero. In the case of the maximally stable perceptron inputs with $x^\mu \neq 0$ were referred to as the *active* examples; in the present more general framework they are called the *support vectors*. Only the explicit values of the embedding strengths of these support vectors have to be determined in the learning process and consequently it is the ratio between the number of support vectors and the total number of examples rather than the dimension of the feature space which is the crucial quantity for bounding the generalization error [155]. Moreover, as discussed in section 3.5 the explicit determination of the coupling vector of the maximally stable perceptron can be effectively accomplished by using the powerful methods of convex optimization

[46]. Taken together this ensures that meaningful learning from examples is possible in principle even in extremely high dimensional feature spaces.

The second important point concerns the more practical question of how to explicitly construct the non-linear mapping $\Phi(\mathbf{S})$ suitable for a concrete problem under consideration. Quite surprisingly it turns out that the complete form of $\Phi(\mathbf{S})$ is not needed at all [237, 238]. Instead it is sufficient to know the scalar product of the feature vectors $\Phi(\mathbf{S})$ and $\Phi(\mathbf{S}')$ corresponding to two inputs $\mathbf{S}$ and $\mathbf{S}'$, which is specified by the so-called *kernel*

$$K(\mathbf{S}, \mathbf{S}') = \Phi(\mathbf{S})\,\Phi(\mathbf{S}') = \sum_i \Phi_i(\mathbf{S})\,\Phi_i(\mathbf{S}'). \qquad (14.2)$$

This is because in the learning process (cf. (3.24)) the determination of the coupling vector $\mathbf{J}$ only requires the knowledge of the correlation matrix

$$C_{\mu\nu} = \Phi(\boldsymbol{\xi}^\mu)\,\Phi(\boldsymbol{\xi}^\nu)\sigma_T^\mu\sigma_T^\nu, \qquad (14.3)$$

which using (14.2) may be written in the form

$$C_{\mu\nu} = K(\boldsymbol{\xi}^\mu, \boldsymbol{\xi}^\nu)\sigma_T^\mu\sigma_T^\nu. \qquad (14.4)$$

Moreover, in order to determine the classification of a new example $\mathbf{S}$ after learning is completed one has to calculate $\mathrm{sgn}(\mathbf{J}\,\Phi(\mathbf{S}))$, which with the help of (14.1) acquires the form

$$\mathrm{sgn}(\mathbf{J}\,\Phi(\mathbf{S})) = \mathrm{sgn}\left(\sum_\mu x^\mu K(\boldsymbol{\xi}^\mu, \mathbf{S})\sigma_T^\mu\right), \qquad (14.5)$$

and is therefore also solely determined by the kernel K. It is hence not necessary to deal with all the complications of the full mapping Φ. Instead it is much more convenient to choose a suitable kernel $K(\mathbf{S}, \mathbf{S}')$ representing e.g. a polynomial decision surface in input space and to work directly with equations (14.4) and (14.5). Of course not every function $K(\mathbf{S}, \mathbf{S}')$ can be written in the form (14.2), but the mathematical conditions to ensure this decomposition are well known (Mercer's theorem, see e.g. [239]). In this way even infinite dimensional feature spaces may be treated without much more effort than needed for the perceptron of maximal stability. A simple example is provided by the so-called *radial basis function networks*, see e.g. [240], which are defined by

$$K(\mathbf{S}, \mathbf{S}') = \exp\left(-\frac{|\mathbf{S} - \mathbf{S}'|^2}{2}\right) \qquad (14.6)$$

corresponding to an infinite dimensional Hilbert space as feature space.

The statistical mechanics analysis of support vector machines builds on the close connection with the perceptron of optimal stability. The desired couplings

$\mathbf{J}$ performing the linearly separable classification in feature space with the largest margin minimize the norm $\mathbf{J}^2$ under the constraints $\mathbf{J}\Phi(\xi^\mu)\sigma_T^\mu > 1$. We are hence led to introduce the partition function

$$Z = \int d\mu(\mathbf{J})\, e^{-\beta \mathbf{J}^2/2} \prod_\mu \theta(\mathbf{J}\Phi(\xi^\mu)\sigma_T^\mu - 1) \tag{14.7}$$

and to consider the zero-temperature limit $\beta \to \infty$ of the free energy $f = -\langle\!\langle \ln Z \rangle\!\rangle / \beta$. The target labels σ_T^μ are provided by a teacher support vector machine with the same function Φ and an unknown coupling vector T performing the classification in feature space.

This program was carried through in [241] for polynomial kernels of the form

$$K(\mathbf{S}, \mathbf{S}') = g\left(\frac{\mathbf{S}\,\mathbf{S}'}{N}\right) \tag{14.8}$$

with

$$g(x) = \sum_l a_l x^l. \tag{14.9}$$

The resulting behaviour of the generalization error shows a *hierarchy of plateaus* corresponding to the different scaling regimes $p \sim N^l$ of the training set size p with the dimension of the input space N. This is similar to what was discussed in section 12.6 for the fully connected committee machine. An analogous behaviour is also found for perceptrons with higher order interactions, e.g. those including terms of the form $J_{ij} S_i S_j$ in the expression for the local field at the output [242]. Roughly speaking for $p \sim N$ the examples are just sufficient to learn the linear components of (14.9), for $p \sim N^2$ the quadratic part is adapted and so on. This should, however, not be taken literally since from the decomposition (14.1) it is clear that for all scaling regimes of p non-linear features of Φ also contribute to $\mathbf{J}$.

As in the case of the perceptron, the statistical mechanics analysis allows exact calculation of several interesting quantities in the thermodynamic limit. In this way it contributes decisively to the quantitative characterization of the performance of support vector machines. In [241], e.g., not only the learning curve $\varepsilon(\alpha)$ but also the average number of support vectors was calculated. Moreover it was shown that a support vector network with quadratic kernel performs rather well on a linearly separable task, verifying that despite larger capacity the generalization ability is remarkably high. Also the storage problem was considered and the results of Cover [72] on *polynomial* decision surfaces were re-derived.

The concept of support vector machines was developed by V. N. Vapnik and co-workers in the 1990s [171, 243]. A pedagogical introduction is given in [244]. In the statistical mechanics of learning also, support vector machines constitute a modern and promising field.

14.2 Complex optimization

Problems of combinatorial optimization occur in large variety in everyday engineering practice, e.g. in logistics, scheduling and design, and IC chip placement and wiring. Quite generally these problems may be formulated as the minimization of a cost function with many parameters and a large number N of variables. Different choices of the parameters correspond to different instances of the problem.

Well known examples include the travelling salesman problem, the number partitioning problem and the knapsack problem. In the travelling salesman problem a list of N cities and the costs for travelling between any pair of them is given and a tour for a salesman is sought which passes through each city exactly once, returns to the starting point, and minimizes the total cost. In the number partitioning problem $2N$ real numbers are given and a partition into two subsets is wanted with the difference between the sums of the numbers in each subset as small as possible. In the knapsack problem one is given N items with different "utilities" and "loads" and the problem is to find a subset of items with maximal utility not exceeding a given load limit.[1] A problem related to the main topic of this book is learning in a neural network with discrete degrees of freedom (see section 7.4).

Practical experience shows that some of these problems are easy to solve, others are notoriously difficult, and for others some instances are hard whereas others are easy. The theory of algorithmic complexity [245, 246] aims at tightening up these loose statements into mathematical theorems. To do so it is crucial to study how the time t an algorithm needs to solve a problem depends on the problem size N.

If for a problem there is an algorithm for which this time grows only like a power of N, i.e. $t \sim N^\gamma$, the problem is said to be *polynomial* and belongs to the class P. Note that a universal and rather obvious algorithm to solve any combinatorial optimization problem is given by *exhaustive search*, i.e. calculating the cost function for *all* possible configurations and selecting the minimum. The time scaling of such an algorithm is (at least) *exponential* with N. Knowing a polynomial algorithm hence implies a deeper understanding of the problem, which is then exploited for a much more effective solution.

For many relevant problems, however, no polynomial algorithm is known and hence there are instances for which the time necessary to obtain a solution increases exponentially with N, rendering an exact solution impractical even for rather small sizes. An obvious and at the same time rather uninteresting reason for this exponential scaling may be that the evaluation of the cost function for a specific configuration of the N variables is computationally very costly. The more challenging situation concerns problems for which the evaluation of the cost

---

[1] It is very instructive to try to solve randomly generated instances of these problems for moderate N between 10 and 50.

function itself is easy, i.e. polynomial in the system size. The exponential scaling of the time needed for the solution is then really due to the intrinsic difficulty of the problem. Hence one may still hope to improve on the understanding of the problem and of finding a more effective algorithm. Problems of this type are called *non-deterministic polynomial* and form the class NP.

Among all NP problems some stand out in the sense that every instance of an NP problem may be mapped on one of the instances of these problems in polynomial time. This subclass of NP problems is called NP-*complete* and forms the core of all NP problems. The first problem which was shown to be NP-*complete* is the *satisfiability problem* concerning the question of whether an assignment of values to N logical variables may be found which makes a long logical expression involving these variables and their negation true [247], see also [248] for a pedagogical introduction.

One of the basic issues in the theory of computational complexity is the question whether the classes P and NP are really distinct. In view of the above definitions this is equivalent to the question whether an algorithm exists which solves at least one NP-*complete* problem in polynomial time. Although it is generally believed that no such algorithm exists no proof for this statement is available up to now.

Because they involve the minimization of a cost function, optimization problems are at first sight easy to link to statistical mechanics techniques. Considering the number partitioning problem, e.g., we may introduce binary variables $S_i = \pm 1$, $i = 1, \ldots, 2N$ specifying to which subset the i-th number a_i belongs, so that the solution of the problem corresponds to the ground state of an Ising spin system with energy

$$H(\mathbf{S}) = \sum_{i,j} a_i a_j S_i S_j. \qquad (14.10)$$

The knapsack problem with utilities a_i and loads b_i may be formulated in a similar fashion by introducing variables c_i which are either 1 (put item i in the knapsack) or 0 (do not include this item) and looking for the minimum of the energy function

$$H(c) = -\sum_i a_i c_i \qquad (14.11)$$

under the constraint $\sum_i b_i c_i < B$. The constraint may be included into the energy by a Lagrange multiplier playing the role of a chemical potential. Likewise the travelling salesman problem [17] and the satisfiability problem [249] may be mapped onto the determination of the ground state of appropriate Ising spin systems.

Despite these formal similarities, however, the focus in the theory of algorithmic complexity and complex optimization is rather different from that of statistical mechanics. In the former all details of an instance are known and the full (microscopic) solution is needed. On the contrary, in statistical mechanics only partial information on the system is available and average (macroscopic) characteristics are looked for. The connection may nevertheless become fruitful if one considers the statistical mechanics of *ensembles* of *randomly* generated instances of complex optimization problems. As in the learning scenarios discussed in the present book, it turns out that many interesting quantities characterizing optimization problems, e.g. the minimal tour length in a travelling salesman problem, are *self-averaging* and hence the same for almost all instances. Therefore statistical mechanics again tries to characterize *typical* properties, and is thus complementary to the theory of algorithmic complexity, which concentrates on *worst case* situations (hardest instances). Often the typical hardness of an optimization problem may be more relevant for practical purposes than an over-pessimistic worst case result. In fact it is known that for some NP-complete problems the majority of instances may be solved easily and only very few realizations really require the complete enumeration of all possible configurations [250, 251].

Results from statistical mechanics may be useful for optimization tasks in several ways. First an estimate of the typical minimal value of the cost function is clearly useful as a guide to the solution of a particular instance since it allows one to judge how far an intermediate result might still be from the true optimum. Moreover *bounds* for the typical ground state cost, e.g. those resulting from the annealed approximation, may be extremely useful in branch-and-bound algorithms used for the explicit solution of a problem. Additionally the ground state entropy and more generally the density of states near the ground state specify the typical number of optimal and near optimal solutions respectively. With the help of this information one may be able to compare the efforts needed to find the real optimum and an almost optimal solution. In practical situations it might be advisable to be content with a nearly optimal solution which can be easily determined instead of insisting on the hard-to-find true optimum offering only a slight additional improvement. In addition the mutual relation between near optimal solutions of an optimization problem may be characterized by overlap parameters between different configurations with low energies [252]. This allows one to obtain an impression of the topology of the solution space, which may be very useful for the design of appropriate algorithms. In particular a family of algorithms called *simulated annealing* deriving from standard Monte-Carlo methods used in statistical mechanics has been put forward [98]. Their efficiency depends crucially on the location and nature of possible dynamical phase transitions which in turn are related to the organization of the solution space. We finally mention that finite size scaling techniques, being a standard tool for the numerical investigation of phase transitions in statistical mechanics, have been found extremely valuable for the quantitative investigation of sudden transitions in the algorithmic complexity of the satisfiability problem [253].

Statistical mechanics techniques developed in the theory of disordered systems may hence be useful for the analysis of complex optimization problems and the corresponding results are often complementary to those obtained within mathematics and theoretical computer science. An example of a concrete calculation is [17] which includes a discussion of the travelling salesman problem. The knapsack problem was analysed in the framework of statistical mechanics in [254, 255] by exploiting an analogy with the Ising perceptron discussed in section 6.3. A very detailed statistical mechanics analysis using methods rather similar to those introduced for learning problems in neural networks was performed for the satisfiability problem in [249, 256] by building on previous work in statistical mechanics [257] and computer science [253]. A nice and concise discussion of some surprising aspects of the number partitioning problem is given in [258, 259].

14.3 Error-correcting codes

Since Shannon's seminal work on information theory [260, 261], the study of coding and transmission of messages has become a discipline of its own. One of Shannon's great achievements was to show that a noisy transmission channel can in fact transmit *errorless* information at a certain maximum rate referred to as the channel capacity. As an example consider the case of a noisy binary channel, in which a bit has a probability $(1 - a)/2$ of being inverted during the transmission. The information contained in such a noisy bit is given by

$$\frac{1}{\alpha_c} = 1 - \left(-\frac{1-a}{2} \log_2 \frac{1-a}{2} - \frac{1+a}{2} \log_2 \frac{1+a}{2} \right). \tag{14.12}$$

The term between brackets represents the information loss as a result of the noisy flipping. According to Shannon, one can, using appropriate error-correcting codes, recover without error a message of N bits from a transmitted message of $\alpha_c N$ noisy bits (in the limit $N \to \infty$) [164].

Recently, a new family of codes has been suggested by Sourlas [262], in which the message is encoded as the lowest energy state or ground state of a spin model. Methods of statistical mechanics, similar to those used in spin glass theory and neural networks, can be used to analyse the efficiency of these codes and to explore and construct novel coding methods.

The basic idea is the following. The message consists of an N-dimensional binary vector $\boldsymbol{\xi}$. Instead of sending this signal, one transmits an encoded message consisting of binary coupling vectors of the following form

$$J^0_{i_1 i_2 \dots i_K} = \xi_{i_1} \xi_{i_2} \dots \xi_{i_K}, \tag{14.13}$$

i.e. the product of K components with indices $i_1, i_2, \dots, i_K$ of the signal $\boldsymbol{\xi}$. Let us denote by $J_{i_1 i_2 \dots i_K}$ the transmitted version of the binary variable $J^0_{i_1 i_2 \dots i_K}$. The purpose is to retrieve the original message as the lowest state of the following energy function with K-spin interactions described by the J-couplings

$$H(\mathbf{S}) = -\sum_K \sum_{(i_1 i_2 \dots i_K)} c_{i_1 i_2 \dots i_K} J_{i_1 i_2 \dots i_K} S_{i_1} S_{i_2} \dots S_{i_K}. \tag{14.14}$$

Here $\mathbf{S}$ is an N-dimensional spin variable and the inner sum runs over all the $\binom{N}{K}$ possible different choices of the indices for a given connectivity K and c is the connectivity matrix with elements taking the value 1 if the corresponding K-spin interaction is present and 0 otherwise. To understand the motivation for this construction, consider first the case of a full connectivity $c \equiv 1$ and suppose that the channel is not noisy. It is then clear that the minimum of the energy H is attained for $\mathbf{S} = \boldsymbol{\xi}$. This however is not a very efficient procedure since the amount of bits that is being transmitted, namely that of all the coupling components, is much larger than N. One expects however, thanks to the redundant and "distributed" way in which the information about the signal is stored, that the correct ground state will be preserved when the channel becomes noisy and, more importantly, when one removes redundant information by *randomly diluting* connections between the spins. This is done by setting the corresponding elements of the connectivity matrix c equal to zero. Concomitantly, only those coupling components corresponding to non-zero components have to be transmitted. According to Shannon's bound, it might be possible to bring their number down to $\alpha_c N$ in the limit $N \to \infty$.

To investigate this question in detail, one considers the sampling of spin states $\mathbf{S}$ from the Boltzmann distribution

$$\text{Prob}(\mathbf{S}) = \frac{1}{Z} e^{-\beta H(\mathbf{S})}. \tag{14.15}$$

One defines the corresponding free energy by

$$f(\beta) = -\frac{1}{\beta} \lim_{N \to \infty} \frac{1}{N} \langle\!\langle \ln Z \rangle\!\rangle \tag{14.16}$$

where the average is taken over the random choices of the dilution, over the random flippings of the synaptic vector and over the randomly chosen message. The properties of the ground state may now be investigated by taking the zero-temperature limit $\beta \to \infty$. In the process of calculating f by the replica trick, one encounters the following self-averaging order parameter

$$R(\beta) = \frac{1}{N} \sum_{i=1}^{N} S_i \xi_i. \tag{14.17}$$

If this overlap tends to 1 in the limit $\beta \to \infty$ the signal is indeed recovered with no error, or, more precisely, with a number of errors that is not extensive. To rephrase the same question in terms of spin systems, we first note that one can without loss of generality choose[2] the signal to have all its components equal to 1. The basic quantity to be evaluated is then the magnetization

$$m(\beta) = \frac{1}{N} \sum_{i=1}^{N} S_i \tag{14.18}$$

and full recovery of the signal corresponds to a ferromagnetic ground state.

The problem described above has been investigated for a number of scenarios, differing mainly in the way in which the spin connections are diluted, i.e. in the choice of the connectivity matrix c. Sourlas [262] considered the problem in which only one term in the sum over K is allowed, but with high connectivity, namely the number of connections per spin proportional to $\binom{N-1}{K-1}$. For $K = 2$ it can be mapped to the Sherrington–Kirkpatrick model [264] while the random energy model [79] is obtained for $K \to \infty$. In the latter case, it is found that Shannon's bound is indeed saturated. The case of sparse connectivity, with the number of connections per spin of order 1, is investigated in [265] and Shannon's bound is again recovered in a limiting case. Motivated by the idea of parity-checking codes, the case of an energy function consisting of a sum over the coordination number K going from 1 to some maximal value $N\alpha$ has been considered, with a single (randomly chosen) spin interaction for every degree of coordination K [266].

Interestingly, one can show by working in a Bayesian framework that the Sourlas ground state maximizes the posterior probability, i.e. it is the most likely choice for the message. However, just as learning from a noisy teacher is sub-optimal at zero temperature, see chapter 5, it turns out that zero-temperature decoding does not necessarily lead to the lowest error rate. In fact, Ruján [267] proposed to choose as the best approximation for the message the clipped magnetization observed in the spin system at a finite temperature, namely the so-called Nishimori temperature T_N with

$$\frac{1}{T_N} = \frac{1}{2} \ln \frac{1+a}{1-a}. \tag{14.19}$$

It was proved subsequently [268] that the error rate is in this case always lower than

---

[2] This may be achieved by switching to new spin variables $\tilde{S}_i = \xi_i S_i$ and purely ferromagnetic interactions $\mathbf{J}^0$ as in the Mattis model of spin glasses [263].

or equal to that of the ground state. The same type of idea has also been applied to image restoration [269]. The major difference from error-correcting codes is that one usually does not receive additional redundant information, but one can use *a priori* knowledge about the images to remove the noise.

It should be emphasized that the *practical* implementation of the different proposals for error-correcting codes is usually far from being straightforward. For the codes using a mapping on a spin system one observes e.g. a trade-off between accuracy, i.e. the final magnetization, and the basin of attraction of the ground state. If the latter is rather small the code is practically useless although it may theoretically still saturate the Shannon bound. Ideas for a possible solution of this dilemma are discussed in [270].

We finally turn to yet another type of coding, namely one which is suggested by a neural network model studied in this book. We mentioned that the Ising reversed wedge perceptron learning from a similar teacher saturates the information-theoretic bound for generalization when the specific width $\gamma = \gamma_c = \sqrt{2 \ln 2}$ of the wedge is considered, see section 7.3. Hence the N-dimensional binary teacher vector $\mathbf{T}$ can in principle be reconstructed on the basis of the classifications $\sigma_T^\mu = g_{\mathrm{RW}}(\mathbf{T}\boldsymbol{\xi}^\mu/\sqrt{N})$ of randomly chosen examples $\boldsymbol{\xi}^\mu$, $\mu = 1, \ldots, p = \alpha N$ for $\alpha = 1$ where $g_{\mathrm{RW}}(\lambda) = \mathrm{sgn}(\lambda - \gamma)\,\mathrm{sgn}(\lambda)\,\mathrm{sgn}(\lambda + \gamma)$ is the reversed wedge transfer function. If these classifications are sent through a noisy channel, the problem becomes equivalent to learning from a teacher with output noise $\sigma'^\mu_T = \eta^\mu \sigma_T^\mu$, cf. chapter 5, with η^μ being -1 or $+1$ depending on whether the channel makes an error or not. To reconstruct the teacher in this case, we define the energy function $H(\mathbf{J})$ that counts the number of errors of the student $\mathbf{J}$ on the noisy classifications

$$H(\mathbf{J}) = \sum_{\mu=1}^{p} \theta\left(-g_{\mathrm{RW}}\left(\frac{\mathbf{J}\boldsymbol{\xi}^\mu}{\sqrt{N}}\right) g_{\mathrm{RW}}\left(\frac{\mathbf{T}\boldsymbol{\xi}^\mu}{\sqrt{N}}\right) \eta^\mu\right). \tag{14.20}$$

Building on our experience of finite-temperature learning, we will sample $\mathbf{J}$ from a Boltzmann ensemble

$$\mathrm{Prob}(\mathbf{J}) = \frac{1}{Z} e^{-\beta H(\mathbf{J})} \tag{14.21}$$

at the analogue of the inverse Nishimori temperature, namely $\beta = \beta_N = \ln(1 + a)/(1-a)$, cf. (5.32). At this temperature, those students will be selected that make as many mistakes with respect to the noisy classifications σ'^μ_T as the teacher. This restores the symmetry between students and teacher, allowing an $n \to 1$ rather than an $n \to 0$ calculation in the replica trick with the concomitant symmetry property $q = R$. By performing these calculations for the specific wedge size $\gamma = \gamma_c$ one finds moreover that $q = R = 0$ for $\alpha \le \alpha_c$, with α_c defined by (14.12), and the annealed approximation becomes exact. In particular for $\alpha \le \alpha_c$ the entropy is given by

$$s(\alpha) = \ln 2 \left(1 - \frac{\alpha}{\alpha_c} \right).$$ (14.22)

At $\alpha = \alpha_c$ the entropy becomes zero and a first order transition to perfect general-ization $R = 1$ takes place. The teacher can thus in principle be reconstructed from the $p = \alpha_c N$ noisy classifications. The reversed wedge coding therefore saturates the Shannon bound.

14.4 Game theory

Game theory aims at modelling in mathematical terms problems of decision-making typically arising in economics, sociology, or politics. Although first attempts with this goal are apparently rather old, game theory became an estab-lished field of mathematics only after the seminal work of John von Neumann collected in the influential book [271]. Meanwhile, after several interesting results have been obtained, including the characterization of equilibria [272] and the emergence of cooperation [273], game theory has developed into a flourishing field of mathematics with growing influence on economic research.[3]

The generic game theoretic setup is characterized by a set of *players* $\{X, Y, \dots\}$ choosing between different *strategies* $\{X_i\}, \{Y_j\}, \dots$. The outcome of the game is specified by the *payoffs* $P_X(X_i, Y_j, \dots), P_Y(X_i, Y_j, \dots), \dots$ every player is going to receive. The game is repeated many times and every player strives to maximize his cumulative payoff. The important point is that the payoff of every individual player depends on the *whole set* of strategies including those chosen by all the other players. In order to maximize his payoff every player has hence to optimize his own strategy without having control over the actions of the other players.

Several realizations of this basic scenario, usually involving a small number of players each having just a few strategies at their disposal, have been studied (see, e.g., [271, 274]). The aspect relevant in the present context is that the number of possible strategies may often be rather large and that the dependence of the payoffs on the strategies is in general very complex and involves many parameters. It is then sensible to ask whether the payoffs may be modelled by *random* functions and whether interesting self-averaging quantities may be identified which characterize the *typical* properties of the game.

This approach has recently been shown to be fruitful for matrix games [275] and for some aspects of bi-matrix games [276, 277]. Matrix games are a classical and simple realization of zero-sum games between two players which also formed

---

[3] The 1994 Nobel prize for economics was awarded to J. C. Harsanyi, J. S. Nash and R. Selten for their work in game theory.

the basis of von Neumann's early investigations. The two players X and Y may choose between N strategies X_i and M strategies Y_j respectively and the payoffs $P_X(X_i, Y_j) =: c_{ij}$ and $P_Y(X_i, Y_j) := -c_{ij}$ always add to zero and are coded in the *payoff matrix* c_{ij}. Hence what one player gains is always the other player's loss and the goals of the players are completely conflicting.

In order to get some intuitive feeling for the situation it is helpful to consider a simple example. Let the payoff matrix be given by

$$c_{ij} = \begin{pmatrix} -8 & 2 & -4 & -11 \\ 6 & 4 & 2 & 17 \\ 12 & 7 & 1 & 3 \end{pmatrix}. \tag{14.23}$$

It is sensible for player X to proceed as follows: Playing strategy i he will receive *at least* the payoff $\min_j c_{ij}$, i.e. in the example choosing strategy 1, 2 or 3 would guarantee him payoffs -11, 2 and 1 respectively. It is then best to choose the *maximum* of these and to play the strategy i^* satisfying $\min_j c_{i^*j} = \max_i \min_j c_{ij}$. In the example this is strategy 2. Likewise player Y in his attempt to maximize his payoff first looks for the *largest* losses he may encounter when playing a given strategy, i.e. he determines $\max_i c_{ij}$ for all j. In this example he may lose 12, 7, 2 and 17 when playing strategies 1, 2, 3 and 4 respectively. He therefore chooses the strategy j^* satisfying $\max_i c_{ij^*} = \min_j \max_i c_{ij}$ *minimizing* the maximal possible loss. In the example the best choice for player Y would therefore be to play strategy 3. The matrix game specified by (14.23) therefore represents a rather simple situation. Player X should always play his second strategy and player Y always his third. If one player deviates from this prescription and the other one stays with it the payoff of the deviating player will decrease. This is the most elementary example of a *Nash equilibrium* [272, 274].

It is not difficult to prove that for a given matrix c_{ij} one has always

$$\max_i \min_j c_{ij} \leq \min_j \max_i c_{ij}. \tag{14.24}$$

Equality holds only if the matrix c has a *saddle point*, i.e. if a pair i^*, j^* exists for which

$$\max_i \min_j c_{ij} = c_{i^*j^*} = \min_j \max_i c_{ij} \tag{14.25}$$

as in the example (14.23). For payoff matrices without saddle points the situation is more interesting. Then, as implied by the inequality (14.24), the gain guaranteed for player X is *less* than the loss player Y is expecting . Intuitively it is clear that the players should try to move into this gap left by their pessimistic reasonings described above. However, deviating from their respective strategies in a way which may be anticipated by the opponent might result in dramatic losses. A crucial idea of von Neumann was that the players may improve their payoffs if they *mix* their strategies *at random*. This allows them, in a manner unpredictable for the other player, to use all their strategies including those promising high gain at the risk of equally high losses.

Accordingly a vector of probabilities $\boldsymbol{x} = \{x_1, \ldots, x_N\}$ for playing the different strategies $X_1, \ldots, X_N$ is called a *mixed strategy* of player X. Being probabilities the vectors $\boldsymbol{x}$ must of course satisfy the normalization condition

$$\sum_i x_i = 1. \tag{14.26}$$

The famous *minmax–theorem* of von Neumann states that for all payoff matrices c_{ij} there exists a *saddle point of mixed strategies*, i.e. there are *optimal mixed strategies* $\boldsymbol{x}^*$ and $\boldsymbol{y}^*$ such that (cf. (14.25))

$$\max_{\boldsymbol{x}} \min_{\boldsymbol{y}} \sum_{i,j} c_{ij}\, x_i\, y_j = \sum_{i,j} c_{ij}\, x_i^*\, y_j^* = \min_{\boldsymbol{y}} \max_{\boldsymbol{x}} \sum_{i,j} c_{ij}\, x_i\, y_j. \tag{14.27}$$

The expected payoff for the optimal mixed strategies

$$v_c := \sum_{i,j} c_{ij}\, x_i^*\, y_j^* \tag{14.28}$$

is called the *value of the game*. For games with saddle points the optimal strategies are realized as *pure strategies* which are of the form $x_i = \delta(i, m)$, $y_j = \delta(j, n)$ with the Kronecker symbol defined by (A1.13) and the value of the game is just the respective element c_{mn} of the payoff matrix.

Besides their existence little is known about the optimal mixed strategies. If the numbers N and M of strategies available to the players are large one may gain some general insight by considering payoff matrices generated at random in the thermodynamic limit $N, M \to \infty$. If the different entries c_{ij} of the payoff matrix are independent random variables it is easy to show that the probability of a saddle point in pure strategies vanishes exponentially with the size of the matrix. The optimal mixed strategies are therefore non-trivial with probability 1. In order to proceed, the following simple result is very helpful. A necessary and sufficient condition for the mixed strategy $\boldsymbol{x}^*$ of player X to be optimal is that

$$\sum_i c_{ij} x_i^* \geq v_c \qquad \text{for all } j. \tag{14.29}$$

The condition is necessary since if it were violated for some j player Y could increase his payoff by always playing j. It is sufficient since multiplying the equation by y_j and summing over j one finds that the payoff for player X playing $\boldsymbol{x}^*$ is never smaller than v_c.

Using this condition we may introduce the *indicator function* for an optimal mixed strategy

$$\chi(\boldsymbol{x}) = \prod_{j=1}^{M} \theta\left(\sum_i c_{ij}x_i - v_c\right). \tag{14.30}$$

This is 0 if (14.29) is violated for at least one j and 1 otherwise. Placing this function under an integral over all possible mixed strategies $\boldsymbol{x}$ satisfying the normalization condition (14.26) would hence project out all optimal strategies of player X. Nevertheless, in the form (14.30) the indicator function is not yet of much help since v_c is a complicated function of the payoff matrix not known in advance. However, guided by our experience with optimal stability neural networks (cf. sections 4.1 and 6.1) we may introduce the quenched entropy

$$s(v) = \lim_{N \to \infty} \frac{1}{N} \left\langle\!\!\left\langle \ln \int_0^1 \prod_{i=1}^{N} dx_i \, \delta\left(\sum_i x_i - 1\right) \prod_{j=1}^{M} \theta\left(\sum_i c_{ij}x_i - v\right) \right\rangle\!\!\right\rangle \tag{14.31}$$

describing the typical variability in strategies which fulfil (14.29) with v_c replaced by a general threshold v. The average is here over the distribution of the elements of the payoff matrix. From the definition (14.28) of the expected payoff v_c we expect $s(v) \to -\infty$ for $v \to v_c$ since with increasing v the number of available mixed strategies decreases until at $v = v_c$ only the optimal mixed strategy $\boldsymbol{x}^*$ is left (cf. also fig. 4.1). Calculating the quenched entropy (14.31) and taking appropriate order parameter limits corresponding to $s(v) \to -\infty$ one may therefore characterize the typical value of a random game and typical properties of the optimal stabilities. The explicit calculation [275] is rather similar to the one performed in section 6.1 for the storage problem of the spherical perceptron, with the notable difference that the spherical constraint (2.1) for the perceptron couplings is to be replaced by the simplex constraint (14.26) for the probabilities x_i.

As an interesting example the fraction of zero components in the optimal strategy was calculated in [275]. As it turns out, an *extensive fraction* of the N strategies available to player X are *never played at all* within the optimal strategy, i.e. they are characterized by $x_i^* = 0$. The dependence of this fraction on the ratio M/N between the *a priori* variabilities of the two players is a non-trivial result accessible to statistical mechanics and interesting for game theory.

Matrix games are among the simplest systems in game theory and many interesting aspects of games are beyond this basic setup. Nevertheless methods of statistical mechanics may still be of value in the investigation of more advanced situations whenever complex relations may be modelled by random parameters and interesting quantities turn out to be self-averaging in an appropriately defined thermodynamic limit. A first step towards the analysis of more complicated game theoretic problems is the analysis of bi-matrix games, for which the typical number of Nash equilibria was calculated in [276] and [277]. For the application of statistical mechanics techniques to related systems see also [278, 279], [280] and [281].

Appendix 1

Basic Mathematics

The purpose of this appendix is to collect some of the basic mathematical tools which are used in this book. For more details, we refer to standard texts [282, 283].

A1.1 Gaussian integrals

Let $\mathbf{t}$ and $\mathbf{b}$ be N-dimensional real vectors, and A an $N \times N$ positive definite matrix. Then

$$
\begin{aligned}
\int d\mathbf{t}\, e^{-\frac{1}{2}\mathbf{t}A\mathbf{t}+\mathbf{t}\mathbf{b}} &= \int_{-\infty}^{\infty} dt_1 \ldots \int_{-\infty}^{\infty} dt_N \exp\left(-\frac{1}{2}\sum_{i,j=1}^{N} t_i A_{ij} t_j + \sum_{i=1}^{N} t_i b_i\right) \\
&= \frac{(2\pi)^{N/2}}{\sqrt{\det A}} \exp\left(\frac{1}{2}\sum_{i,j=1}^{N} b_i (A^{-1})_{ij} b_j\right) \\
&= \frac{(2\pi)^{N/2}}{\sqrt{\det A}} e^{\frac{1}{2}\mathbf{b}A^{-1}\mathbf{b}},
\end{aligned}
\tag{A1.1}
$$

with A^{-1} denoting the inverse matrix of A. Integrals of this type occur very frequently in the statistical mechanics of neural networks. It has therefore become customary to introduce the abbreviation

$$
Dt := \frac{dt}{\sqrt{2\pi}} \exp(-t^2/2),
\tag{A1.2}
$$

for the Gaussian measure, with the help of which the simplest case of (A1.1) corresponding to $N = 1$ may be written in the form

$$
\int Dt\, e^{bt} = e^{b^2/2}.
\tag{A1.3}
$$

Using this equation from right to left is usually called a *Hubbard–Stratonovich transformation*. It allows an expression with b^2 in the exponent to be replaced by one with b occurring linearly in the exponent at the expense of an additional integration over an auxiliary variable t. This is particularly useful to factorize integrals when b is a sum of integration variables.

Another frequently occurring construction is the incomplete integral over the Gaussian measure (A1.2), which is abbreviated as

$$H(x) := \int_x^\infty Dt = \int_x^\infty \frac{dt}{\sqrt{2\pi}} \exp(-t^2/2). \tag{A1.4}$$

The function $H(x)$ defined in this way is related to the complementary error function $\mathrm{erfc}(x)$ by

$$H(x) = \frac{1}{2}\mathrm{erfc}\left(\frac{x}{\sqrt{2}}\right) = \frac{1}{2}\left(1 - \mathrm{erf}\left(\frac{x}{\sqrt{2}}\right)\right). \tag{A1.5}$$

Of particular importance are the asymptotic forms of $H(x)$ for small and large argument given by

$$H(x) \sim \begin{cases} \dfrac{1}{2} - \dfrac{1}{\sqrt{2\pi}}\left(x - \dfrac{x^3}{6} + \cdots\right) & \text{for } x \to 0 \\[2ex] \dfrac{1}{\sqrt{2\pi}\,x} \exp\left(-\dfrac{x^2}{2}\right)\left(1 - \dfrac{1}{x^2} + \dfrac{3}{x^4} + \cdots\right) & \text{for } x \to \infty. \end{cases} \tag{A1.6}$$

We also collect some useful integrals involving the Gaussian measure and the H-function where a denotes a real parameter

$$\int Dt\, H(at) = \frac{1}{2}$$

$$\int Dt\, t\, H(at) = -\frac{a}{\sqrt{2\pi(1+a^2)}}$$

$$\int Dt\, t^2\, H(at) = \frac{1}{2}$$

$$\int_0^\infty Dt\, H(at) = \frac{1}{2\pi}\mathrm{arccot}(a)$$

$$\int_0^\infty Dt\, t\, H(at) = \frac{1}{2\sqrt{2\pi}}\left(1 - \frac{a}{\sqrt{1+a^2}}\right)$$

$$\int_0^\infty Dt\, t^2\, H(at) = \frac{1}{2\pi}\mathrm{arccot}(a) - \frac{a}{2\pi(1+a^2)}.$$

A1.2 Jensen's inequality

For $f(x)$ a concave function, i.e. $f''(x) \geq 0$, for all x the inequality

$$f(x) \geq f(x_0) + (x - x_0)f'(x_0) \tag{A1.7}$$

holds for all x and x_0. Consider now the case of a random variable x. By averaging over x and choosing $x_0 = \langle x \rangle$, one finds

$$\langle f(x) \rangle \geq f(\langle x \rangle). \tag{A1.8}$$

For a convex function, the inequality is just the other way round. Notable applications of this inequality are $\langle x \rangle \langle 1/x \rangle \geq 1$ and

$$\langle \ln x \rangle \leq \ln \langle x \rangle. \tag{A1.9}$$

A1.3 The δ- and θ-functions

The δ-function was introduced by P. A. M. Dirac in connection with quantum mechanics. Since its precise mathematical definition requires some more advanced concepts we will here be content to understand it intuitively and "define" it by

$$\delta(x) = \begin{cases} 0 & \text{for } x \neq 0 \\ \infty & \text{for } x = 0, \end{cases} \tag{A1.10}$$

such that at the same time $\int dx\, \delta(x) = 1$. The δ-function therefore represents an "extremely sharp peak" at $x = 0$. The main property following from this description is

$$\int dx\, f(x)\, \delta(x - x_0) = f(x_0) \tag{A1.11}$$

for every sufficiently smooth function $f(x)$. Some useful consequences are

$$f(x)\, \delta(x - x_0) = f(x_0)\, \delta(x - x_0)$$
$$x\, \delta(x) = 0$$
$$\delta(ax) = \frac{1}{|a|}\, \delta(x).$$

Of particular interest is the integral representation of the δ-function, which is of the form

$$\delta(x) = \int \frac{d\hat{x}}{2\pi}\, e^{i\hat{x}x}. \tag{A1.12}$$

A related function for discrete variables is the δ-symbol due to Kronecker which is defined by

$$\delta(m, n) = \begin{cases} 0 & \text{for } n \neq m \\ 1 & \text{for } n = m, \end{cases} \tag{A1.13}$$

where n and m are integer numbers. The discrete analogue of (A1.11) is clearly

$$\sum_n a_n\, \delta(m, n) = a_m. \tag{A1.14}$$

Like the Dirac δ-function the Kronecker symbol has an integral representation, which is of the form

$$\delta(m, n) = \int_{-\pi}^{\pi} \frac{d\hat{x}}{2\pi} e^{i\hat{x}(n-m)}. \tag{A1.15}$$

In order to show the usefulness of manipulations involving the δ-function we consider a simple example. Assume we have to calculate an integral of the form

$$\int \prod_{i=1}^{N} dx_i \prod_{i=1}^{N} g(x_i) f\left(\sum_{i=1}^{N} x_i\right). \tag{A1.16}$$

Clearly the individual integrals are coupled to each other by the dependence of f on the sum of all x_i. Using (A1.11) and (A1.12) we may however perform the transformations

$$\int \prod_{i=1}^{N} dx_i \prod_{i=1}^{N} g(x_i) f\left(\sum_{i=1}^{N} x_i\right) = \int dy\, \delta\left(y - \sum_i x_i\right) \int \prod_{i=1}^{N} dx_i \prod_{i=1}^{N} g(x_i)\, f(y)$$

$$= \int \frac{dy\, d\hat{y}}{2\pi} e^{i\hat{y}y} f(y) \int \prod_{i=1}^{N} dx_i \prod_{i=1}^{N} g(x_i)\, e^{-i\hat{y}\sum_i x_i}$$

$$= \int \frac{dy\, d\hat{y}}{2\pi} e^{i\hat{y}y} f(y) \left[\int dx\, g(x)\, e^{-i\hat{y}x}\right]^N.$$

The introduction of the δ-function has therefore led to a simple way to factorize the x_i-integrals. This is particularly useful for large N, which in turn is characteristic of statistical mechanics calculations.

The θ-function is defined by

$$\theta(x) = \begin{cases} 0 & \text{for } x \leq 0 \\ 1 & \text{for } x > 0. \end{cases} \tag{A1.17}$$

It is also often referred to as the Heaviside or step function. The θ-function is quite convenient for the incorporation of inequality constraints, cf. (2.13). From the obvious relation with the δ-function

$$\theta(x - x_0) = \int_{x_0}^{\infty} dy\, \delta(x - y) \tag{A1.18}$$

one infers the integral representation of the θ-function

$$\theta(x - x_0) = \int_{x_0}^{\infty} dy \int \frac{d\hat{y}}{2\pi} e^{i\hat{y}(x-y)}. \tag{A1.19}$$

A1.4 The saddle point method

Because they rely heavily on the thermodynamic limit, statistical mechanics calculations are often confronted with the problem of extracting the *asymptotic* behaviour of integrals of the form

$$I = \int_{x_1}^{x_2} dx \, g(x) \, e^{N f(x)} \tag{A1.20}$$

in the limit $N \to \infty$. A method going back to Laplace is built on the observation that for large N those regions in the integral contribute most for which the function f attains its largest values. In fact if the maximum $f(x_0)$ of f lies *inside* the integration interval, i.e. if $x_1 < x_0 < x_2$, we find by using Taylor expansions of f and g around x_0, extending the integration to the complete axis and using (A1.1)

$$I \cong \int_{x_1}^{x_2} dx \, (g(x_0) + g'(x_0)(x - x_0) + \cdots)$$

$$\times \exp\left(N \left[f(x_0) + \frac{1}{2} f''(x_0)(x - x_0)^2 + \cdots \right] \right)$$

$$\cong g(x_0) e^{N f(x_0)} \sqrt{\frac{2\pi}{N |f''(x_0)|}},$$

where the prime denotes differentiation. Using more sophisticated methods one may indeed prove that this argument yields the correct asymptotic form

$$\ln \int_{x_1}^{x_2} dx \, g(x) \, e^{N f(x)} =$$

$$N f(x_0) - \frac{1}{2} \ln N + \frac{1}{2} \ln \frac{2\pi}{|f''(x_0)|} + \ln g(x_0) + O\left(\frac{1}{\sqrt{N}} \right). \tag{A1.21}$$

In many cases only the dominant term proportional to N is of interest. The calculation of the integral is thus reduced to finding the maximal value of the function f in the interval of integration. Assuming that all occurring functions are differentiable this is done by determining all solutions $x_0^{(1)}, \ldots, x_0^{(k)}$ of the equation $f'(x) = 0$ and comparing the corresponding values $f(x_0^{(i)})$ with each other *and with the values of f at the boundary*, i.e. $f(x_1)$ and $f(x_2)$. The latter is necessary since the maximum of f may well occur at one of the boundary values, which are usually not solutions of $f'(x) = 0$.

As an example we consider the integral representation of the gamma function $\Gamma(N + 1)$ for $N > 0$ given by

$$\Gamma(N + 1) = \int_0^\infty dx \, e^{-x} x^N. \tag{A1.22}$$

The integrand is zero at the boundaries of the integration interval and attains its maximum at $x_0 = N$. This suggests introducing the integration variable $y = x/N - 1$ and writing the integral in the form

$$\Gamma(N + 1) = N e^{-N + N \ln N} \int_{-1}^{\infty} dy \, e^{N[-y + \ln(1+y)]}. \tag{A1.23}$$

The function in the exponent is maximal for $y = y_0 = 0$, giving rise to

$$\ln \Gamma(N + 1) = \ln N! \sim N \ln N - N + \frac{1}{2} \ln N + \frac{1}{2} \ln(2\pi) \tag{A1.24}$$

which is nothing but the famous Stirling formula for the asymptotic behaviour of the Γ-function. This simple example also shows that it is in general a good idea to try to find a representation of the integral for which the location of the maximum x_0 is independent of N in order to keep track of the different powers of N.

The described method may be easily generalized to functions of several variables. From the appearance of the determinant in (A1.1) it is clear, however, that the number of integration variables should not diverge with N.

It is often convenient to extend the Laplace method to integrals of the form

$$\int_{\mathcal{C}} dz \, g(z) \, e^{N f(z)} \tag{A1.25}$$

for a *complex* variable z along an integration path $\mathcal{C}$ in the complex plane. To appreciate the new features which arise in this case let us first focus on the behaviour of a complex function $f(z)$ in the vicinity of the analogue of an extremum for a function of a real variable, namely an analytic point z_0 with $f'(z_0) = 0$. The first terms in the Taylor expansion then read

$$f(z_0) = f(z_0) + \frac{1}{2}(z - z_0)^2 f''(z_0) + \cdots. \tag{A1.26}$$

A simple calculation reveals that the functions $u(x, y) = \text{Re} \, f(z)$ and $v(x, y) = \text{Im} \, f(z)$ of the two variables $x = \text{Re} \, z$ and $y = \text{Im} \, z$ actually have, in the vicinity of z_0, the form of two saddles, with respective axes rotated by $\pi/4$. Therefore z_0 is called a *saddle point* of the function $f(z)$.

In order to find the asymptotic behaviour of the integral (A1.25) the integration contour $\mathcal{C}$ is deformed to $\mathcal{C}'$ running through the saddle point z_0 without crossing singularities of $f(z)$. Then, two conditions must hold for the integral

$$\int_{\mathcal{C}'} dz \, g(z) \, e^{N u(z) + i N v(z)} \tag{A1.27}$$

to be dominated by the vicinity of z_0. Firstly, $u(z)$ must go through a *maximum* when moving along $\mathcal{C}'$ through z_0. This is similar to the case of a real valued function. Moreover from (A1.21) it is clear that the best approximation will be obtained if C' follows the direction of *steepest descent* of $u(z)$. Secondly, $v(z)$ must be *constant* in order to avoid violent oscillations of the integrand which would result in cancellations and make the contribution to the integral small even though $u(z)$ is maximal at z_0. As if by a miracle, the latter condition is equivalent to the requirement that C' follows the direction of *steepest descent* of $u(z)$.

Consider for simplicity the case $z_0 = f(z_0) = 0$ and $f''(z_0) = 1$, which may always be achieved by a translation, rotation and rescaling of the coordinate system. Then $u = (x^2 - y^2)/2$ and $v = xy$. The imaginary part is constant along the x- and the y-axis. Only along the y-axis, however, does u really go through a maximum. The integration contour has hence to follow the y-axis in the vicinity of z_0.

The calculation of the asymptotic behaviour of an integral of the form (A1.25) is hence possible by the saddle point method if the integration path C may be deformed without crossing singularities of f in such a way that it runs through a saddle point z_0, which is a solution of $f'(z_0) = 0$, follows locally the direction of steepest descent of the real part of f and ensures that the absolute maximum of the real part of f along the *complete* integration path is at z_0. The result is then given by a similar expression to (A1.21).

If the function $f(z)$ depends on a parameter a it may happen that a given prescription for the deformed contour C' works for $a < a_c$ but fails for $a > a_c$ because for $a > a_c$ it picks up the "wrong direction" of constant imaginary part along which the real part is *minimal* instead of maximal. The saddle point is then said to become *unstable* at $a = a_c$.

Appendix 2

The Gardner Analysis

In this appendix we perform the detailed calculation of the quenched entropy

$$S = \langle\!\langle \ln \Omega(\boldsymbol{\xi}^{\mu}, \mathbf{T}) \rangle\!\rangle_{\boldsymbol{\xi}^{\mu}, \mathbf{T}} \tag{A2.1}$$

for a spherical perceptron $\mathbf{J}$ with N inputs trained by random examples $\boldsymbol{\xi}^{\mu}$, $\mu = 1, \ldots, p = \alpha N$ classified by a random spherical teacher perceptron with coupling vector $\mathbf{T}$. We will consider the probability distributions

$$P_{\xi}(\boldsymbol{\xi}^{\mu}) = \prod_{i} \left[\frac{1}{2}\delta(\xi_i^{\mu} + 1) + \frac{1}{2}\delta(\xi_i^{\mu} - 1) \right] \tag{A2.2}$$

for the components ξ_i^{μ} of the examples and

$$P_{\mathbf{T}}(\mathbf{T}) = (2\pi e)^{-N/2} \delta(\mathbf{T}^2 - N) \tag{A2.3}$$

for the teacher's coupling vector $\mathbf{T}$. The components of $\boldsymbol{\xi}^{\mu}$ are hence ± 1 with equal probability whereas $\mathbf{T}$ is uniformly distributed over the N-sphere.

Using the replica trick we relate $\langle\!\langle \ln \Omega(\boldsymbol{\xi}^{\mu}, \mathbf{T}) \rangle\!\rangle_{\boldsymbol{\xi}^{\mu}, \mathbf{T}}$ to $\langle\!\langle \Omega^n(\boldsymbol{\xi}^{\mu}, \mathbf{T}) \rangle\!\rangle_{\boldsymbol{\xi}^{\mu}, \mathbf{T}}$ via

$$\langle\!\langle \ln \Omega(\boldsymbol{\xi}^{\mu}, \mathbf{T}) \rangle\!\rangle = \lim_{n \to 0} \frac{\langle\!\langle \Omega^n(\boldsymbol{\xi}^{\mu}, \mathbf{T}) \rangle\!\rangle_{\boldsymbol{\xi}^{\mu}, \mathbf{T}} - 1}{n}, \tag{A2.4}$$

so the crucial quantity to calculate is

$$\Omega^{(n)} := \langle\!\langle \Omega^n(\boldsymbol{\xi}^{\mu}, \mathbf{T}) \rangle\!\rangle_{\boldsymbol{\xi}^{\mu}, \mathbf{T}} = \left\langle\!\!\!\left\langle \int \prod_{a=1}^{n} d\mu(\mathbf{J}^a) \prod_{a,\mu} \theta\left(\frac{\mathbf{T}\boldsymbol{\xi}^{\mu}}{\sqrt{N}} \frac{\mathbf{J}^a\boldsymbol{\xi}^{\mu}}{\sqrt{N}} \right) \right\rangle\!\!\!\right\rangle_{\boldsymbol{\xi}^{\mu}, \mathbf{T}}, \tag{A2.5}$$

where

$$d\mu(\mathbf{J}) := \prod_{i=1}^{N} \frac{dJ_i}{\sqrt{2\pi e}} \delta\left(\sum_{i=1}^{N} J_i^2 - N \right) \tag{A2.6}$$

denotes the spherical measure defined in (2.11).

To calculate $\Omega^{(n)}$ we first introduce the variables

$$\lambda_\mu^a = \frac{\mathbf{J}^a \boldsymbol{\xi}^\mu}{\sqrt{N}} \qquad \text{and} \qquad u_\mu = \frac{\mathbf{T} \boldsymbol{\xi}^\mu}{\sqrt{N}} \tag{A2.7}$$

by δ-functions to obtain

$$\Omega^{(n)} = \int \prod_a d\mu(\mathbf{J}^a) \int \prod_{a,\mu} d\lambda_\mu^a \int \prod_\mu du_\mu \prod_{a,\mu} \theta(u_\mu \lambda_\mu^a) \tag{A2.8}$$

$$\times \left\langle\!\!\left\langle \delta\!\left(\lambda_\mu^a - \frac{\mathbf{J}^a \boldsymbol{\xi}^\mu}{\sqrt{N}}\right) \delta\!\left(u_\mu - \frac{\mathbf{T}\boldsymbol{\xi}^\mu}{\sqrt{N}}\right) \right\rangle\!\!\right\rangle_{\boldsymbol{\xi}^\mu, \mathbf{T}}$$

and use the integral representation (A1.12) of the δ-functions. We then find

$$\Omega^{(n)} = \int \prod_a d\mu(\mathbf{J}^a) \int \prod_{a,\mu} \frac{d\lambda_\mu^a d\hat{\lambda}_\mu^a}{2\pi} \int \prod_\mu \frac{du_\mu d\hat{u}_\mu}{2\pi} \tag{A2.9}$$

$$\times \prod_{a,\mu} \theta(u_\mu \lambda_\mu^a) \exp\!\left(i \sum_{\mu,a} \lambda_\mu^a \hat{\lambda}_\mu^a + i \sum_\mu u_\mu \hat{u}_\mu\right)$$

$$\times \left\langle\!\!\left\langle \exp\!\left(-\frac{i}{\sqrt{N}} \sum_{a,\mu} \hat{\lambda}_\mu^a \mathbf{J}^a \boldsymbol{\xi}^\mu - \frac{i}{\sqrt{N}} \sum_\mu \hat{u}_\mu \mathbf{T} \boldsymbol{\xi}^\mu\right) \right\rangle\!\!\right\rangle_{\boldsymbol{\xi}^\mu, \mathbf{T}}.$$

With the help of (A2.2) we find for the average in this expression because of the statistical independence of the components ξ_i^μ

$$\left\langle\!\!\left\langle \prod_{i,\mu} \left\langle\!\!\left\langle \exp\!\left(-\frac{i}{\sqrt{N}} \Big(\sum_a \hat{\lambda}_\mu^a J_i^a + \hat{u}_\mu T_i\Big) \xi_i^\mu\right) \right\rangle\!\!\right\rangle_{\boldsymbol{\xi}^\mu} \right\rangle\!\!\right\rangle_{\mathbf{T}} \tag{A2.10}$$

$$= \left\langle\!\!\left\langle \prod_{i,\mu} \cos\!\left(\frac{1}{\sqrt{N}} \Big(\sum_a \hat{\lambda}_\mu^a J_i^a + \hat{u}_\mu T_i\Big)\right) \right\rangle\!\!\right\rangle_{\mathbf{T}}$$

$$= \left\langle\!\!\left\langle \exp\!\left(\sum_{i,\mu} \ln \cos\!\left(\frac{1}{\sqrt{N}} \Big(\sum_a \hat{\lambda}_\mu^a J_i^a + \hat{u}_\mu T_i\Big)\right)\right) \right\rangle\!\!\right\rangle_{\mathbf{T}}.$$

The asymptotic behaviour of this expression for large N is given by[1]

$$\left\langle\!\!\left\langle \exp\!\left(\sum_{i,\mu} \ln\!\left(1 - \frac{1}{2N}\Big(\sum_a \hat{\lambda}_\mu^a J_i^a + \hat{u}_\mu T_i\Big)^2\right)\right) \right\rangle\!\!\right\rangle_{\mathbf{T}} \tag{A2.11}$$

$$= \left\langle\!\!\left\langle \exp\!\left(-\frac{1}{2} \sum_\mu \sum_{a,b} \hat{\lambda}_\mu^a \hat{\lambda}_\mu^b \frac{1}{N} \sum_i J_i^a J_i^b - \sum_\mu \sum_a \hat{\lambda}_\mu^a \hat{u}_\mu \frac{1}{N} \sum_i J_i^a T_i \right.\right.$$

$$\left.\left. - \frac{1}{2} \sum_\mu \hat{u}_\mu^2 \frac{1}{N} \sum_i T_i^2 \right) \right\rangle\!\!\right\rangle_{\mathbf{T}}.$$

---

[1] Note that this expansion cannot be justified for all values of the integration variables $\hat{\lambda}_\mu^a$, $\hat{u}_\mu$, J_i^a and T_i. The contributions to $\Omega^{(n)}$ from regions with $(\hat{\lambda}_\mu^a J_i^a + \hat{u}_\mu T_i) = O(\sqrt{N})$ are, however, negligible for $N \to \infty$.

Obviously the dominant terms for large N are the same for any distribution of examples with the first two moments

$$\langle\!\langle \xi_i^\mu \rangle\!\rangle = 0 \qquad \text{and} \qquad \langle\!\langle \xi_i^\mu \xi_j^\nu \rangle\!\rangle = \delta(\mu, \nu)\delta(i, j). \tag{A2.12}$$

Using $\mathbf{J}^2 = \mathbf{T}^2 = N$ we obtain after inserting (A2.11) back into (A2.9)

$$\Omega^{(n)} = \int \prod_a d\mu(\mathbf{J}^a) \int \prod_{a,\mu} \frac{d\lambda_\mu^a d\hat{\lambda}_\mu^a}{2\pi} \int \prod_\mu \frac{du_\mu d\hat{u}_\mu}{2\pi} \prod_{a,\mu} \theta(u_\mu \lambda_\mu^a) \tag{A2.13}$$

$$\times \left\langle\!\!\left\langle \exp\left(i \sum_{\mu,a} \lambda_\mu^a \hat{\lambda}_\mu^a + i \sum_\mu u_\mu \hat{u}_\mu - \frac{1}{2}\sum_{\mu,a}(\lambda_\mu^a)^2 \right.\right.\right.$$

$$\left.\left.\left. - \frac{1}{2}\sum_\mu \sum_{(a,b)} \hat{\lambda}_\mu^a \hat{\lambda}_\mu^b \frac{1}{N}\sum_i J_i^a J_i^b - \frac{1}{2}\sum_\mu \hat{u}_\mu^2 - \sum_{\mu,a} \hat{\lambda}_\mu^a \hat{u}_\mu \frac{1}{N}\sum_i J_i^a T_i \right) \right\rangle\!\!\right\rangle_{\mathbf{T}}.$$

Here $\sum_{(a,b)}$ denotes the sum over all terms with $a \neq b$. To make further progress we introduce the auxiliary variables

$$q^{ab} = \frac{1}{N}\sum_i J_i^a J_i^b \qquad \text{and} \qquad R^a = \frac{1}{N}\sum_i T_i J_i^a \tag{A2.14}$$

to decouple the J- from the λ-u-integrals. We then find

$$\Omega^{(n)} = \int \prod_{a<b} N\, dq^{ab} \int \prod_a N\, dR^a \tag{A2.15}$$

$$\times \int \prod_a d\mu(\mathbf{J}^a) \left\langle\!\!\left\langle \prod_a \delta(\mathbf{J}^a \mathbf{T} - N R^a) \right\rangle\!\!\right\rangle_{\mathbf{T}} \prod_{a<b} \delta(\mathbf{J}^a \mathbf{J}^b - N q^{ab})$$

$$\times \int \prod_{a,\mu} \frac{d\lambda_\mu^a d\hat{\lambda}_\mu^a}{2\pi} \int \prod_\mu \frac{du_\mu d\hat{u}_\mu}{2\pi} \prod_{a,\mu} \theta(u_\mu \lambda_\mu^a) \exp\left(i \sum_{\mu,a} \lambda_\mu^a \hat{\lambda}_\mu^a + i \sum_\mu u_\mu \hat{u}_\mu \right.$$

$$\left. - \frac{1}{2}\sum_{\mu,a}(\hat{\lambda}_\mu^a)^2 - \frac{1}{2}\sum_\mu \sum_{(a,b)} \hat{\lambda}_\mu^a \hat{\lambda}_\mu^b q^{ab} - \sum_{\mu,a} \hat{\lambda}_\mu^a \hat{u}_\mu R^a - \frac{1}{2}\sum_\mu \hat{u}_\mu^2 \right).$$

The remaining average over $\mathbf{T}$ is trivial since the integral over $\mathbf{J}^a$ gives the same result for almost all choices of $\mathbf{T}$. Having averaged over the examples the teacher average is hence redundant due to the isotropy of the example distribution.

We finally introduce integral representations for the remaining δ-functions in (A2.15), including those contained in the integration measures $d\mu(\mathbf{J}^a)$, and perform the Gaussian $\hat{u}_\mu$-integral. In this way we end up with

$$\Omega^{(n)} = \int \prod_a \frac{d\hat{k}^a}{4\pi} \int \prod_{a<b} \frac{dq^{ab} d\hat{q}^{ab}}{2\pi/N} \int \prod_a \frac{dR^a d\hat{R}^a}{2\pi/N}$$

$$\times \exp\left(i\frac{N}{2}\sum_a \hat{k}^a + iN\sum_{a<b} q^{ab}\hat{q}^{ab} + iN\sum_a R^a\hat{R}^a\right)$$

$$\times \int \prod_{i,a} \frac{dJ_i^a}{\sqrt{2\pi e}} \exp\left(-\frac{i}{2}\sum_a \hat{k}^a \sum_i (J_i^a)^2 - i\sum_{a<b}\hat{q}^{ab}\sum_i J_i^a J_i^b\right.$$

$$\left. - i\sum_a \hat{R}_a \sum_i J_i^a\right)$$

$$\times \int \prod_\mu Du_\mu \int \prod_{\mu,a} d\lambda_\mu^a \int \prod_{\mu,a} \frac{d\hat{\lambda}_\mu^a}{2\pi} \prod_{a,\mu} \theta(u_\mu \lambda_\mu^a)$$

$$\times \exp\left(-\frac{1}{2}\sum_a (1 - (R^a)^2) \sum_\mu (\hat{\lambda}_\mu^a)^2\right.$$

$$\left. - \frac{1}{2}\sum_\mu \sum_{(a,b)} \hat{\lambda}_\mu^a \hat{\lambda}_\mu^b (q^{ab} - R^a R^b) + i\sum_{\mu,a} \lambda_\mu^a \hat{\lambda}_\mu^a - i\sum_\mu u_\mu \sum_a \hat{\lambda}_\mu^a R^a\right).$$

$$(A2.16)$$

Now the J_i^a-integrals factorize in i, i.e. they give rise to a single J^a-integral to the power N. Similarly the u_μ-λ_μ^a-$\hat{\lambda}_\mu^a$-integrals factorize in μ and can hence be reduced to a single u-λ^a-$\hat{\lambda}^a$-integral to the power $p = \alpha N$. Altogether this yields

$$\Omega^{(n)} = \int \prod_a \frac{d\hat{k}^a}{4\pi} \int \prod_{a<b} \frac{dq^{ab} d\hat{q}^{ab}}{2\pi/N} \int \prod_a \frac{dR^a d\hat{R}^a}{2\pi/N}$$

$$\times \exp\left(N\left[\frac{i}{2}\sum_a \hat{k}^a + i\sum_{a<b} q^{ab}\hat{q}^{ab} + i\sum_a R^a\hat{R}^a + G_S(\hat{k}^a, \hat{q}^{ab}, \hat{R}^a)\right.\right.$$

$$\left.\left. + \alpha G_E(q^{ab}, R^a)\right]\right) \quad (A2.17)$$

with

$$G_S(\hat{k}^a, \hat{q}^{ab}, \hat{R}^a) = \ln \int \prod_a \frac{dJ^a}{\sqrt{2\pi e}} \exp\left(-\frac{i}{2}\sum_a \hat{k}^a (J^a)^2 - i\sum_{a<b} \hat{q}^{ab} J^a J^b\right.$$

$$\left. - i\sum_a \hat{R}^a J^a\right) \quad (A2.18)$$

and

$$G_E(q^{ab}, R^a) = \ln \int \frac{du}{\sqrt{2\pi}} \int \prod_a d\lambda^a \int \prod_a \frac{d\hat{\lambda}^a}{2\pi} \prod_a \theta(u\lambda^a)$$

$$\times \exp\left(-\frac{u^2}{2} - \frac{1}{2}\sum_a (1 - (R^a)^2)(\hat{\lambda}^a)^2\right.$$

$$\left. - \frac{1}{2}\sum_{(a,b)} \hat{\lambda}^a \hat{\lambda}^b (q^{ab} - R^a R^b) + i \sum_a \lambda^a \hat{\lambda}^a - iu \sum_a \hat{\lambda}^a R^a\right). \quad \text{(A2.19)}$$

G_S is called the *entropic part* since it just measures how many spherical coupling vectors **J** fulfil the constraints (A2.14). On the other hand G_E is referred to as the *energetic part* since it is specific to the cost function or learning rule which is being used (cf. chapter 4).

We now proceed to evaluate the asymptotic behaviour of the integrals over the auxiliary parameters q^{ab}, $\hat{q}^{ab}$, R^a, $\hat{R}^a$ and $\hat{k}^a$ for $N \to \infty$ by the saddle point method discussed in section A1.4.

The extremum with respect to $\hat{k}^a$, $\hat{q}^{ab}$ and $\hat{R}^a$ can be found in closed form since the J^a-integration are Gaussian. Introducing the $n \times n$ matrices A and B by

$$A_{ab} = i\hat{k}^a \delta(a,b) + i\hat{q}^{ab}(1 - \delta(a,b))$$

$$B_{ab} = \delta(a,b) + q^{ab}(1 - \delta(a,b)), \quad \text{(A2.20)}$$

the J^a-integration in the entropic part can be performed to yield[2]

$$G_S(\hat{k}^a, \hat{q}^{ab}, \hat{R}^a) = -\frac{n}{2} - \frac{1}{2}\ln(\det A) - \frac{1}{2}\sum_{a,b} \hat{R}^a (A^{-1})_{ab} \hat{R}^b). \quad \text{(A2.21)}$$

Using $\ln \det A = \text{Tr} \ln A$ the part of the exponent in (A2.17) which depends on $\hat{k}^a$, $\hat{q}^{ab}$ and $\hat{R}^a$ may be written as

$$-\frac{n}{2} - \frac{1}{2}\text{Tr} \ln A - \frac{1}{2}\sum_{a,b} \hat{R}^a (A^{-1})_{ab} \hat{R}^b + \frac{1}{2}\text{Tr} AB + i \sum_a R^a \hat{R}^a. \quad \text{(A2.22)}$$

To find the extremum with respect to $\hat{R}^a$ and the elements of A we set the derivative of this expression with respect to $\hat{R}^c$ and A_{cd} to zero

$$0 = -\sum_a (A^{-1})_{ac} \hat{R}^a + i R^c \quad \text{(A2.23)}$$

$$0 = -\frac{1}{2}(A^{-1})_{cd} + \frac{1}{2}\sum_{a,b} \hat{R}^a (A^{-1})_{ac}(A^{-1})_{bd} \hat{R}^b + \frac{1}{2}B_{cd}. \quad \text{(A2.24)}$$

---

[2] The transformation $\hat{k}^a \to \hat{k}^a - i\varepsilon$ makes the integral convergent for all $\varepsilon > 0$ and does not change the asymptotic behaviour since the extremum with respect to $\hat{k}^a$ lies on the negative imaginary axis.

This gives

$$\hat{R}^a = i \sum_b A_{ab} R^b \tag{A2.25}$$

and

$$(A^{-1})_{cd} = B_{cd} - R^c R^d =: C_{cd}. \tag{A2.26}$$

Using these results we find that (A2.22) is at the saddle point simply given by $\frac{1}{2} \mathrm{Tr} \ln C$. Therefore (A2.17) simplifies to

$$\Omega^{(n)} \sim \exp\left(N \underset{q^{ab}, R^a}{\mathrm{extr}} \left[\frac{1}{2} \mathrm{Tr} \ln C + \alpha G_E(q^{ab}, R^a) \right] \right). \tag{A2.27}$$

Determining the remaining extremum with respect to q^{ab} and R^a is not straightforward, particularly in view of the analytic continuation $n \to 0$ to be performed at the end. The subtleties of the general case are discussed in detail in [17]. In our case it turns out that the values of q^{ab} and R^a at the extremum are *replica symmetric*, i.e. they obey

$$q^{ab} = q \quad \text{and} \quad R^a = R, \tag{A2.28}$$

which simplifies the further analysis considerably.

First we note that in this case the matrix C defined in (A2.26) has an $(n-1)$-fold degenerated eigenvalue $(1-q)$ and an additional one $(1-q) + n(q - R^2)$. This gives

$$\frac{1}{2} \mathrm{Tr} \ln C = \frac{n}{2} \ln(1-q) + \frac{1}{2} \ln\left(1 + n \frac{q - R^2}{1 - q} \right). \tag{A2.29}$$

We then use the θ-functions in (A2.19) to restrict the integration range of u and λ^a and simplify the energetic part using a Hubbard–Stratonovich transformation (A1.3). With the shorthand notation (A1.2) we find

$$G_E = \ln 2 \int Dt \int_0^\infty Du \int_0^\infty \prod_a d\lambda^a \int \prod_a \frac{d\hat{\lambda}^a}{2\pi} \exp\left(-\frac{1-q}{2} \sum_a (\hat{\lambda}^a)^2 \tag{A2.30} \right.$$

$$\left. + i \sum_a \hat{\lambda}^a (\lambda^a - uR - \sqrt{q - R^2} t) \right)$$

$$= \ln 2 \int Dt \int_0^\infty Du$$

$$\times \left[\int_0^\infty \frac{d\lambda}{\sqrt{2\pi(1-q)}} \exp\left(-\frac{1}{2(1-q)} (\lambda - uR - \sqrt{q - R^2} t)^2 \right) \right]^n$$

$$= \ln 2 \int Dt \int_0^\infty Du \, H^n\left(-\frac{\sqrt{q - R^2} t + Ru}{\sqrt{1-q}} \right).$$

Shifting the integration variable $t \to (\sqrt{q - R^2}\,t + uR)/\sqrt{q}$ the u-integral may be performed and we get

$$G_E = \ln 2 \int Dt\, H\left(-\frac{Rt}{\sqrt{q - R^2}}\right) H^n\left(-\sqrt{\frac{q}{1-q}}\,t\right). \tag{A2.31}$$

Extracting the dominant terms in (A2.29) and (A2.31) for $n \to 0$ is now a simple matter and we find

$$\Omega^{(n)} \sim \exp\left(Nn \underset{q,R}{\mathrm{extr}}\left[\frac{1}{2}\ln(1-q) + \frac{q - R^2}{2(1-q)}\right.\right.$$
$$\left.\left. + 2\alpha \int Dt\, H\left(-\frac{Rt}{\sqrt{q - R^2}}\right) \ln H\left(-\sqrt{\frac{q}{1-q}}\,t\right)\right]\right). \tag{A2.32}$$

Using (A2.4) this finally gives

$$\frac{1}{N}\langle\!\langle \ln \Omega(\boldsymbol{\xi}^\mu, \mathbf{T})\rangle\!\rangle = \underset{q,R}{\mathrm{extr}}\left[\frac{1}{2}\ln(1-q) + \frac{q - R^2}{2(1-q)}\right.$$
$$\left. + 2\alpha \int Dt\, H\left(-\frac{Rt}{\sqrt{q - R^2}}\right) \ln H\left(-\sqrt{\frac{q}{1-q}}\,t\right)\right]. \tag{A2.33}$$

Setting to zero the derivatives with respect to q and R of the right hand side of this expression we find after some partial integration

$$\frac{q - R^2}{1 - q} = \frac{\alpha}{\pi}\int Dt\, H\left(-\frac{Rt}{\sqrt{q - R^2}}\right) \frac{\exp(-\frac{q}{1-q}t^2)}{H^2(-\sqrt{\frac{q}{1-q}}\,t)} \tag{A2.34}$$

and

$$\frac{R\sqrt{q - R^2}}{\sqrt{q}\sqrt{1 - q}} = \frac{\alpha}{\pi}\int Dt\, \frac{\exp(-\frac{t^2}{2}(\frac{R^2}{q-R^2} + \frac{q}{1-q}))}{H(-\sqrt{\frac{q}{1-q}}\,t)}. \tag{A2.35}$$

These two equations coincide for $q = R$. The intuitive reason for this was discussed in section 2.3. There is hence always a solution determined by

$$q = R = \frac{\alpha}{\pi}\sqrt{1 - R}\int Dt\, \frac{\exp(-Rt^2/2)}{H(\sqrt{R}\,t)}. \tag{A2.36}$$

For the entropy we get for $q = R$ from (A2.33)

$$\frac{1}{N}\langle\!\langle \ln \Omega(\boldsymbol{\xi}^\mu, \mathbf{T})\rangle\!\rangle = \underset{R}{\mathrm{extr}}\left[\frac{1}{2}\ln(1 - R) + \frac{R}{2}\right.$$
$$\left. + 2\alpha \int Dt\, H\left(-\sqrt{\frac{R}{1-R}}\,t\right) \ln H\left(-\sqrt{\frac{R}{1-R}}\,t\right)\right]. \tag{A2.37}$$

The last two equations are identical to (2.42) and (2.41) respectively.

Appendix 3

Convergence of the Perceptron Rule

In this appendix our purpose is to show that the perceptron rule will converge if there exists a vector $\mathbf{J}^*$ which correctly performs all the classifications with at least a stability κ, i.e. which fulfils

$$\frac{1}{\sqrt{N}}\mathbf{J}^*\boldsymbol{\xi}^\mu\sigma_T^\mu \geq \kappa > 0 \qquad \text{for all} \quad \mu = 1, \ldots, p. \tag{A3.1}$$

Without loss of generality we assume that $\mathbf{J}^*$ obeys the usual normalization $|\mathbf{J}^*|^2 = N$. Consider now the vector $\mathbf{J}_X$ obtained through the perceptron rule after a total number of X updates, starting from $\mathbf{J} = 0$. It has the form, cf. (3.11),

$$\mathbf{J}_X = \frac{1}{\sqrt{N}}\sum_\mu x^\mu \boldsymbol{\xi}^\mu \sigma_T^\mu, \tag{A3.2}$$

where the embedding strength x^μ is equal to the number of times that an updating was performed upon presentation of example μ. By definition, one has

$$\sum_\mu x^\mu = X. \tag{A3.3}$$

Multiplying all equations (A3.1) by x^μ and summing over μ and squaring both sides one therefore finds

$$X^2\kappa^2 \leq \left(\frac{1}{\sqrt{N}}\sum_\mu x^\mu \mathbf{J}^*\boldsymbol{\xi}^\mu\sigma_T^\mu\right)^2$$
$$= (\mathbf{J}^*\mathbf{J}_X)^2 \leq |\mathbf{J}^*|^2|\mathbf{J}_X|^2 = N|\mathbf{J}_X|^2, \tag{A3.4}$$

where the Schwarz inequality has been used. Let us now focus on the last example that was updated, say the one with label ν. Since the perceptron rule only performs an update when an error has occurred, it is clear that $\mathbf{J}_{X-1}\boldsymbol{\xi}^\nu\sigma_T^\nu < \kappa\sqrt{N}$. One can therefore write

$$|\mathbf{J}_X|^2 = |\mathbf{J}_{X-1} + \frac{1}{\sqrt{N}}\boldsymbol{\xi}^\nu \sigma_T^\nu|^2 = |\mathbf{J}_{X-1}|^2 + 2\frac{1}{\sqrt{N}}\mathbf{J}_{X-1}\boldsymbol{\xi}^\nu \sigma_T^\nu + \frac{1}{N}|\boldsymbol{\xi}^\nu|^2$$

$$\leq |\mathbf{J}_{X-1}|^2 + 2\kappa + 1 \tag{A3.5}$$

so the maximal increase in the square of the size of the vector is $2\kappa + 1$. We conclude from (A3.4) and (A3.5) that

$$X^2\kappa^2 \leq N|\mathbf{J}_X|^2 \leq NX(2\kappa + 1), \tag{A3.6}$$

from which it follows that the number of updates fulfils

$$X \leq \left(\frac{2}{\kappa} + \frac{1}{\kappa^2}\right) N \tag{A3.7}$$

and must hence be finite.

Appendix 4

Stability of the Replica Symmetric Saddle Point

In this appendix the calculations necessary to investigate the stability of a replica symmetric (RS) saddle point are summarized. As explained in section 2.3 the stability check of the saddle point is an important part of any replica calculation. As an illustrative example we use the storage problem for the Ising perceptron as discussed in section 6.3 and mainly follow [25].

We start with the saddle point expression (6.22) for the averaged replicated phase space volume

$$\langle\langle \Omega^n \rangle\rangle = \int \prod_{a<b} \frac{dq^{ab}\, d\hat{q}^{ab}}{2\pi/N} \exp(NG(q^{ab}, \hat{q}^{ab})), \qquad (A4.1)$$

where

$$G(q^{ab}, \hat{q}^{ab}) = i \sum_{a<b} q^{ab}\hat{q}^{ab} + G_S(\hat{q}^{ab}) + \alpha G_E(q^{ab}) \qquad (A4.2)$$

with

$$G_S(\hat{q}^{ab}) = \ln \sum_{\{J^a=\pm1\}} \exp\left(-i \sum_{a<b} \hat{q}^{ab} J^a J^b\right) \qquad (A4.3)$$

and

$$G_E(q^{ab}) = \ln \int_\kappa^\infty d\lambda^a \int \frac{d\hat{\lambda}^a}{2\pi} \exp\left(i \sum_a \lambda^a \hat{\lambda}^a - \frac{1}{2}\sum_a (\hat{\lambda}^a)^2 - \frac{1}{2}\sum_{(a,b)} \hat{\lambda}^a \hat{\lambda}^b q^{ab}\right).$$
$$(A4.4)$$

In the limit $N \to \infty$ the integrals in (A4.1) are calculated by the saddle point method which requires the *maximum* of $G(q^{ab}, \hat{q}^{ab})$ to be found. The RS ansatz assumes that at this maximum one has $q^{ab} = q$ and $-i\hat{q}^{ab} = \hat{q}$ for all pairs of replicas $a < b$ giving rise to the RS saddle point equations

$$q = \int Dz \tanh^2(\sqrt{\hat{q}}z)$$

$$\hat{q} = \frac{\alpha}{2\pi(1-q)} \int Dt \, \frac{\exp\left(-\frac{(\kappa-\sqrt{\hat{q}}t)^2}{1-q}\right)}{H^2\left(\frac{\kappa-\sqrt{\hat{q}}t}{\sqrt{1-q}}\right)} \tag{A4.5}$$

that fix q and $\hat{q}$ as functions of α.

In order to check whether the solution of (A4.5) is in fact a maximum of $G(q^{ab}, \hat{q}^{ab})$ we set

$$q^{ab} = q + \delta q^{ab}, \qquad \hat{q}^{ab} = i\hat{q} + i\delta\hat{q}^{ab} \tag{A4.6}$$

and expand G around $q, \hat{q}$ in $\delta q^{ab}, \delta\hat{q}^{ab}$. Forming an $n(n-1)$-dimensional vector $(\delta q^{ab}, \delta\hat{q}^{ab})$ from the fluctuations of both q^{ab} and $\hat{q}^{ab}$ we then find up to second order

$$G(q + \delta q^{ab}, \hat{q} + \delta\hat{q}^{ab}) = G(q, \hat{q}) + \frac{1}{2} \sum_{a<b,c<d} (\delta q^{ab}, \delta\hat{q}^{ab}) M^{ab,cd} (\delta q^{cd}, \delta\hat{q}^{cd}). \tag{A4.7}$$

Note that the terms linear in $\delta q^{ab}, \delta\hat{q}^{ab}$ must vanish because q and $\hat{q}$ are chosen such that $\partial G/\partial q = \partial G/\partial \hat{q} = 0$ (cf. (A4.5)). For $(q, \hat{q})$ to be a local maximum of G it is necessary that the Hessian matrix $M^{ab,cd}$ is negative definite, i.e. all of its eigenvalues must be negative.

The determination of the spectrum of a matrix like $M^{ab,cd}$ is a non-trivial task, and to succeed we have to exploit its symmetries under permutations of the replica indices. From the form (A4.2) of $G(q^{ab}, \hat{q}^{ab})$ it is clear that $M^{ab,cd}$ is a block matrix of four $n(n-1)/2 \times n(n-1)/2$ matrices of the form

$$M = \begin{pmatrix} \alpha A & I \\ I & B \end{pmatrix}, \tag{A4.8}$$

where I denotes the unit matrix and

$$A^{ab,cd} = \frac{\partial^2 G_E}{\partial q^{ab} \partial q^{cd}} \tag{A4.9}$$

and

$$B^{ab,cd} = \frac{\partial^2 G_S}{\partial \hat{q}^{ab} \partial \hat{q}^{cd}} \tag{A4.10}$$

with the derivatives calculated at the RS saddle point $q^{ab} = q$, $\hat{q}^{ab} = i\hat{q}$.

The determination of the eigenvalues of M proceeds in three steps. We first calculate the elements of the matrices A and B, and in particular we determine their symmetry structure with respect to permutations of the replicas. We then determine the eigenvalues of A and B and verify that their eigenvectors are parallel. This will enable us in the final step to deduce the eigenvalues of M from those of A and B.

First step

We start with the elements of A. The formulas can be written in the most compact form by introducing the average $\langle g(\lambda^c)\rangle$ of some function $g(\lambda^c)$ with the following abbreviation

$$\langle g(\lambda^c)\rangle :=$$
$$\frac{\int_\kappa^\infty d\lambda^a \int \frac{d\hat{\lambda}^a}{2\pi} \exp\left(i\sum_a \lambda^a\hat{\lambda}^a - \frac{1}{2}\sum_a(\hat{\lambda}^a)^2 - \frac{1}{2}\sum_{(a,b)} \hat{\lambda}^a\hat{\lambda}^b q^{ab}\right) g(\lambda^c)}{\int_\kappa^\infty d\lambda^a \int \frac{d\hat{\lambda}^a}{2\pi} \exp\left(i\sum_a \lambda^a\hat{\lambda}^a - \frac{1}{2}\sum_a(\hat{\lambda}^a)^2 - \frac{1}{2}\sum_{(a,b)} \hat{\lambda}^a\hat{\lambda}^b q^{ab}\right)}\Bigg|_{q^{ab}=q}.$$

We then find from (A4.4)

$$\frac{\partial^2 G_E}{\partial q^{cd}\partial q^{ef}}\Bigg|_{q^{ab}=q} = \langle\hat{\lambda}^c\hat{\lambda}^d\hat{\lambda}^e\hat{\lambda}^f\rangle - \langle\hat{\lambda}^c\hat{\lambda}^d\rangle\langle\hat{\lambda}^e\hat{\lambda}^f\rangle. \tag{A4.11}$$

At the RS saddle point all replica indices are equivalent and since $c < d$ and $e < f$ there are *only three* different values possible for this second derivative

$$P := \langle(\hat{\lambda}^c)^2(\hat{\lambda}^d)^2\rangle - \langle\hat{\lambda}^c\hat{\lambda}^d\rangle^2 \tag{A4.12}$$

corresponding to $c = e$ and $d = f$;

$$Q := \langle(\hat{\lambda}^c)^2\hat{\lambda}^d\hat{\lambda}^f\rangle - \langle\hat{\lambda}^c\hat{\lambda}^d\rangle\langle\hat{\lambda}^c\hat{\lambda}^f\rangle = \langle(\hat{\lambda}^c)^2\hat{\lambda}^d\hat{\lambda}^f\rangle - \langle\hat{\lambda}^c\hat{\lambda}^d\rangle^2 \tag{A4.13}$$

corresponding to $c = e$ and $d \neq f$, or $d = e$, or $c \neq e$ and $d = f$, or $c = f$; and

$$R := \langle\hat{\lambda}^c\hat{\lambda}^d\hat{\lambda}^e\hat{\lambda}^f\rangle - \langle\hat{\lambda}^c\hat{\lambda}^d\rangle\langle\hat{\lambda}^e\hat{\lambda}^f\rangle = \langle\hat{\lambda}^c\hat{\lambda}^d\hat{\lambda}^e\hat{\lambda}^f\rangle - \langle\hat{\lambda}^c\hat{\lambda}^d\rangle^2 \tag{A4.14}$$

corresponding to the case in which all four indices are different from each other.

Let us calculate the first term of P explicitly:

$$\langle (\hat{\lambda}^c)^2 (\hat{\lambda}^d)^2 \rangle$$

$$= \frac{\int_\kappa^\infty d\lambda^a \int \frac{d\hat{\lambda}^a}{2\pi} \exp\left(i\sum_a \lambda^a \hat{\lambda}^a - \frac{1}{2}\sum_a (\hat{\lambda}^a)^2 - \frac{1}{2}\sum_{(a,b)} \hat{\lambda}^a \hat{\lambda}^b q^{ab}\right) (\hat{\lambda}^c)^2 (\hat{\lambda}^d)^2}{\int_\kappa^\infty d\lambda^a \int \frac{d\hat{\lambda}^a}{2\pi} \exp\left(i\sum_a \lambda^a \hat{\lambda}^a - \frac{1}{2}\sum_a (\hat{\lambda}^a)^2 - \frac{1}{2}\sum_{(a,b)} \hat{\lambda}^a \hat{\lambda}^b q^{ab}\right)} \Bigg|_{q^{ab}=q}$$

$$= \frac{\int_\kappa^\infty d\lambda^a \int \frac{d\hat{\lambda}^a}{2\pi} \exp\left(i\sum_a \lambda^a \hat{\lambda}^a - \frac{1-q}{2}\sum_a (\hat{\lambda}^a)^2 - \frac{q}{2}(\sum_a \hat{\lambda}^a)^2\right) (\hat{\lambda}^c)^2 (\hat{\lambda}^d)^2}{\int_\kappa^\infty d\lambda^a \int \frac{d\hat{\lambda}^a}{2\pi} \exp\left(i\sum_a \lambda^a \hat{\lambda}^a - \frac{1-q}{2}\sum_a (\hat{\lambda}^a)^2 - \frac{q}{2}(\sum_a \hat{\lambda}^a)^2\right)}$$

$$= \frac{\int Dt\, H^{n-2}\left(\frac{\kappa - \sqrt{q}t}{\sqrt{1-q}}\right) \left[\int_\kappa^\infty d\lambda \int \frac{d\hat{\lambda}}{2\pi} \exp\left(i\hat{\lambda}(\lambda - \sqrt{q}t) - \frac{1-q}{2}\hat{\lambda}^2\right)\hat{\lambda}^2\right]^2}{\int Dt\, H^n\left(\frac{\kappa - \sqrt{q}t}{\sqrt{1-q}}\right)}$$

$$= \frac{\int Dt\, H^{n-2}\left(\frac{\kappa - \sqrt{q}t}{\sqrt{1-q}}\right) \left[\int_\kappa^\infty \frac{d\lambda}{\sqrt{2\pi(1-q)}} \exp\left(-\frac{(\lambda - \sqrt{q}t)^2}{2(1-q)}\right) \frac{1}{1-q}\left(1 - \frac{(\lambda - \sqrt{q}t)^2}{1-q}\right)\right]^2}{\int Dt\, H^n\left(\frac{\kappa - \sqrt{q}t}{\sqrt{1-q}}\right)}$$

$$= \frac{1}{(1-q)^2} \frac{\int Dt\, H^{n-2}(\kappa') \left[\int_{\kappa'}^\infty D\lambda'(1 - \lambda'^2)\right]^2}{\int Dt\, H^n(\kappa')}$$

$$\tag{A4.15}$$

where

$$\kappa' = \frac{\kappa - \sqrt{q}t}{\sqrt{1-q}} \qquad \text{and} \qquad \lambda' = \frac{\lambda - \sqrt{q}t}{\sqrt{1-q}}. \tag{A4.16}$$

The limit $n \to 0$ is finally taken yielding

$$\langle (\hat{\lambda}^c)^2 (\hat{\lambda}^d)^2 \rangle = \frac{1}{(1-q)^2} \int Dt \frac{\left[\int_\kappa^\infty D\lambda'(1 - \lambda'^2)\right]^2}{H^2(\kappa')}. \tag{A4.17}$$

In an analogous fashion we obtain

$$\langle \hat{\lambda}^c \hat{\lambda}^d \rangle = \frac{1}{(1-q)} \int Dt \frac{\left[\int_{\kappa'}^\infty D\lambda'\, i\lambda'\right]^2}{H^2(\kappa')}$$

$$\langle (\hat{\lambda}^c)^2 \hat{\lambda}^d \hat{\lambda}^f \rangle = \frac{1}{(1-q)^2} \int Dt \frac{\int_{\kappa'}^\infty D\lambda'(1 - \lambda'^2) \left[\int_{\kappa'}^\infty D\lambda'\, i\lambda'\right]^2}{H^3(\kappa')}$$

$$\tag{A4.18}$$

and

$$\langle \hat{\lambda}^c \hat{\lambda}^d \hat{\lambda}^e \hat{\lambda}^f \rangle = \frac{1}{(1-q)^2} \int Dt \frac{\left[\int_{\kappa'}^\infty D\lambda'\, i\lambda'\right]^4}{H^4(\kappa')} \tag{A4.19}$$

from which P, Q and R can be determined.

The elements of B may be obtained in an analogous way. Introducing the abbreviation

$$\langle g(J^c) \rangle := \frac{\sum\limits_{\{J^a\}} \exp\left(-i \sum_{a<b} \hat{q}^{ab} J^a J^b\right) g(J^c)}{\sum\limits_{\{J^a\}} \exp\left(-i \sum_{a<b} \hat{q}^{ab} J^a J^b\right)} \Bigg|_{\hat{q}^{ab}=i\hat{q}} \tag{A4.20}$$

we find

$$-\frac{\partial^2 G_s}{\partial \hat{q}^{cd} \partial \hat{q}^{ef}} = \langle J^c J^d J^e J^f \rangle - \langle J^c J^d \rangle \langle J^e J^f \rangle. \tag{A4.21}$$

Again only three different values are possible

$$\begin{aligned}
-P' &:= \langle (J^c)^2 (J^d)^2 \rangle - \langle J^c J^d \rangle^2 \\
-Q' &:= \langle (J^c)^2 J^d J^f \rangle - \langle J^c J^d \rangle^2 \quad \text{and} \\
-R' &:= \langle J^c J^d J^e J^f \rangle - \langle J^c J^d \rangle^2
\end{aligned} \tag{A4.22}$$

where different replica indices are assumed to denote different natural numbers between 1 and n. Explicitly we find, e.g.

$$\begin{aligned}
\langle J^c J^d \rangle &= \frac{\sum\limits_{\{J^a\}} \exp\left(-i \sum_{a<b} \hat{q}^{ab} J^a J^b\right) J^c J^d}{\sum\limits_{\{J^a\}} \exp\left(-i \sum_{a<b} \hat{q}^{ab} J^a J^b\right)} \Bigg|_{\hat{q}^{ab}=i\hat{q}} \\[2mm]
&= \frac{\sum\limits_{\{J^a\}} \exp\left(\frac{\hat{q}}{2}\left(\sum_a J^a\right)^2 - n\frac{\hat{q}}{2}\right) J^c J^d}{\sum\limits_{\{J^a\}} \exp\left(\frac{\hat{q}}{2}\left(\sum_a J^a\right)^2 - n\frac{\hat{q}}{2}\right)} \\[2mm]
&= \frac{\int Dz \sum\limits_{\{J^a\}} \exp\left(\sqrt{\hat{q}}z \sum_a J^a\right) J^c J^d}{\int Dz \sum\limits_{\{J^a\}} \exp\left(\sqrt{\hat{q}}z \sum_a J^a\right)} \\[2mm]
&= \frac{\int Dz \left[2\cosh\sqrt{\hat{q}}z\right]^{n-2} \left[2\sinh\sqrt{\hat{q}}z\right]^2}{\int Dz \left[2\cosh\sqrt{\hat{q}}z\right]^n}
\end{aligned} \tag{A4.23}$$

and for $n \to 0$

$$\langle J^c J^d \rangle = \int Dz \tanh^2 \sqrt{\hat{q}}z = q \tag{A4.24}$$

where in the last step (A4.5) has been used. By similar algebra we finally obtain

$$P' = q^2 - 1$$
$$Q' = q^2 - q \qquad (A4.25)$$
$$R' = q^2 - \int Dz \tanh^4 \sqrt{\hat{q}}z$$

which completes the first step of calculating the elements of the matrices A and B.

Second step

We now calculate the eigenvalues and corresponding eigenvectors of the matrices A and B. In a remarkable paper [284] de Almeida and Thouless showed that these are almost entirely determined by the properties of the matrix elements under permutations of the replicas. Let us consider an $n(n-1)/2 \times n(n-1)/2$ matrix $C^{ab,cd}$, $a, b, c, d = 1, \ldots, n$, $a < b$, $c < d$ with a structure similar to A and B, i.e. there are only three different elements P, Q, R according to

$$C^{ab,cd} = P \qquad \text{if} \quad a = c, \ b = d$$
$$C^{ab,cd} = Q \qquad \text{if exactly two indices coincide} \qquad (A4.26)$$
$$C^{ab,cd} = R \qquad \text{if all indices are different from each other.}$$

We determine the eigenvalues by explicit construction of the eigenvectors. First we observe that the sum of the elements in one row of $C^{ab,cd}$ is the same for all rows:

$$\sum_{c<d} C^{ab,cd} = P + (2n-4)Q + \frac{(n-2)(n-3)}{2}R. \qquad (A4.27)$$

Therefore the vector $\boldsymbol{\zeta}_1$ defined by

$$\zeta_1^{ab} = \zeta \qquad \text{for all} \quad a < b \qquad (A4.28)$$

is an eigenvector of $C^{ab,cd}$ with eigenvalue

$$\lambda_1 = P + (2n-4)Q + \frac{(n-2)(n-3)}{2}R. \qquad (A4.29)$$

This eigenvector is replica symmetric itself, since all replicas are treated in the same way.

Consider next vectors $\boldsymbol{\zeta}_2$ in which *one* replica index, l, is special

$$\zeta_2^{ab} = \begin{cases} \zeta & \text{if} \quad a = l \quad \text{or} \quad b = l \\ \varepsilon & \text{otherwise.} \end{cases} \qquad (A4.30)$$

Vectors of this type span an n-dimensional subspace of the $n(n-1)/2$-dimensional space of all eigenvectors. This subspace contains $\boldsymbol{\zeta}_1$ (for $\zeta = \varepsilon$). However, choosing $\zeta = (1 - n/2)\varepsilon$ all vectors of type (A4.30) are orthogonal to $\boldsymbol{\zeta}_1$. We then find

$$\sum_{c<d} C^{ab,cd} \zeta_2^{cd} = (P + (n - 4)Q - (n - 3)R)\, \zeta_2^{ab} \tag{A4.31}$$

which means there is an $(n - 1)$-times degenerate eigenvalue

$$\lambda_2 = P + (n - 4)Q - (n - 3)R. \tag{A4.32}$$

We continue with vectors $\boldsymbol{\zeta}_3$ for which *two* replica indices, $k < l$, are special

$$\zeta_3^{ab} = \begin{cases} \zeta & \text{if} \quad a = k, b = l \\ \varepsilon & \text{if} \quad a = k, b \neq l \quad \text{or} \quad a = l \quad \text{or} \quad b = k \quad \text{or} \quad b = l, a \neq k \\ \vartheta & \text{otherwise.} \end{cases}$$

$$\tag{A4.33}$$

These vectors span *the whole* $n(n - 1)/2$-dimensional space. Orthogonality with respect to $\boldsymbol{\zeta}_1$ and all $\boldsymbol{\zeta}_2$ can be ensured by choosing $\zeta = (2-n)\varepsilon$ and $\varepsilon = (3-n)\vartheta/2$ in (A4.33). After same algebra one then finds

$$\sum_{c<d} C^{ab,cd} \zeta_3^{cd} = (P - 2Q + R)\zeta_3^{ab} \tag{A4.34}$$

and hence there is a third eigenvalue

$$\lambda_3 = P - 2Q + R \tag{A4.35}$$

with degeneracy $n(n - 3)/2$.

This gives one eigenvector $\boldsymbol{\zeta}_1$, $(n - 1)$ eigenvectors $\boldsymbol{\zeta}_2$ and $n(n - 3)/2$ eigenvectors $\boldsymbol{\zeta}_3$, i.e. altogether $(n - 1)/2$ linearly independent eigenvectors and hence we are done!

We are therefore able to determine the eigenvalues of the matrices A and B. Note that the corresponding eigenvectors do not depend at all on the entries P, Q, R of the matrices, so A and B have *parallel* eigenvectors entirely determined by their replica structure. Also, $\boldsymbol{\zeta}_1$ describes for both A and B so-called *longitudinal* fluctuations which lie *within* the replica symmetric subspace. They hence merely test whether the replica symmetric saddle point equations have been solved correctly and cannot signal a breakdown of the RS assumption itself. This can only be done by *transversal* fluctuations as described by $\boldsymbol{\zeta}_2$ and $\boldsymbol{\zeta}_3$. In the limit $n \to 0$, however, λ_2 becomes degenerate with λ_1. It is hence λ_3, the so-called *replicon* eigenvalue given by (A4.35), that may change sign and thereby signal the local instability of the RS saddle point.

Third step

Assume now that φ is an eigenvector of both A and B with corresponding eigenvalues λ_A and λ_B. We form two $n(n-1)$-dimensional vectors $\phi = (\varphi, \varphi)$ and $\bar{\phi} = (\varphi, -\varphi)$ and look for eigenvalues Λ of M with eigenvectors of the form $a\phi + b\bar{\phi}$

$$
\begin{aligned}
0 = (M - \Lambda I)(a\phi + b\bar{\phi}) &= \begin{pmatrix} \alpha A - \Lambda I & -I \\ -I & B - \Lambda I \end{pmatrix} \begin{pmatrix} (a+b) & \varphi \\ (a-b) & \varphi \end{pmatrix} \\
&= \begin{pmatrix} [(\alpha\lambda_A - \Lambda)(a+b) - (a-b)] & \varphi \\ [-a-b+(\lambda_B - \Lambda)(a-b)] & \varphi \end{pmatrix} \\
&= \begin{pmatrix} [(\alpha\lambda_A - \Lambda - 1)a + (\alpha\lambda_A - \Lambda + 1)b] & \varphi \\ [(\lambda_B - \Lambda - 1)a - (\lambda_B - \Lambda + 1)b] & \varphi \end{pmatrix}.
\end{aligned}
$$

Non-trivial solutions for a and b require

$$
\begin{vmatrix} \alpha\lambda_A - \Lambda & \Lambda \\ \Lambda & \lambda_B - \Lambda \end{vmatrix} = 0 \tag{A4.36}
$$

or equivalently

$$
\Lambda^2 - (\alpha\lambda_A + \lambda_B)\Lambda + \alpha\lambda_A\lambda_B - 1 = 0. \tag{A4.37}
$$

To elucidate the stability of the RS saddle point it is convenient to consider the product of the eigenvalues

$$
\Lambda_1\Lambda_2 = \alpha\lambda_A\lambda_B - 1. \tag{A4.38}
$$

For $\alpha = 0$ we find $\Lambda_1\Lambda_2 = -1 < 0$. But this is impossible at a maximum! On the other hand for this case the calculation of $\langle\langle\Omega^n\rangle\rangle$ is trivial and RS should be stable. The reason for the "wrong" sign is that the integration over the $\hat{q}^{ab}$ in (A4.1) is along the *real* axis whereas the ansatz (A4.6) introduces *imaginary* fluctuations of $\hat{q}^{ab}$. Because of well known properties of analytic functions the second derivatives of the real part of G along the real and imaginary $\hat{q}^{ab}$-axes just differ by the sign, so all is well.

Starting with $\Lambda_1\Lambda_2 < 0$ at $\alpha = 0$ the instability of the RS saddle point will hence show up by $\Lambda_1\Lambda_2 \geq 0$ or equivalently by

$$
\alpha\lambda_A\lambda_B \geq 1. \tag{A4.39}
$$

Inserting the replicon eigenvalues (A4.35) $P - 2Q + R$ and $P' - 2Q' + R'$ this finally gives rise to the following equation fixing the de Almeida–Thouless value

α_{AT} of α beyond which RS becomes unstable

$$\frac{1}{\alpha_{AT}} = \frac{1}{(1-q)^2} \int Dt \, H^{-4}(\kappa') \left[H(\kappa') \int_{\kappa'}^{\infty} D\lambda (1 - \lambda^2) + \left(\int_{\kappa'}^{\infty} D\lambda \, \lambda \right)^2 \right]^2$$

$$\times \int Dz (1 - \tanh^2 \sqrt{\hat{q}} z)^2 \quad \text{(A4.40)}$$

with

$$\kappa' = \frac{\kappa - \sqrt{q} t}{\sqrt{1 - q}} \quad \text{(A4.41)}$$

as before.

For the numerical evaluation of α_{AT} one has to determine q and $\hat{q}$ from (A4.5) for every trial value of α. One finds $\alpha_{AT} \sim 1.015$ with $q \sim 0.721$ and $\hat{q} \sim 7.366$.

By analogous considerations one can also investigate the local stability of solutions with one or more steps of replica symmetry breaking at the expense of an increasing complexity of the algebra. Meanwhile the crucial steps have been formalized to a certain extent [285] and appropriate mathematical tools have been formulated [286] which help to make the calculations more transparent.

Let us finally note an additional strange feature of the replica trick. For natural $n \geq 1$ the correct application of the saddle point method to the calculation of the solution space volume as given by (A4.1) requires finding the maximum of $G(q^{ab}, \hat{q}^{ab})$. This maximum is identified by the eigenvalues of the corresponding Hessian matrix $M^{ab,cd}$ being all negative. We have retained this requirement for the sign of the eigenvalues as the relevant criterion for the stability of the RS saddle point in the limit $n \to 0$ and this is indeed the correct procedure [17]. However, the function G depends on $n(n-1)$ variables and this number becomes negative for $n < 1$! It turns out that in this regime negative eigenvalues of the Hessian correspond to a *minimum* instead of a maximum of G. This is the reason why the solution q of the RS saddle point equation *minimizes* the RS expression for the quenched entropy.

Appendix 5

One-step Replica Symmetry Breaking

In this appendix we study the storage problem for the Ising perceptron with $\kappa = 0$ within the framework of one-step RSB. The starting point is again the general expression (6.22) for the replicated solution volume

$$\langle\langle \Omega^n \rangle\rangle = \int \prod_{a<b} \frac{dq^{ab}\, d\hat{q}^{ab}}{2\pi/N} \, \exp\left(N\left[i \sum_{a<b} q^{ab}\hat{q}^{ab} + G_S(\hat{q}^{ab}) + \alpha G_E(q^{ab}) \right] \right). \tag{A5.1}$$

For small enough storage ratio α the solution space is connected and can be correctly described within the replica symmetric ansatz $q^{ab} = q$, $-i\hat{q}^{ab} = \hat{q}$. For sufficiently large values of α, however, this ansatz is known to fail. As discussed in section 6.3 an ansatz suitable for the description of a disconnected solution space consisting of several individual patches must involve at least *two* overlap parameters. One, denoted by q_1, specifies the overlap between different solutions belonging to the *same* patch and the other, denoted by $q_0 \leq q_1$, characterizes the overlap between two solutions belonging to *different* patches.

Explicitly, the ansatz referred to as one-step RSB is defined by [86, 17]

$$q^{ab} = \begin{cases} q_1 & \text{if } 0 < |a - b| < m \\ q_0 & \text{otherwise} \end{cases} \tag{A5.2}$$

and similarly

$$-i\hat{q}^{ab} = \begin{cases} \hat{q}_1 & \text{if } 0 < |a - b| < m \\ \hat{q}_0 & \text{otherwise.} \end{cases} \tag{A5.3}$$

At this stage, the parameter m is an integer factor of n and is called the block size. Its physical interpretation becomes clear only after the limit $n \to 0$ as will be

300

discussed below. As an example we give the form of q^{ab} for $n = 6$ and $m = 2$

$$
\begin{pmatrix}
0 & q_1 & q_0 & q_0 & q_0 & q_0 \\
q_1 & 0 & q_0 & q_0 & q_0 & q_0 \\
q_0 & q_0 & 0 & q_1 & q_0 & q_0 \\
q_0 & q_0 & q_1 & 0 & q_0 & q_0 \\
q_0 & q_0 & q_0 & q_0 & 0 & q_1 \\
q_0 & q_0 & q_0 & q_0 & q_1 & 0
\end{pmatrix}
\tag{A5.4}
$$

Note that for $q_1 = q_0$ and $\hat{q}_1 = \hat{q}_0$, or $m = n$, we recover the replica symmetric ansatz.

Let us see how this ansatz simplifies expression (A5.1) for the replicated solution volume. It is easy to see that

$$
i \sum_{a<b} q^{ab}\hat{q}^{ab} = -\frac{n}{2}(m-1)q_1\hat{q}_1 - \frac{n}{2}(n-m)q_0\hat{q}_0.
\tag{A5.5}
$$

To simplify $G_S(\hat{q}^{ab})$ and $G_E(q^{ab})$ it is convenient to rewrite the replica indices in the form $a = Am + \alpha$ where $A = 1, \ldots, n/m$ gives the number of the block a belongs to and $\alpha = 1, \ldots, m$ specifies the position inside the blocks.[1] We then find

$$
\begin{aligned}
G_S &= \ln \sum_{\{J^a\}} \exp\left(-\frac{i}{2} \sum_{(a,b)} \hat{q}^{ab} J^a J^b\right) \\
&= \ln \sum_{\{J^a\}} \exp\left(\frac{\hat{q}_0}{2} \sum_{A,B} \sum_{\alpha,\beta} J^{Am+\alpha} J^{Bm+\beta} + \frac{\hat{q}_1 - \hat{q}_0}{2} \sum_A \sum_{\alpha,\beta} J^{Am+\alpha} J^{Am+\beta}\right. \\
&\qquad \left. -\frac{\hat{q}_1}{2} \sum_A \sum_\alpha (J^{Am+\alpha})^2\right) \\
&= \ln \sum_{\{J^a\}} \exp\left(\frac{\hat{q}_0}{2}\left(\sum_A \sum_\alpha J^{Am+\alpha}\right)^2 + \frac{\hat{q}_1 - \hat{q}_0}{2} \sum_A \left(\sum_\alpha J^{Am+\alpha}\right)^2 - n\frac{\hat{q}_1}{2}\right)
\end{aligned}
\tag{A5.6}
$$

---

[1] This position index α is not to be confused with the storage ratio α.

and using appropriate Hubbard–Stratonovich transformations

$$
G_S = -n\frac{\hat{q}_1}{2} + \ln \int Dz_0 \int \prod_A Dz_A \sum_{\{J^a\}} \exp\left(\sqrt{\hat{q}_0}z_0 \sum_A \sum_\alpha J^{Am+\alpha} +\right.
$$

$$
\left. \sqrt{\hat{q}_1 - \hat{q}_0} \sum_A z_A \sum_\alpha J^{Am+\alpha}\right)
$$

$$
= -n\frac{\hat{q}_1}{2} +
$$

$$
\ln \int Dz_0 \int \prod_A Dz_A \prod_A \sum_{\{J^{Am+\alpha}\}} \prod_A \exp\left((\sqrt{\hat{q}_0}z_0 + \sqrt{\hat{q}_1 - \hat{q}_0}z_A) \sum_\alpha J^{Am+\alpha}\right),
$$

$$
\tag{A5.7}
$$

where $\sum_{\{J^{Am+\alpha}\}}$ denotes the sum over all the 2^m configurations with $J^{Am+\alpha} = \pm 1$ for $\alpha = 1, \dots, m$ and *fixed A*. Evaluating this sum we finally obtain

$$
G_S = -n\frac{\hat{q}_1}{2} + \ln \int Dz_0 \left[\int Dz_1 \sum_{\{J^a\}} \exp\left((\sqrt{\hat{q}_0}z_0 + \sqrt{\hat{q}_1 - \hat{q}_0}z_1) \sum_\alpha J^\alpha\right)\right]^{n/m}
$$

$$
= -n\frac{\hat{q}_1}{2} + \ln \int Dz_0 \left[\int Dz_1 [2\cosh(\sqrt{\hat{q}_0}z_0 + \sqrt{\hat{q}_1 - \hat{q}_0}z_1)]^m\right]^{n/m}
$$

$$
= -n\frac{\hat{q}_1}{2} + \frac{n}{m} \int Dz_0 \ln \int Dz_1 \left[2\cosh(\sqrt{\hat{q}_0}z_0 + \sqrt{\hat{q}_1 - \hat{q}_0}z_1)\right]^m + O(n^2).
$$

$$
\tag{A5.8}
$$

By similar means we simplify the expression for $G_E(q^{ab})$

$$
G_E = \ln \int_0^\infty d\lambda^a \int \frac{d\hat{\lambda}^a}{2\pi} \exp\left(i\sum_a \lambda^a\hat{\lambda}^a - \frac{1}{2}\sum_a (\hat{\lambda}^a)^2 - \frac{1}{2}\sum_{(a,b)} \hat{\lambda}^a\hat{\lambda}^b q^{ab}\right)
$$

$$
= \ln \int_0^\infty d\lambda^a \int \frac{d\hat{\lambda}^a}{2\pi} \exp\left(i\sum_{A,\alpha} \lambda^{Am+\alpha}\hat{\lambda}^{Am+\alpha} - \frac{q_0}{2}\sum_{A,B}\sum_{\alpha,\beta} \hat{\lambda}^{Am+\alpha}\hat{\lambda}^{Bm+\beta}\right.
$$

$$
\left. -\frac{q_1 - q_0}{2}\sum_A\sum_{\alpha,\beta} \hat{\lambda}^{Am+\alpha}\hat{\lambda}^{Am+\beta} - \frac{1 - q_1}{2}\sum_A\sum_\alpha (\hat{\lambda}^{Am+\alpha})^2\right)
$$

$$= \ln \int Dt_0 \int \prod_A Dt_A \int_0^\infty d\lambda^a \int \frac{d\hat{\lambda}^a}{2\pi} \exp\left(i \sum_{A,\alpha} \lambda^{Am+\alpha} \hat{\lambda}^{Am+\alpha} - \right.$$

$$i\sqrt{q_0} t_0 \sum_{A,\alpha} \hat{\lambda}^{Am+\alpha} - i\sqrt{q_1 - q_0} \sum_A t_A \sum_\alpha \hat{\lambda}^{Am+\alpha} - \frac{1-q_1}{2} \sum_{A,\alpha} (\hat{\lambda}^{Am+\alpha})^2 \bigg)$$

$$= \ln \int Dt_0 \left[Dt_1 \int_0^\infty d\lambda^\alpha \int \frac{d\hat{\lambda}^\alpha}{2\pi} \exp\left(i \sum_\alpha \lambda^\alpha \hat{\lambda}^\alpha - \right.\right.$$

$$\left.\left. i\sqrt{q_0} t_0 \sum_\alpha \hat{\lambda}^\alpha - i\sqrt{q_1 - q_0} t_1 \sum_\alpha \hat{\lambda}^\alpha - \frac{1-q_1}{2} \sum_\alpha (\hat{\lambda}^\alpha)^2 \right) \right]^{n/m}$$

$$= \ln \int Dt_0 \left[\int Dt_1 H^m \left(-\frac{\sqrt{q_0} t_0 + \sqrt{q_1 - q_0} t_1}{\sqrt{1-q_1}} \right) \right]^{n/m}$$

$$= \frac{n}{m} \int Dt_0 \ln \int Dt_1 H^m \left(-\frac{\sqrt{q_0} t_0 + \sqrt{q_1 - q_0} t_1}{\sqrt{1-q_1}} \right) + O(n^2). \tag{A5.9}$$

We have finally to take the limit $n \to 0$. It is not obvious how to treat m in this limit. As part of the ansatz it is assumed that m, which was an integer between 1 and n for integer n, becomes a real number between 0 (to which n tends) and 1, which before the limit was the minimal value of m [86]. Its concrete value has to be determined self-consistently from the saddle point equations. One can then show that m gives the probability that two coupling vectors chosen at random from the solution space belong to different patches. In view of (A5.2) this is not completely unexpected.[2]

We finally get after letting $n \to 0$

$$\frac{1}{N} \langle\!\langle \ln \Omega \rangle\!\rangle = \underset{q_0, q_1, \hat{q}_0, \hat{q}_1, m}{\text{extr}} \left[\frac{m}{2} (q_0 \hat{q}_0 - q_1 \hat{q}_1) - \frac{\hat{q}_1}{2}(1-q_1) \right.$$

$$+ \frac{1}{m} \int Dz_0 \ln \int Dz_1 \left[2\cosh\left(\sqrt{\hat{q}_0} z_0 + \sqrt{\hat{q}_1 - \hat{q}_0} z_1\right) \right]^m \tag{A5.10}$$

$$\left. + \frac{\alpha}{m} \int Dt_0 \ln \int Dt_1 H^m \left(-\frac{\sqrt{q_0} t_0 + \sqrt{q_1 - q_0} t_1}{\sqrt{1-q_1}} \right) \right].$$

This expression is evaluated by solving the saddle point equations for the order parameters q_0, q_1, $\hat{q}_0$, $\hat{q}_1$ and m.

---

[2] For a more complete motivation of the many assumptions and the physical interpretation of the RSB ansatz consult [17].

Appendix 6

The Cavity Approach

Most of the statistical mechanics calculations in this book use the replica method to deal with the problem of quenched random variables. The replica method is compact and fairly straightforward; on the other hand, since it is rather formal it is often not easy to grasp the intuitive meaning of the manipulations done and some-times even of the results obtained. The cavity method, which we will describe in its simplest version in this appendix, was devised in the theory of disordered systems as a complementary approach, highlighting the physical content of the calculations and giving intuitive meaning to the quantities introduced. Cavity derivations are often less direct than replica calculations and relying on self-consistency arguments they usually require a fairly clear idea of what the final result might be. On the other hand they frequently allow a deeper understanding of the mechanisms behind the formal manipulations of the replica method and facilitate the interpretation of the results.

The central tool of the cavity method is to analyse the reaction of a macroscopic system when a single degree of freedom is added. In the case of a system of $N \gg 1$ spins this would e.g. concern the reorganization of local fields due to the addition of another spin together with the corresponding couplings. From the very existence of the thermodynamic limit this reaction is expected to be small and therefore amenable to a perturbative treatment. In very simple systems as e.g. a ferromagnet, the reaction is completely negligible. However, as was realized first by Onsager in the calculation of the electric polarization in crystals [287], in somewhat more complicated settings it is important to properly treat correlations induced by the presence of the new degree of freedom. This is particularly crucial in systems with quenched disorder [288], for which the cavity method represents by now a rather elaborate and powerful version of mean-field theory [17]. The central idea is to determine first the so-called cavity field, which is the local field of the new spin *neglecting* these correlations. From the absence of correlations this cavity field usually has simple probabilistic properties; in mean field models it is

304

often Gaussian by the central limit theorem. Taking into account the reaction of the system on the new spin the true local field can then be determined.

In the framework of learning in neural network models the cavity method usually studies the reorganization of the coupling vector upon adding a new example ξ^p to the training set. For simplicity we will lay out the basic ideas of the method for the simple case of an unsupervised perceptron learning from unstructured inputs, following the analysis given in [289].[1] This will allow us to compare the results with those obtained in section 8.2 by using the replica method.

The role of the cavity field in learning problems is played by the aligning field t of the new example *before* learning, i.e. before adjusting the coupling vector $\mathbf{J}$ to this example. Since the new example is usually assumed to be uncorrelated with the previous examples t is by the central limit theorem a Gaussian random variable. By determining the small modifications of the synaptic vector when the new pattern is included into the training set the stability λ of the new example *after* learning can be calculated. The main idea of the method is that λ is for given training set size a universal, self-averaging function of the cavity field t which can be determined self-consistently and which fixes the order parameters describing the learning process.

Let us start then by considering the vector $\mathbf{J}$ which minimizes a given cost function

$$E(\mathbf{J}) = \sum_{\mu=1}^{p-1} V(\lambda^{\mu}) \qquad (A6.1)$$

specifying the learning rule, subject to the normalization

$$\mathbf{J}^2 - N = 0. \qquad (A6.2)$$

The examples ξ^{μ} are sampled at random on the N-sphere and the stabilities

$$\lambda^{\mu} = \frac{\mathbf{J}\xi^{\mu}}{\sqrt{N}} \qquad (A6.3)$$

are defined as in 8.5.

By minimizing $E(\mathbf{J}) - (\mathbf{J}^2 - N)/2\Gamma$, we find that $\mathbf{J}$ obeys the equation

$$\mathbf{J} = \frac{\Gamma}{\sqrt{N}} \sum_{\mu=1}^{p-1} V'(\lambda^{\mu})\xi^{\mu}, \qquad (A6.4)$$

where the prime denotes the derivative with respect to the argument. The Lagrange multiplier Γ is determined by the normalization (A6.2).

---

[1] For somewhat different versions of the cavity method in neural network contexts see [290] and [291].

Now consider adding a new example $\boldsymbol{\xi}^p$. The cavity field is the aligning field

$$t^p = \frac{\mathbf{J}\boldsymbol{\xi}^p}{\sqrt{N}} \tag{A6.5}$$

with the $\mathbf{J}$-vector constructed in the *absence* of this example. From the statistical independence between $\boldsymbol{\xi}^p$ and $\mathbf{J}$ it follows that t^p is a Gaussian random variable with zero mean and unit variance.

Now that $\boldsymbol{\xi}^p$ is included into the training set the $\mathbf{J}$-vector will slightly adjust from $\mathbf{J}$ to $\mathbf{J}_+$ satisfying

$$\mathbf{J}_+ = \frac{\Gamma_+}{\sqrt{N}} \sum_{\mu=1}^{p} V'(\lambda_+^\mu)\boldsymbol{\xi}^\mu. \tag{A6.6}$$

Together with the shift in $\mathbf{J}$ there is a correction of the Lagrange multiplier and a modification of the stabilities $\lambda^\mu \mapsto \lambda_+^\mu$ of the previously learned examples.

Enforcing the spherical normalization condition for both $\mathbf{J}$ and $\mathbf{J}_+$ one can prove that $|\Gamma - \Gamma_+| = O(1/\sqrt{N})$. For the following manipulations this implies that the change in the Lagrange multiplier can be neglected. Moreover, the corrections $\lambda_+^\mu - \lambda^\mu$ of the stabilities of the previously learned examples are likewise of order $1/\sqrt{N}$ and we may hence expand $V'(\lambda_+^\mu)$ around λ^μ. This gives rise to

$$\mathbf{J}_+ - \mathbf{J} = \frac{\Gamma}{\sqrt{N}} V'(\lambda_+^p)\boldsymbol{\xi}^p + \frac{\Gamma}{\sqrt{N}} \sum_{\mu=1}^{p-1} V''(\lambda^\mu)(\lambda_+^\mu - \lambda^\mu)\boldsymbol{\xi}^\mu. \tag{A6.7}$$

The first term derives from the direct cost of incorporating the new example into the training set; the second term describes the indirect contributions coming from the slight realignment of the previous examples.[2] Multiplying (A6.7) by $\boldsymbol{\xi}^p/\sqrt{N}$ and using the definitions (A6.3) and (A6.5) we find

$$\lambda_+^p - t^p = \Gamma V'(\lambda_+^p) + \frac{\Gamma}{N} \sum_{\mu=1}^{p-1} V''(\lambda^\mu)(\lambda_+^\mu - \lambda^\mu)\boldsymbol{\xi}^\mu\boldsymbol{\xi}^p. \tag{A6.8}$$

We therefore obtain an equation for the difference between the aligning field of the new example before and after learning as a function of the stability shifts of all the other patterns.

As in all forms of mean-field theory we transform this relation into a self-consistent equation by observing that the p-th pattern is in no way special. Hence an equivalent relation must hold between the stability and the cavity field of every other example in the training set. More precisely we will assume that there is a universal, self-averaging function, which for consistency with the main text will

---

[2] Incidentally, we note that the main difference between the off-line learning scenario considered here and the on-line learning discussed in chapter 9 is precisely the absence of the latter adjustments in on-line learning.

be denoted by $\lambda_0(t, \alpha)$, specifying the stability λ after learning one of $p = \alpha N$ examples as a function of the aligning field t of that example before learning.

With the help of this assumption we may simplify the reaction term in (A6.8) in the following way. We denote by $\mathbf{J}^{\setminus \mu}$ and $\mathbf{J}_+^{\setminus \mu}$ the coupling vectors constructed from the corresponding training sets after *removing example* $\boldsymbol{\xi}^\mu$ and introduce

$$t_+^\mu = \frac{\mathbf{J}_+^{\setminus \mu} \boldsymbol{\xi}^\mu}{\sqrt{N}} \quad \text{and} \quad t^\mu = \frac{\mathbf{J}^{\setminus \mu} \boldsymbol{\xi}^\mu}{\sqrt{N}} \tag{A6.9}$$

as the cavity fields of example $\boldsymbol{\xi}^\mu$ with and without inclusion of example $\boldsymbol{\xi}^p$ respectively. Since $\lambda_+^\mu - \lambda^\mu = O(1/\sqrt{N})$ we get by Taylor expansion of the universal function $\lambda_0(t, \alpha)$ in both variables

$$\lambda_+^\mu - \lambda^\mu = \lambda_0\left(t_+^\mu, \alpha + \frac{1}{N}\right) - \lambda_0(t^\mu, \alpha) \tag{A6.10}$$

$$= \lambda_0'(t^\mu, \alpha)(t_+^\mu - t^\mu) + O(1/N), \tag{A6.11}$$

where the prime denotes differentiation with respect to the first argument. Using these expressions the reaction term in (A6.8) may be written in the form

$$\frac{\Gamma}{N} \sum_{\mu=1}^{p-1} V''(\lambda^\mu) \lambda_0'(t^\mu, \alpha) \sum_{i,j} \frac{(J_{+i}^{\setminus \mu} - J_i^{\setminus \mu})}{\sqrt{N}} \xi_i^\mu \xi_j^\mu \xi_j^p =$$

$$\frac{\Gamma}{N} \sum_{\mu=1}^{p-1} V''(\lambda^\mu) \lambda_0'(t^\mu, \alpha) \left[\sum_i \frac{(J_{+i}^{\setminus \mu} - J_i^{\setminus \mu})}{\sqrt{N}} \xi_i^p + \sum_{i \neq j} \frac{(J_{+i}^{\setminus \mu} - J_i^{\setminus \mu})}{\sqrt{N}} \xi_i^\mu \xi_j^\mu \xi_j^p \right].$$

Using now the analogue of (A6.7) in the absence of input μ one verifies that the two terms in the brackets coming from the diagonal and the off-diagonal parts of the i, j-sum respectively are both of order 1. However, due to the random μ-dependence of $\xi_i^\mu \xi_j^\mu$ and the fact that $J^{\setminus \mu}$ does not depend on $\boldsymbol{\xi}^\mu$ the contribution of the second term *after summing over* μ is negligible. Finally, to the required order we may replace in the first term $(J_{+i}^{\setminus \mu} - J_i^{\setminus \mu})$ by $(J_{+i} - J_i)$ and obtain

$$\lambda_+^p - t^p = \Gamma V'(\lambda_+^p) + (\lambda_+^p - t^p) \frac{\Gamma}{N} \sum_{\mu=1}^{p-1} V''(\lambda^\mu) \lambda_0'(t^\mu, \alpha). \tag{A6.12}$$

We therefore find, not surprisingly, that the reaction term is proportional to its cause, namely $(\lambda_+^p - t^p)$. Introducing the auxiliary quantity

$$x = \frac{\Gamma}{1 - \frac{\Gamma}{N} \sum_{\mu=1}^{p-1} V''(\lambda_0(t_\mu)) \lambda_0'(t_\mu)} \tag{A6.13}$$

we obtain from (A6.12)

$$\lambda_0(t, \alpha) - t = x\, V'(\lambda_0), \tag{A6.14}$$

which is equivalent to the extremum condition for λ in (8.18) with the dependence of λ_0 on α parameterized by x.

To finally derive the equation fixing x as a function of α we recall that the cavity fields t^μ are uncorrelated Gaussian variables with zero mean and unit variance. This implies for large N

$$\frac{\Gamma}{N} \sum_{\mu=1}^{p-1} V''(\lambda_0(t^\mu))\lambda_0'(t^\mu) = \Gamma\alpha \int Dt\, V''(\lambda(t))\, \lambda_0'(t) \tag{A6.15}$$

$$= \frac{\Gamma\alpha}{x} \int Dt\, (\lambda_0'(t) - 1), \tag{A6.16}$$

where the last equality follows from the derivative of (A6.14). Combining this result with the definition (A6.13) of x we find

$$x = \Gamma\left(1 + \alpha \int Dt\, (\lambda_0'(t) - 1)\right). \tag{A6.17}$$

The value of Γ follows from the normalization condition. Multiplying (A6.4) by $\mathbf{J}/N$, we get

$$1 = \frac{\Gamma}{N} \sum_{\mu=1}^{p-1} V'(\lambda^\mu)\frac{\mathbf{J}\boldsymbol{\xi}^\mu}{\sqrt{N}} \tag{A6.18}$$

$$= \Gamma\alpha \int Dt\, V'(\lambda_0(t))\lambda_0(t) \tag{A6.19}$$

$$= \frac{\Gamma\alpha}{x} \int Dt\, (\lambda_0(t) - t)\, \lambda_0(t), \tag{A6.20}$$

where we have again used (A6.14). Substituting the value (A6.17) for x, the Lagrange multiplier Γ drops out, and we finally obtain after a partial integration

$$\alpha \int Dt\, (\lambda_0(t) - t)^2 = 1, \tag{A6.21}$$

which is identical to the saddle point equation corresponding to (8.18).

Using similar arguments it is also possible to find a self-consistency criterion for the general reasoning employed. The central assumption of the cavity approach is that the correction $(\mathbf{J}_+ - \mathbf{J})$ of the coupling vector induced by the new example is small. Multiplying (A6.7) by $(\mathbf{J}_+ - \mathbf{J})$ and using similar arguments to those which led to (A6.12) we obtain

$$(\mathbf{J}_+ - \mathbf{J})^2 = \frac{\Gamma V'(\lambda_+^p)(\lambda_+^p - t^p)}{1 - \frac{\Gamma}{N} \sum_{\mu=1}^{p-1} V''(\lambda_0(t_\mu))(\lambda_0'(t_\mu, \alpha))^2}. \tag{A6.22}$$

Using (A6.14) and its derivative with respect to t this may be written as

$$(\mathbf{J}_+ - \mathbf{J})^2 = \frac{(\lambda_+^p - t^p)^2}{1 - \alpha \int Dt \, (\lambda_0'(t) - 1)^2}, \tag{A6.23}$$

which diverges for $\alpha \to \alpha_{AT}$ with the de Almeida–Thouless threshold given by

$$\frac{1}{\alpha_{AT}} = \int Dt \, (\lambda_0'(t) - 1)^2. \tag{A6.24}$$

If α approaches α_{AT} the correction to the coupling vector $\mathbf{J}$ induced by a single additional example therefore becomes macroscopic and the reasoning of the cavity method breaks down. The result (A6.24) is for the present problem equivalent to the condition for local stability of the replica symmetric saddle point derived in problem 4.13. For more details about this connection with the replica formalism consult [292] and [17].

Appendix 7
The VC theorem

Many results from statistics are based on inequalities for probability distributions which are valid independently of the specific value of some unknown parameter. The Vapnik–Chervonenkis bound introduced in section 10.3 is a beautiful and successful illustration of this idea. The first step in the proof of this important theorem is to eliminate the dependence on the unknown generalization errors of the test functions. To do so, we first rewrite the probability (10.3) as

$$\text{Prob}(\sup_{f \in \mathcal{F}} |v_f^p - \varepsilon_f| > \delta) = \langle \theta(\sup_{f \in \mathcal{F}} |v_f^p - \varepsilon_f| - \delta) \rangle$$

$$= \langle \sup_{f \in \mathcal{F}} \theta(|v_f^p - \varepsilon_f| - \delta) \rangle$$

$$= \langle \sup_{f \in \mathcal{F}} [\theta(v_f^p - \varepsilon_f - \delta) + \theta(\varepsilon_f - v_f^p - \delta)] \rangle, \quad (A7.1)$$

with $\theta(x)$ again denoting the step function defined in (A1.17). The brackets $\langle \cdots \rangle$ denote the average over the choice of the p examples determining the value of v_f^p. One of the main steps in the proof of the theorem is to construct an inequality such that one can eliminate the ε_f dependence in the mean value. This can be achieved by introducing a new training set with p' examples for which the function f gives a frequency of errors $v_f^{p'}$. Since $\theta(x)\theta(x') \leq \theta(x + x')$, one finds

$$\theta(v_f^p - \varepsilon_f - \delta)\theta\left(\varepsilon_f - v_f^{p'} + \frac{1}{p'}\right) \leq \theta\left[v_f^p - v_f^{p'} - \left(\delta - \frac{1}{p'}\right)\right].$$

This inequality is valid for any value of $v_f^{p'}$ and hence also for the average $\langle \cdots \rangle'$ over the choices of the p' new and independent examples, i.e.

$$\theta(v_f^p - \varepsilon_f - \delta)\left\langle \theta\left(\varepsilon_f - v_f^{p'} + \frac{1}{p'}\right) \right\rangle' \leq \left\langle \theta\left[v_f^p - v_f^{p'} - \left(\delta - \frac{1}{p'}\right)\right] \right\rangle'. \quad (A7.2)$$

Recalling that $p'v_f^{p'}$ is a random variable with binomial distribution and mean value $p'\varepsilon_f$ one can prove [155] that

$$\left\langle \theta\left(\varepsilon_f - v_f^{p'} + \frac{1}{p'}\right)\right\rangle' = \mathrm{Prob}\left[0 \le v_f^{p'} < \varepsilon_f + \frac{1}{p'}\right] \ge \frac{1}{2},$$

which together with (A7.2) leads to

$$\theta(v_f^p - \varepsilon_f - \delta) \le 2\left\langle \theta\left[v_f^p - v_f^{p'} - \left(\delta - \frac{1}{p'}\right)\right]\right\rangle'. \tag{A7.3}$$

In a similar way one may easily prove that

$$\theta(\varepsilon_f - v_f^p - \delta) \le 2\left\langle \theta\left[v_f^{p'} - v_f^p - \left(\delta - \frac{1}{p'}\right)\right]\right\rangle'. \tag{A7.4}$$

Finally, combining (A7.1), (A7.3) and (A7.4) yields

$$\mathrm{Prob}\left(\sup_{f \in \mathcal{F}} |v_f^p - \varepsilon_f| > \delta\right) \le 2\left\langle\left\langle \sup_{f \in \mathcal{F}} \theta\left[|v_f^p - v_f^{p'}| - \left(\delta - \frac{1}{p'}\right)\right]\right\rangle\right\rangle'$$

or

$$\mathrm{Prob}\left(\sup_{f \in \mathcal{F}} |v_f^p - \varepsilon_f| > \delta\right) \le 2\,\mathrm{Prob}\left[\sup_{f \in \mathcal{F}} |v_f^p - v_f^{p'}| > \left(\delta - \frac{1}{p'}\right)\right]. \tag{A7.5}$$

This result is called the basic lemma by Vapnik and Chervonenkis [168]. The derivation here follows [160].

We can now introduce the classification diversity of our class of functions $\mathcal{F}$: for a given choice of these examples the functions $f \in \mathcal{F}$ can be grouped into equivalence classes $\widehat{f}$, such that all functions within a given equivalence class $\widehat{f}$ have an identical classification of the $p + p'$ examples. Since the functions in $\mathcal{F}$ induce at most $\Delta(p + p')$ different classifications of any $p + p'$ training examples, the total number of equivalence classes is bounded by $\Delta(p + p')$ for any choice of the examples. Since the outcome on the examples and hence also the observed error frequencies are the same for all the elements belonging to the same class $\widehat{f}$, one may write

$$\left\langle\left\langle \sup_{f \in \mathcal{F}} \theta\left[|v_f^p - v_f^{p'}| - \left(\delta - \frac{1}{p'}\right)\right]\right\rangle\right\rangle' \le \left\langle\left\langle \sum_{\widehat{f}} \theta\left[|v_f^p - v_f^{p'}| - \left(\delta - \frac{1}{p'}\right)\right]\right\rangle\right\rangle',$$

where the sum in the right hand side runs over all the equivalence classes. Note that these equivalence classes depend on the choice of the examples but not on the order in which they appear in the total sample. On the other hand, the total mean value is also invariant under permutations of the $p + p'$ examples. It is possible to write then

$$\left\langle\left\langle \sum_{\hat{f}} \theta\left[|v_{\hat{f}}^m - v_{\hat{f}}^{m'}| \left(\delta - \frac{1}{p'}\right)\right]\right\rangle\right\rangle'$$

$$= \left\langle\left\langle \sum_{\hat{f}} \frac{1}{(p+p')!} \sum_{\sigma} \theta\left[|\sigma(v_{\hat{f}}^p) - \sigma(v_{\hat{f}}^{p'})| - \left(\delta - \frac{1}{p'}\right)\right]\right\rangle\right\rangle',$$

where the sum runs over all the possible permutations σ of the $p+p'$ examples and $\sigma(v_{\hat{f}}^p)$ and $\sigma(v_{\hat{f}}^{p'})$ are the frequencies resulting in the two subsamples considered after permuting the examples of the whole sample. Note that the composition of each subsample can be modified by the permutation.

It turns out that the quantity

$$\Gamma_\delta = \frac{1}{(p+p')!} \sum_{\sigma} \theta\left[|\sigma(v_{\hat{f}}^p) - \sigma(v_{\hat{f}}^{p'})| - \delta\right]$$

can be bounded for all the possible outcomes. We will consider two different bounds for Γ. The first one is valid for $p = p'$ and may be found in [155]:

$$\Gamma_\delta < 3e^{-p\delta^2}. \tag{A7.6}$$

The second one, derived in [154] and [159], is weaker for the special case $p = p'$ but gives stronger results when $p' \gg p$. It reads

$$\Gamma_\delta \le 2\exp\left[-2p\left(\frac{p'}{p+p'}\delta\right)^2\right]. \tag{A7.7}$$

Finally, combining (A7.5) with the bound (A7.6), one immediately obtains equation (10.9). By playing on the choice of p and p' combined with (A7.7), one may obtain a sharper bound, and in particular the sharper accuracy threshold mentioned in chapter 10.

Bibliography

[1] W. S. McCulloch and W. Pitts. A logical calculus of ideas immanent in nervous activity. *Bull. Math. Biophys.*, 5:115–133, 1943.

[2] D. J. Amit. *Modelling Brain Function*. Cambridge University Press, Cambridge, 1989.

[3] J. A. Hertz, A. Krogh, and R. G. Palmer. *Introduction to the Theory of Neural Computation*. Addison-Wesley, Redwood City, 1991.

[4] B. Müller and J. Reinhard. *Neural Networks – An Introduction*. Springer, Berlin, 1991.

[5] P. Peretto. *An Introduction to the Modeling of Neural Networks*. Cambridge University Press, Cambridge, 1992.

[6] F. Rosenblatt. *Principles of Neurodynamics*. Spartan, New York, 1962.

[7] M. L. Minsky and S. A. Papert. *Perceptrons*. MIT Press, Cambridge, MA, 1969.

[8] Patarnello and P. Carnevali. Exhaustive thermodynamical analysis of Boolean learning networks. *Europhys. Lett.*, 4:503, 1987.

[9] T. J. Sejnowski and C. R. Rosenberg. Parallel networks that learn to pronounce english text. *Complex Systems*, 1:145, 1987.

[10] D. E. Rummelhart and J. E. McClelland, editors. *Parallel Distributed Processing*. MIT Press, Cambridge MA, 1986.

[11] E. Levin, N. Tishby, and S. Solla. A statistical approach to learning and generalization in layered neural networks. In R. Rivest, D. Haussler, and M. K. Warmuth, editors. *Proceedings of the 2nd Workshop on Computational Learning Theory*, page 245. Morgan Kaufmann, San Mateo, 1989.

[12] M. Opper and W. Kinzel. Statistical mechanics of generalization. In E. Domany, J. L. van Hemmen, and K. Schulten, editors. *Models of Neural Networks III*, pages 151–209. Springer, New York, 1996.

[13] L. G. Valiant. A theory of the learnable. *Commun. ACM*, 27:1134, 1984.

[14] E. W. Montroll and M. F. Shlesinger. Maximum entropy formalism, fractals, scaling phenomena, and $1/f$ noise: a tale of tails. *J. Stat. Phys.*, 32:209, 1983.

[15] M. Talagrand. Self averaging and the space of interactions in neural networks. *Random Struct. Alg.*, 14:199, 1999.

[16] K. Binder and A. P. Young. Spin glasses: experimental facts, theoretical concepts, and open questions. *Rev. Mod. Phys.*, 58:801, 1986.

[17] M. Mézard, G. Parisi, and M. A. Virasoro. *Spin Glass Theory and Beyond*. World Scientific, Singapore, 1987.

[18] M. Kac. On certain Toeplitz-like matrices and their relation to the problem of

lattice vibrations. *Ark. Det. Fys. Seminar i Trondheim*, 11:1–21, 1968.

[19] S. F. Edwards. Statistical mechanics of polymerized materials. In R. W. Douglass and B. Ellis, editors. *Proc. Third Int. Conf. on the Physics of Non-crystalline Solids*, pages 279–300. Wiley, New York, 1972.

[20] S. F. Edwards and P. W. Anderson. Theory of spin glasses. *J. Phys. F*, 5:965, 1975.

[21] M. S. Seung, H. Sompolinsky, and N. Tishby. Statistical mechanics of learning from examples. *Phys. Rev. A*, 45:6056, 1992.

[22] B. Schwartz, V. K. Samalam, S. A. Solla, and J. S. Denker. Exhaustive learning. *Neural Computation*, 2:371, 1990.

[23] C. Van den Broeck and R. Kawai. Learning in feedforward Boolean networks. *Phys. Rev. A*, 42:6210, 1990.

[24] E. Gardner. The space of interactions in neural network models. *J. Phys. A*, 21:257, 1988.

[25] E. Gardner and B. Derrida. Optimal storage properties of neural network models. *J. Phys. A*, 21:271, 1988.

[26] E. Gardner. Optimal basins of attraction in randomly sparse neural network models. *J. Phys. A*, 22:1969, 1989.

[27] E. Gardner and B. Derrida. Three unfinished works on the optimal storage capacity of networks. *J. Phys. A*, 22:1983, 1989.

[28] P. Del Giudice, S. Franz, and M. A. Virasoro. Perceptron beyond the limit of capacity. *J. Physique*, 50:121, 1989.

[29] F. Vallet. The Hebb rule for learning linearly separable Boolean functions: learning and generalization. *Europhys. Lett.*, 8:747, 1989.

[30] G. Györgyi and N. Tishby. Statistical theory of learning a rule. In K. Theumann and W. K. Koeberle, editors. *Workshop on Neural Networks and Spin Glasses*, pages 3–36. World Scientific, Singapore, 1990.

[31] M. Bouten and C. Van den Broeck. Nearest-neighbour classifier for the perceptron. *Europhys. Lett.*, 26:69, 1994.

[32] D. O. Hebb. *The Organization of Behavior*. Wiley, New York, 1949.

[33] R. Meir and J. F. Fontanari. Calculation of learning curves for inconsistent algorithms. *Phys. Rev. A*, 45:8874, 1992.

[34] J. Berg and A. Engel. A multifractal phase-space analysis of perceptrons with biased patterns. *J. Phys. A*, 31:2509, 1998.

[35] S. Seung, M. Opper, and H. Sompolinsky. Query by committee. In *Vth Annual Workshop on Computational Learning Theory (COLT92)*, page 287, San Mateo, 1992.

[36] P. Ruján. Playing billiards in version space. *Neural Computation*, 9:99, 1995.

[37] T. L. H. Watkin. Optimal learning with a neural network. *Europhys. Lett*, 21:871, 1993.

[38] T. Kohonen. Analysis of a simple self-organizing process. *Biol. Cyb.*, 44:135, 1982.

[39] L. Personnaz, I. Guyon, and G. Dreyfus. Information storage and retrieval in spin-glass like neural networks. *J. Phys. Lett.*, 46:4217, 1985.

[40] B. Widrow and M. E. Hoff. Adaptive switching circuits. *WESCON convention report*, (4):96, 1960.

[41] M. Opper. Learning in neural networks: solvable dynamics. *Europhys. Lett.*, 8:389, 1989.

[42] S. Diederich and M. Opper. Learning of correlated patterns in spin-glass networks by local learning rules. *Phys. Rev. Lett.*, 58:949, 1987.

[43] W. Krauth and M. Mézard. Learning algorithms with optimal stability in neural

networks. *J. Phys. A*, 20:L745, 1987.

[44] M. Opper. Learning times of neural networks: exact solution for a perceptron algorithm. *Phys. Rev. A*, 38:3824, 1988.

[45] J. F. Fontanari and A. Theumann. Learning times of a perceptron that learns from examples. *J. Phys. A*, 27:379, 1994.

[46] R. Fletcher. *Practical Methods of Optimization*. John Wiley and Sons, New York, 1996.

[47] J. K. Anlauf and M. Biehl. The adatron: an adaptive perceptron algorithm. *Europhys. Lett.*, 10:687, 1989.

[48] P. Ruján. A fast method for calculating the perceptron with maximal stability. *J. Physique I*, 3:277, 1993.

[49] J. Imhoff. A polynomial training algorithm for calculating perceptrons of optimal stability. *J. Phys. A*, 28:2173, 1995.

[50] D. Haussler, M. Kearns, and R.E. Schapire. Bounds on the sample complexity of Bayesian learning using information theory and the VC dimension. In *Machine Learning*, volume 14, page 83, 1994.

[51] J. A. Anderson and E. Rosenfeld. *Neurocomputing: Foundations of Research*. MIT Press, Cambridge, MA, 1988.

[52] W. Kinzel and G. Reents. *Physics by Computer*. Springer, Berlin, 1998.

[53] S. Solla. A Bayesian approach to learning in neural networks. *Intl. J. of Neural Systems*, 6:161, 1995.

[54] M. Bouten, J. Schietse, and C. Van den Broeck. Gradient descent learning in perceptrons: a review of its possibilities. *Phys. Rev. E*, 52:1958, 1995.

[55] O. Kinouchi and N. Caticha. Learning algorithm that gives the Bayes generalization limit for perceptrons. *Phys. Rev. E*, 54:R54, 1996.

[56] A. Buhot, J.-M. T. Moreno, and M. B. Gordon. Finite size scaling of the Bayesian perceptron. *Phys. Rev. E*, 55:7434, 1997.

[57] N. Caticha and O. Kinouchi. Time ordering in the evolution of information processing and modulation systems. *Phil. Mag. B*, 77:1565, 1998.

[58] M. Opper, W. Kinzel, J. Kleinz, and R. Nehl. On the ability of the optimal perceptron to generalize. *J. Phys. A*, 23:581, 1990.

[59] M. Opper and D. Haussler. Generalization performance of Bayes optimal classification algorithm for learning a perceptron. *Phys. Rev. Lett.*, 66:2677, 1991.

[60] J. M. Parrondo and C. Van den Broeck. Error vs. rejection curve for the perceptron. *Europhys. Lett.*, 22:319, 1993.

[61] I. Derényi, T. Geszti, and G. Györgyi. Generalization in the programed teaching of a perceptron. *Phys. Rev. E*, 50:3192, 1994.

[62] P. Majer, A. Engel, and A. Zippelius. Perceptrons above saturation. *J. Phys. A*, 26:7405, 1993.

[63] T. L. H. Watkin and A. Rau. Learning unlearnable problems with perceptrons. *Phys. Rev. A*, 45:4102, 1992.

[64] P. Kuhlmann and K.-R. Müller. On the generalization ability of diluted perceptrons. *J. Phys. A*, 27:3759, 1994.

[65] D. Nabutovsky and E. Domany. Learning the unlearnable. *Neural Comp.*, 3:604, 1991.

[66] G. Györgyi. Inference of a rule by a neural network with thermal noise. *Phys. Rev. Lett.*, 64:2957, 1990.

[67] D. Hansel and H. Sompolinsky. Learning from examples in a single-layer neural network. *Europhys. Lett.*, 11:687, 1990.

[68] G. Parisi. A memory which forgets. *J. Phys. A*, 19:L617, 1986.

[69] J. L. van Hemmen, G. Keller, and R. Kühn. Forgetful memories. *Europhys. Lett.*, 5:663, 1988.

[70] M. Mézard, J. P. Nadal, and G. Toulouse. Solvable models of working memories. *J. Physique*, 47:1457, 1986.

[71] J. P. Nadal, G. Toulouse, J. P. Changeux, and S. Dehaene. Networks of formal neurons and memory palimpsests. *Europhys. Lett.*, 1:535, 1986.

[72] T. M. Cover. Geometrical and statistical properties of systems of linear inequalities with applications in pattern recognition. *IEEE Trans. Electron. Comput.*, EC-14:326, 1965.

[73] J. G. Wendel. A problem in geometric probability. *Math. Scand.*, 11:109, 1962.

[74] L. Schläfli. Theorie der vielfachen Kontinuität. In Steiner-Schläfli-Komitee Basel, editor. *Gesammelte Mathematische Abhandlungen*. Birkhäuser, Basel, 1852.

[75] M. Bouten. Replica symmetry instability in perceptron models. *J. Phys. A*, 27:6021, 1994.

[76] D. J. Gross and M. Mézard. The simplest spin glass. *Nucl. Phys. B*, 240:431, 1984.

[77] W. Krauth and M. Opper. Critical storage capacity of the $j = \pm 1$ neural network. *J. Phys. A*, 22:L519, 1989.

[78] B. Derrida, R. B. Griffith, and A. Prügel-Bennett. Finite-size effects and bounds for perceptron models. *J. Phys. A*, 24:4907, 1991.

[79] B. Derrida. Random-energy model: an exactly solvable model of disordered systems. *Phys. Rev. B*, 24:2613, 1981.

[80] M. Bouten, A. Komoda, and R. Serneels. Storage capacity of a diluted neural network with Ising couplings. *J. Phys. A*, 23:2605, 1990.

[81] T. B. Kepler and L. F. Abbott. Domains of attraction in neural networks. *J. Physique*, 49:1657, 1988.

[82] L. Ein-Dor and I. Kanter. Confidence in prediction by neural networks. *Phys. Rev. E*, 60:799, 1999.

[83] W. Whyte and D. Sherrington. Replica-symmetry breaking in perceptrons. *J. Phys. A*, 29:3063, 1996.

[84] M. Griniasty and H. Gutfreund. Learning and retrieval in attractor neural networks above saturation. *J. Phys. A*, 24:715, 1991.

[85] R. Erichsen and W. K. Theumann. Optimal storage of a neural network model: a replica symmetry-breaking solution. *J. Phys. A*, 26:L61, 1993.

[86] G. Parisi. The order parameter for spin glasses: A function on the interval 0–1. *J. Phys. A*, 13:L115, 1101 and 1887, 1980.

[87] G. Györgyi and P. Reimann. Parisi phase in a neuron. *Phys. Rev. Lett.*, 79:2746, 1997.

[88] G. Györgyi and P. Reimann. Beyond storage capacity in a single model neuron: Continuous replica symmetry breaking. *Journ. Stat. Phys.*, 101:673, 2000.

[89] G. Györgyi. Techniques of replica symmetry breaking and the storage problem of the McCulloch–Pitts neuron. *Phys. Rep.*, to appear, 2001.

[90] D. J. Amit, K. Y. M. Wong, and C. Campbell. Perceptron learning with sign-constrained weights. *J. Phys. A*, 22:2039, 1989.

[91] D. J. Amit, C. Campbell, and K. Y. M. Wong. The interaction space of neural networks with sign-constrained synapses. *J. Phys. A*, 22:4687, 1989.

[92] C. Campbell and A. Robinson. On the storage capacity of neural networks with sign-constrained weights. *J. Phys. A*, 24:L93, 1991.

[93] I. Kanter and E. Eisenstein. On the capacity per synapse. *J. Phys. A*, 23:L935, 1990.

[94] H. Gutfreund and Y. Stein. Capacity of neural networks with discrete synaptic

couplings. *J. Phys. A*, 23:2613, 1990.

[95] B. López and W. Kinzel. Learning by dilution in a neural network. *J. Phys. A*, 30:7753, 1997.

[96] R. Meir and J. F. Fontanari. Learning from examples in weight-constrained neural networks. *J. Phys. A*, 25:1149, 1992.

[97] D. M. L. Barbato and J. F. Fontanari. The effects of lesions on the generalization ability of a perceptron. *J. Phys. A*, 26:1847, 1993.

[98] S. Kirkpatrick, C. D. Gelatt, and M. P. Vecci. Optimization by simulated annealing. *Science*, 220:671, 1983.

[99] H. Horner. Dynamics of learning for the binary perceptron problem. *Z. Phys. B*, 86:291, 1992.

[100] S. Mertens. Exhaustive search for low-autocorrelation binary sequences. *J. Phys. A*, 29:L199, 1996.

[101] L. Pitt and L. G. Valiant. Computational limitations on learning from examples. *J. Assoc. Comput. Macinary*, 35:965, 1988.

[102] R. W. Penney and D. Sherrington. The weight-space of the binary perceptron. *J. Phys. A*, 26:6173, 1993.

[103] L. Reimers, M. Bouten, and B. Van Rompaey. Learning strategy for the binary perceptron. *J. Phys. A*, 29:6247, 1996.

[104] R. E. Mayer. *Thinking and Problem Solving: An Introduction to Human Cognition and Learning*. Scott, Foresman and Company, Glenview, 1977.

[105] G. Györgyi. First-order transition to perfect generalization in a neutral network with binary synapses. *Phys. Rev. A*, 41:7097, 1990.

[106] G. Boffetta, R. Monasson, and R. Zecchina. Symmetry breaking in nonmonotonic neural networks. *J. Phys. A*, 26:L507, 1993.

[107] A. Engel and L. Reimers. Reliability of replica symmetry for the generalization problem in a toy multilayer neural network. *Europhys. Lett.*, 28:531, 1994.

[108] G. J. Bex, R. Serneels, and C. Van den Broeck. Storage capacity and generalization error for the reversed-wedge Ising perceptron. *Phys. Rev. E*, 51:6309, 1995.

[109] J. Schietse, M. Bouten, and C. Van den Broeck. Training binary perceptrons by clipping. *Europhys. Lett.*, 32:279, 1995.

[110] R. O. Duda and P. E. Hart. *Pattern Classification and Scene Analysis*. Wiley, New York, 1973.

[111] E. Oja. A simplified neuron model as a principal component analyser. *J. Math. Biology*, 15:267, 1992.

[112] M. Biehl and A. Mietzner. Statistical mechanics of unsupervised learning. *Europhys. Lett.*, 24:421, 1993.

[113] R. Linsker. Towards an organizing principle for perception: the role of Hebbian synapses in the emergence of feature-analyzing function. In *1987 IEEE Conference on Neural Information Processing Symstems – Natural and Synthetic*. IEEE, Denver, page 10, 1987.

[114] P. Reimann, C. Van den Broeck, and G. J. Bex. A Gaussian scenario for unsupervised learning. *J. Phys. A*, 29:3521, 1996.

[115] F. Spitzer. *Principles of a Random Walk*. Van Nostrand, Princeton, New Jersey, 1964.

[116] W. Feller. *An Introduction to Probability Theory and its Applications*, volume 1. John Wiley and Sons, New York, 1950.

[117] M. Biehl and A. Mietzner. Statistical mechanics of unsupervised structure recognition. *J. Phys. A*, 27:1885, 1994.

[118] T. L. H. Watkin and J-P. Nadal. Optimal unsupervised learning. *J. Phys. A*,

27:1899, 1994.

[119] A. Buhaut, J.-M. T. Moreno, and M. Gordon. Finite size scaling of the Bayesian perceptron. *Phys. Rev. E*, 55:7434, 1997.

[120] E. Lootens and C. Van den Broeck. Analysing cluster formation by replica method. *Europhys. Lett.*, 30:381, 1995.

[121] P. R. Krishnaiah and L. N. Kanal. *Classification, Pattern Recognition, and Reduction of Dimensionality*, volume 2. North Holland, Amsterdam, 1982.

[122] S. Grossberg. *Studies of the Mind and Brain*. Reidel, Boston, 1982.

[123] K. Rose, E. Gurewitz, and G. C. Fox. Statistical mechanics and phase transitions in clustering. *Phys. Rev. Lett.*, 65:945, 1990.

[124] N. Barkai and H. Sompolinsky. Statistical mechanics of the maximum-likelihood density estimation. *Phys. Rev. E*, 50:1766, 1994.

[125] M. Blatt, S. Wiseman, and E. Domany. Superparamagnetic clustering of data. *Phys. Rev. Lett.*, 76:3251, 1996.

[126] N. Barkai, H. S. Seung, and H. Sompolinsky. Scaling laws in learning of classification tasks. *Phys. Rev. Lett.*, 70:3167, 1993.

[127] P. Reimann and C. Van den Broeck. Learning by examples from a nonuniform distribution. *Phys. Rev. E*, 53:3989, 1996.

[128] C. Marangi, M. Biehl, and S. A. Solla. Supervised learning from clustered input examples. *Europhys. Lett.*, 30:117, 1995.

[129] D. Herschkowitz and M. Opper. Retarded learning: rigorous results from statistical mechanics. *Phys. Rev. Lett.*, to appear, 2001.

[130] P. Reimann. Unsupervised learning of distributions. *Europhys. Lett*, 40:251, 1997.

[131] G. Reents and R. Urbanczik. Self-averaging and on-line learning. *Phys. Rev. Lett*, 80:5445, 1998.

[132] E. B. Baum. The perceptron algorithm is fast for nonmalicious distributions. *Neural Comp.*, 2:248, 1990.

[133] D. Saad, editor. *On-line Learning in Neural Networks*. Cambridge University Press, Cambridge, 1998.

[134] M. Biehl and H. Schwarze. Learning by on-line gradient descent. *J. Phys. A*, 28:643, 1995.

[135] W. Kinzel and P. Ruján. Improving a network generalization ability by selecting examples. *Europhys. Lett.*, 13:473, 1990.

[136] T. Heskes and B. Kappen. Learning processes in neural networks. *Phys. Rev. A*, 44:2718, 1990.

[137] S. Amari and S. C. Douglas. Why natural gradient? In *Proceedings of the 1998 IEEE International Conference on Acoustics, Speech and Signal Processing*, page 1213, 1998.

[138] O. Kinouchi and N. Caticha. Lower bounds on generalization errors for drifting rules. *J. Phys. A*, 26:2878, 1992.

[139] M. Biehl and P. Riegler. On-line learning with a perceptron. *Europhys. Lett.*, 28:525, 1994.

[140] N. Barkai, H. S. Seung, and H. Sompolinsky. Local and global convergence of on-line learning. *Phys. Rev. Lett.*, 75:1415, 1995.

[141] M. Biehl and H. Schwarze. Learning drifting concepts with neural networks. *J. Phys. A*, 26:2651, 1993.

[142] O. Kinouchi and N. Caticha. Lower bounds on generalization errors for drifting rules. *J. Phys. A*, 26:6161, 1993.

[143] O. Kinouchi. Biased learning in Boolean perceptrons. *Physica A*, 185:411, 1992.

[144] T. L. H. Watkin and A. Rau. Selecting examples for perceptrons. *J. Phys. A*,

25:113, 1992.

[145] J.-I. Inoue, H. Nishimori, and Y. Kabashima. On-line learning of non-monotonic rules by simple perceptron. *J. Phys. A*, 30:3795, 1997.

[146] C. Van den Broeck and P. Reimann. Unsupervised learning by examples: on-line versus off-line. *Phys. Rev. Lett.*, 76:2188, 1996.

[147] M. Opper. On-line versus off-line learning from random examples: general results. *Phys. Rev. Lett.*, 77:4671, 1996.

[148] M. Rattray, D. Saad, and S. Amari. Natural gradient descent for on-line learning. *Phys. Rev. Lett.*, 81:5461, 1998.

[149] C. W. H. Mace and A. C. C. Coolen. Statistical mechanical analysis of the dynamics of learning in perceptrons. *Statistics and Computing*, 8:55, 1998.

[150] J. W. Kim and H. Sompolinsky. On-line Gibbs learning. *Phys. Rev. Lett*, 76:3021, 1996.

[151] W. Kinzel and R. Urbanczik. On-line learning in a discrete state space. *J. Phys. A*, 31:L27, 1998.

[152] P. Riegler, M. Biehl, S. A. Solla, and C. Marangi. In M. Marinaro and R. Tagliaferri, editors. On-line learning from clustered input examples. *Proc. 7th Italian Workshop on Neural Networks*. World Scientific, Singapore, 1996.

[153] W. Hoeffding. On the distribution of the number of successes in independent trials. *Ann. Math. Statist.*, 27:713, 1956.

[154] G. R. Shorak and J. A. Wellner. *Empirical Processes with Applications to Statistics*. Wiley, New York, 1986.

[155] V. N. Vapnik. *Estimation of Dependences Based on Empirical Data*. Springer, Berlin, 1982.

[156] N. Sauer. On the density of families of sets. *J. Comb. Th. A*, 13:145, 1972.

[157] M. Anthony and N. Biggs. *Computational Learning Theory*. CUP, Cambridge, 1992.

[158] E. Baum and D. Haussler. What size net gives valid generalization? *Neur. Comput.*, 1:151, 1989.

[159] L. Devroye. Bounds for the uniform deviation of empirical measures. *J. Multivariate Anal.*, 12:72–79, 1982.

[160] J. M. Parrondo and C. Van den Broeck. Vapnik–Chervonenkis bounds for generalization. *J. Phys. A*, 26:2211, 1993.

[161] A. Engel and C. Van den Broeck. Replica calculation of the Vapnik–Chervonenkis bound for the perceptron. *Physica A*, 200:636–643, 1993.

[162] A. Engel and C. Van den Broeck. Systems that can learn from examples: replica calculation of uniform convergence bounds for perceptrons. *Phys. Rev. Lett.*, 71:1772, 1993.

[163] D. Haussler, M. Kearns, and R. Schapire. Bounds on the sample complexity of Bayesian learning using information theory and the VC dimension. In *Proceedings of the Fourth Annual Workshop on Computational Learning Theory*, page 61. Morgan Kaufmann, San Mateo, 1991.

[164] T. Cover and J. Thomas. *Elements of Information Theory*. Wiley, New York, 1991.

[165] A. Engel and W. Fink. Statistical mechanics calculation of Vapnik–Chervonenkis bounds for perceptrons. *J. Phys. A*, 26:6893, 1993.

[166] A. Blumer, A. Ehrenfeucht, D. Haussler, and M. K. Warmuth. Learnability and the Vapnik–Chervonenkis dimension. *J. Assoc. Comput. Machinery*, 36:929, 1989.

[167] Y. S. Abu-Mostafa. The Vapnik–Chervonenkis dimension: information versus complexity in learning. *Neur. Comput.*, 1:312–317, 1989.

[168] V. N. Vapnik and A. Y. Chervonenkis. Theory of uniform convergence of

frequency of appearance, attributes to their probabilities and problems of defining optimal solution by empiric data. *Avtomatika i Telemekhanika.*, 2:42, 1971.

[169] M. Biehl and M. Opper. Perceptron learning: the largest version space. In J.-H. Oh, C. Kwon, and S. Cho, editors. *Neural Networks: The Statistical Mechanics Perspective*, page 59. World Scientific, Singapore, 1995.

[170] M. Anthony and P. L. Bartlett. *Neural Network Learning: Theoretical Foundations*. Cambridge University Press, Cambridge, 1999.

[171] V. N. Vapnik. *The Nature of Statistical Learning Theory*. Springer, 1995.

[172] J. Feder. *Fractals*. Plenum, New York, 1988.

[173] T. Tél. Fractals, multifractals, and thermodynamics. *Z. Naturforsch.*, 43a:1154, 1988.

[174] A. Engel and M. Weigt. Multifractal analysis of the coupling space of feedforward neural networks. *Phys. Rev. E*, 53:R2064, 1996.

[175] U. Frisch and G. Parisi. Fully developed turbulence and intermittency. In M. Ghil, R. Benzi, and G. Parisi, editors. *Turbulence and Predictability in Geophysical Fluid Dynamics and Climate Dynamics*. North-Holland, 1985.

[176] T. C. Halsey, M. H. Jensen, L. P. Kadanoff, I. Procaccia, and B. I. Shraiman. Fractal measures and their singularities: the characterization of strange sets. *Phys. Rev. A*, 33:1141, 1986.

[177] R. Monasson and D. O'Kane. Domains of solutions and replica symmetry breaking in multilayer neural networks. *Europhys. Lett.*, 27:85, 1994.

[178] M. Weigt. Multifractal analysis of perceptron learning with errors. *Phys. Rev. E*, 57:955, 1998.

[179] M. Weigt and A. Engel. Multifractality and percolation in the phase space of neural networks. *Phys. Rev. E*, 55:4552, 1997.

[180] P. Riegler and H. S. Seung. Vapnik–Chervonenkis entropy of the spherical perceptron. *Phys. Rev. E*, 55:3283, 1997.

[181] C. Van den Broeck and G. J. Bex. Multifractal a-priori probability distribution for the perceptron. *Phys. Rev. E*, 57:3660–3663, 1998.

[182] L. Reimers and A. Engel. Weight space structure and generalization in the reversed-wedge-perceptron. *J. Phys. A*, 29:3923, 1996.

[183] G. J. Bex and C. Van den Broeck. Domain sizes of the Gardner volume for the Ising reversed wedge perceptron. *Phys. Rev. E*, 56:870, 1997.

[184] R. Monasson and R. Zecchina. Weight space structure and internal representations: a direct approach to learning and generalization in multilayer neural networks. *Phys. Rev. Lett.*, 75:2432, 1995.

[185] R. Monasson and R. Zecchina. Learning and generalization theories of large committee-machines. *Mod. Phys. Lett. B*, 9:1887, 1996.

[186] S. Cocco, R. Monasson, and R. Zecchina. Analytical and numerical study of internal representations in multilayer neural networks with binary weights. *Phys. Rev. E*, 54:717, 1996.

[187] M. Opper, P. Kuhlmann, and A. Mietzner. Convexity, internal representations and the statistical mechanics of neural networks. *Europhys. Lett.*, 37:31, 1997.

[188] J. S. Denker, D. Schwartz, B. Wittner, S. Solla, R. Howard, L. Jackel, and J. Hopfield. Large automatic learning, rule extraction, and generalization. *Complex Systems*, 1:877, 1987.

[189] G. Cybenko. Approximation by superpositions of a sigmoidal function. *Math. Contr. Sign. Syst.*, 2:303, 1989.

[190] A. N. Kolmogorov. On the representation of continuous functions of many variables by superposition of continuous functions of one variable and addition.

Dokl. Akad. Nauk SSSR, 114:953, 1957.

[191] A. Priel, M. Blatt, T. Grossmann, E. Domany, and I. Kanter. Computational capabilities of restricted two-layered perceptrons. *Phys. Rev. E*, 50:577, 1994.

[192] N. J. Nilson. *Learning Machines*. McGraw-Hill, New York, 1965.

[193] M. Opper. Learning and generalization in a two-layer neural network: the role of the Vapnik–Chervonenkis dimension. *Phys. Rev. Lett.*, 72:2113, 1994.

[194] G. Mato and N. Parga. Generalization properties of multilayered neural networks. *J. Phys. A*, 25:5047, 1992.

[195] G. J. Mitchison and R. M. Durbin. Bounds on the learning capacity of some multi-layer networks. *Biol. Cybern.*, 60:345, 1989.

[196] M. Opper. Statistical-physics estimates for the complexity of feedforward neural networks. *Phys. Rev. E*, 51:3613, 1995.

[197] E. Barkai, D. Hansel, and I. Kanter. Statistical mechanics of a multilayered neural network. *Phys. Rev. Lett.*, 65:2312, 1990.

[198] E. Barkai, D. Hansel, and H. Sompolinsky. Broken symmetries in multilayered perceptrons. *Phys. Rev. A*, 45:4146, 1992.

[199] A. Engel, H. M. Köhler, F. Tschepke, H. Vollmayr, and A. Zippelius. Storage capacity and learning algorithm for two-layer perceptrons. *Phys. Rev. A*, 45:7590, 1992.

[200] A. Engel. Correlation of internal representations in feed-forward neural networks. *J. Phys. A*, 29:L323, 1996.

[201] D. Malzahn and A. Engel. Correlations between hidden units in multilayer neural networks and replica symmetry breaking. *Phys. Rev. E*, 60:2097, 1999.

[202] D. Malzahn, A. Engel, and I. Kanter. Storage capacity of correlated perceptrons. *Phys. Rev. E*, 55:7369, 1997.

[203] R. Urbanczik. Storage capacity of the fully-connected committee machine. *J. Phys. A*, 30:L387, 1997.

[204] Y. S. Xiong, C. Kwon, and J.-H. Oh. Storage capacity of a fully-connected parity machine with continuous weights. *J. Phys. A*, 31:7043, 1998.

[205] H. Schwarze. Learning a rule in a multilayer neural network. *J. Phys. A*, 26:5781, 1993.

[206] D. Hansel, G. Mato, and C. Meunier. Memorization without generalization in a multilayered neural network. *Europhys. Lett.*, 20:471, 1992.

[207] H. Schwarze and J. Hertz. Generalization in a large committee machine. *Europhys. Lett.*, 20:375, 1992.

[208] H. Schwarze and J. Hertz. Learning from examples in fully connected committee machines. *J. Phys. A*, 26:4919, 1993.

[209] K. Kang, J.-H. Oh, C. Kwon, and Y. Park. Generalization in a two-layer neural network. *Phys. Rev. E*, 48:4805, 1993.

[210] B. Schottky. Phase transitions in the generalization behaviour of multilayer neural networks. *J. Phys. A*, 28:4515, 1995.

[211] H. Schwarze, M. Opper, and W. Kinzel. Generalization in a two-layer neural network. *Phys. Rev. A*, 46:R6185, 1992.

[212] O. Winther, B. Lautrup, and J.-B. Zhang. Optimal learning in multilayer neural networks. *Phys. Rev. E*, 55:836, 1997.

[213] R. De Figueviedo. *J. Math. Anal.*, 38:1227, 1980.

[214] M. Biehl and M. Opper. Tiling-like learning in the parity machine. *Phys. Rev. A*, 44:6888, 1991.

[215] M. Copelli and N. Caticha. Universal asymptotics in committee machines with tree architecture. In D. Saad, editor. *On-line Learning in Neural Networks*, page 165.

Cambridge University Press, Cambridge, 1998.

[216] R. Simonetti and N. Caticha. On-line learning in parity machines. *J. Phys. A*, 29:4859, 1996.

[217] S. Saad and S. Solla. Exact solution for on-line learning in multilayer neural networks. *Phys. Rev. Lett.*, 74:4337, 1995.

[218] D. Saad and S. Solla. On-line learning in soft committee machines. *Phys. Rev. E*, 52:4225, 1995.

[219] M. Biehl, P. Riegler, and C. Wohler. Transient dynamics of on-line learning in two-layered neural networks. *J. Phys. A*, 29:4769, 1996.

[220] Y. Chauvin and D. E. Rumelhart, editors. *Backpropagation: Theory, Architectures, and Applications*. Erlbaum, Hillsdale, NJ, 1995.

[221] P. Riegler and M. Biehl. On-line backpropagation in two-layered neural networks. *J. Phys. A*, 28:L507, 1995.

[222] M. J. Shervish. *Theory of Statistics*. Springer, New York, 1995.

[223] O. Winther and S. Solla. Optimal Bayesian on-line learning. In K. Y. M. Wong, I. King, and D.-Y. Yeung, editors. *Theoretical Aspects of Neural Computation*, page 61. Springer, Berlin, 1997.

[224] S. Solla and O. Winther. Optimal perceptron learning: an on-line Bayesian approach. In D. Saad, editor. *On-line Learning in Neural Networks*, page 379. Cambridge University Press, Cambridge, 1998.

[225] Y. Kabashima. Perfect loss of generalization due to noise in $K = 2$ parity machines. *J. Phys. A*, 27:1917, 1994.

[226] M. Copelli and N. Caticha. On-line learning in the committee machine. *J. Phys. A*, 28:1615, 1995.

[227] M. Copelli, O. Kinouchi, and N. Caticha. Equivalence between learning in noisy perceptrons and tree committee machines. *Phys. Rev. E*, 53:1615, 1996.

[228] M. Copelli, R. Eichorn, O. Kinouchi, M. Biehl, R. Simonetti, P. Riegler, and N. Caticha. Noise robustness in multilayer neural networks. *Europhys. Lett.*, 37:427, 1997.

[229] D. Saad and M. Rattray. Optimal on-line learning in multilayer neural networks. In D. Saad, editor. *On-line Learning in Neural Networks*, page 135. Cambridge University Press, Cambridge, 1998.

[230] H. Sompolinsky and J. W. Kim. On-line Gibbs learning. i. general theory. *Phys. Rev. E*, 58:2335, 1998.

[231] J. W. Kim and H. Sompolinsky. On-line Gibbs learning. ii. application to perceptron and multilayer networks. *Phys. Rev.*, (58):2348, 1998.

[232] H. C. Rae, P. Sollich, and A. C. C. Coolen. On-line learning with restricted training sets: an exactly solvable case. *J. Phys. A*, 32:3321, 1999.

[233] A. C. C. Coolen and D. Saad. Dynamics of supervised learning with restricted training sets. In D. Saad, editor. *On-line Learning in Neural Networks*, page 303. Cambridge University Press, Cambridge, 1998.

[234] S. E. Fahlman. Fast-learning variations on back-propagation: an empirical study. In *Proceedings of the 1988 Connectionist Models Summer School*, page 38. Morgan Kaufmann, San Mateo, CA, 1988.

[235] D. Ruelle and F. Takens. On the nature of turbulence. *Comm. Math. Phys.*, 20:167, 1971.

[236] A. Lapedes and R. Farber. How neural nets work. In D. Anderson, editor. *Neural Information Processing Systems*, page 442. American Institute of Physics, New York, 1988.

[237] M. A. Aizerman, E. M. Braverman, and L. I. Rozonoer. Theoretical foundations of

the potential function method in pattern recognition learning. *Automation and Remote Control*, 25:821, 1964.

[238] B. E. Boser, I. Guyon, and V. N. Vapnik. A training algorithm for optimal margin classifiers. In *Proceedings of the 5th Workshop on Computational Learning Theory*, page 144, Pittsburgh, 1992. ACM.

[239] R. Courant and D. Hilbert. *Methoden der mathematischen Physik*. Springer, Berlin, 1993.

[240] C. M. Bishop. *Neural Networks for Pattern Recognition*. Cambridge University Press, Cambridge, 1995.

[241] R. Dietrich, M. Opper, and H. Sompolinsky. Statistical mechanics of support vector networks. *Phys. Rev. Lett.*, 82:2975, 99.

[242] H. Yoon and J.-H. Oh. Learning of higher-order perceptrons with tunable complexities. *J. Phys. A*, 31:7771, 1998.

[243] V. N. Vapnik. *Statistical Learning Theory*. John Wiley and Sons, New York, 1997.

[244] N. Christianini and J. Shawe-Taylor. *An Introduction to Support Vector Machines*. Cambridge University Press, Cambridge, 2000.

[245] A. R. Garey and D. S. Johnson. *Computers and Intractability: A Guide to the Theory of NP-completeness*. Freeman, San Francisco, 1979.

[246] C. H. Papadimitriou. *Computational Complexity*. Addison-Wesley, Reading, MA, 1994.

[247] S. A. Cook. The complexity of theorem-proving procedures. In *Proceedings of the 3rd Annual ACM Symposium on Theory of Computing*, page 151, 1971.

[248] B. Hayes. Can't get no satisfaction. *American Scientist*, 85:108, 1997.

[249] R. Monasson and R. Zecchina. Entropy of the K-satisfiability problem. *Phys. Rev. Lett.*, 76:3881, 1996.

[250] K.-H. Borgwardt. Some distribution-independent results about the asymptotic order of the average number of pivot steps of the simplex method. *Math. Oper. Res.*, 7(3):441–462, 1982.

[251] K.-H. Borgwardt. *The Simplex Method*. Springer, Berlin, 1987.

[252] S. Kirkpatrick and G. Toulouse. Configuration space analysis of travelling salesman problems. *J. Physique*, 46:1277, 1985.

[253] S. Kirkpatrick and B. Selman. Critical behavior in the satisfiability of random Boolean expressions. *Science*, 264:1297, 1994.

[254] E. Korutcheva, M. Opper, and B. López. Statistical mechanics of the knapsack problem. *J. Phys. A*, 27:L645, 1994.

[255] J. Inoue. Statistical mechanics of the multi-constraint continuous knapsack problem. *J. Phys. A*, 30:1047, 1997.

[256] R. Monasson and R. Zecchina. Statistical mechanics of the random K-satisfiability model. *Phys. Rev. E*, 56:1357, 1997.

[257] S. Kirkpatrick, G. Györgyi, N. Tishby, and L. Troyansky. The statistical mechanics of k-satisfaction. In J. Cowan, G. Tesauro, and L. Troyansky, editors. *Advances in Neural Information Processing Systems*, volume 6, page 439. Morgan Kaufmann, San Mateo, 1994.

[258] S. Mertens. Phase transition in the number partitioning problem. *Phys. Rev. Lett.*, 81:4281, 1998.

[259] S. Mertens. Random costs in combinatorial optimization. *Phys. Rev. Lett.*, 84:1347, 2000.

[260] C. E. Shannon. A mathematical theory of communication: I. *Bell. Sys. Tech. J.*, 27:379, 1948.

[261] C. E. Shannon. A mathematical theory of communication: II. *Bell. Sys. Tech. J.*,

27:623, 1948.

[262] N. Sourlas. Spin-glass models as error-correcting codes. *Nature*, 339:693, 1989.

[263] D. C. Mattis. Solvable spin systems with random interactions. *Phys. Lett.*, 56A:421, 1976.

[264] D. Sherrington and S. Kirkpatrick. Solvable model of a spin glass. *Phys. Rev. Lett.*, 35:1792, 1975.

[265] Y. Kabashima and D. Saad. Statistical mechanics of error-correcting codes. *Europhys. Lett.*, 45:97, 1999.

[266] N. Sourlas. Spin glasses, error-correcting codes and finite-temperature decoding. *Europhys. Lett.*, 25:159, 1994.

[267] P. Ruján. Finite temperature error-correcting codes. *Phys. Rev. Lett.*, 70:2968, 1993.

[268] H. Nishimori. Optimum decoding temperature for error-correcting codes. *J. Phys. Soc. Jpn.*, 62:2973, 1993.

[269] H. Nishimori and K. Y. M. Wong. Statistical mechanics of image restoration and error-correcting codes. *Phys. Rev. E*, 60:132, 1999.

[270] I. Kanter and D. Saad. Error-correcting codes that nearly saturate Shannon's bound. *Phys. Rev. Lett.*, 83:2660, 2000.

[271] J. von Neumann and O. Morgenstern. *Theory of Games and Economic Behavior*. Princeton Press, Princeton, 1953.

[272] J. F. Nash. Non-cooperative games. *Annals of Mathematics*, 54(2):286–95, 1951.

[273] R. Axelrod. *The Evolution of Cooperation*. Basic Books, New York, 1984.

[274] W. Jianhua. *The Theory of Games*. Oxford University Press, Oxford, 1988.

[275] J. Berg and A. Engel. Matrix games, mixed strategies, and statistical mechanics. *Phys. Rev. Lett.*, 81:4999, 1998.

[276] J. Berg and M. Weigt. Entropy and typical properties of Nash equilibria in two-player games. *Europhys. Lett.*, 48:129, 1999.

[277] J. Berg. Statistical mechanics of random two-player games. *Phys. Rev. E*, 61:2327, 2000.

[278] S. Diederich and M. Opper. Replicators with random interactions: a solvable model. *Phys. Rev. A*, 39:4333, 1989.

[279] M. Opper and S. Diederich. Phase transition and 1/f noise in a game dynamical model. *Phys. Rev. Lett.*, 69:1616, 1992.

[280] V. Peter. Minimax games, spin glasses, and the polynomial-time hierarchy of complexity classes. *Phys. Rev. E*, 57:6487, 1998.

[281] D. Challet, M. Marsili, and R. Zecchina. Statistical mechanics of systems with heterogeneous agents: minority games. *Phys. Rev. Lett.*, 84:1824, 2000.

[282] J. Mathews and R. L. Walker. *Mathematical Methods of Physics*. Addison-Wesley, Redwood City, 1970.

[283] C. M. Bender and S. A. Orszag. *Advanced Mathematical Methods for Scientists and Engineers*. McGraw-Hill, Auckland, 1978.

[284] J. R. L. de Almeida and D. Thouless. Stability of the Sherrington–Kirkpatrick solution of a spin glass model. *J. Phys. A*, 11:983, 1978.

[285] T. Temesvári, C. De Dominicis, and I. Kondor. Block diagonalizing ultrametric matrices. *J. Phys. A*, 27:7569, 1994.

[286] C. De Dominicis, M. Carlucci, and T. Temesvári. Replica fourier transforms on ultrametric trees, and block-diagonalizing multi-replica matrices. *J. Physique I*, 7:105, 1997.

[287] L. Onsager. Electric moments of molecules in liquids. *J. Am. Chem. Soc.*, 58:1486–1493, 1936.

[288] D. J. Thouless, P. W. Anderson, and R. G. Palmer. Solution of 'solvable model of a spin glass'. *Phil. Mag.*, 35:593, 1977.

[289] K. Y. M. Wong. Microscopic equations and stability conditions in optimal neural networks. *Europhys. Lett.*, 30:245, 1995.

[290] M. Mézard. The space of interactions in neural networks: Gardner's computation with the cavity method. *J. Phys. A*, 22:2181, 1989.

[291] M. Griniasty. 'Cavity-approach' analysis of the neural-network learning problem. *Phys. Rev. E*, 47:4496, 1993.

[292] T. Plefka. Convergence condition of the TAP equation for the infinite-ranged Ising spin glass model. *J. Phys. A*, 15:1971, 1982.

Index

Printed in the United States
By Bookmasters